# English Grammar and Composition

**HERITAGE EDITION**

FIFTH COURSE

# English Grammar and Composition

## HERITAGE EDITION

## FIFTH COURSE

John E. Warriner
Joseph Mersand
Francis Griffith

HARCOURT BRACE JOVANOVICH

New York   Chicago   San Francisco
Atlanta   Dallas   and   London

**THE SERIES:**

English Grammar and Composition: First Course
English Grammar and Composition: Second Course
English Grammar and Composition: Third Course
English Grammar and Composition: Fourth Course
English Grammar and Composition: Fifth Course
English Grammar and Composition: Complete Course

Test booklet and teacher's manual for each above title.

**CORRELATED SERIES:**

English Workshop: First Course
English Workshop: Second Course
English Workshop: Third Course
English Workshop: Fourth Course
English Workshop: Fifth Course
English Workshop: Review Course

Composition: Models and Exercises, First Course
Composition: Models and Exercises, Second Course
Composition: Models and Exercises, Third Course
Composition: Models and Exercises, Fourth Course
Composition: Models and Exercises, Fifth Course
Advanced Composition: A Book of Models for Writing, Complete
  Course

**John E. Warriner** taught English for thirty-two years in junior and senior high schools and in college. He is chief author of the *English Grammar and Composition* series, coauthor of the *English Workshop* series, and general editor of the *Composition: Models and Exercises* series. His coauthors are all active in English education.

ISBN   0–15–311904–7

# To the Student

Travelers who have been abroad several times and are planning yet another trip and a longer one know something about what to expect, but because the next trip will take them to places they have not visited, they know they will encounter much that will be new. So it is with each successive course in English. Because you have studied English before, you have, as you start another English course, a fairly good idea of what lies ahead. However, since each succeeding course is more advanced than the one preceding it, you know that, like the travelers, you will encounter much that will be new. You will learn more of the conventions of standard usage. You will refresh your knowledge of language skills you have already studied and go on to the study of the more advanced skills that must be mastered by anyone who, like you, wishes to speak and write with clarity and force.

Command of one's language comes in two ways. It comes first from everyday experience in using the language —in speaking it, reading it, and writing it—and, second, it comes with the regular practice of skills that a course in English provides. Your teacher and your textbook are your guides in this work. By following their directions, you will improve your competence in self-expression.

As you continue to study English, you will find more and more emphasis on learning to *write* well. This is because the skills involved in writing are harder to master than those involved in speaking. You probably learned to speak English before you went to school, but only in school have you learned to write it and only in English class is direct attention given to how to write. Teachers of other subjects judge your writing, but very few can take the time to help you to improve it. This is the responsibility of the English teacher and the English textbook. If you follow your teacher's instructions carefully and study the textbook on your own, as well as when you are assigned work in it, you will have a greater command of English at the end of this course than you had at the beginning.

The phrase "on your own" in the preceding sentence means literally what it says. This book is not only a guide and storehouse of practice materials. It is also designed for use as a reference book. This means that by referring to the book, you can on your own find out the answer to any question that arises when you are writing a composition, whether the question be about a minor matter like the use of a comma or about a major matter like the organization of a composition. Familiarize yourself with the contents of the book and make full use of the index.

J. W.

# Contents

**Preface**         v

## PART ONE: GRAMMAR

1. **The Parts of Speech**     3
   Their Identification and Function

2. **The Parts of a Sentence**     24
   Subjects, Predicates, and Complements

3. **The Phrase**     40
   Kinds of Phrases and Their Functions

4. **The Clause**     56
   Adjective, Noun, and Adverb Clauses

## PART TWO: USAGE

5. **The Varieties of English**     75
   Levels of Usage; Appropriateness

   *Standard English · Formal Standard English ·
   Informal Standard English · Nonstandard English*

6. **Correct Agreement**     81
   Subject and Verb, Pronoun and Antecedent

   *Agreement of Subject and Verb · Intervening Phrases
   and Clauses · Indefinite Pronouns · Compound
   Subjects · Other Problems in Agreement ·
   Agreement of Pronoun and Antecedent*

### 7. Correct Pronoun Usage 103
Case Forms of Pronouns

*Nominative Forms · Objective Forms · Who and
Whom · Pronouns in Incomplete Constructions ·
Other Problems in the Use of Pronouns*

### 8. Correct Verb Usage 122
Principal Parts; Tense, Voice, Mood

*Kinds of Verbs · Principal Parts of Verbs · Regular
Verbs · Irregular Verbs · Six Troublesome Verbs ·
Tense · Special Problems in the Use of Tenses ·
Sequence of Tenses · The Present and the Perfect
Infinitive · Active and Passive Voice · The Retained
Object · Use of the Passive Voice · The Subjunctive
Mood*

### 9. Correct Use of Modifiers 163
Form of Adjectives and Adverbs; Comparison

*Adjective and Adverb Forms · Bad and Badly ·
Well and Good · Slow and Slowly · Comparison of
Adjectives and Adverbs · Comparative and
Superlative Forms · Irregular Comparison · Use of
Comparatives and Superlatives*

### 10. Glossary of Usage 174

# PART THREE: COMPOSITION:
## SENTENCE STRUCTURE

### 11. Complete Sentences 199
Fragments and Run-on Sentences

*Sentence Fragments · The Phrase Fragment · The
Appositive Fragment · The Subordinate Clause
Fragment · Run-on Sentences*

## 12. Coordination and Subordination    213
Emphasis and Relationship of Ideas

*Coordinate Ideas · Subordinate Ideas · Subordinate
Adverb Clauses · Adjective Clauses · Correcting
Faulty Coordination*

## 13. Clear Reference    226
Pronouns and Antecedents

*Ambiguous Reference · General Reference · Weak
Reference · Indefinite Use of Pronouns*

## 14. Placement of Modifiers    235
Misplaced and Dangling Modifiers

*Misplaced Modifiers · Dangling Modifiers · Two-Way
Modifiers*

## 15. Parallel Structure    242
Matching Idea to Form

## 16. Sentence Variety    248
Interest and Emphasis

# PART FOUR: COMPOSITION: PARAGRAPHS AND LONGER PAPERS

## 17. The Paragraph    259
Structure and Development of Paragraphs

*The Topic Sentence · The Concluding Sentence ·
Developing a Paragraph · Unity in the Paragraph ·
Coherence in the Paragraph · Chronological Order ·
Spatial Order · Order of Importance · Linking
Expressions and Connectives · Checklist for
Paragraph Revision*

## 18. The Whole Composition 284

Selecting a Subject; Planning and Writing the Composition

*The Subject · Organizing and Arranging Material · Outlining · Writing the Composition · The Introduction · The Body · The Conclusion · Revising the Composition · Summary of the Stages of Composition · Topics for Composition*

## 19. Clear Thinking 313

*The Fallacy of Overgeneralizing · Generalization and the Scientific Hypothesis · Overgeneralizing and Prejudice · The Fallacy in Some Cause-and-Effect Reasoning · The Fallacy of the False Analogy · The Fallacy of Attacking the Man Instead of the Issues · The Fallacy of Rationalizing · The Fallacy of "Either-Or" · The Fallacy of Circular Thinking— Begging the Question*

## 20. Exercises in Writing Prose 327

The Essay, the Book Review, the Précis

*The Essay · The Informal Personal Essay · The Essay of Opinion · Choosing an Arguable Subject · Gathering Your Material · Organizing Your Material · Style and Tone · The Book Review · Before You Read · As You Read · Writing the Review · The Précis*

## 21. The Research Paper 348

Research Techniques; The Formal Composition

*Preparing the Research Paper · Writing the Research Paper · Footnotes · The Bibliography · Charts, Diagrams, and Illustrations · The Complete Paper*

## 22. The Business Letter 382

Standard Practice in Business Correspondence

*Form in a Business Letter · The Letter of Inquiry or Request · The Letter of Adjustment or Complaint · The Letter of Application · The Personal Résumé*

# PART FIVE: MECHANICS

## 23. Capitalization
### Rules of Standard Usage

*Other Problems in Capitalization · Summary Style
Sheet*

407

## 24. Punctuation
### End Marks and Commas

*End Marks · The Comma · Items in a Series ·
Commas Between Independent Clauses ·
Nonessential Elements · Participial Phrases ·
Introductory Elements · Interrupters · Conventional
Uses · Unnecessary Commas · Summary of the
Uses of the Comma*

422

## 25. Punctuation
### Other Marks of Punctuation

*The Semicolon · The Colon · The Dash ·
Parentheses · Brackets · Underlining (Italics) ·
Quotation Marks · The Apostrophe · The Hyphen*

443

## 26. Manuscript Form
### Rules for Preparing a Final Draft

*The Manuscript · Revising First Draft · Numbers ·
Dividing a Word at the End of a Line · Correction
Symbols*

463

# PART SIX: AIDS TO GOOD ENGLISH

## 27. The Library
### Arrangement and Resources of the Library

*Arrangement of Books in the Library · Fiction ·
Nonfiction: The Dewey Decimal System · Locating
Information in the Library · The Card Catalogue ·
The Parts of a Book · The Readers' Guide · The
Vertical File*

475

## 28. Reference Books 492

The Principal Reference Books and Their
Uses

*Encyclopedias · Encyclopedias in Many Volumes ·
One-Volume Encyclopedias · General Reference
Books · Yearbooks and Almanacs · Atlases ·
Biographical Reference Books · General Biography ·
Books About Authors · Literary Reference Books ·
Books of Quotations · Indexes and Collections of
Poetry · Other Reference Books*


## 29. The Dictionary 503

Content and Uses of Dictionaries

*Kinds of Dictionaries · Unabridged Dictionaries ·
College Dictionaries · Content and Arrangement of
Dictionaries · Dictionary Information About a Word ·
Spelling · Other Information in Dictionaries ·
Dictionaries of Synonyms*


## 30. Vocabulary 520

Meaning Through Context and Word Analysis

*The Kinds of Vocabulary · How Our Vocabularies Are
Formed · Common Clues to Meaning · Word
Analysis · How Words Are Divided · Prefixes ·
Suffixes · Roots · Word List*


## 31. Spelling 542

Improving Your Spelling

*Good Spelling Habits · Spelling Rules · ie and ei ·
—cede, —ceed, and —sede · Adding Prefixes ·
Adding Suffixes · The Plural of Nouns · Words Often
Confused · Commonly Misspelled Words*

# PART SEVEN: AMERICAN ENGLISH

## 32. American English 569

*American English Dialects · Eastern New England
and Southern · Midland: South and North ·
Northern · The Mississippi and Beyond ·*

*Characteristics of American English · Vocabulary · Pronunciation · Grammar · "Standard" American · Loan Words · American Indian Loan Words · Loan Words from Other Languages · Americanisms · The Richness of Our Language*

# PART EIGHT: COLLEGE ENTRANCE AND OTHER EXAMINATIONS

## 33. College Entrance and Other Examinations    593

Tests of Vocabulary, Reading, and English Composition

**Index**    621

**Tab Key Index**    639

# Grammar

PART ONE

# Chapter 1

# The Parts of Speech

## Their Identification and Function

Noah Webster, the American lexicographer who gave his name to many dictionaries, was concerned with more than definitions and pronunciations. In his *Rudiments of English Grammar,* published in 1790, he wrote

> What is English grammar? The art of speaking and writing the English language correctly, according to the rules and general practice.
>
> Where are the rules of the language to be found? In the language itself.

This seems a simple principle at first, but in order to speak and write "according to the rules" we must first discover what those rules are. And just as a mechanic, in discussing how a car or an engine works, will use certain words to describe the mechanism and its parts, so, in stating the "rules" of language, we use certain terms — *parts of speech* and *parts of the sentence* — to describe the mechanism of language.

You have been studying the way our language works since elementary school. In order to test your knowledge, each of the first four chapters in this book begins with a diagnostic test on what you have learned. If you make scores on these tests that are satisfactory to your teacher, you will not have to spend much time studying things you already know. If the diagnostic tests show that you need to review something, you can do that by working through each chapter carefully and attentively.

To discover whether or not your knowledge of the parts of speech is adequate, take the diagnostic test below. Analyze the results to find out which of the parts of speech you should review.

## Diagnostic Test

Copy in a column on your paper the italicized words in the following sentences, numbering them as they are numbered in the test. Study the way each word is used in its sentence; then write after it what part of speech it is.[1]

Thursday, April 4th, 1974, (1) *was* a day that will (2) *always* be remembered in the history of (3) *baseball*. At 2:40 P.M. in Riverfront Stadium in Cincinnati, Henry Aaron (4) *of* the Atlanta Braves tied Babe Ruth's (5) *unbroken* record of 714 home runs during a major league baseball career. Aaron, (6) *forty* years old, was at bat for the first time in the (7) *baseball* season. It was the first inning. He (8) *hit* a 3-1 pitch (9) *which* sailed (10) *solidly* out to left center field, and it traveled four hundred feet, zooming (11) *neatly* over the twelve-foot fence and driving in the first runs of the 1974 baseball season. Anonymous Braves rooters cried (12) *"Bravo!"* from the packed stands as the crowd rose to its feet. The (13) *horsehide* ball was caught on the first bounce by Clarence Williams, a 22-year-old Cincinnati (14) *police officer,* while he was covering the area (15) *behind* the fence. "I couldn't see what was going on," said Williams, (16) *one* of Aaron's fans, (17) *"but* I knew he was up when I saw 44 on the scoreboard under the at-bat sign." After the game, while being interviewed by the press, Aaron (18) *pointedly* (19) *mentioned* his disappointment that the (20) *brief* pre-game ceremonies had not included homage (21) *to* Martin Luther King, Jr., on the (22) *sixth* anniversary of (23) *his* assassination, (24) *although* a number of

[1] The word *his,* which is the possessive form of the pronoun *he,* is called a pronoun throughout this book. Some teachers, however, prefer to think of *his* and other possessive pronouns (*your, their, her, its, our,* etc.) as adjectives. Follow your teacher's direction in labeling these words.

the players had requested a moment of (25) *silent* tribute. But in his (26) *usual* gracious (27) *fashion,* Aaron smiled (28) *and* said he was (29) *simply* delighted to have tied the Babe's (30) *long-standing* record. "It's a load off my back," he (31) *said.* Such great events (32) *seldom* occur, and there will always be (33) *someone* eager to tell the story of that day.

# THE NOUN

**1a. A *noun* is a word used to name a person, place, thing, or idea.**

Nouns may be classified as *proper* or *common, abstract* or *concrete,* and *collective.*

A *proper noun* is the name of a particular person, place, or thing. Proper nouns are always capitalized: *Naomi Sims, N. Scott Momaday, Iceland, Chicago, Golden Gate Bridge, Boulder Dam, United Nations.*

A *common noun* is a noun which does not name a particular person, place, or thing. Common nouns are not capitalized: *girl, country, city, bridge, dam.*

An *abstract noun* names a quality, a characteristic, an idea: *popularity, coldness, efficiency, beauty, power.*

A *concrete noun* names an object that can be perceived by the senses: *book, rose, cottage, cathedral.*

A *collective noun* names a group: *herd* (of cattle), *flock* (of sheep), *orchestra, army, jury.*

With reference to all these classifications, the noun *orchestra* is a common, concrete, collective noun.

Sometimes two or more words will be joined together to form a *compound noun.* They may be written as one word (*doorstep*), as two words (*training school*), or with hyphens (*sister-in-law*).

# THE PRONOUN

**1b. A *pronoun* is a word used in place of one or more nouns.**

EXAMPLES  The graduate accepted the diploma proudly. **She** had
worked hard for **it**.  [The pronoun *she* takes the place
of the noun *graduate*. The pronoun *it* takes the place
of the noun *diploma*.]

That boy and girl are older, but **they** do not try to
take advantage.  [The pronoun *they* takes the place
of the nouns *boy* and *girl*.]

The word to which a pronoun refers (whose place it
takes) is the *antecedent*[1] of the pronoun. In the preceding
example *graduate* is the antecedent of *she*, and *diploma* is
the antecedent of *it*.

► **NOTE**  A pronoun may also take the place of another pronoun.

EXAMPLE  **Some** of the students wore red sweaters. **They** were
celebrating Valentine's Day.  [The pronoun *they* takes
the place of the pronoun *some*.]

There are several kinds of pronouns: *personal* (which includes the *possessive* and *reflexive* forms), *relative, interrogative, demonstrative,* and *indefinite*.

### Personal Pronouns

*Personal pronouns* are so called because they refer to first
person (*I*), second person (*you*), and third person (*it, he*).
See page 104 for a more complete explanation of person.

| | | | |
|---|---|---|---|
| I, me | he, him | it | they, them |
| you | she, her | we, us | |

### Possessive Forms

| | | | |
|---|---|---|---|
| my, mine | his | its | their, theirs |
| your, yours | her, hers | our, ours | |

Personal pronouns combined with *–self, –selves* may be
used in two ways:

[1] Not all pronouns have antecedents. For example, in the sentence "*Nobody* was in the room," the pronoun *nobody* does not stand for a specific
noun. However, it is used "in place of" a noun in the sense that it is
used in a sentence in the place where a noun would ordinarily occur, as
in the sentence "A *woman* was in the room."

(1) They may be used *reflexively*.

EXAMPLE   Jack burned **himself** during the experiment.

(2) They may be used *intensively* for emphasis.

EXAMPLE   Maria **herself** is directing the entire play.

### Reflexive and Intensive Forms

| | | | |
|---|---|---|---|
| myself | himself, herself | ourselves | themselves |
| yourself | itself | yourselves | |

## Relative Pronouns

*Relative pronouns* are used to introduce subordinate clauses (see pages 59–60).

| | | |
|---|---|---|
| who | whose | that |
| whom | which | |

EXAMPLES   The book **that** you gave me was the one I wanted.

The woman **whose car you borrowed** wants to sell you a horse.

## Interrogative Pronouns

*Interrogative pronouns* are used in questions.

| | | |
|---|---|---|
| who | which | whose |
| whom | what | |

EXAMPLES   **What** will you give her now?
**Whose** did you borrow?

## Demonstrative Pronouns

*Demonstrative pronouns* point out a particular person or thing. When they are used before nouns, they are considered adjectives (*these houses, that flag, those books*).

| | | | |
|---|---|---|---|
| this | these | that | those |

EXAMPLES   **These** are her books.
**That** is the road she took.

## *Commonly Used Indefinite Pronouns*

*Indefinite pronouns* refer generally, not specifically, to persons, places, or things.

| | | | |
|---|---|---|---|
| all | either | more | one |
| another | everybody | much | several |
| any | everyone | neither | some |
| anybody | everything | nobody | somebody |
| anyone | few | none | someone |
| both | many | no one | such |
| each | | | |

EXAMPLES   **Few** of the players made points.

**Nobody** was there to welcome him.

**EXERCISE 1.**   Select the pronouns in each of the following sentences, and write them in order after the appropriate number.

1. I do not consider myself one of those who seem thoroughly satisfied with the world as it is.
2. Individuals themselves have to decide what their attitude is toward this sort of thing.
3. It has been said that humorists are those who laugh at one or more of the world's foibles.
4. Some of the famous contemporary humorists are women who write both prose and poetry.
5. Phyllis McGinley has written humorously about suburban life as she has known it.
6. Dorothy Parker, who was one of the few to have a book of verse on the best-seller list, frequently wrote about the subject of heartbreak, which she treated with ironic humor.
7. Shirley Jackson wrote either bizarre stories like "The Lottery" or humorous ones about her family life.
8. Few of the people who have seen Jean Kerr's comedies on Broadway have failed to find amusement in them.
9. Nearly everybody is familiar with P. L. Travers' stories about Mary Poppins, a character ever-popular with young people.
10. Mother Goose rhymes provided the topics for some of Eve Merriam's satires, which are in a book called *The Inner City Mother Goose.*

# THE ADJECTIVE

**1c. An *adjective* is a word used to modify a noun or a pronoun.**

*To modify* means "to describe or make more definite" the meaning of a word. The most frequently used adjectives are *a, an,* and *the,* which are called *articles*. Adjectives may modify nouns or pronouns in any one of three different ways.

1. By telling *what kind:*
   **green** eyes, **high** plains, **sunken** ship

2. By pointing out *which one:*
   **that** plane, **this** drugstore

3. By telling *how many:*
   **ten** sticks, **many** barrels of flour

Usually an adjective precedes the noun it modifies. Sometimes, for emphasis, a writer may place it after the noun.

EXAMPLE   This land, so **rich** and **flourishing,** gave a new life to the immigrants.

A *predicate adjective* (see page 35) is separated from the word it modifies by a verb.

EXAMPLES   Leroy was **late.**

The heat was **insufferable.**

Paris is **wonderful** in the spring.

Thomas seems **lazy.**

## The Same Word as Adjective and as Pronoun

A word may be used as more than one part of speech. This is especially true of the following words, which may be used as either *pronouns* or *adjectives:*

| | | | |
|---|---|---|---|
| all | few | one | this |
| another | many | other | those |
| any | more | several | what |
| both | most | some | which |
| each | much | that | |
| either | neither | these | |

ADJECTIVE  **Which** museum did you visit in Florence?  [*Which* modifies the noun *museum*.]

PRONOUN  **Which** did you visit?  [*Which* takes the place of the noun *museum*.]

ADJECTIVE  Leslie Silko wrote **these** stories.  [*These* modifies *stories*.]

PRONOUN  Leslie Silko wrote **these**.  [*These* takes the place of the noun *stories*.]

## Nouns Used as Adjectives

Sometimes nouns are used as adjectives.

**cattle** ranch    **bank** owner
**animal** trainer    **barn** door

When you are identifying parts of speech in any of the exercises in this book and find a noun used as an adjective, call it an adjective.

**EXERCISE 2.**  Some of the nouns, pronouns, and adjectives in the following sentences are italicized. For each sentence, list these words in order in a column, numbering as in the example. After each word, tell what part of speech it is. If a word is an adjective, write after it the word the adjective modifies.

EXAMPLE  1. *Many* tourists to America admire the *vast* plains and constantly praise *them*.

1. *many, adj., tourists*
   *vast, adj., plains*
   *them, pron.*

1. "A *little learning* is a *dangerous* thing."
2. "*What* is so *rare* as a day in June? . . ."

3. A *political leader* should be an *effective* speaker.

4. *Coleridge* left *several* of *his* most fascinating *poems* unfinished.

5. The *astronaut* of today receives the *same* kind of admiration *that* was showered upon the *great* explorers of the *fifteenth* and sixteenth *centuries*.

6. Thanks to the development of *quadrophonic* recording, symphony *performances* can now be recorded with even higher fidelity.

7. Whenever they felt in good *condition*, the gymnasts would twist *their* lithe bodies and entertain their *audience*.

8. I could not recall *that* answer.

9. *Many* of the *delegates* were *eager* to make speeches supporting the *presidential* candidate.

10. *Each* was asked to speak for only *five* minutes.

## THE VERB

**1d. A *verb* is a word that expresses action or otherwise helps to make a statement.**

Some verbs make a statement by expressing action. The action may be physical, as in *push, crush, throw, send*, or mental, as in *remember* and *believe*.

### Action Verbs

Action verbs may or may not take an object. An object is a noun or pronoun that completes the action by telling who or what is affected by the action. Action verbs that take objects are called *transitive* verbs. The verbs in the following examples are transitive.

EXAMPLES   The rider **lost** her stirrups.   [*Stirrups* is the object of *lost*.]

The actor **appreciated** the applause.   [*Applause* is the object of *appreciated*.]

Everyone at the outing **played** touch football. [*Touch football* is the object.]

*Intransitive verbs* can express action without an object.

EXAMPLES    The rider **fell.**

The actor **laughed.**

Everyone **played.**

Although some verbs are transitive only (*avoid*) and some intransitive only (*fall*), most verbs can be either.

EXAMPLES    The sudden cold **froze** the ground.   [transitive]
Suddenly the ground **froze.**   [intransitive]

The pianist **practiced** her scales daily.   [transitive]
The pianist **practiced** daily.   [intransitive]


## Linking Verbs

Some intransitive verbs that do not express action are called *linking verbs*. They connect, or link, to the subject a noun, pronoun, or adjective that identifies or describes it. The word that is linked to the subject is called the *subject complement.*

EXAMPLES    The crane **is** the Chinese symbol for long life.
[*Symbol* is the *subject complement* that refers to the subject *crane.*]

She **became** our representative. [*Representative* refers to *she.*]

The pie **smelled** too spicy.   [*Spicy* refers to *pie.*]

The subject complement may identify the subject, as in the first two examples, or describe it, as in the third.

Linking verbs are sometimes called state-of-being verbs because they help to describe the condition or state of being of a person or thing. The most common linking verb is the verb *be*[1]: *am, is, are, was, were, be, being, been,* and all verb phrases ending in *be, being,* or *been;* for example, *have been, could have been, can be, should be,* etc. Other common linking verbs are

[1] The verb *be,* and some other linking verbs, can also be followed by certain adverbs of place: He was *there,* She stayed *home.* In these instances the verbs are not linking verbs.

| appear | grow | seem | stay |
|--------|------|------|------|
| become | look | smell | taste |
| feel | remain | sound | |

EXAMPLES   She **is** a graduate of the University of Florida.

Edmonia Lewis **became** a highly respected sculptor in America.

The waiting **seemed** endless to me.

In these sentences the verbs do not express action; they act as a link between the subject and the words following the verb.

Some verbs may be used as either action or linking verbs.

ACTION   The chemist **smelled** the new compound.
LINKING   The roses **smelled** sweet.
ACTION   Mr. Jordan **grows** many varieties of black orchids.
LINKING   After a storm passes, the sea **grows** calm.

In general, a verb is a linking verb if you can substitute *is* or *was* for it. For instance, in the sentence *The milk tasted sour,* you can substitute *was* for *tasted:* The milk **was** sour. You cannot make the substitution, however, in a sentence with an action verb.

EXAMPLE   The queen never **tasted** a dish until after her vizier had tried it first.

## The Helping Verb and the Verb Phrase

A *verb phrase* is a verb of more than one word. It is made up of a main verb and one or more *helping verbs.* Helping verbs are so called because they help the main verb to express action or make a statement. The helping verbs in the following verb phrases[1] are printed in bold-faced type:

---

[1] A word ending in –*ing* may be used as part of a verb phrase or as an adjective:

They thought that a ghost *was haunting* the house.   [*Haunting* is part of a verb phrase.]

That melody was *haunting.* [*Haunting* is an adjective modifying *melody.*]

**have** written                     **will be** promoted
**should be** studying           **might have been** lost

## Common Helping Verbs

| | | |
|---|---|---|
| do | has | can (may) have |
| did | had | could (would, should) be |
| does | can | could (would, should) have |
| am | may | will (shall) have been |
| are | will (shall) be | might have |
| is | will (shall) have | might have been |
| was | has (had) been | must have |
| were | can (may) be | must have been |
| have | | |

The parts of a verb phrase may be separated from one another by other words; i.e., the helping verb may be separated from the main verb.

**Did** you **hear** the announcement?
She **could** hardly **believe** the fantastic story.

**EXERCISE 3.** List in order the verbs and verb phrases in the following sentences, placing before each the number of the sentence in which it appears. After each verb, tell whether it is a *transitive* (*v.t.*), *intransitive* (*v.i.*), or *linking* (*l.v.*) verb. Be sure to list all parts of a verb phrase.

1. Hawaii, the newest and most exotic of the fifty states, houses its legislature in a former palace.
2. Before the United States annexed the Islands, kings and queens reigned there.
3. The ruling clan was the Kamehameha family, who had come into power in the late eighteenth century.
4. Their rule lasted until the end of the nineteenth century, when Hawaii became a territory.

5. When American missionaries arrived in 1820, they converted the natives to Christianity, taught them writing, and introduced the rulers to democratic principles.

6. Many of the most important families in the Islands today are descendants of missionaries and Hawaiians.

7. A name like Keokila Dowsett or Keola Bishop may seem strange to some Americans, but to a Hawaiian it is a name full of prestige.

8. The original language of Hawaii was aboriginal Polynesian.

9. Hawaii relinquished its independence for the benefits of statehood on August 21, 1959.

10. Many of the islanders could hardly believe the news.

## THE ADVERB

**1e. An *adverb* is a word used to modify a verb, an adjective, or another adverb.**

The adverb is used most commonly as the modifier of a verb. It may tell *how, when, where,* or *to what extent* (*how often* or *how much*) the action of the verb is done.

EXAMPLES   Marian Anderson sang **beautifully.** [*Beautifully* tell *how* Marian Anderson sang.]

Marian Anderson sang **then.** [*Then* tells *when* Marian Anderson sang.]

Marian Anderson sang **here.** [*Here* tells *where* Marian Anderson sang.]

Marian Anderson sang **daily.** [*Daily* tells *how often* Marian Anderson sang.]

An adverb may modify an adjective.

EXAMPLE   Philippa is **unusually** clever. [*Unusually* modifies the adjective *clever,* telling *how* clever she is.]

An adverb may modify another adverb.

EXAMPLE   Jesse Owens ran **very** rapidly. [*Very* modifies the adverb *rapidly,* telling *to what extent* Jesse Owens ran rapidly, or *how* rapidly he ran.]

Adverbs like *really, truly, actually, indeed,* etc., which are used primarily for emphasis, should be classified as adverbs of extent.

EXAMPLES   She can **really** bowl.   [*Really* emphasizes the extent of her bowling ability.]

A friend in need is a friend **indeed.**   [*Indeed* emphasizes the extent of true friendship.]

## Nouns Used as Adverbs

Some nouns may be used adverbially.

We decided to stay **home.**   [tells *where*]

Our vacation starts **tomorrow.**   [tells *when*]

In identifying parts of speech, label nouns used in this way as adverbs.

► **NOTE**   To avoid possible confusion, you should know that *not* is classified as an adverb. Because it is so commonly used, you may ignore it in doing the exercises on parts of speech.

**EXERCISE 4.**   On your paper list in order the adverbs in the following sentences, placing before each the number of the sentence in which it appears. After each adverb, write the word or words it modifies and be prepared to state whether the adverb tells *how, when, where,* or *to what extent.* For this exercise you need not list the adverb *not.*

1. I knew that I had seen her before.
2. Our star runner could not have done better if he had practiced daily.
3. Students were advised to come to the game early.
4. "Place your books here," said the librarian.
5. "Do not take my advice lightly," warned the stranger.
6. Jet planes fly so rapidly that whole continents can be crossed in hours.
7. "That was not very polite," I responded when he spoke sarcastically.

8. If you do very well on college entrance tests, you may be able to enter the college of your choice.

9. "This group is too noisy," said the teacher to the unruly class.

10. Although the U.S. space project is an extremely costly one, we feel it to be quite valuable.

**EXERCISE 5.** Copy in a column on your paper the italicized words in the following sentences, placing before each word the number of the sentence in which it appears. After each word, tell what part of speech it is; after each adjective or adverb, tell what word or words it modifies.

1. *Everyone* entering the *theater received* a booklet describing how and where the film was made.

2. Luis Tiant *threw* the ball from the *mound* without any difficulty.

3. After *ten* hours, the jury *finally agreed* on a verdict.

4. The *class* as a group scored *well* on the examination, but a *few students* received *very poor* grades.

5. When the early morning mist had cleared away sufficiently, I *saw* the *lovely* valley *below*.

6. Though the large *building* with *seventy* rooms *is* now a furniture warehouse, it *was then* a well-known hospital.

7. *She found* the book about Sacajawea although she had not been able to remember the *title*.

8. "Do not put off until tomorrow what you can do *today*," is *still* a wise adage.

9. Lincoln frequently convinced his *listeners* by *simple*, humorous *anecdotes*.

10. Scientists *who* study the origins of the human species use *radioactive* materials in establishing the *age* of bones and tools

11. Fearing that she would be late, she left *early* in order to get *her* ticket from the *reserve* window.

12. *Some* people seem *always* to be concerned with the *minute*, specific points, while *others* see *quickly* the large, general *meanings* of the *things they* read.

# THE PREPOSITION

**1f. A *preposition* is a word used to show the relationship of a noun or pronoun to some other word in the sentence.**

In the following sentences the prepositions are shown in bold-faced type. The words related by the preposition are in italics. Note that the sentences are alike in wording except for the prepositions *to, around,* and *near.* The change in relationship between *walked* and *house* is due to the change in preposition.

> Joan *walked* **to** her aunt's *house.*
> Joan *walked* **around** her aunt's *house.*
> Joan *walked* **near** her aunt's *house.*

A preposition always introduces a phrase (see page 41). The noun or pronoun that ends a prepositional phrase is the *object* of the preposition which introduces the phrase.

## *Commonly Used Prepositions*

| | | |
|---|---|---|
| about | between | over |
| above | beyond | past |
| across | but (meaning *except*) | since |
| after | by | through |
| against | concerning | throughout |
| along | down | to |
| amid | during | toward |
| among | except | under |
| around | for | underneath |
| at | from | until |
| before | in | unto |
| behind | into | up |
| below | like | upon |
| beneath | of | with |
| beside | off | within |
| besides | on | without |

Sometimes a group of words may act as a preposition: *on account of, in spite of, along with, together with.*

**EXERCISE 6.** Write ten sentences, each containing one of the following prepositions. Draw a line under the phrase which each preposition introduces and draw a circle around the object of the preposition.

| | |
|---|---|
| around | since |
| at | through |
| between | under |
| except | upon |
| into | without |

## THE CONJUNCTION

**1g. A *conjunction* is a word that joins words or groups of words.**

In the following sentences the conjunctions are printed in bold-faced type; the words or groups of words which the conjunctions join are underlined.

I completed all preparations **before** the party began.
Pearl Buck **and** Selma Lagerlöf won the Nobel Prize.
No one knows **when** opportunity will knock.
Mary's health has improved **since** she began doing daily exercises.
A good teacher **both** encourages **and** helps students.

There are three kinds of conjunctions: *coordinating, correlative,* and *subordinating.*

### *Coordinating Conjunctions*

| | | | | | |
|---|---|---|---|---|---|
| and | but | or | nor | for | yet |

### *Correlative Conjunctions*

| | |
|---|---|
| either . . . or | not only . . . but (also) |
| neither . . . nor | whether . . . or |
| both . . . and | |

Correlative conjunctions are always used in pairs:

**Both** native ability **and** long practice are necessary for success in a musical career.

"**Either** you work after school **or** you go out for baseball," the understanding mother said to her son.

Subordinating conjunctions are used to begin subordinate clauses (see page 65), usually adverb clauses.

In the following sentences the subordinating conjunctions are printed in bold-faced type, and the subordinate clauses which the conjunctions begin are underlined.

The police kept the crowd away **until** the fire had died.

Many new nations have been formed in Asia and Africa **since** World War II ended.

We could stand talking for hours, even in the rain, **when** we were young.

A subordinating conjunction need not come between the sentence parts it joins. It may come at the beginning of a sentence.

**When** we were young, we could stand talking for hours, even in the rain.

### Commonly Used Subordinating Conjunctions[1]

| | | | | |
|---|---|---|---|---|
| after | before | provided | though | whenever |
| although | how | since | till | where |
| as | if | so that | unless | wherever |
| as much as | inasmuch as | than | until | while |
| because | in order that | that | when | |

## THE INTERJECTION

**1h. An** *interjection* **is a word that expresses emotion and has no grammatical relation to other words in the sentence.**

---

[1] Some of these words may also be used as prepositions: *after, before, since, until;* others may also be used as adverbs: *how, when, where. That* is often used as a pronoun or an adjective.

EXAMPLES   Help!  Ouch!  Ah!  Well!  Hurrah!

# THE SAME WORD AS DIFFERENT PARTS OF SPEECH

You have already learned that a word may be used as more than one part of speech. For instance, you learned in your study of pronouns and adjectives that a word like *those* may be an adjective (*those* books) or a pronoun (She asked for *those*); *home* may be a noun (Our *home* is comfortable) or an adverb (We decided to stay *home*); *green* may be a noun (*Green* is my favorite color) or an adjective (a *green* umbrella). Many words cannot be classified by part of speech until you see them in a sentence.

EXAMPLES   She asked the librarian if the book was in **print**. [*Print* is the name of something, a noun.]

The editor **printed** the brochure.   [*Printed* expresses action; it is a verb.]

Gloria wore a **print** dress yesterday.   [*Print* modifies the noun *dress;* it is an adjective.]

She was a **fast** runner.   [*Fast* is an adjective.]

She ran **fast**.   [*Fast* is an adverb.]

Some Hindu holy men **fast** frequently.   [*Fast* is a verb.]

Mahatma Gandhi would often use a **fast** to achieve his goals.   [*Fast* is a noun.]

**EXERCISE 7.**  In this exercise you are to identify the uses of the same word as different parts of speech. Copy on your paper the twenty italicized words in the following sentences, writing the number of the sentence before each. After each word, write what part of speech it is. Be prepared to explain your answers.

1. The employer will *fire* whoever was responsible for the *fire* in the store.
2. The pioneers worked *hard* to cultivate the *hard* ground they farmed.

3. After turning to the *left,* we found that the engineers had *left* their tractor on the *left* side of the road.
4. *That* is what you can expect when you engage in *that* sort of behavior.
5. *Might* does not make *right,* but it *might* lead to the *right* goal.
6. If *home* is where the heart is, why don't more people stay *home* when they have a holiday?
7. The average *fly* can always *fly* away before you can catch it.
8. The woman with the *head* for figures used to *head* the sales department at the *head* office in Chicago.

## SUMMARY

| Rule | Part of Speech | Use | Examples |
|------|------|------|------|
| 1a | noun | names | volume, Bible, literature |
| 1b | pronoun | takes the place of a noun | I, her, theirs, who, it |
| 1c | adjective | modifies a noun or pronoun | happy, sponta- neous, odd |
| 1d | verb | shows action or otherwise helps to make a statement | give, could go, was |
| 1e | adverb | modifies a verb, an adjective, or another adverb | usually, slightly, happily, very |
| 1f | preposition | relates a noun or a pronoun to an- other word | into, from, of |
| 1g | conjunction | joins words or groups of words | and, but, or, although |
| 1h | interjection | shows emotion | Oh! |

**REVIEW EXERCISE.** Copy in a column on your paper the italicized words in the following passage. (Treat a verb phrase as one word.) Consider carefully the way each word is used in its sentence; write after it what part of speech it is.

(1) "*Brush* fire down at the (2) *lean-to!*" the scout called (3) *to* Maria as she (4) *passed* her on the trail. Maria blew (5) *three* blasts on her whistle, the (6) *signal* that there was an emergency and (7) *that* (8) *all* must return to the campsite. A (9) *few* minutes later, twelve (10) *excited* girls appeared. "Is the lean-to (11) *in* (12) *danger?*" Maria asked (13) *urgently.* "Yes," the girls answered.

Maria (14) *had experienced* such an emergency (15) *once,* and she remembered (16) *vividly* what steps (17) *her* leader had taken at (18) *that* time. She told the girls to break camp and to carry (19) *all* equipment and foodstuffs (20) *down* the trail to a (21) *small* cave they had come upon earlier in the day. After that, (22) *she* and the twelve girls walked to the (23) *edge* of the fire. Maria decided that it had to be kept (24) *from* jumping the trail. (25) *That* was the (26) *only* way to save the lean-to. She showed the girls how to make (27) *improvised* brooms from twigs and (28) *some* string. (29) *These* were to be used to brush back the (30) *burning* leaves that would (31) *soon* be blowing (32) *across* the trail.

The method succeeded for a while, (33) *but* (34) *then* the wind (35) *grew* (36) *stronger.* The fire jumped the trail and started moving (37) *toward* the lean-to. There was nothing that could be done (38) *now,* and rather than endanger the girls (39) *further,* Maria led them down the trail (40) *toward* the cave. Then, as though (41) *from* nowhere, a group of fire fighters carrying equipment ran toward them.

They went to work immediately and soon restrained the fire (42) *until* it was confined to a single area that would soon burn (43) *itself* out. The lean-to had been saved (44) *after* all! (45) *Night* had come by then, and the girls had staked their tents (46) *again.* (47) "*Whew!*" the girls sighed (48) *as* they prepared their bedding. They were (49) *too* tired for the usual campfire and marshmallows. Anyway, they had seen (50) *enough* fire for one day!

# Chapter 2

# The Parts
# of a Sentence

## Subjects, Predicates,
## and Complements

Much of Winston Churchill's success in leading England during World War II was due to the impact that his speeches made upon the minds and hearts of his countrymen. In his school days Churchill was considered a dull pupil, unable to cope with the complexities of Latin. He was made to repeat his English courses instead. He described the effect of this in his own words:

> I gained an immense advantage over the cleverer boys . . . I got into my bones the essential structure of the ordinary British sentence — which is a noble thing.[1]

Since your elementary school days you too have been "getting into your bones" the structure of the ordinary sentence. You began by dividing the sentence into two parts — *subject* and *predicate*. Later you learned the terms *object, predicate nominative,* and *predicate adjective* to fill out the description of the predicate. These elements form the essential structure of all the English sentences you will ever speak, read, or hear, no matter how varied or complex.

The following test is in two parts. It is designed to show how much information you have remembered about these terms and how much you should review.

---

[1] From *Roving Commission: My Early Life* by Winston Churchill. Copyright 1930 by Charles Scribner's Sons.

## Diagnostic Test

**A.** Number your paper 1–10. After the corresponding number, write the simple subject and the verb of each of the sentences below. (The italicizing applies only to Exercise B.)

1. Some decisions require little *thought*.
2. Other decisions are more *difficult*.
3. You can send *me* the *bill* later.
4. We can now send television *programs* across the Atlantic by means of communication satellites.
5. The Shakespeare Festival at Stratford, Connecticut, has become *famous*.
6. The Pulitzer Prize Committee gave *Gwendolyn Brooks* the *prize* for poetry in 1950.
7. Bowling attracts *millions* of fans.
8. Many women become *lawyers* now.
9. Ecologists study an animal's *relation* to its environment.
10. Eudora Welty, who won the Pulitzer Prize in 1973, is a distinguished *novelist*.

**B.** List all the italicized words in sentences 1–10. After each word write the kind of complement it is: direct object (*d.o.*), indirect object (*i.o.*), predicate nominative (*p.n.*), predicate adjective (*p.a.*).

# THE SENTENCE

**2a. A *sentence* is a group of words expressing a complete thought.**

Consider the following group of words:

The victorious team

According to the definition, a sentence must express a *complete* thought. It is true that the words *The victorious team* create a mental image; but, in terms of communicating a thought to the reader, something is lacking.

To complete the thought started by the words, you must tell what the team *did,* or what *happened to* the team, or what the team *is.*

| INCOMPLETE THOUGHT | COMPLETE THOUGHT |
|---|---|
| | left the field. |
| | was praised by the coach. |
| | is from our school. |
| The victorious team | lifted the coach high on their shoulders. |
| | remained calm. |
| | won the county championship. |

| | |
|---|---|
| NOT A SENTENCE | Millions of American students now attending our colleges . . . [thought not complete] |
| SENTENCE | Millions of American students are now attending our colleges. [complete thought] |
| NOT A SENTENCE | The orchestra working together for five years . . . [thought not complete] |
| SENTENCE | The orchestra has been working together for five years. [complete thought] |
| NOT A SENTENCE | Billions each year for space research . . . [thought not complete] |
| SENTENCE | Billions are appropriated each year for space research. [complete thought] |

# SUBJECT AND PREDICATE

**2b. A sentence consists of two parts: the *subject* and the *predicate*. The subject is that part about which something is being said. The predicate is that part which says something about the subject.**

| *subject* | *predicate* |
|---|---|
| Time | flies. |

| *predicate* | *subject* |
|---|---|
| Into the silent sea sailed | the ancient mariner. |

## The Simple Predicate, or Verb

**2c.  The principal word or group of words in the predicate is called the *simple predicate,* or the *verb.***

EXAMPLES    Ana **ate** her breakfast silently and hastily.  [The
complete predicate is *ate her breakfast silently and
hastily.* The simple predicate, or verb, is *ate.*]
History **repeats** itself in a most unusual manner.
[The complete predicate is *repeats itself in a most
unusual manner.* The verb is *repeats.*]

## The Simple Subject

**2d.  The *simple subject* is the main word or combination of words naming the person, place, thing, or idea about which something is being said.**

EXAMPLES    The **idea** of transmigration of souls is believed by
many in India.  [The complete subject is *the idea of
transmigration of souls.* The simple subject is *idea.*]
**Immigrants** from many lands contributed to America.
[The complete subject is *immigrants from many
lands.* The simple subject is *immigrants.*]

► **NOTE**  Throughout this book the term *subject,* when used in
connection with the sentence, refers to the simple subject; the
term *verb* refers to the simple predicate.

## Compound Subjects and Compound Verbs

**2e.  A *compound subject* consists of two or more subjects that are joined by a conjunction and have the same verb. The usual connecting words are *and* and *or.***

EXAMPLES    Faster **service** and greater **courtesy** help increase
sales.  [compound subject: *service . . . courtesy*]

Neon, argon, and krypton are elements that do not easily combine with other materials. [compound subject: *neon . . . argon . . . krypton*]

**2f. A *compound verb* consists of two or more verbs that are joined by a conjunction and have the same subject.**

EXAMPLES The librarian **stamped** the book and **gave** it to the student. [compound verb: *stamped . . . gave*]

Charity **bears** all things, **believes** all things, **hopes** all things. [compound verb: *bears . . . believes . . . hopes*]

## How to Find the Subject of a Sentence

Most often we expect to find the subject at the beginning of the sentence and the verb following the subject. But this need not be so. For example, in the sentence "Out of the stillness came the sound of laughter," the verb precedes the subject. A simple way to identify the subject is as follows:

1. First find the verb (the simple predicate).
2. Then ask yourself the question "Who or what . . .?"

EXAMPLE Driven by instinct, the herd of reindeer moves south each winter. [The verb is *moves*. Who or what moves? The answer is *herd*, the subject.]

This procedure will aid you in selecting the subject from the most complicated and involved sentences. There are several additional ways to help you locate the subject in certain special cases.

1. In sentences expressing a command or request, the subject is always understood to be *you*, even though the word *you* may not appear in the sentence.

EXAMPLES You sit down this very minute. [*You* is expressed.]

Don't forget to write. [*You* is understood.]

Please take this letter, Kate. [*You* is understood.]

2. The subject of a sentence is never in a prepositional phrase.

EXAMPLES    Flocks of birds surrounded the tower.   [Verb: *surrounded*. Who surrounded? *Flocks. Flocks* is the subject. *Birds* is not the subject. It is in the phrase *of birds*.]

Neither of the scientists could give an explanation of the phenomena.   [Verb: *could give*. Who could give? *Neither. Neither* is the subject. *Scientists* is not the subject. It is in the phrase *of the scientists*.]

3. To find the subject in a question, turn the question into statement form.

QUESTION    Do you know Helen Keller's birthplace?

STATEMENT    You do know Helen Keller's birthplace.   [verb: *do know;* subject: *you*]

4. The word *there* (or *here*) is never the subject of a sentence except in a sentence like the one you are now reading.

EXAMPLES    **There** is the famous *Mona Lisa*.   [Verb: *is;* subject: *Mona Lisa*. In this sentence the word *there* is an adverb indicating location.]

**There** is a famous writer in this little town.   [Verb: *is;* subject: *writer. There* in this sentence is called an *expletive*. It indicates that a subject will follow the verb. Sometimes the word *it* may be used as an expletive: *It is annoying to wait for someone*.]

**EXERCISE 1.** Number your paper 1–20. After the proper number write the simple subject and verb of each sentence. Identify the verb, but first copy the subject and then write the verb after it. Be certain to include all parts of compound forms and all words in a verb phrase.

1. There are many unverified legends and conjectures about the life of William Shakespeare.
2. Actual facts concerning his life remain few.
3. He was born in 1564 in Stratford-on-Avon, a market town about eighty miles from London.

4. Records establish the dates of the baptisms of his children as 1583 and 1585.
5. Another known fact is the date of his death, April 23, 1616.
6. None of Shakespeare's contemporaries set down a record of the poet's life.
7. The life and works of a mere dramatist were not thought important enough to merit a biography.
8. In the eighteenth century James Boswell wrote *The Life of Samuel Johnson,* an entertaining account of the life and times of the great English lexicographer and wit.
9. This classic has been read with enjoyment for nearly two hundred years.
10. Boswell's book, unlike many of the full-length biographies of the next century, was an accurate and faithful record.
11. Many nineteenth-century biographers relied on their imagination, not on real facts.
12. One example of a nineteenth-century biography is the life of George Washington by Parson Weems.
13. The lack of adequate research and the use of imaginary facts make this account of America's first President very unreliable.
14. Lytton Strachey revolutionized the writing of biography with the publication of *Eminent Victorians* in 1918.
15. Strachey's biographical portraits used some imaginary details but were based on careful historical research.
16. This combination of well-documented fact and psychologically true detail soon became popular.
17. Today biographies, autobiographies, and memoirs flood the bookstores.
18. The private lives of politicians, generals, and other notables fascinate the reading public.
19. Have you read any good biographies lately?
20. Borrow a good biography from the library.

## COMPLEMENTS

By definition a sentence expresses a complete thought. Some sentences express a complete thought by means of a subject and verb only.

|  |  |
|---|---|
| S | V |
| Duty | calls. |
| S | V |
| She | arrived. |

Sometimes even briefer sentences are possible, like *Stop!*, or *Run!*, in which the subject *you* is understood. Most sentences, however, have in the predicate one or more words that complete the meaning of the subject and verb. These completing words are called *complements*.

EXAMPLES
| The legislature passed | the **bill**. |
|---|---|
| The President gave | the **astronaut** a **medal**. |
| Virginia Woolf was | a well-read **woman**. |
| The sea looks | **choppy**. |
| The group elected | **Consuela president**. |

## Direct and Indirect Objects

Transitive verbs require a direct object to complete their meaning. They may also be followed by an indirect object.

**2g. The *direct object* of the verb receives the action of the verb or shows the result of the action. It answers the question "What?" or "Whom?" after an action verb.**

Except when it ends in –*self* (*myself, himself*), the object of a verb never refers to the same person or thing as the subject.

EXAMPLES    Susan defeated **Steve** at tennis. [Susan defeated *whom?*]

Drought destroyed the **crops**. [Drought destroyed *what?*]

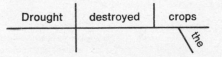

▶ **NOTE**    The diagrams are given to help those students who have already studied diagraming. No attempt is made in this book to teach diagraming. However, for review purposes, the following principles should be remembered. On the main horizontal line the subject is followed by a vertical line which crosses the main line and separates the subject from the verb. Another vertical line, which does not cross the main line, follows the verb and separates it from the direct object. A single-word modifier slants downward from the word it modifies. An indirect object (p. 33) is represented on a horizontal line attached to the verb by a slanted line. The following diagram illustrates the basic sentence pattern.

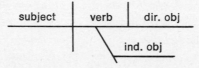

A predicate nominative or predicate adjective (p. 35) is separated from the verb by a slanting line:

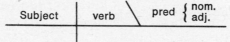

Sometimes there may be a compound direct object:

Beethoven composed sonatas and symphonies.

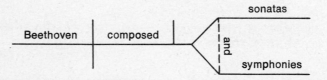

**2h. The *indirect object* of the verb precedes the direct object and usually tells to whom or for whom the action of the verb is done.**[1]

---

[1] If the word *to* or *for* is used, the pronoun or noun following it is part of a prepositional phrase; it is not an indirect object. Like subjects, objects of verbs are never part of a prepositional phrase.

The principal gave **her** the award. [*Her* is the indirect object.]
The principal gave the award **to her.** [*Her* is part of a phrase.]

The indirect objects in these sentences are in bold-faced type.

EXAMPLES   His artistic skill won **him** many honors.

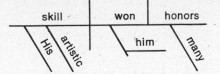

The senator gave **Jaime** and **me** a copy of her speech.

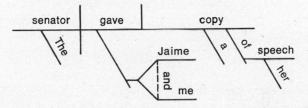

## The Objective Complement

To complete their meaning, some action verbs require an additional complement following their objects. This additional complement is called an *objective complement* because it refers to the object; it may be a noun or an adjective.

They named Mary **secretary**.   [The noun *secretary* refers to the direct object *Mary* and helps to complete the meaning of the verb *named*. It is an objective complement.]

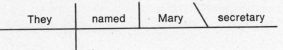

Everyone considered him **foolish**.   [The adjective *foolish* modifies the direct object *him* and helps to complete the meaning of the verb *considered*. It is an objective complement.]

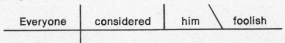

Only a few verbs meaning "make" or "consider" take an objective complement: *elect, appoint, name, choose, render, make, consider,* etc.

His refusal to pay rendered the contract **null** and **void**.   [*made* the contract null and void]

He scrubbed the floor **clean**.   [*made* the floor clean]

**EXERCISE 2.**   Number your paper 1–10. Copy after the proper number the objects of the verb in each sentence (do not include modifiers). After each object write *d.o.* for a direct object or *i.o.* for an indirect object. Some sentences contain more than one object.

1. Meteorologists are discovering more secrets about the weather every year.
2. Often the weather defies prediction.
3. But meteorologists serve us well, by and large.
4. Weather bureaus save travelers much time and effort.
5. The daily weather maps in the newspapers offer everyone benefits undreamt of in the past.
6. They chart the weather on a national and sometimes global scale.
7. Sometimes jet travel yields strange results because of meteorologists.
8. Travelers boarding planes in the bright sun carry raincoats to protect themselves from rain 500 miles away.
9. Meteorology has put the weather more or less in order.
10. At least, it has guaranteed us a certain amount of predictability in a risky situation.

## Subject Complements

A complement that follows a linking verb[1] is either a *predicate nominative* or a *predicate adjective*. These complements refer to (describe or explain) the subject.

---

[1] The common linking verbs are the forms of the verb *be* (*am, is, are, was, were, be, been*) and the following: *become, seem, grow, appear, feel, smell, taste, remain, sound, stay.*

**2i.** A *predicate nominative* **is a noun or pronoun complement that refers to the same person or thing as the subject of the verb. It follows a linking verb.**

EXAMPLES   Adele Rogers St. John is a famous **journalist.** [*Journalist* refers to the subject *Adele Rogers St. John.*]

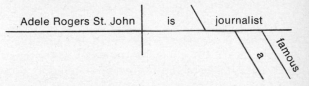

The Twin Cities are **St. Paul** and **Minneapolis.** [compound predicate nominative]

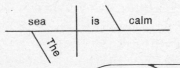

**2j.** A *predicate adjective* **is an adjective complement that modifies the subject of the verb. It follows a linking verb.**

EXAMPLES   The sea is **calm.** [The predicate adjective *calm* modifies the subject *sea.*]

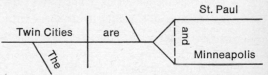

Illuminated manuscripts are **rare** and **valuable.** [compound predicate adjective]

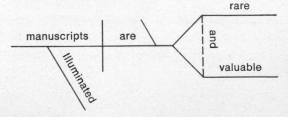

Normally, complements follow the verb. Occasionally, they may precede the verb for the purpose of emphasis.

**Sweet** are the uses of adversity. [*Sweet* is a predicate adjective modifying the noun *uses*. Normal order: The uses of adversity are sweet.]

► **NOTE** Like subjects and objects, predicate nominatives and predicate adjectives are never in a prepositional phrase.

**EXERCISE 3.** Number your paper 1–15. After the proper number, write the predicate nominatives or predicate adjectives in each of the following sentences; identify each with the abbreviation *p.n.* or *p.a.*

1. The Mississippi River is one of the world's longest rivers.
2. Was Ferber the author of *Giant* and *So Big?*
3. After the five-mile march, the soldiers felt tired.
4. Jeanette Rankin was a congresswoman of action and willpower.
5. Studying is an art that can be learned.
6. A well-designed room should be beautiful and functional.
7. The people of the Renaissance were eager for knowledge of Greece and Rome.
8. Because of the long ordeal, she looked wan and weary.
9. The Tower of London is an ancient fortress.
10. The gray skies became clear at noon.
11. In his later years King Henry VIII grew enormously fat.
12. The cavalry horses remained quiet under fire.
13. My aunt seemed happy that afternoon.
14. The playwright Ibsen grew bitter with the years.
15. The modern scientist is an expert in research methods.

## CLASSIFICATION OF SENTENCES

**2k. Sentences may be classified according to their purpose.**

Sentences may have four purposes: (1) to make a statement; (2) to ask a question; (3) to command or request; (4) to exclaim.

(1) A *declarative sentence* is a sentence that makes a statement.

EXAMPLE    Nuclear physics has become a new branch of learning since 1945.

(2) An *interrogative sentence* is a sentence that asks a question.

EXAMPLE    Have you seen a sculpture by Augusta Savage?

(3) An *imperative sentence* is a sentence that gives a command or makes a request.

EXAMPLES    Be ready to leave at noon.
            Please pick up your term paper in my office.

(4) An *exclamatory sentence* is a sentence that expresses strong feeling or emotion.

EXAMPLE    Oh, what a week it was!

One advantage of speech over writing is that by a change of tone or emphasis we can convey different meanings with the same words.

Shakespeare is the greatest writer the world has ever known. [declarative]

Shakespeare is the greatest writer the world has ever known? [Interrogative; the speaker is questioning the statement.]

Shakespeare is the greatest writer the world has ever known! [Exclamatory; you can almost hear the speaker's voice rise for emphasis.]

Without the inflection of the speaker's voice, the different meanings of this sentence are communicated by punctuation.

**REVIEW EXERCISE.**  Number your paper 1–10. Copy after the proper number the subject, the verb, and the complements in each sentence. After each complement, tell what kind it is, using abbreviations as follows: direct object, *d.o.;* indirect object, *i.o.;* predicate nominative, *p.n.;* predicate adjective, *p.a.*

1. The story of the Donner Party is tragic and terrible.
2. In 1846 a schemer gave the pioneers directions for a new route to California.
3. A heroic story of that journey is the story of Tamsen Donner.
4. Tamsen Donner was a forty-five-year-old woman from Illinois.
5. She carried books, school supplies, and water colors for a new school in California.
6. In the Sierra Nevadas snow trapped the pioneers.
7. Tamsen Donner's husband injured his hand, and he became so ill that he could not travel with the rescue team.
8. Forced to choose between husband and children, Tamsen Donner gave the rescue team her three young girls.
9. Tamsen Donner attended her husband until his death.
10. Tamsen Donner lost her life also, but the children reached California safely.

## SUMMARY OF SENTENCE PATTERNS

Every sentence has two basic parts—subject and predicate. Within the subject there is a simple subject, usually called just the subject; within each predicate there is a simple predicate, usually called the verb. Some sentences consist of subject and verb only.

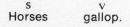

Modifiers may be added to the subject and verb without changing the basic pattern of such a sentence.

$$\overset{s}{\text{The swift horses}} \overset{v}{\text{gallop}} \text{ over the plains.}$$

Complements, which are additions to the predicate, create other sentence patterns. Because there are different kinds of complements, each produces a different sentence pattern. The seven common sentence patterns are

| S | V | | |
|---|---|---|---|
| Mary | reads. | | |

| S | V | D.O. | |
|---|---|---|---|
| Mary | reads | fairy tales. | |

| S | V | I.O. | D.O. |
|---|---|---|---|
| Mary | reads | John | fairy tales. |

| S | V | D.O. | OBJ. COMP. (ADJ.) |
|---|---|---|---|
| Fairy tales | make | John | dreamy. |

| S | V | D.O. | OBJ. COMP. (NOUN) |
|---|---|---|---|
| He | imagines | himself | king. |

| S | V | P.N. | |
|---|---|---|---|
| John | is | a dreamer. | |

| S | V | P.A. | |
|---|---|---|---|
| He | looks | sleepy. | |

# Chapter 3

# The Phrase

## Kinds of Phrases
## and Their Functions

One of the most famous prose compositions in the English language is a brief essay, about a page in length, called simply "Of Studies" by Francis Bacon. Many of his other essays were similarly introduced by the preposition *of*. Likewise, one of the noblest pieces of Latin prose is Cicero's "De Senectute," which might be translated "Of Old Age." These expressions introduced by a preposition are not sentences, but *phrases*.

A phrase is a group of related words not containing a subject and predicate. A phrase may serve as a subject, as an object, as a predicate nominative, or as a modifier. You have already learned the *verb phrase* (a verb of more than one word, *am writing, could have gone*). In this chapter you will review the other types of phrases and how they function in the sentence.

To determine how much you already know about phrases and what parts of this chapter you have to review, give yourself the following two-part test.

## Diagnostic Test

**A.** Number your paper 1–5. Copy in order the ten prepositional phrases in the following sentences. After each phrase indicate whether it is an adjective or an adverb phrase.

1. Edgar Allan Poe died in the charity ward of a Baltimore hospital.
2. "Bring Me the Sunset in a Cup" was written by Emily Dickinson.
3. Armed with the oldest weapons of preservation, the cockroach lives on.
4. She hopes to win the election in Ohio by a large majority.
5. His trips to Italy on important diplomatic missions broadened Chaucer's knowledge.

**B.** Copy on your paper one participial phrase and one infinitive phrase from the sentences above. Label each phrase.

**3a. A *phrase* is a group of related words used as a single part of speech and not containing a verb and its subject.**

Five types of phrases are explained in the following pages: *prepositional phrases* (adjective and adverb), *participial phrases, gerund phrases, infinitive phrases,* and *appositive phrases*.

## THE PREPOSITIONAL PHRASE

**3b. A *prepositional phrase* is a group of words beginning with a preposition and usually ending with a noun or a pronoun.**

EXAMPLES  on the roof     inside the house
under the sea    over the hill

The noun or pronoun that ends the phrase is the object of the preposition that begins the phrase.

Prepositional phrases do not stand by themselves (except in such commands as *At ease!, On the double!,* and in titles, like "Of Studies"); they are parts of a sentence and are used as modifiers, sometimes as adjectives and at other times as adverbs.

## The Adjective Phrase

**3c.** An *adjective phrase* **is a prepositional phrase that modifies a noun or a pronoun.**

EXAMPLE    That tall building **with the red tower** is our new library.    [The prepositional phrase *with the red tower* modifies—describes or limits the meaning of—the noun *building* and is, therefore, an adjective phrase.]

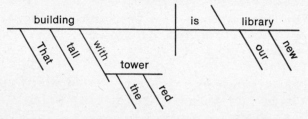

In diagraming a prepositional phrase, the preposition that begins the phrase is placed on a line slanting downward from the word the phrase modifies. The object of the preposition is placed on a horizontal line extending to the right from the line with the preposition. Single-word modifiers in the phrase are diagramed in the usual way.

**EXERCISE 1.** Copy in a column the adjective phrases from the following sentences. Before each phrase, place the number of the sentence in which it appears. After each phrase, write the noun or pronoun the phrase modifies.

1. The first attempt at lunar exploration took place over 500 years ago.
2. A scholar in China named Wan Hoo wanted to make a trip to the moon.
3. The apparatus for the trip was very simple.
4. Wan Hoo took one of his largest chairs and attached forty-seven rockets to it.
5. His servants were to set off the rockets on the chair when he was seated in it.
6. He planned to steer by means of two kites, one on each side of the chair.

7. His plans for the trip back have not been recorded.
8. On the day of the flight, he strapped himself securely into the chair.
9. "I'm off to the moon!" he cried, and signaled his servants with a wave of his hand.
10. There was a gigantic explosion of all forty-seven rockets; the chair disappeared, and with it Wan Hoo.

## The Adverb Phrase

**3d. An *adverb phrase* is a prepositional phrase that modifies a verb, an adjective, or another adverb.**

Notice in the following sentences the different ways in which an adverb phrase can modify a verb.

Louisa May Alcott wrote **with great care.**  [how she wrote]

Louisa May Alcott wrote **in the nineteenth century.**  [when she wrote]

Louisa May Alcott wrote **for thirty years.**  [how long she wrote]

Louisa May Alcott wrote **in America.**  [where she wrote]

Louisa May Alcott wrote **for her own pleasure.**  [why she wrote]

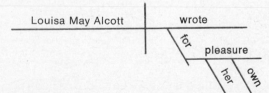

In the sentence below the adverb phrase modifies an adjective.

The old manor was rich **in traditions.**

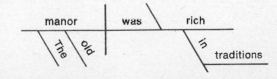

In the next sentence an adverb phrase modifies an adverb.

Thomas Hardy wrote poetry late in life.

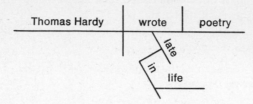

**EXERCISE 2.** Number your paper 1–10. After the proper number, copy the adverb phrases in the following sentences. After each phrase, write the word it modifies.

1. At fifteen Jascha Heifetz played like a master.
2. After years of practice, she played tennis with great ease.
3. Sarah Caldwell conducted with verve.
4. Louise dribbled across the court.
5. The Beatles sang by long-playing record to the world.
6. Television brings matter for thought into the living room.
7. Cleopatra was filled with anger when she heard about Antony's marriage.
8. Lightning never strikes twice in the same way.
9. Death Valley looks attractive in the pale moonlight.
10. Earlier in the day, its terrain casts less of a spell.

## VERBALS AND VERBAL PHRASES

Verbals are so called because they are formed from verbs. Although they act like verbs in some ways—showing action, having modifiers, taking complements—they are not used as verbs in a sentence. Instead, they are used as nouns, adjectives, or adverbs.

The three verbals are *participles* (verbal adjectives), *gerunds* (verbal nouns), and *infinitives* (which can serve as verbal adjectives, verbal nouns, or verbal adverbs). A *verbal phrase* is a phrase consisting of a verbal and its complements or modifiers.

## The Participle

**3e. A *participle* is a word that is formed from a verb and used as an adjective.**

EXAMPLES   The **shouting** sailors threw their hats in the air.

**Shouting,** the sailors threw their hats in the air. [In these sentences, *shouting,* like the verb *shout,* expresses action; like an adjective, it modifies the noun *sailors.*]

The teacher saw a student **sleeping.** [Here *sleeping* expresses action, like a verb; it also modifies the noun *student.*]

There are two forms of participles: *present participles* and *past participles.* The perfect tense of a participle is formed with the helping verb *having.*

having given        having been given

Present participles end in *–ing.* Past participles end in *–ed, –d, –t, –en, –n:* talk*ed,* sav*ed,* crep*t,* bitt*en,* se*en.*

PRESENT PARTICIPLE   They heard Buffy Sainte-Marie **playing.**

PAST PARTICIPLE   The landlord, **satisfied,** left the apartment.

The words *playing* and *satisfied* modify nouns and hence are used as adjectives. Notice carefully that they show action but do not serve as verbs in the sentences. The verbs are *heard* and *left.* A participle may, however, be part of a verb phrase when it is used with a helping verb.

The **singing** waiter earned many tips. [*Singing* modifies *waiter.*]

The waiter was **singing** to please the customers. [The verb phrase *was singing* consists of the helping verb *was* and the present participle *singing.*]

Think of the participle in a verb phrase as part of the verb, not as an adjective modifying the subject.

Like verbs, participles may be modified by adverbs.

EXAMPLE   **Struggling vigorously,** she managed to swim to safety.

[The participle *struggling* is modified by the adverb *vigorously*.]

Participles, again like verbs, may take an object.

EXAMPLE **Calling the name repeatedly,** she shouted, "Heathcliff, Heathcliff!" [The object of the participle *calling* is *name*. It answers the question, *Calling what?* Notice that *repeatedly* is an adverb modifying *calling*.]

## The Participial Phrase

**3f. A *participial phrase* is a phrase containing a participle and any complements or modifiers it may have.**

The participle[1] introduces the phrase, and the entire phrase acts as an adjective to modify a noun or a pronoun.

EXAMPLES **Nodding his head,** the defendant acknowledged his guilt. [The participial phrase is made up of the participle *nodding* and the complement *head,* which is the direct object of *nodding*.]

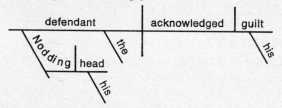

**Disturbed by his letter,** she telephoned him. [The participial phrase is made up of the participle *disturbed* and its modifier *by his letter,* which is an adverb phrase modifying *disturbed*.]

**EXERCISE 3.** List on your paper the participial phrases in the following sentences. Before each phrase, write the number of the sentence in which it appears. After each phrase, write the word it modifies.

---

[1] For work on the participial phrase as a sentence fragment, see pages 202–03. For exercises on the dangling participle, see pages 237–38.

1. Staking her reputation on her success, Junko Tabei climbed Mt. Everest, hoping to reach the top in May.
2. Delighted by penicillin's discovery, Fleming duplicated his experiments with Florey.
3. Their procedure, arrived at with such great care and effort, made their reputations.
4. Nellie Melba, thrilled by her successful career, retired repeatedly.
5. Delayed by wind and rain, the Spanish Armada arrived too late.
6. Drumming his wings wildly, the male pheasant tries to attract the female's attention.
7. The male pheasant, once firmly convinced of the female's interest, begins to accelerate the drumbeats expressing his excitement.
8. Socrates, preparing for a calm, self-administered death, seemed certain that his effort to liberate others would succeed, and that he would be remembered.

**EXERCISE 4.** In the following sentences, prepositional and participial phrases are italicized. Copy each phrase and indicate which kind (prepositional or participial) it is. After each phrase, write the word it modifies. Consider each italicized group as one phrase.

EXAMPLE   1. *Delighted by the new symphony,* the critic applauded *with great enthusiasm.*

1. *Delighted by the new symphony, critic, participial with great enthusiasm, applauded, prepositional*

1. Mahalia Jackson, *called the greatest potential blues singer since Bessie Smith,* would sing only religious songs.
2. Her version of "Silent Night" was one *of the all-time best-selling records* in Denmark.
3. *Acting as interpreter,* Sacajawea, a member *of the Shoshones,* aided the expedition *mapping the Northwest Territory.*
4. *Having been rejected by six publishers,* the story *of Peter Rabbit* was finally published privately *by Beatrix Potter.*
5. *Known for his imaginative style,* architect Minoru Yamasaki designed the World Trade Center *located in New York City.*

6. Elizabeth Blackwell, *ridiculed by nearly everyone,* became *in 1849* the first woman medical graduate *in the world.*

7. Maria Tallchief, an Osage, was the prima ballerina *of the New York Ballet Company.*

8. *Dancing to unanimous acclaim in the United States and Europe,* she was known *for her interpretation* of Stravinsky's *Firebird.*

9. The street *named for Mary McLeod Bethune* is *in New York City.*

10. *Widely honored as an educator,* she died *in 1955.*

## The Gerund

**3g. A *gerund* is a word ending in *–ing* that is formed from a verb and used as a noun.**

While both are formed from verbs, the gerund differs from the participle in that it is used as a noun, while the participle is used as an adjective.

EXAMPLE **Editing** is hard work. [*Editing* is formed from the verb *edit* and, as the subject of the sentence, is used as a noun.]

A gerund is a verbal noun. Like any other noun, it may be used as a subject, as the direct or indirect object of a verb, as a predicate nominative, or as the object of a preposition.

**Daydreaming** is her favorite pastime.   [gerund as subject]

We enjoy **swimming** here.   [gerund as direct object]

She gave her **editing** her full attention.   [gerund as indirect object]

Roberto's greatest pleasure was **composing.**   [gerund as predicate nominative]

By **planning** carefully, she managed to complete her thesis on time.   [gerund as object of a preposition]

**EXERCISE 5.** List the numbers 1–10. From each of the following sentences, select the participles and gerunds and write them in order after the numbers. Indicate by writing *p* or *g* whether the words you select are participles or gerunds.

1. Using the penname "Nellie Bly," Elizabeth Seaman became a famous journalist in the late 1800's.
2. Traveling alone around the world in seventy-two days, she beat the hero of Jules Verne's novel.
3. A task of the Shaker women was designing furniture.
4. Being the publisher of the *Washington Post* has made Katharine Graham one of the country's most influential people.
5. Mary Shelley, who wrote *Frankenstein*, liked reading ghost stories with friends at night.
6. The plot of *Frankenstein* came to her in a dream after a conversation about creating life.
7. Accepting an offer to do a TV program, La Deva Davis said she was no Julia Child but knew her way around the burners.
8. Keeping the costs of her recipes low, Ms. Davis gained wide popular appeal.
9. *Sylvia Porter's Money Book,* by the columnist, became a best seller by giving sound financial advice.
10. Taking her title from the Bible, actress Ethel Waters wrote her now-famous autobiography, *His Eye Is on the Sparrow.*

## The Gerund Phrase

**3h. A *gerund phrase* is a phrase consisting of a gerund and any modifiers or complements it may have.**

EXAMPLE    **Boiling an egg properly** is not easy for an inexperienced cook.   [The gerund *boiling* has *egg* as its direct object and is modified by the adverb *properly*.]

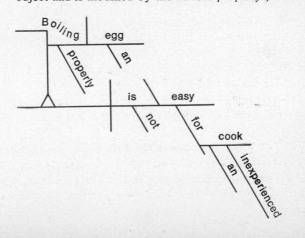

Like the gerund alone, the gerund phrase may be used in
any place that a noun would fit.

EXAMPLES   **Playing the piano** was his greatest accomplishment.
[gerund phrase as subject]

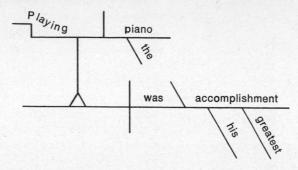

The general admitted **sending the order.** [gerund
phrase as object of the verb *admitted—order* is the
object of the gerund *sending*]

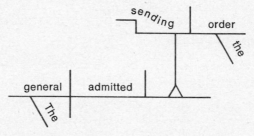

The judge warned him about **telling lies.** [gerund
phrase as object of preposition *about*]

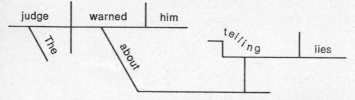

**Voting regularly** is **accepting a responsibility of citizenship.** [gerund phrases as subject and predicate
nominative]

## The Infinitive

**3i. An *infinitive* is a verb form, usually preceded by *to*, that is used as a noun or a modifier.**

to explore     to worry     to live

An infinitive is generally used as a noun, but it may also be used as an adjective or as an adverb.

THE INFINITIVE USED AS A NOUN

**To err** is human.   [infinitive as subject]

Samuel Johnson liked **to argue**.   [infinitive as direct object]

The soldier's duty is **to obey orders**.   [infinitive as predicate nominative]

THE INFINITIVE USED AS AN ADJECTIVE

The surgeon had not a minute **to lose**.   [The infinitive modifies the noun *minute*.]

THE INFINITIVE USED AS AN ADVERB

Radium in its pure state is hard **to find**.   [The infinitive modifies the adjective *hard*.]

► **NOTE**   Do not confuse the infinitive, which is a verbal beginning with *to*, and the prepositional phrase beginning with *to*, which consists of *to* plus a noun or pronoun.

| INFINITIVES | PREPOSITIONAL PHRASES |
|---|---|
| to smile | to them |
| to predict | to the theater |
| to walk | to the museum |

The word *to*, the sign of the infinitive, is sometimes omitted.

I saw her [to] **raise** her hand.

Let me [to] **give** this to Sophia.

Please [to] **stay** here.

Will you help me [to] **pack**?

**EXERCISE 6.**   Number your paper 1–20. From each of the following sentences, select the participles, gerunds, and infinitives and list them in order. After each, tell what it is. For each participle, state the word it modifies. For each gerund, state whether it is used as the subject, direct object, predicate nominative, or object of a preposition. For each infinitive, indicate whether it is used as a noun, adjective, or adverb.

EXAMPLES  1. Earhart spoke of flying across the ocean.
1. *flying, gerund, object of preposition*
2. Cordelia hoped to help her father.
2. *to help, infinitive, noun*
3. Rosalind went to the Forest of Arden to escape her menacing cousin.
3. *to escape, infinitive, adverb*
*menacing, participle, cousin*

1. Each of Portia's suitors wanted to choose the right casket.
2. To incite the Roman mobs, Antony praised Caesar.
3. The dying Hamlet begged Horatio for literary immortality.
4. Reading Shakespeare is a creditable pastime.
5. Juliet did not wish to survive Romeo.
6. Desdemona was eager to keep the love of Othello.
7. Frowning and spreading its arms, the ghost of Hamlet's father disappeared.
8. Amiens enjoyed entertaining his fellow musicians.
9. Calpurnia tried to discourage the ambition of her husband.
10. We who now behold these present days have eyes to wonder, but lack tongues to praise.
11. To win retribution was her insoluble problem of justice.
12. We admire Katharina for showing her conviction to marry only for love.
13. To compose effective drama is quite difficult.
14. Falling to utter disaster left Olivia nothing but hope.
15. Lady Macbeth wanted to understand herself, but she failed to succeed.
16. A perfect bowling score is difficult to achieve.
17. Mercutio's strong point was spinning fairy tales.
18. When the time came for courting Miranda, Ferdinand was carrying logs.

19. Shakespeare knew acting from his own personal experience.
20. Have you seen him performed?

## The Infinitive Phrase

**3j. An *infinitive phrase* consists of an infinitive and any complements or modifiers it may have.**

> She offered **to cook breakfast.**    [*Breakfast* is the object of the infinitive *to cook.*]
>
> Actors must learn **to speak clearly.**    [*Clearly* is an adverb modifying *to speak.*]

Like infinitives alone, the infinitive phrase may serve as the subject of a verb or as the direct object of a verb. It may also be used as an adjective or an adverb.

EXAMPLES    **To write a good term paper** is a difficult task.    [infinitive phrase as subject]

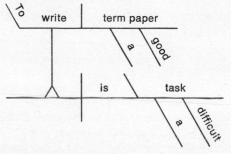

> Rosetta decided **to attend business school.**    [infinitive phrase as object of verb]
>
> She had a great desire **to see Paris.**    [infinitive phrase used as adjective, modifying the noun *desire*]
>
> The attorney labored **to free her client.**    [infinitive phrase as adverb modifying the verb *labored*]

## The Infinitive Clause

Unlike other verbals, an infinitive may have a subject as well as complements and modifiers.

EXAMPLES  The judge ordered **the district attorney to drop the charges.**  [*The district attorney* is the subject of the infinitive *to drop*. The entire group of words *the district attorney to drop the charges* is the object of the verb *ordered.*]

The police officer asked **them to leave quietly.**  [*Them* is the subject of the infinitive *to leave.*]

When an infinitive has a subject, as in the preceding examples, the construction is called an *infinitive clause.* Notice that the subject of the infinitive in the second sentence (*them*) is in the objective case.[1]

**REVIEW EXERCISE A.** Number your paper 1–15. In the following sentences most of the phrases have been numbered and italicized. After each number, write the kind of phrase: prepositional, participial, gerund, or infinitive.

EXAMPLE  (1) *Winning a scholarship* is the result (2) *of hard work.*

1. *gerund*
2. *prepositional*

a. (1) *Shocked by his mother's illness,* Gian made reservations (2) *to return home* (3) *on Monday.*

b. (4) *Running down the steps,* she discovered that the burglar had tried (5) *to open the safe* (6) *in the library.*

c. (7) *Hoping for an early victory,* the general decided (8) *to attack the enemy* (9) *before midnight.*

d. (10) *Understanding the position,* the dean granted a delay for (11) *filing the application* (12) *for Annapolis.*

e. She decided (13) *to wait for the results* (14) *of the exam* before (15) *giving a party.*

# THE APPOSITIVE[2]

**3k. An *appositive* is a noun or pronoun that follows another noun or pronoun to identify or explain it. An**

---

[1] For rules concerning the use of the objective case, see pages 108–10.
[2] For rules on the punctuation of appositives, see page 437. For the use of appositives in the subordination of ideas, see pages 252–53.

*appositive phrase* **is made up of an appositive and its modifiers.**

In the following sentences the appositives and appositive phrases are in bold-faced type.

> Her sister **Nancy** was a year older.
> We stopped at Stonehenge, **an historic site.**
> George Washington, **our first President,** was a great military leader.

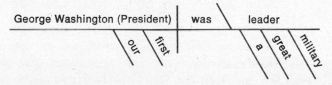

George Washington (President) | was | leader
our first | a great military

**REVIEW EXERCISE B.** Number your paper 1–20. In the following sentences most of the phrases have been numbered and italicized. After each number, write the kind of phrase: prepositional, participial, gerund, infinitive, or appositive.

[1] *Searching for energy* has become more complex [2] *in recent years.* [3] *Sobered by the energy crunch,* governments have been urged [4] *to take careful planning measures.* [5] *To ensure future supplies,* new sources have been sought [6] *for raw materials.* [7] *Preparing for the next century,* the Canadian National Energy Board and the United States Federal Power Commission, [8] *agencies with jurisdiction in such matters,* guided the Arctic Pipeline project from Prudhoe Bay across Alaska to the fjord of Valdez. [9] *Building the pipeline* at all, said some consumer groups, would be equivalent [10] *to ecological suicide.* Cost-cutting, [11] *a euphemism for exploitation of the land surface,* would again lead to drastic destruction of the natural chain [12] *of life* disrupted by the pipeline. [13] *After long and complicated negotiations* between all parties, the various ecological, industrial, and governmental agencies managed to agree [14] *to the basic principles* [15] *governing the construction project.* [16] *Depleting the earth's natural resources* is not an unimportant affair that can be ignored [17] *by any single group* [18] *with an interest* in the future. [19] *Enlightened by our new understanding* of the global web of life, all of us must cooperate [20] *to give the whole earth what it requires* for its health.

# Chapter 4

# The Clause

## Adjective, Noun, and Adverb Clauses

When we first begin to write, we use simple sentences: *Last Saturday we went to the theater. The play was very funny. I liked the last act best.* However, as we grow older and more mature in our thinking, we write more complicated sentences, in order to express our thoughts more effectively. One sign of maturity in writing is the use of subordination. We might now write:

Last Saturday we went to the theater **because it was my birthday.** [An adverbial clause shows the reason for doing something.]

The play, **which the critics had praised highly,** was very funny. [An adjective clause modifies the word *play*.]

Afterwards, I told my parents **that I liked the last act best.** [The original sentence has become a noun clause used as a direct object of the verb *told*.]

Each of these three sentences contains a subordinate clause. Studying the different kinds of subordinate clauses — the adjective, the adverb, and the noun clause — will help you to write sentences that will have more clarity, smoothness, and force.

## Diagnostic Test

Give yourself this diagnostic test. There are ten subordinate clauses in the following sentences. Copy them in order on your paper. After each clause, tell whether it is an adjective, adverb, or noun clause.

1. Whoever forgot the matches on our hike was probably the one who was most relieved by the accident.
2. After the lightning struck Dick's transistor radio antenna on the pine tree, our plans for the barbecue were saved.
3. The burning pine cones which fell closest to us kindled our cardboard food cartons.
4. Jane found a cool, high rock where we ate our burnt hot dogs and our toasted rolls separately.
5. At the time we hoped the soda would cool again if we let it stand awhile.
6. When fall came, the trees that had been charred made a remarkable comeback.
7. Few of us will forget that you don't always need plans for a barbecue.

**4a. A *clause* is a group of words containing a subject and a predicate and used as part of a sentence.**

An *independent clause*[1] expresses a complete thought and can stand alone as a sentence. A *subordinate clause* does not express a complete thought and cannot stand alone.

## INDEPENDENT CLAUSES

When an independent clause stands alone, it is called a simple sentence.

> The lecturer discussed the causes of the French Revolution.

It is called an independent clause only when it is combined with one or more additional clauses in a sentence.

> The lecturer discussed the causes of the French Revolution, but she purposely neglected to mention the influence of the American Revolution on European politics. [The conjunction *but* joins two independent clauses.]
>
> When the lecture was over, she asked for questions from the class. [In this sentence the independent clause *she asked for questions from the class* is combined with a subordinate clause.]

---

[1] *Independent* clauses are sometimes called *main* clauses.

## SUBORDINATE CLAUSES

Subordinate clauses[1] cannot stand alone as sentences. They are always joined in some way to an independent clause.

> that she bought yesterday
> who she was
> when she retired

Combined with an independent clause, each of these subordinate clauses plays its part in completing the meaning of the sentence.

> Rita liked the book **that she bought yesterday.**
> We told the teacher **who she was.**
> My aunt went to Florida **when she retired.**

**EXERCISE 1.** Number your paper 1–10. If the italicized clause is an independent clause, write *I* after the proper number; if it is a subordinate clause write *S*.

1. Do you know *that our capacity for swallowing is weak compared to that of animals?*
2. When a human swallows, *food passes from the mouth to the stomach.*
3. There are three stages *that are involved in swallowing.*
4. First the tongue pushes food into the oral pharynx *while the soft palate seals off the nasal cavities.*
5. Then the upper esophageal sphincter relaxes to admit food to the esophagus *as the glottis seals off the passageway to the lungs.*
6. *Finally, rhythmic contractions in the esophagus carry food to the stomach,* where the cardiac sphincter relaxes and the cardiac valve opens.
7. Nobody can breathe *while food is entering the esophagus.*
8. Liquids take less time to swallow *when we are standing upright.*
9. Once the reflex begins, *no conscious effort is required.*
10. It is a relief to know *that practically all these reflexes take care of themselves.*

---

[1] *Subordinate* clauses are sometimes called *dependent* clauses.

## The Adjective Clause

**4b. An *adjective clause* is a subordinate clause that, like an adjective, modifies a noun or a pronoun.**

EXAMPLES    Here is the book **that I want** you to read.

The place **where they found** the gold is farther west.

The first man **who circumnavigated the globe** was Magellan. [The subordinate clause *who circumnavigated the globe* modifies the noun *man*.][1]

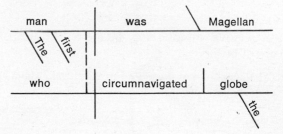

## Relative Pronouns

Adjective clauses often begin with the pronouns *who, whom, whose, which, that.* Pronouns used in this way refer to, or are *related to,* some word or idea which has preceded them. Because of this relationship they are called *relative pronouns.*[2]

**4c. A *relative pronoun* is a pronoun that begins a subordinate clause and is related to another word or idea.**

---

[1] Since a subordinate clause has a verb and a subject and may contain complements and modifiers, it is diagramed very much like a sentence. Adjective and adverb clauses are placed on a horizontal line below the main line. An adjective clause introduced by a relative pronoun is joined to the word it modifies by a broken line drawn from the modified word to the relative pronoun.

[2] The compound relative pronouns *whoever, whomever, whichever, whatever* may also begin clauses. Occasionally, an adjective clause may begin with a relative adverb, for example, *This is the place* where *they found the treasure.*

A relative pronoun may be the subject of the clause it begins.

> The President decorated the astronaut **who had orbited the earth.** [The relative pronoun *who* is the subject of the verb *had orbited.*]

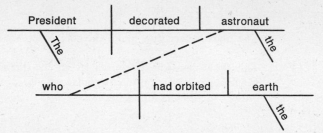

A relative pronoun may be the object of the verb in the clause it begins.

> The bouquet was presented to the singer, **whom everyone was applauding wildly.**

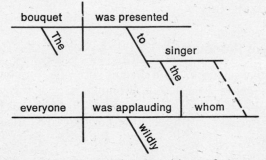

A relative pronoun may be the object of a preposition in the clause.

> She is the doctor **for whom you called.**

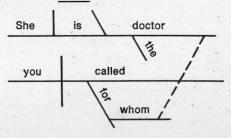

**EXERCISE 2.** Copy in order on your paper the adjective clauses in the following sentences. After each clause, write the noun or pronoun that the clause modifies. Be prepared for your teacher to ask you whether the relative pronoun is used as the subject, object of the verb, or object of the preposition.

1. The time for complaints about marks which were recorded last year has already passed.
2. Decisions that the Supreme Court has made become part of the law of the land.
3. Her cousin David is the only person whom Delia trusts completely.
4. Algebra, which was first used by the Arabs, was brought to Europe during the crusades.
5. The United States has sent billions of dollars' worth of supplies to countries that needed them.
6. The woman whom I introduced you to at the party heads this committee.
7. The Secretary-General of the United Nations is a person who has heavy responsibilities.
8. I have just finished reading the book that you mentioned.
9. As her executive secretary, the mayor appointed a man who had been in public service for twenty years.
10. This story has a plot that is difficult to follow.
11. That is a subject about which I know nothing.
12. Some magazines are written especially for those who hold a particular point of view.
13. This book is one that you cannot put down.
14. The earthquake, which began so suddenly, stopped just as suddenly.
15. Prescribed drugs that may have harmful side effects must be used with great caution.

## The Noun Clause

**4d. A *noun clause* is a subordinate clause used as a noun.**

EXAMPLE  We appreciated **what the violinist played.**[1]

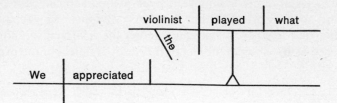

The entire clause *what the violinist played* is the direct object of the verb *appreciated.* Study the following pairs of sentences to see how a noun clause may be the subject of a verb, a predicate nominative, or the object of a preposition.

> Her **guilt** was obvious.  [*Guilt* is a noun used as the subject of the verb *was.*]
>
> **That she was guilty** was obvious.  [*That she was guilty* is a noun clause used as the subject of the verb *was.*]
>
> Chemistry is her favorite **subject.**  [*Subject* is a noun used as a predicate nominative.]
>
> Chemistry is **what she likes best in school.**  [*What she likes best in school* is a noun clause used as a predicate nominative.]
>
> Degrees are awarded by the **principal.**  [*Principal* is a noun used as the object of the preposition *by.*]
>
> Degrees are awarded by **whoever is in charge of the school.** [*Whoever is in charge of the school* is a noun clause used as object of the preposition *by.*]

Adjective and noun clauses are frequently used without an introductory relative pronoun or other joining word. Note that the introductory word is omitted in the second sentence in each of the following pairs.

> Washington said **that he wanted no third term.**
>
> Washington said **he wanted no third term.**

---

[1] In diagraming, a noun clause is pictured as a unit by being placed at the top of a vertical line, like a pedestal, rising from that part of the diagram (subject, object, predicate nominative) to which the clause belongs.

We pitied the little boy **whom everybody had ridiculed.**[1]

We pitied the little boy **everybody had ridiculed.**

**EXERCISE 3.** List in order on your paper the subordinate clauses in the following sentences. Before each clause, place the number of the sentence in which it appears. After each clause, tell what kind it is—adjective or noun. Be prepared to tell what word each adjective clause modifies and how each noun clause is used in the sentence—as a subject, an object of a verb or of a preposition, or a predicate nominative.

1. Until recently, scientists believed that the giant sequoias of California were the oldest living trees on earth.

2. Now, however, that honor is given to the bristlecone pine, a tree that few people have ever heard of.

3. Everyone who respects hardiness and pluck respects the bristlecone pine.

4. Its leaves or needles last on the branches for twelve to fifteen years, a length of time that is considered extraordinary.

5. Botanists know that the bristlecone is a member of the family of foxtail pines.

6. What its needle-clusters resemble gives the foxtail pine its name.

7. In the north temperate zone there are over ninety species of pine, a tree that is central to the economy of most northerly nations.

8. Species which are native to North America are divided into two types, hard pines and soft pines.

9. Bristlecone is a species of soft pine that is valued for its resin.

10. The southern Rockies are where it thrives naturally.

## The Adverb Clause

**4e. The *adverb clause* is a subordinate clause that, like an adverb, modifies a verb, an adjective, or an adverb.**

[1] For exercises on *who* and *whom* in standard usage, see pages 113–15.

In the following examples the adverb clauses modify the verb by telling *how, when, where, why, to what extent,* or *under what conditions.*

> Mary Lou Williams played the piano **as though she were inspired.** [*how* she played]
>
> The committee announced the new tax plan **after the election was over.** [*when* they announced the plan]
>
> The soprano practiced **where she could.** [*where* she practiced]
>
> Some people learn to cook **because they enjoy good food.** [*why* they learn]
>
> The Harrisons play bridge more **than we do.** [*how much* or *to what extent* they play]
>
> Will you go **if the weather is nice?**[1] [*under what conditions* you will go]

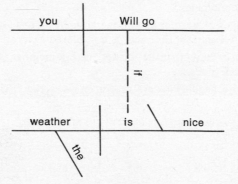

**ADVERB CLAUSE MODIFYING AN ADJECTIVE**

> Alexander the Great was sure **that he would conquer the world.** [The adverb clause *that he would conquer the world* modifies the adjective *sure.*]

**ADVERB CLAUSE MODIFYING AN ADVERB**

> Jane plays the piano better **than I do.** [The adverb clause *than I do* modifies the adverb *better.*]

---

[1] In diagraming, an adverb clause is written on a horizontal line below the main line of the diagram. The subordinating conjunction beginning the clause is written on a broken line which links the verb of the clause to the word the clause modifies.

## The Subordinating Conjunction

**4f. A conjunction that begins an adverb clause is called a** *subordinating conjunction.* **It joins the clause to the rest of the sentence.**

### Common Subordinating Conjunctions[1]

| | | | |
|---|---|---|---|
| after | as though | since | when |
| although | because | so that | whenever |
| as | before | than | where |
| as if | if | though | wherever |
| as long as | in order that | unless | while |
| as soon as | provided that | until | |

## The Elliptical (Incomplete) Clause

Sometimes in our writing and speaking, we do not complete the adverb clauses we use.

EXAMPLES    Bacon was more learned in the classics than Shakespeare [was].

While [he was] painting, Rembrandt could concentrate completely.

In these adverb clauses the part of the clause given in brackets has been omitted. The complete clause, however, is in the writer's and the reader's mind. Such incomplete clauses are said to be *elliptical.* (For the correct use of pronouns in elliptical clauses see page 116.)

An elliptical clause is diagramed as if the missing element were present.

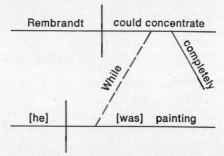

[1] Many of these words may also be used as other parts of speech.

**EXERCISE 4.** Copy on your paper the adverb clauses in the following sentences. Before each clause, write the number of the sentence in which it appears. Draw a line under the subordinating conjunction that introduces the clause. After each clause, write the word or expression that the clause modifies. Be prepared to state whether the clause describes *how, when, where, why, to what extent,* or *under what conditions.* (Since interpretations of the meaning may differ, more than one correct answer is sometimes possible.)

1. When there is contentment, there is no rebellion.
    — CONFUCIUS

2. Arachne was the best of the mortal weavers until her pride destroyed her.

3. She ran until she dropped.

4. Agriculture in many of the African countries is sometimes especially difficult because crops will not grow in the bricklike soil.

5. In scientific research all variables must be controlled so that no errors will be introduced.

6. If Professor King's theory is true, then the Chinese might have been the first to discover America.

7. While commercial television must depend on its sponsors for profit, it must still consider the public interest.

8. A family physician should be available whenever an emergency arises.

9. Since there are so many good paperbacks, almost any student can now have a good library at home.

10. A sailfish can swim faster than a person can run.

# SENTENCES CLASSIFIED ACCORDING TO STRUCTURE

**4g. Classified according to their structure, there are four kinds of sentences—*simple, compound, complex,* and *compound-complex.***

**(1)** A *simple sentence* **is a sentence with one independent clause and no subordinate clauses.**

EXAMPLE    The defeat of Napoleon at Waterloo was a victory for England.

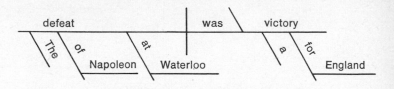

**(2)** A *compound sentence* **is a sentence which is composed of two or more independent clauses but no subordinate clauses.**

EXAMPLE    The defeat of Napoleon was a victory for England, but it meant the end of an era of French grandeur.

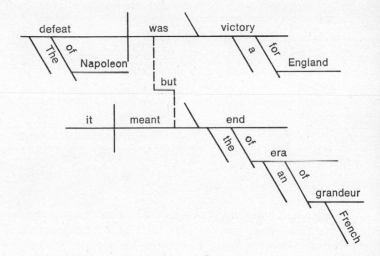

► **NOTE**    Be careful not to confuse the compound subject or predicate of a simple sentence with the clauses of a compound sentence.

The archaeological discovery was made in the spring and was widely acclaimed in the fall.  [simple sentence with compound predicate]

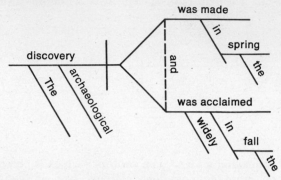

The archaeological discovery was made in the spring, and it was widely acclaimed in the fall.  [compound sentence with two subjects and two verbs]

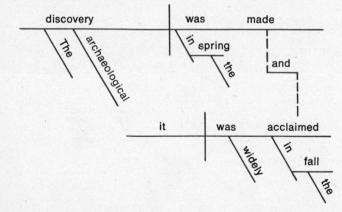

Independent clauses may be joined by coordinating conjunctions (*and, but, nor, or, for, yet*) or by conjunctive adverbs (*accordingly, also, besides, consequently, furthermore, hence, however, moreover, nevertheless, then, therefore, thus, still*).

**(3) A *complex sentence* is a sentence that contains one independent clause and one or more subordinate clauses.**

The man who looks for trouble often finds it. [The independent clause is *the man often finds it.* The subordinate clause is *who looks for trouble.*]

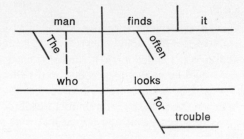

**(4) A** *compound-complex sentence* **is a sentence that contains two or more independent clauses and one or more subordinate clauses.**

The man who looks for trouble often finds it, but then he does not want it.

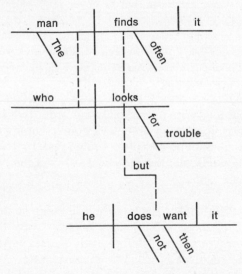

**EXERCISE 5.** Number your paper 1–10. After the proper number, tell what kind of sentence each of the following is: simple, compound, complex, compound-complex.

1. Charles Drew did research on blood plasma and helped develop blood banks.
2. The rain water will be gathered in barrels and used for emergencies.
3. After the advertisement appeared in the newspapers, Dr. Scott declared that she would never change her mind.
4. When World War I ended in 1918, almost everybody thought that there would be no more wars; but twenty-one years later World War II began.
5. In his letter to Mrs. Bixby, Abraham Lincoln consoled her for the loss of several sons and hoped that time would ease her sorrow.
6. When the speaker saw how pleased her audience looked, she felt more at ease and spoke more distinctly.
7. Those who want to have an otter for a pet must be prepared to share their life with a playful, destructive, eccentric creature.
8. The great English philosopher Thomas Hobbes once aspired to be a mathematician, but he never really seemed to grasp the point of mathematics.
9. It was generally believed that Queen Elizabeth's hair was red, but no one knew for sure because she always wore a wig.
10. Lee Trevino is considered by many to be one of the best golf players in America.

**EXERCISE 6.** Write in the following order two simple sentences, two compound sentences, four complex sentences, and two compound-complex sentences. In the complex and compound-complex sentences, draw a line under each subordinate clause.

**REVIEW EXERCISE.** Each of the following sentences contains one or more subordinate clauses. Copy the clauses in order on your paper. Before each clause, write the number of the sentence in which it appears. After each clause, write what kind it is — adjective, noun, adverb.

1. Mecca, which is the spiritual center of Islam, is visited by thousands of pilgrims each year.

2. The settlers abandoned their cabins before the first volcanoes erupted on the islands.

3. Many of the antibiotics that are used today are produced by organisms called *Streptomyces,* which have some of the characteristics of bacteria and some of the characteristics of molds.

4. Samuel F. B. Morse, the man who invented the telegraph, painted the portrait of President James Monroe that hangs in the White House.

5. Although the Japanese borrowed their writing system from the Chinese, they used it to write a language that is completely unlike Chinese.

6. Changes in the law are slow because changes in people's values are also slow.

7. The judge who decided to dismiss the case was influenced by what the defendant's supervisor had illegally done.

8. Whenever she spoke, the oracle was heard with attention.

9. Soon after he had married a new wife, Henry VIII concluded that she was unsatisfactory.

10. The senator failed to realize that the trouble was in the local government and not in the state capital.

11. I didn't know that the trouble was in the sparkplug and not in the distributor.

12. Little League baseball teams which refused to admit girls when they applied were ordered to change their policy after Judith S. Weis sued the State of New Jersey in 1972.

13. Whenever a comet passes through the solar system and loses a little of its outermost layer, we are the ones who gain materially.

14. Students who know what they want to learn are students who will succeed.

15. If we read one book a day, it would still take us many years to read all the books published in a single year.

# Usage

# PART TWO

# Chapter 5

# The Varieties of English

## Levels of Usage; Appropriateness

Because you speak English, you can communicate with all other English-speaking people. This does not mean, however, that the English you speak is identical in every way with the English that others speak. Differences exist in pronunciation, idioms, vocabulary, grammar, and usage.

The varieties of a language are called dialects. All of us naturally speak a dialect that reflects the speech of those from whom we learned to speak — parents, family, and friends. A dialect may be regional. We distinguish differences between the English spoken in New England and the English spoken in the Midwest or in the South or in the West. A dialect may be local. The English used by people who grew up in a big city is likely to be different from that spoken by people who grew up in a small town or in the suburbs. A dialect may be ethnic, carrying over into English the idioms and syntax of another language. A dialect may reflect one's education. The more schooling people have, the greater their exposure to different bodies of knowledge and to uses of the language that may differ from their own. This increased knowledge is often reflected in their speech.

Dialects are not thought of as good or bad, correct or incorrect English. They are simply natural, healthy varieties of English reflecting differences in the environment in which the language was learned. It is just as natural for a person to say, for example, "It don't make no difference to me" as it is for another person to say, "It doesn't make any difference to me." For the former, the ungrammatical "it don't" and the double negative "don't make no" are acceptable English in the place where they were learned.

Nevertheless, everyone is familiar with the expression "good English." An employer may ask about an applicant, "Does she speak good English?" Sometimes we hear it said of a person, "His English isn't very good." What is meant by such remarks is that their English is in some way a departure from what we call standard English.

## STANDARD ENGLISH

In school students are encouraged to learn so-called "good English." This is standard English, or the standard dialect.

Why are you encouraged to learn standard English? In the simplest terms it is the most generally accepted form of the language spoken and written in this country. It is, for example, the language most used in mass communication. Standard English is the language of newspapers and magazines, of most books and journals. Standard English is usually spoken by newscasters and disc jockeys, movie and television personalities; it is often the language spoken in the programs, plays, and films in which they perform. Standard English is the spoken and written language of the business world, the medical and technological fields, and is the language of politics and politicians.

The language you use conveys to a listener more than just the ideas you are expressing. It often implies, sometimes unjustly, the extent of your general education and your general sophistication. Authorities on the modern problems of urban renewal and the television reporter who interviews them may be very familiar with dialects that are quite different from standard English. Indeed they may themselves occasionally use nonstandard dialects in some circumstances, but they will probably not use them on a television program, where it would be inappropriate. If they did use them on such a television program, listeners might question the educational backgrounds and the competence of the speakers.

## Two Kinds of Standard English

One aim of this book, and of all English teaching, is to develop your ability to use standard English with ease. The chapters on usage will increase your understanding of the conventions of standard English. But standard English is not one set of words or expressions or pronunciations; it can be broken down into two main divisions: *formal* and *informal.*

### Formal Standard English

Formal standard English is English that is appropriate to serious essays, formal reports, research papers, some literary criticism, essay answers on some examinations, and addresses on serious or solemn occasions. It is almost always written. Many of the words used are not the ordinary words of everyday speech. Sentences are often long and elaborately constructed. Contractions are rarely used and slang almost never.

In the following example of formal English, note the length of sentences, the repetition, and certain expressions —the use of *go forth* and *ask not,* for example—not usually used in ordinary conversation.

> . . . Let the word go forth from this time and place, to friend and foe alike, that the torch has been passed to a new generation of Americans—born in this century, tempered by war, disciplined by a hard and bitter peace, proud of our ancient heritage, and unwilling to witness or permit the slow undoing of those human rights to which we are committed today at home and around the world.
>
> Let every nation know, whether it wishes us well or ill, that we shall pay any price, bear any burden, meet any hardship, support any friend, oppose any foe, to assure the survival and success of liberty. . . . And so my fellow Americans:

ask not what your country can do for you; ask what you can do for your country.

. . . Finally, whether you are citizens of America or citizens of the world, ask of us here the same high standards of strength and sacrifice which we ask of you. With a good conscience our only sure reward, with history the final judge of our deeds, let us go forth to lead the land we love, asking His blessing and His help, but knowing that here on earth God's work must truly be our own.[1]

## Informal Standard English

Informal English is the language knowledgeable people use most of the time. It is the language of newspapers, magazines, and most books, and of business letters and talks for a general audience. It is also the language of most contemporary novels, short stories, and plays.

The conventions of informal English are not as rigid as those of formal English. Sentences may be long or short and often imitate the rhythms of everyday conversations rather than the stately and regular rhythms of formal prose. Contractions often appear and slang is sometimes used.

In the following example of informal standard English, notice that the speech patterns are the familiar everyday ones, the words simple and the sentences varied in length.

> Ever since I bit a circus lion, believing him to be another dog like myself, only larger, I have been what Doc Watson calls a Public Character in our town.
>
> Freckles, my boy, was a kind of Public Character, too. He went around bragging about my noble blood and bravery, and all the other boys and dogs in town sort of looked up to him and thought how lucky he was to belong to a dog like me. And he deserved whatever glory he got out of it, Freckles did. For, if I do say it myself, there's not a dog in town got a better boy than my boy Freckles, take him all in all. I'll back him against any dog's boy that is anywhere near his size, for fighting, swimming, climbing, foot-racing, or throwing

[1] "Inaugural Address," January 20, 1961, by John F. Kennedy.

stones farthest and straightest. Or I'll back him against any stray boy, either.[1]

# NONSTANDARD ENGLISH

Nonstandard English is the term used to describe variations in usage that are best avoided in all but the most casual writing and speaking.

Speakers of nonstandard English can, and often do, rise to positions of importance in business, government, and elsewhere, but they generally master standard English along the way.

Nonstandard English can be found in literature in many novels, short stories, and stage and television plays. In John Steinbeck's compelling novel *Grapes of Wrath,* the author records in the speech, thoughts, and actions of the Joad family the hopes and frustrations of the thousands of poor migrant farmers who were victims of the Depression and the drought that blighted southwestern farmlands in the thirties.

Tom slowly made a cigarette, and inspected it and lighted it. He took off his ruined cap and wiped his forehead. "I got an idear," he said. "Maybe nobody gonna like it, but here she is: The nearer to California our folks get, the quicker they's gonna be money rollin' in. Now this here car'll go twicet as fast as that truck. Now here's my idea. You take out some a that stuff in the truck, an' then all you folks but me an' the preacher get in an' move on. Me an' Casy'll stop here an' fix this here car an' then we drive on, day an' night, an' we'll catch up, or if we don't meet on the road, you'll be a-workin' anyways. An' if you break down, why, jus' camp 'longside the road till we come. You can't be no worse off, an' if you get through, why, you'll be a-workin', an' stuff'll be easy. Casy can give me a lif' with this here car, an' we'll come a-sailin'."[2]

[1] From "Being a Public Character" by Don Marquis. Reprinted by permission of Doubleday & Company, Inc.
[2] From *The Grapes of Wrath* by John Steinbeck. Copyright 1939, Copyright © renewed 1967 by John Steinbeck. Reprinted by permission of The Viking Press, Inc., and McIntosh & Otis, Inc.

## Sources of Information on Usage

To find out whether or not a particular expression is standard usage, consult a usage reference book or a dictionary. The *American Heritage Dictionary of the English Language* is especially rich in current information on usage.

One or more of the following reference books may be available in your school or public library.

> Copperud, Roy H., *American Usage: The Consensus*
> Evans, Bergen and Cornelia, *A Dictionary of Contemporary American Usage*
> Morris, William and Mary, *Harper's Dictionary of Contemporary Usage*

**EXERCISE 1.** Bring to class two examples of formal standard and two examples of informal standard writing from books, magazines, and newspapers. Be prepared to give your reasons for labeling each as you have done.

**EXERCISE 2.** The words and expressions listed below present usage problems that trouble many people. Look them up in this and whatever other textbooks and reference books are available to you — most will be listed in the index.

1. double negative
2. *between, among*
3. *It's me.* [pronoun usage]
4. *like, as*
5. *bring, take*
6. *good, well*
7. *imply, infer*
8. *(the) reason is because . . .*
9. *could of*
10. *fewer, less*

**Chapter 6**

# Correct Agreement

## Subject and Verb, Pronoun and Antecedent

Certain words in English that are closely related in sentences have matching forms. When the forms match, they are said to *agree*. A subject and verb agree if both are singular or both plural. Pronouns and their antecedents (the words the pronouns stand for) agree in the same way. In the following sentences the forms do not match:

Two planes *is* flying overhead.

Each girl won *their* varsity letter.

In order to correct these sentences, we would have to change the italicized words:

Two planes **are** flying overhead.

Each girl won **her** varsity letter.

## AGREEMENT OF SUBJECT AND VERB

**6a. A word that refers to one person or thing is *singular* in number. A word that refers to more than one thing is *plural* in number.**

SINGULAR   house, woman,
               that, he, she, it

PLURAL   houses, women,
              those, they

## 6b. A verb agrees with its subject in number.

### (1) Singular subjects take singular verbs.

The **typewriter was** new.
Either **car performs** economically.

### (2) Plural subjects take plural verbs.

The **typewriters were** new.
Both **cars perform** economically.

Not many students have difficulty in distinguishing between the singular and plural forms of nouns and pronouns. Almost without thinking, you can tell which of the words in the following list refer to one thing or person, and which refer to more than one.[1]

| | |
|---|---|
| bird | birds |
| child | children |
| hat | hats |
| race | races |
| he | they |

Similarly, most students can easily tell the difference between the singular and plural forms of a verb.

| | |
|---|---|
| sings | sing |
| throws | throw |
| seems | seem |
| is | are |
| was | were |

From the above examples, you will note that most nouns form their plural by adding the letter s, as in *birds, hats, races*. With nouns, then, the final s is a clue to the *plural* form.

With many verbs, however, the opposite is true. An s ending on a verb is associated with the *singular* form, not the plural, as in *sings, throws, is, was. Are, were, have* and

---

[1] Detailed rules for the formation of the plural forms of nouns are given on pages 548–51.

most verbs not ending in single *s* are plural: they *are*, they *play*, they *sing*. The exceptions, which are not difficult to remember, are verbs used with *I* and singular *you:* I *play*, you *sing*.

All the verbs that have been used as examples so far are in the present tense. All past tense verbs have the same form in the singular and the plural with the exception of *be*, which has the special form *was* (with the *s* sign for the singular) that is used with *he, she, I,* and *it,* and all singular nouns.

| SINGULAR | PLURAL |
|----------|--------|
| I played. | They played. |
| He sang. | We sang. |
| You were. | You were. |
| She was. | They were. |

Although most students are familiar with the singular and plural forms of nouns, pronouns, and verbs, beginning writers still commit "agreement errors" often in their sentences. Why do these errors occur? Often the writers have failed to analyze their own sentences correctly; more specifically, they have failed to see the *true* subjects of the sentences. Certain constructions tend to make the number of the subject obscure. Those constructions which cause most agreement problems will be taken up separately below.

## Intervening Phrases and Clauses

In many sentences a phrase intervenes between the subject and the verb. When the noun in this phrase does not agree in number with the subject, writers often become confused about the number of the verb.

A clause can also come between the subject and the verb. Just as with the phrase, the intervening clause tends to confuse the writer in choosing the correct form of the verb. Remember the basic principle of agreement: the verb must agree with its *subject*, not with any modifiers the subject may have.

## 6c. The number of the subject is not changed by a phrase or clause following the subject.

EXAMPLES    This **book** is by Eudora Welty.

This **book** of short stories **is** by Eudora Welty.    [*Book* is still the subject.]

The **girl** is our next-door neighbor.

The **girl** who sells eggs **is** our next-door neighbor. [*Girl is*, not *eggs are*.]

In formal writing, the number of the subject is not changed when it is followed by such explanatory or parenthetical phrases as *along with, as well as, accompanied by, in addition to, together with*, etc.

EXAMPLES    Our English **class**, accompanied by Mrs. Strauss, **attends** several plays each year.

Our English **classes**, as well as the drama club, **attend** several plays each year.

All English **classes** other than the freshman class **attend** several plays each year.

## EXERCISE 1.    Number your paper 1–20. After each number, write the subject of the corresponding sentence. After the subject, write the one of the two verbs that agrees in number with the subject.

1. The author of the stories (is, are) Leslie Silko.
2. The yearly sales of paperback books in the United States (is, are) astronomical.
3. Sleeping sickness, the common name for diseases that put the patient into a sleeplike condition, (attacks, attack) both humans and animals.
4. Many inventions, as well as the discovery of certain scientific principles, (has, have) often been ascribed to accident or chance.
5. The inability to sleep naturally, accompanied by restlessness and anxiety, (is, are) called *insomnia*.
6. The popularity of television programs (is, are) reflected in the ratings.

7. The protection of forests, together with other natural resources, (concerns, concern) all the citizens of a country.

8. The government of the United States (grants, grant) aid for advanced study to scientists.

9. Sundews, a fascinating group of plants, (traps, trap) insects for food.

10. Long after machines for weaving cotton and wool fabric (was, were) invented, home weavers remained at their solitary looms.

11. Speeding in restricted zones (endangers, endanger) both driver and pedestrian.

12. Small amounts of fat (provides, provide) considerable heat for the body.

13. Mica, one of the best insulating materials, (resists, resist) high temperatures.

14. Other animals than the cow (gives, give) milk for human consumption.

15. The state of Idaho, best known for its potatoes, also (produces, produce) great quantities of small grains, fruit, and other vegetables.

16. Model-making, one of the most popular of hobbies, (develops, develop) one's dexterity.

17. Susan B. Anthony, along with Lucy Stone and Elizabeth C. Stanton, (was, were) an early suffragist.

18. Carl's excuses for not having completed his assignment on time always (depresses, depress) me.

19. The infantry, which fights with easily portable weapons, (constitutes, constitute) the largest division of the ground force in most armies.

20. One typewriter for two or three students (seems, seem) adequate.


## Indefinite Pronouns

The indefinite pronouns like *some, any, someone, many, everything* can present usage problems. Some of these words are always singular, some always plural, and some can be either, depending on the meaning of the sentence.

In addition, many of these words are followed by phrases, as in this sentence (*many of these words*). Remember to determine the number of the subject pronoun alone without considering the intervening phrase before you choose your verb.

### 6d. The following common words are singular: *each, either, neither, one, everyone, no one, nobody, anyone, anybody, someone, somebody, everybody, much.*

**Neither** of the horses **is** [not *are*] there.

Such a construction is easier to analyze if *neither* is treated as an adjective or made to stand alone as a pronoun:

**Neither** horse **is** there.
**Neither is** there.

**No one** of the designs **seems** [not *seem*] good enough to win.
**No one** design **seems** good enough to win.
**No one seems** good enough to win.

**Everyone** on both teams **has** [not *have*] to follow certain rules.
**Everyone has** to follow certain training rules.

### 6e. The following common words are plural: *several, few, both, many, others.*

EXAMPLES  **Both** of the cars **start** readily in cold weather.
**Few** of the members **were** at the meeting.
**Many** of our animals **are** becoming extinct.
**Others** besides Ann **admire** Rita's courage.
**Several** of the assignments **require** outside reading.

### 6f. The words *some, any, none, all,* and *most* may be either singular or plural, depending on the meaning of the sentence.

When the words *some, any, all,* and *most* refer to a singular word, they are singular. When they refer to a plural word, they are plural.

**Some** of the money **was** saved.   [*Some* refers to *money*, which is singular.]

**Some** of the tickets **were** sold.   [*Some* refers to *tickets*, which is plural.]

**Most** of the country **is** in the temperate zone.   [*Most* refers to *country*, which is singular.]

**Most** of the countries **are** in the temperate zone.   [*Most* refers to *countries*, which is plural.]

**All** of the food **tastes** delicious.   [*All* refers to *food*, which is singular.]

**All** the meals **taste** delicious.   [*All* refers to *meals*, which is plural.]

Even when it refers to a plural, the word *none* may be considered singular, meaning *not one,* or it may be considered plural, meaning *not any.*

**None** of the dishes **was** broken.   [*not one* was]

**None** of the dishes **were** broken.   [*not any* were]

**EXERCISE 2.**  Number your paper 1–15. After the proper number on your paper, write the one of the two verbs in parentheses that agrees in number with the subject. Be prepared to explain your decision.

1. Somebody – I think it was Ann or Jo – (has, have) nominated me for "Junior most likely to be a distinguished police officer."

2. Each of the team members (agrees, agree) that strict training regulations are necessary for maximum performance.

3. Many of the methods used to preserve food (involves, involve) the halting of enzyme action.

4. It seems to me that neither of the political parties (is, are) entirely right on any issue.

5. Although many try out for the yearbook, only one in three (succeeds, succeed) in making the staff.

6. All of the courses recommended for college preparatory work (is, are) recognized by the state university.

7. Everybody in France, it sometimes seems to tourists, (regards, regard) cooking as a fine art.

8. Some of the books on the reserve shelf (has, have) mysteriously disappeared.

9. (Do, Does) each of the campers have a knapsack and a sleeping bag?

10. Nobody, not even my best friends, (realizes, realize) the troubles that I have had trying to pass English.

11. None of the land behind the levees (was, were) affected by the flood.

12. Some of the reporting of supposedly objective newspaper writers (appears, appear) to be prejudiced.

13. Both of the paintings (shows, show) the influence of the work of Emilio Sanchez.

14. Several on the board (refuses, refuse) to attend the public meeting on the referendum.

15. Others besides you and me (objects, object) to the pollution of lakes and rivers.

**EXERCISE 3.** *Oral Drill.* These sentences should be read *aloud* many times to fix the habit of using the correct form. Ear training is important in correcting faulty usage. In reading aloud, stress the italicized words. Be sure that you understand the rule of agreement that each sentence illustrates.

1. *Neither* of these answers *is* correct.

2. The *cost* of the cars *was* high.

3. *One* of my friends *has* the flu.

4. *Are all* of the books on the shelf?

5. Every *one* of the reports *is* due today.

6. *Several* of the games *were* canceled.

7. The *view* of the mountains *was* splendid.

8. *Most* of the snow *has* melted.

9. Not *one* of the glasses *has* been broken.

10. The *last* of the assignments *is* complete.

## Compound Subjects

In Chapter 2 you learned that two words or groups of words may be connected to form the *compound subject* of a verb. These words are usually joined by *and* or *or* and may take singular or plural verbs depending on what the connecting word is and on whether the words joined are singular or plural.

### 6g. Subjects joined by *and* take a plural verb.

EXAMPLES   A **hot dog and mustard seem** to belong together.

**Aries, Taurus, Gemini, and Cancer are** signs of the zodiac.

EXCEPTION   When a compound subject is considered as a unit, not as two or more distinct things, it takes a singular verb.

**Broadway and Forty-second Street** [one place] **is** where Times Square begins.

**Apple pie and ice cream** [one dish] **is** a favorite American dessert.

### 6h. Singular subjects joined by *or* or *nor* take a singular verb.

EXAMPLES   **Has** your **mother or** your **father** given permission to use the car?

**Neither snow nor ice keeps** the mail carriers from their appointed rounds.

**Either Alice or Felicia** plans to attend the performance.

### 6i. When a singular subject and a plural subject are joined by *or* or *nor*, the verb agrees with the nearer subject.

ACCEPTABLE   Neither the **students** nor their **teacher regrets** the approach of summer.

Whenever possible, this awkward construction should be avoided:

BETTER   The **students do** not regret the approach of summer, and neither **does** their **teacher**.

Another reason for avoiding this construction is that the subjects may be different in person as well as in number.

When that is the case, the verb must agree with the nearer subject. In the following example, the verb must not only be singular to agree with *I;* it must also have the form that matches *I* as a subject:

ACCEPTABLE    Neither my **sisters** nor **I am** planning to attend.

BETTER    My **sisters are** not planning to attend, and neither **am I.**

**EXERCISE 4.**    Number your paper 1–25. Read each of the following sentences aloud. If the verb agrees with the subject, write *C* (for correct). If the verb does not agree, write the correct form on your paper.

1. Both the lake and the body of water connecting it to the ocean have been discussed repeatedly.
2. The view from the top of the surrounding hills are unforgettable.
3. One or both of the beautiful expanses of water are likely to be destroyed.
4. Some of the signs of destruction are already clearly visible.
5. Indisputable symptoms of decay which should be recognized by every visitor includes the littered appearance of the shoreline as well as the absence of wildlife.
6. The date for effective application of the new regulations have not yet been determined.
7. Not one of the participants in the discussions was eager to bring that issue to a vote.
8. And not one of the disputing parties seem particularly anxious to compromise.
9. Every one of the attempts to establish principles have ended in failure.
10. Neither the statement of the problems nor the solution suggested for them satisfies the Committee.
11. The terms *filibuster* and *point of order* seem to be synonymous with the word *discussion.*
12. The local City Planning Council and the Union of Shore Industries together constitutes the Committee.
13. The idea of further discussion and delay, as well as the rising costs involved, anger the local citizens.

14. Somebody, either a local resident or some other concerned party, have notified the Environmental Protection Agency.

15. Assistant Director Gray, with a number of her staff, is expected to tour the area.

16. A waterside community hemmed in by mountains change its local habits and customs more slowly than one less dependent on the sea.

17. Heavy industrial use, as well as community sewage disposal, has affected the capacity of the water to sustain wildlife and provide breeding grounds.

18. Besides having a financial interest in the waters, tourists and the local community uses it for sports and other recreational purposes.

19. Most of the city budget — at least two thirds — consist of water-related income and expenditures.

20. Neither the proposals of the mayor's special task force nor the recommendation of the Planning Council have been put into effect.

21. Pollution and water are associated in the minds of most local residents.

22. Fish and chips is the specialty of the restaurant trade.

23. Each of the shorefront families have a dock on the beach.

24. A number of the members of the Planning Council refuse to back the recommendations of the majority.

25. The discussion of issues seem useless in helping the community come to grips with the problem.

## OTHER PROBLEMS IN AGREEMENT

**6j. When the subject follows the verb, as in questions and sentences beginning with *there* and *here,* be careful to determine the subject and make sure that the verb agrees with it.**

NONSTANDARD   Here's two letters for you.
STANDARD   Here **are** two letters for you.

NONSTANDARD   Where is the hammer and nails?
STANDARD   Where **are** the hammer and nails?

## 6k. Collective nouns may be either singular or plural.

A collective noun is singular in form but names a group of persons, animals, or things: *crowd, flock, chorus, jury, family.* By its very nature, any collective noun may have either a singular or a plural meaning. When the speaker or writer is thinking of the group as a *single unit,* it takes a singular verb; when the speaker or writer is thinking of the *individual parts* or *members* of the group, it takes a plural verb.

> The football **team practices** every day.   [The speaker is thinking of the team as a unit, as though it were a single person.]
>
> The football **team buy** their own uniforms.   [The speaker is thinking of the individual members of the team, each of whom buys his own uniform.]
>
> The **herd** of elk **is** in the meadow.   [the herd as a unit]
>
> The **herd** of elk **disperse** at the slightest noise.   [Each individual elk bounds in a different direction.]
>
> The **majority** of the party **has** given its assent.   [The majority as a unit has given its assent.]
>
> The **majority** of the party **have** cast negative votes.   [The speaker is thinking of all those individual members — a majority — whose votes were negative.]

## 6l. Expressions stating amount (time, money, measurement, weight, volume, fractions) are usually singular.

EXAMPLES   **Four score and seven years equals** eighty-seven years. [a single period]

**Twenty-three inches is** a tiny waist measurement. [one length]

**Fifty dollars seems** a reasonable price.   [a single sum of money]

When, however, an amount is considered to be individual parts rather than a single unit, a plural verb is used.

EXAMPLES   **Two silver dollars do** not fit in my coin purse.   [The dollars are thought of separately.]

**Seven years is** a hard sentence. [The prison term is thought of as a unit.]

**Seven years have** passed since we last saw him. [Each year is thought of separately.]

Fractions followed by phrases can sometimes cause problems. In the examples immediately following, the form of the verb seems to be determined by the number of the noun in the phrase.

Four fifths of the problem is complete.
Four fifths of the problems are complete.

This, like rule 6f on page 86, is an exception to rule 6c on page 84, which says the number of the subject is not changed by the phrase following it. A fraction is singular when it refers to a singular word—*problem* in the first example above. It is plural when it refers to a plural word—*problems* in the second example.

**EXERCISE 5.** Number your paper 1–20. After the proper number on your paper, write the verb in parentheses that agrees in number with the subject. Be prepared to defend your choice.

1. Upon the hunters (rests, rest) the responsibility of buying their licenses.
2. Ten dollars (is, are) a high price for a theater ticket.
3. The public education system for boys and girls in the United States (is, are) principally supported by local taxes.
4. As the curtain falls, the audience, as one body, (stands, stand) to applaud Chita Rivera's splendid performance.
5. Either snow or ice or fog (makes, make) driving a hazardous undertaking.
6. There (is, are) the papers I was looking for.
7. The return of his gold coins (was, were) a shock to Silas Marner.
8. Mental fitness, as well as physical fitness, (is, are) taken into account by army recruiting officers.
9. Perhaps the best thing about birthdays (is, are) looking forward to them.

10. There (is, are) almost seven million volumes in the New York Public Library.

11. On our block alone, ninety-five dollars (was, were) collected for the March of Dimes.

12. Few of the excuses given by students for careless and sloppy handwriting (is, are) valid.

13. Of the earth's surface, three tenths (is, are) land.

14. Contemporary painting, with its distortion of traditional materials, (puzzles, puzzle) many people.

15. Many of the parents of our students (attends, attend) Back-to-School Night.

16. Frustration, failure, and lack of opportunity (leads, lead) to school dropouts.

17. Either fruit juice or milk (serves, serve) as a healthful in-between-meals snack.

18. The poetry and plays of today's writers (is, are) tomorrow's "classics."

19. Every one of the dresses and coats (is, are) selling at half price.

20. Twenty percent of each tax dollar (goes, go) toward the maintenance of roads.

## 6m. The title of a work of art or the name of an organization, or a country, even when plural in form, takes a singular verb.

EXAMPLES    Chaucer's *Canterbury Tales* **includes** many humorous characterizations.

"Tales from the Vienna Woods" **is** one of Strauss's most popular waltzes.

The Malay States **is** now part of the Federation of Malaysia.

EXCEPTION    Some organizations (*Girl Scouts, New York Mets, Elks,* etc.) customarily take a plural verb.

The Sons of Italy **are** giving this benefit.

## 6n. A few nouns, although plural in form, take a singular verb.

Three classes of confusing words are described below. Examine these carefully. Whenever you encounter a similar word, and are uncertain of its usage, consult your dictionary.

1. *Words that are plural in form but singular in usage:*

EXAMPLES  aeronautics   mathematics   news
          civics        measles       physics
          economics     mumps         genetics

Keep in mind that the examples given above do not make a rule that can be consistently followed. For example, the following similar words are more often plural than singular: *acoustics, athletics, statistics, tactics.* The word *politics* may be either singular or plural. For a detailed discussion of the usage of words ending in *–ics,* look up *–ics* in your dictionary.

2. *Words that have no singular forms:*

EXAMPLES  pliers      shears
          scissors    trousers

Notice that these plural nouns refer to *pairs* of things. If they are preceded by the word *pair,* use a singular verb.

EXAMPLE   **The pliers are** on the workbench.
          **The pair of pliers is** on the workbench.

3. *Plural forms of foreign nouns:*

Certain English nouns of foreign origin retain their foreign plural forms, especially in scientific and technical writing. *Always* consult your dictionary when you do not know whether a specific form is singular or plural, or when you do not know how to write the plural form of any word.

|  SINGULAR  |  PLURAL  |
|  ---  |  ---  |
|  analysis  |  analyses  |
|  nucleus  |  nuclei  |
|  parenthesis  |  parentheses  |
|  phenomenon  |  phenomena  |
|  radius  |  radii  |

## 6o. When the subject and the predicate nominative are different in number, the verb agrees with the subject, not with the predicate nominative.

EXAMPLES  Crocuses **are** one of the first signs of spring.

One of the first signs of spring **is** crocuses.

Quite often this construction, although correct, is somewhat awkward.

AWKWARD  The best thing about solitary country walks **is** the chances to observe nature's wonders quietly.

The chances to observe nature's wonders quietly **are** the best thing about solitary country walks.

BETTER  Best of all, solitary country walks **provide** chances to observe nature's wonders quietly.

## 6p. *Every* or *many a* before a subject is followed by a singular verb.

EXAMPLES  **Every** car and truck **was** stopped by the roadblock.

**Many** a person **chooses** security over adventure, sometimes a regrettable decision.

## 6q. *Doesn't* and *don't* must agree with their subjects.

Speakers and writers sometimes forget that *don't* is a contraction for *do not,* and *doesn't* is a contraction for *does not.* With the subjects *I* and *you,* use *don't.* With other subjects, use *doesn't* when the subject is singular, and *don't* when the subject is plural.

EXAMPLES  **She doesn't** know my name.

**This doesn't** solve the problem.

**It doesn't** run fast enough.

**They don't** always win.

By always using *doesn't* after *he, she, it, this, that,* you can eliminate most of the common errors in the use of *don't* and *doesn't.*

**EXERCISE 6.** Number your paper 1–25. After the proper

number, write the correct one of the two verbs in parentheses in each sentence.

1. *The Oxford Book of English Verse,* one of the best-known anthologies, (contains, contain) some of the most famous poems in English literature.
2. (Does, Do) every boy and girl in kindergarten visit the zoo?
3. The total received from the sale of tickets (was, were) three hundred dollars.
4. Mathematics, as a subject, (doesn't, don't) appeal to many students who excel in English studies.
5. There (is, are) many reasons why I want to go to college.
6. Angela (doesn't, don't) have as much physical work to do as her grandmother had.
7. Ships and sailors, as well as soldiers and armies, (appears, appear) in many of Shakespeare's plays.
8. Neither the plaintiff nor the defendant (has, have) changed his mind about the suit.
9. Many of the examinations that I have taken (asks, ask) for a parroting of facts, not a formulation of ideas derived from facts.
10. "Seventeen Syllables" (recounts, recount) the story of a Japanese-American family.
11. In churches all over the country, the number of enrolled members (has, have) varied widely over the years.
12. Neither of the does in the zoo (has, have) had a fawn this spring.
13. Measles (is, are) now fought by injecting exposed children with gamma globulin.
14. In Roman mythology, the goddess of invention, who was admired for her wisdom by many, (was, were) Minerva.
15. True sonnets, whether Italian or Shakespearean, (has, have) fourteen lines.
16. One of the courses recommended by many colleges (is, are) physics.
17. Neither of my cats (likes, like) cream.
18. Our cat (doesn't, don't) like us to pick up its kittens.
19. More important than some students believe (is, are) the scores on aptitude tests.

20. (Doesn't, Don't) it worry you that everyone else is out of step?

21. Small classes and homogeneous grouping plus an experienced teacher (makes, make) learning a pleasure.

22. The people for whom I baby-sit every weekend (lives, live) next door to my aunt.

23. The unusual phenomena (was, were) explained by astronomers as being caused by exceptionally strong solar radiations.

24. One hundred percent of the sheep inoculated by Pasteur with germs of anthrax (was, were) immune to lethal doses of the disease.

25. It is difficult to know which to buy because there (is, are) so many kinds of soap on the market.

**EXERCISE 7.** *Oral Drill.* To fix the agreement habit in your speech, read each of the following sentences aloud several times, stressing the italicized words. State the reason for each construction.

1. *Has either* of the flowers bloomed?
2. *Both potatoes and rice are* starchy foods.
3. Here *are* the *notes* that I borrowed.
4. *Twelve months is* a year.
5. Not *one* of the nations *is* willing to compromise.
6. Where *are* her *sister and aunt?*
7. The *coach doesn't* like his attitude.
8. *Several* of the squad *were* dropped.
9. *Neither Gina nor Betty shows* favoritism.
10. *Each* of those chairs *is* broken.

# AGREEMENT OF PRONOUN AND ANTECEDENT

## 6r. A pronoun agrees with its antecedent in number and gender.

Pronouns also agree in person (see page 104): *We* ought to have fixed it *ourselves. Ellen* wants *her* book back.

The word to which a pronoun refers or for which it stands is called its antecedent. In the phrase *Jack and his sister,* the pronoun *his* has the proper noun *Jack* as its antecedent.

In the examples below, both pronouns and antecedents are printed in bold-faced type. Like subjects and verbs, antecedents and pronouns agree in *number.* When its antecedent is singular, the pronoun is singular. If its antecedent is plural, the pronoun is plural. Notice, too, that a pronoun is masculine (*he, him, his*) when its antecedent is masculine; feminine (*she, her, hers*) when its antecedent is feminine; neuter (*it, its*) when its antecedent is neuter. This second kind of agreement is agreement in *gender* (see page 104).

**Martha** has done more than **her** share.

The **campers** took **their** food with **them.**

**Neither** of the rooms has **its** furnishings yet.

The **others** are invited if **they** pay for **themselves.**

**(1) The words** *each, either, neither, one, everyone, everybody, no one, nobody, anyone, anybody, someone, somebody* **are referred to by singular pronouns—***he, him, his, she, her, hers, it, its.* **A phrase after the antecedent does not change the number of the antecedent.**

EXAMPLES    **Nobody** is so perfect that **he** can criticize others.

**One** of my sisters is president of **her** class.

► **USAGE NOTE**    When the antecedent may be either masculine or feminine, it is standard in formal writing to use the masculine pronoun in referring to it.

EXAMPLES    **Anyone** may start **his** [not *his or her*] luncheon when **he** [not *he or she*] is ready.

**Everyone** cheered at the top of **his** [not *his or her*] voice.

**(2) Two or more singular antecedents joined by** *and* **should be referred to by a plural pronoun.**

EXAMPLES    If **Sue and Francesca** call, tell **them** that I have left.

Jay, Kay, and Mae have donated their time to the project.

**(3) Two or more singular antecedents joined by *or* or *nor* should be referred to by a singular pronoun.**

EXAMPLES  **Either Rinaldo or Bill** will always do **his** best work under pressure.

**Neither Sharon nor Carla** thinks **she** is ready for the test.

**(4) The number of a relative pronoun is determined by the number of its antecedent.**

EXAMPLES  A letter of welcome is sent to **everyone who** moves into the neighborhood.  [*Who* refers to the singular word *everyone;* therefore, it takes the singular verb *moves.*]

It is the most coveted of all the **awards that** are given each year.  [*That* refers to the plural word *awards.*]

► NOTE  Strict agreement between pronoun and antecedent is sometimes abandoned to prevent an unnatural construction.

The rules of agreement may sometimes lead to absurd constructions. This occurs when a singular pronoun is used to agree with a singular antecedent even though the meaning of the antecedent is clearly plural. When the meaning of the antecedent is plural, a plural pronoun must be used.

ABSURD  **Nobody** left the party early because **he** was enjoying **himself.**  [In this sentence, *nobody* is clearly plural in meaning, and the singular pronouns *he* and *himself,* though grammatically correct, are confusing and unnatural.]

BETTER  **Nobody** left the party early because **they** were enjoying **themselves.**

ABSURD  **Everyone** in the club volunteered to help, although **he** was pressed for time.

BETTER  **Everyone** in the club volunteered to help, although **they** were pressed for time.

**EXERCISE 8.** Number your paper 1–10. After each number, write a pronoun to fill the blank in the corresponding sentence, making sure that it agrees with its antecedent. When your answers have been corrected, use the sentences for oral drill.

1. Each teacher prepares —— own tests.
2. One of the birds built —— nest in the holly tree.
3. Both Jane and Ruth added —— contributions to the fund.
4. If anyone else wishes to go, tell —— to notify Mrs. Hill.
5. Many of the girls have dyed —— hair.
6. Not one of the students turned in —— paper late.
7. Neither Angela nor Alice has lost —— faith in me.
8. Either Mr. Phillips or Mr. Schwartz must give —— permission.
9. Each of the boys brought —— own sandwiches.
10. Everyone in the class has paid —— dues.

**REVIEW EXERCISE.** This exercise covers agreement of both verb and subject and pronoun and antecedent. Number your paper 1–10. If a sentence is correct, write a +; if it is incorrect, write a 0. One error makes a sentence incorrect. Revise all incorrect sentences.

1. Do you know what the differences between human beings and animals is?
2. One of the differences are that human beings can reason.
3. You may ask: Don't dogs and monkeys have the ability to think?
4. Yes, but this kind of thinking and human understanding, although they seem identical, is not really the same thing.
5. When human beings use their minds to reason, they are using their minds in a very complicated manner.
6. Sometimes it seems that there is reasoning processes going on in the minds of particularly smart monkeys and dogs, but they are not really using intelligent understanding.
7. People has the capacity to adapt themselves to their surroundings.

8. This ability to change their surroundings and adapt to them also distinguish human beings from animals.

9. The human abilities to cultivate plants, tame animals, and draw energy from wind and water further distinguishes them.

10. Classified by Linnaeus in 1735 as *Homo sapiens*, which means "man the wise," humanity is thus differentiated from the animals by the ability to understand, or be wise.

**Chapter 7**

# Correct Pronoun Usage

## Case Forms of Pronouns

The correct use of pronouns may be learned in various ways. One method is to depend on your ear: "Which *sounds* right—*I* or *me?*" Another way is to learn the case forms of pronouns and to know when to use each form.

Study the following sentences:

I lent **her my** book.
**He** lent **me his** book.
**She** and **I** lent **him** and **her our** books.
**They** lent books to **him** and to **her.**

The bold-faced words in these sentences are pronouns. Notice the number of different forms these pronouns take. These forms are called *case forms*. A pronoun that acts as the subject of a verb is in the *nominative* (sometimes called the *subjective*) *case;* a pronoun that acts as the object of a verb or preposition is in the *objective case;* and a pronoun that shows possession is in the *possessive case.*

PRONOUN AS SUBJECT   I read the book.
PRONOUN AS OBJECT   The book delighted me.
POSSESSIVE PRONOUN   My delight was genuine.

Notice that the pronoun has a different form (*I*, *me*, *my*) in each case.

**7a. Learn the case forms of pronouns and when to use each form.**

Of all the words in modern English, personal pronouns have the most varied and complex forms.

Pronouns have number. Like nouns, personal pronouns take different forms for singular and plural numbers (*he*, *they*).

Pronouns have person. Pronouns change form in three different persons—first, second, and third (*I, you, he*). The meaning of the three persons is as follows:

*I* (*We*) will leave.   [First person is the person speaking.]

*You* will leave.   [Second person is the person spoken to.]

*He* (*She, It, They*) will leave. [Third person is a person or thing other than the speaker or the one spoken to.]

Pronouns have gender. In the third person singular, personal pronouns have three different genders—masculine (*he*), feminine (*she*), and neuter (*it*).

Pronouns have case. Many personal pronouns take different forms for the nominative, objective, and possessive cases.

### *Case Forms of Personal Pronouns*

| *Singular* | NOMINATIVE CASE | OBJECTIVE CASE | POSSESSIVE CASE |
|---|---|---|---|
| FIRST PERSON | I | me | my, mine |
| SECOND PERSON | you | you | your, yours |
| THIRD PERSON | he (masculine) | him | his |
| | she (feminine) | her | her, hers |
| | it (neuter) | it | its |

| *Plural* | NOMINATIVE CASE | OBJECTIVE CASE | POSSESSIVE CASE |
|---|---|---|---|
| FIRST PERSON | we | us | our, ours |
| SECOND PERSON | you | you | your, yours |
| THIRD PERSON | they | them | their, theirs |

In this chapter we will concentrate on the nominative and objective case forms of the personal pronouns. Since the pronouns *you* and *it* do not have different nominative and objective case forms, you may ignore them. Memorize the following lists of nominative and objective forms.

| NOMINATIVE CASE | OBJECTIVE CASE |
|---|---|
| I | me |
| he | him |
| she | her |
| we | us |
| they | them |

Two other pronouns—*who* and *whoever*—have different forms in the nominative and objective cases. *Who* and *whoever* are not personal pronouns. They may be used either as *interrogative* pronouns, to ask a question, or as *relative* pronouns, to introduce a subordinate clause.

| NOMINATIVE CASE | OBJECTIVE CASE |
|---|---|
| who, whoever | whom, whomever |

The uses of *who* and *whom* are discussed on pages 113–15.

## NOMINATIVE FORMS

### 7b. The subject of a verb is in the nominative case.

When the subject is a single pronoun, you follow this rule without thinking about it. Few of us would ever say or write "Us [objective case form] read that book," instead of the correct "We read that book." When a verb has a compound subject, however, people often become confused about the form to use. We have all heard sentences like "Sally and us have read that book," or "You and me read it first."

Fortunately, there is a simple method for determining the correct forms of pronouns that appear in combinations.

**(1) To determine the correct pronoun form in a compound subject, try each subject separately with the verb adapting the form as necessary. Your ear will tell you which form is correct.**

NONSTANDARD  Sally and me read that book. [*Me* read that book?]

STANDARD  **Sally and I** read that book. [*I* read that book.]

| NONSTANDARD | She and him read that book. [*Him* read that book?] |
|---|---|
| STANDARD | **She and he** read that book. [*She* read. *He* read.] |

**(2) When a pronoun is used with a noun (as in *we girls*), say the sentence without the noun. Your ear will tell you the correct pronoun form.**

| NONSTANDARD | Us girls read the book last semester. [*Us* read?] |
|---|---|
| STANDARD | **We girls** read the book last semester. [*We* read.] |

**EXERCISE 1.** *Oral Drill.* Read each of the following sentences aloud several times, stressing the italicized words. This is an ear-training exercise, designed to fix habits of correct usage of the nominative forms of personal pronouns.

1. You and *I* will leave early.
2. *We* and *they* have an important date.
3. Either John or *he* will play quarterback.
4. Neither *they* nor *we* should "cast the first stone."
5. Both the seniors and *we* juniors took the test.
6. Sally, Irene, and *I* waited at the gym.
7. Which movie did Kay and *he* see?
8. She said that you and *they* were invited.
9. Why are *he* and his brother always late?
10. *We* three are going to the fair.

**7c. A predicate nominative is in the nominative case.**

A predicate nominative is a noun or pronoun in the predicate that refers to the same thing as the subject of the sentence. As its name implies, a predicate nominative is in the nominative case.

Several verbs may be followed by predicate nominatives, but the verb *be* is by far the most important. Thus, in the table below, a verb form in the first column may be followed by one of the pronoun forms in the second column.

Such a verb form should *not* be followed by a personal pronoun in the objective case — *me, him, her, us, them.*

| COMMON FORMS OF <u>BE</u> | | |
|---|---|---|
| am | | I |
| is, are | | he |
| was, were | are | she |
| has been, have been, had been | followed | we |
| will be, may be, can be, etc. | by | they |
| should be, would be, could be | | who |
| want to be, like to be, etc. | | |

EXAMPLES   Was it **he** who won the Merit Scholarship?

If it had been **she,** I might not have talked to her.

The ones you are thinking about might have been **they.**

► **NOTE**   It is now acceptable to use the form *It's me* in informal usage. The plural form (*It's us*) is also generally accepted, but using the objective case for the third person form of the pronoun (*It's him, It's them*) is widely considered to be unacceptable in writing. When you see any of these forms in exercises, take a conservative attitude and use the nominative form.

**EXERCISE 2.**   Number your paper 1–20. After the numbers, write the correct case forms of personal pronouns to fill the blanks in the corresponding sentences. After each pronoun, write *s.* for subject or *p.n.* for predicate nominative, according to the way the pronoun is used. Use as many different pronouns as you can, but do not use *you* or *it*. When your sentences have been corrected, make an oral drill of this exercise by reading each sentence aloud several times.

1. My mother and —— are going to drive to Maine.
2. It was —— who carried the ball across the line.
3. —— and —— will be married on Saturday.
4. Neither —— nor —— can be called a genius.
5. —— (We, Us) three are in the advanced class.
6. Alice and —— are half sisters.

7. The date that —— (we, us) girls have chosen is the first of July.

8. You and —— can continue the reading when Jane and —— finish.

9. If Sally and —— wish to go, let me know at once.

10. Do you believe that —— and —— are guilty?

11. Either Guy or —— will be elected president.

12. —— and —— want to take the same courses.

13. When shall —— (we, us) three meet again?

14. Was it —— whom you saw walking down the street?

15. Did you know that —— and —— went to the opera?

16. Both —— and —— like to go picnicking in the country.

17. It was —— who won the relay race.

18. Either Phil or —— broke the window.

19. Because they live on an old road without streetlights, neither —— nor —— likes to walk home late at night.

20. Among those selected to represent the school were Pia and ——.

## OBJECTIVE FORMS

### 7d. The object of a verb is in the objective case.

The object of a verb answers the question "What?" or "Whom?" after an action verb.

EXAMPLES   They called **him.**  [Called *whom?* Answer: *him*—the direct object.]

They wrote **him** a letter.  [Wrote *whom* a letter? Answer: *him*—the indirect object.]

As their name suggests, the objective forms (*me, him, her, us, them*) are used as objects.

EXAMPLES   The team selected **her** as captain.

They picked **me** as co-captain.

They trusted **us** as leaders.

Can you give **them** the leadership that they need?

Single objects, like single subjects, are usually handled

correctly; few of us would ever say "We like they" or "I picked he for a winner." Like subjects, however, objects are often compound, with a pronoun appearing in combination with a noun or another pronoun. Here, again, we can trust our ear to tell us the correct case form when we let each pronoun stand alone as an object.

NONSTANDARD    They entertained my brother and I.   [They entertained *I?*]

STANDARD    They entertained my brother and **me**.   [They entertained *me*.]

NONSTANDARD    Naomi sent he and she gifts for graduation. [Naomi sent *he* a gift? *she* a gift?]

STANDARD    Naomi sent **him** and **her** gifts for graduation. [Naomi sent *him* a gift. Naomi sent *her* a gift.]

**EXERCISE 3.** *Oral Drill.* Read each of the following sentences aloud several times, stressing the italicized words. This exercise is ear-training in the objective forms of the personal pronouns.

1. The teachers *asked* Carmen and *me* to report after school.
2. Do you *want us* boys to help at the meeting?
3. *Call* either *her* or Ruth about the homework assignment.
4. *Him* I *respect,* but don't *ask me* to *like them.*
5. Do you really *like* my brother and *me?*
6. *Give* the other girls and *her* a medal for effort.
7. Did they *mean them* or *us?*
8. The success of the test *delighted* Mr. Banks and *him.*
9. The company will *hire* Debbie and *her* for the summer.
10. Please *take him* and Jack to town.

**EXERCISE 4.** Number your paper 1–10. After the numbers, write personal pronouns in the correct forms to fill the blanks in the corresponding sentences. Use a variety of pronouns, but do not use *you* or *it.*

1. Did you give Frank and —— the assignment for Wednesday?
2. He showed you and —— a fine example of sportsmanship.

3. I asked Lena, Chris, and —— for help.
4. Please tell —— (we, us) juniors about the PSAT test.
5. I liked his teaching and —— from the first day of class.
6. Please show —— and her father how to find the auditorium.
7. The coach asked Rosa and —— to pick up the equipment.
8. The story gives —— (we, us) students a new idea.
9. My mother is expecting both you and ——.
10. The newspaper article implied that the candidate had attacked both the governor and —— on their records.

### 7e. The object of a preposition is in the objective case.

A preposition takes an object—the noun or pronoun in prepositional phrases. As we would expect from the name, these objects are in the objective case. Thus, if the object of a preposition is a pronoun, the objective case form must be used.[1]

|  |  |
|---|---|
| after **him** | toward **me** |
| against **her** | without **them** |

When a preposition has a single object, most writers use the correct forms; however, pronouns in combinations often cause trouble. The method used for finding the correct pronoun form as the subject or the object of a verb will work here as well. Whenever pronouns are used in the compound object of a preposition, make each stand alone with the preposition. Your ear will tell you the correct form.

NONSTANDARD   Esteban will ride with you and I.

STANDARD   Esteban will ride **with you and me.**   [with *me*]

NONSTANDARD   Will you do a favor for Lorraine and he?

STANDARD   Will you do a favor **for Lorraine and him?**   [for *him*]

**EXERCISE 5.** Number your paper 1–10. In each sentence,

---

[1] A list of commonly used prepositions will be found on page 18. Reminder: *but* is a preposition when it means "except"; *like* is a preposition meaning "similar to."

find the preposition and write it after the corresponding number on your paper. After each preposition, write the correct one of the two pronouns in parentheses. When your paper has been corrected, use these sentences for oral drill.

1. You must have dinner with Eugenio and (I, me) sometime.
2. The posters were made by Kent and (she, her) with our help.
3. We can forget about Peggy and (he, him) as far as help with this project is concerned.
4. I'll save a seat for you next to Ilia and (I, me).
5. There is a strong feeling of rivalry between (them, they) and the Warriors.
6. Boys like Dave and (he, him) are usually respected by their classmates.
7. The final choice must be made by you and (I, me).
8. Will it be possible for me to rely on Mrs. Carpenter and (them, they) for the refreshments?
9. Because of the hard work of (us, we) juniors, the award of fifty dollars went into our treasury.
10. The Zaretskys were seated directly behind (they, them) and the Richardsons.

**EXERCISE 6.** This exercise covers the use of personal pronouns as subjects of verbs, predicate nominatives, and objects of verbs and prepositions. Number your paper 1–25. After each number, write the correct one of the two pronoun forms in parentheses in the corresponding sentence.

1. I was certain that it was (she, her) and Sylvester who wanted the tickets.
2. When do you think that Joy and (I, me) should leave?
3. Because of you and (he, him), the class had to stay after school.
4. For their work as volunteers, Mrs. Hill recommended Sally and (she, her) for the citizenship award.
5. She gave the outline for the chapters to Dave and (I, me).
6. If I were (she, her), I would save the money earned from the part-time job for a vacation.

7. Neither the band nor (they, them) were stopped by the rain.

8. Just between you and (I, me), was that a fair question?

9. My brother and (I, me) always disagree about doing the chores.

10. That was probably (we, us) whom you heard in the hall.

11. Ask (he, him) and Bobby for their opinions.

12. I taught Mrs. White and (she, her) how to play tennis.

13. After the wrestling meet, Mr. Leonard and (I, me) checked the total score.

14. Will you let this silly quarrel come between you and (she, her)?

15. The principal did not say whether it was (he, him) or the other boy.

16. Our history teacher appointed Margaret and (I, me) class recorders during the group discussion.

17. The speakers at the pregame rally will be you and (he, him).

18. (They, Them) I remember, but I cannot recall meeting you.

19. Of all my friends, I find you and (she, her) most congenial.

20. The guidance counselor told us that winning scholarships was the responsibility of (we, us) students.

21. The principal later reported that (we, us) students had won many scholarships.

22. When the game was over, I went home with (she, her) and her sister.

23. When will you learn that (we, us) citizens must obey the law?

24. The man who sat beside Benedetto and (I, me) was a celebrity.

25. Do you think that it could have been (they, them) who painted the goal posts?

**EXERCISE 7.** Write sentences of your own using the following combinations of pronouns and nouns correctly.

1. she and I
2. her and me
3. my friend and I
4. my friend and me
5. he and I
6. him and me
7. you and I
8. you and me
9. Alice and she
10. Alice and her
11. Bill and they
12. Bill and them

13. they and we
14. them and us
15. she and her father
16. her and her father

17. she nor I
18. him nor me
19. they or I
20. them or me

## *WHO* AND *WHOM*

The pronouns *who* and *whom* are used in two ways in English sentences: as *interrogative* pronouns, which ask a question, or as *relative* pronouns, which introduce a subordinate clause.

The rules governing the case forms of the personal pronouns (pages 105–10) also apply to *who* and *whom*. *Who* is nominative; *whom* is objective. The pronoun *who* is correct whenever *he, she, we,* or *they* can be substituted for it. The pronoun *whom* is correct whenever *him, her, us,* or *them* can be substituted for it.

NOMINATIVE   **Who** sent the roses?   [*Who* is the subject of the verb *sent*. She sent the roses.]

**Who** could it be?   [*Who* is a predicate nominative. It could be who.]

OBJECTIVE   **Whom** did you visit today?   [*Whom* is the object of the verb *did visit*. You did visit whom (him) today.]

With **whom** did you go?   [*Whom* is the object of the preposition *with*. Did you go with him?]

► USAGE NOTE   In informal English, the pronoun *whom* is gradually dropping out of use. Consequently, a sentence in which *who* is used in place of *whom* is acceptable in informal speech and writing. However, in formal English the distinction in the nominative and objective forms should be observed.

INFORMAL   **Who** did he mention?

FORMAL   **Whom** did he mention?   [*Whom* is the object of the verb *did mention*.]

INFORMAL   **Who** are you going with?

FORMAL   With **whom** are you going?   [*Whom* is the object of the preposition *with*.]

**7f. The use of *who* or *whom* in a subordinate clause is determined by the pronoun's function in the clause. The case is not affected by any word outside the clause.**

To solve a *who-whom* problem, ask yourself the following three questions:

1. What words make up the subordinate clause?
2. How is the pronoun used in the clause—as subject, predicate nominative, object of the verb, object of the preposition?
3. What is the correct case form for this use of the pronoun?

| | |
|---|---|
| PROBLEM | She was an old friend (who, whom) I had not seen in years. |
| *Step 1* | The subordinate clause is (*who, whom*) *I had not seen in years.* |
| *Step 2* | In this clause the relative pronoun is used as the object of the verb *had seen.* |
| *Step 3* | The object of the verb is in the objective case and the objective form of the pronoun is *whom.* |
| SOLUTION | She was an old friend **whom** I had not seen in years. |

Now see if you can solve the *who-whom* problem in the following sentence.

| | |
|---|---|
| PROBLEM | Do you know (who, whom) he is? |
| *Step 1* | The subordinate clause is ———. |
| *Step 2* | In this clause ——— is the subject; ——— is the verb; the pronoun (*who, whom*) is used as ———. |
| *Step 3* | A predicate nominative is in the ——— case; therefore, ——— is the correct form. |
| SOLUTION | ——— |

In the example above, the pronoun looks like the object of the verb *do know* in the main clause *you do know.* Remember, however, that the case of a pronoun in a subordinate clause is not affected by any word outside the subordinate clause. The real object of the verb *do know* is the entire subordinate clause:

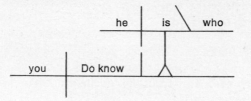

▶ **USAGE NOTE** In determining whether to use *who* or *whom*, do not be misled by a parenthetical expression in the subordinate clause.

EXAMPLES This is the woman **who**, *we believe*, will be our next governor.

There is the police officer **who**, *our guide said*, will know where to find this address.

**EXERCISE 8.** Number your paper 1–10. After each number, write the correct one of the two pronoun forms in parentheses in the corresponding sentences. Use the three-step method on page 114 for determining the case form.

1. Betty Smith, the author of *A Tree Grows in Brooklyn*, was an obscure writer (who, whom) became a celebrity overnight.

2. Her novel is an American classic about a young girl (who, whom) she called Francie Nolan.

3. Francie, (who, whom) we follow from girlhood to adulthood, had only one tree in her city backyard.

4. Carson McCullers, (who, whom) critics describe as a major American writer, wrote a novel about another young girl's coming of age.

5. If anyone can read *The Member of the Wedding* and not be moved, (who, whom) could that person be?

6. Do you know (who, whom) it was that played Frankie in the Broadway production of *A Member of the Wedding*?

7. Pearl Buck is a novelist (who, whom) most Americans are familiar with.

8. The Pulitzer Prize is awarded annually to (whoever, whomever) is selected by the panel of judges.

9. Gwendolyn Brooks, (who, whom) you told me won the Pulitzer Prize for poetry, also wrote a book called *Maud Martha*.

10. Guess (who, whom) Maud Martha really is.

# PRONOUNS IN INCOMPLETE CONSTRUCTIONS

An incomplete, or elliptical, construction is a phrase or clause from which one or more words have been omitted.[1] In English such constructions occur most commonly after the words *than* and *as*.

**7g. After *than* and *as* introducing an incomplete construction, use the pronoun case form that you would use if the construction were completed.**

In the sentence "She sings better than you or I," the verb *sing* is omitted from the clause: "She sings better than you or I (sing)." The pronoun *I* is in the nominative case because it is the subject of the unexpressed verb, *sing*. By supplying missing words, we can determine a correct pronoun form. Similarly, by studying the pronoun forms in incomplete constructions, we can determine what the missing words must be.

EXAMPLES  We like Tom as much as **them**. [The complete clause must be *as we like them*.]

We like Tom as much as **they**. [The complete clause must be *as they like him*.]

**EXERCISE 9.** Number your paper 1–10. After each number, fill out the incomplete construction in the corresponding sentence, supply the missing word or words, and choose the correct pronoun form from the pair of pronouns in the parentheses. In several of the sentences either pronoun form may be correct; the form you use must be correct in the completed construction.

EXAMPLE  1. Jo has longer hair than (I, me).

1. *than I have*

1. Everyone else on the team is taller than (I, me).
2. Do not give Carla a higher grade than (I, me).
3. Can you throw a better curve than (he, him)?

[1] For review of elliptical clauses, see page 65.

4. You will have to run faster than (he, him) if you want to win the race.
5. Our varsity plays as good a game as (they, them).
6. Is everyone else as exhausted as (he, him)?
7. I like Lou more than (she, her).
8. My teacher thought I could get better grades than (he, him).
9. They gave more presents to Mary than (I, me).
10. No one worked harder for the charity than (she, her).

## OTHER PROBLEMS IN THE USE OF PRONOUNS

**7h. In standard formal English the pronouns ending in *–self* and *–selves* should be used only (1) to refer to another word in the sentence or (2) to emphasize another word in the sentence.**

EXAMPLES   I hurt **myself.** [The reflexive pronoun *myself* refers to the subject *I*.]

**Mother** and **Father** bought tickets for **themselves** and me. [The reflexive pronoun *themselves* refers to *Mother and Father*.]

**She herself** will entertain us. [The intensive pronoun *herself* emphasizes *she*.]

**Juan** will do it **himself.** [The intensive pronoun *himself* emphasizes *Juan*.]

Do not use a reflexive or intensive pronoun in place of a simple personal pronoun.

The Knights and we [not *ourselves*] live on the same road.
Did Ruth knit sweaters for herself and **you?** [not *yourself*]

**7i. An appositive is in the same case as the word with which it is in apposition.**

An appositive explains or identifies (but does not modify) the word with which it is in apposition. It is logical, therefore, that both the word and its appositive should be in the same case.

PROBLEM  The decorating committee—Fay, Karen, and (I, me)—will meet during activities period. [The phrase *Fay, Karen, and (I, me)* is in apposition with *committee,* the subject of the verb *will meet.* The subject of a verb is in the nominative case; therefore, the pronoun in the phrase must also be in the nominative case.]

SOLUTION  The decorating committee—**Fay, Karen, and I**—will meet during activities period.

PROBLEM  The principal called the two boys, Hal and (he, him), in for a conference.  [The phrase *Hal and (he, him)* is in apposition with boys, the object of the verb *called.* Therefore, the pronoun should be in the objective case.]

SOLUTION  The principal called the two boys, **Hal and him,** in for a conference.

## 7j. Use the possessive case of a noun or a pronoun before a gerund.

A gerund is a word ending in *–ing* that acts as both a verb and a noun. If you remember that the gerund is a noun form, the use of the possessive case before it is reasonable.

> I was surprised at the **team's** [not *team*] winning so easily.
>
> Everyone was shocked by **their** [not *them*] marrying so young.

Do not confuse the gerund with the present participle, which also ends in *–ing*. A gerund acts as a *noun* and verb. A participle acts as an *adjective* and verb. Like an ordinary adjective, a participle modifies a noun or a pronoun. It can never be used as the subject or object of a verb or as the object of a preposition.

Study the following examples carefully:

PARTICIPLE  Can you imagine **him studying** all night?  [The pronoun *him* is the object of the verb *imagine;* the participle *studying* acts as an adjective modifying *him.* In this sentence the writer is emphasizing the person who is studying rather than the act of studying.]

GERUND    His parents objected to **his studying** all night.    [In this sentence the gerund *studying* is the object of the preposition; the possessive pronoun *his* modifies the gerund. Here the writer is emphasizing the act of studying, not the person who performs the act.]

Distinguish the differences in meaning between the two sentences in each of the following pairs.

Can you imagine **me** winning?

Can you imagine **my** winning?

Think of **their** waiting three whole days in the rain for World Series' tickets.

Think of **them** waiting three whole days in the rain for World Series' tickets.

The **glee club** singing "Hail, Columbia!" got the most applause.

The **glee club's** singing of "Hail, Columbia!" got the most applause.

**EXERCISE 10.**    Number your paper 1–10. After each number, write a + if the pronouns in the corresponding sentence are correct; write a 0 if the pronouns are incorrect. After each 0, write the correct pronoun or pronouns.

1. The officers and myself will draw up a new constitution.
2. Many of the students were happy about his being made principal of the school.
3. The poem had a different meaning for each one of us, Mary, Dawn, and I.
4. Added to the honor roll were two juniors, Frank and she.
5. Both his sister and himself graduated from Purdue.
6. I cannot understand his dropping out of school just before graduation.
7. The new foreign students, Abdul and her, received a friendly welcome at the Student Council party.
8. I have no objection to him singing while he works.
9. The coach has a lot of confidence in both guards, Aretha and she.
10. When I lose my temper, the person I hurt most is myself.

**REVIEW EXERCISE.** Number your paper 1–25. After each number, write the correct one of the two pronouns in the parentheses in the corresponding sentence. Be prepared to explain your choices.

1. To (who, whom) was the letter addressed?
2. Among those who had never been absent from school were Bobby and (I, me).
3. I have always thought that Beth and (he, him) had a lot in common.
4. Listening to Ella Fitzgerald records keeps my friends and (I, me) occupied for hours and hours.
5. There is little doubt about (who, whom) the most popular girl in the class is.
6. Will you help the others and (we, us) with the classwork that we missed?
7. Please use the desk between Lee and (I, me).
8. Was it (she, her) (who, whom) the principal called to his office?
9. It usually is José and (she, her) (who, whom) everyone wants to hear.
10. They have many more possessions than (we, us), but we have more fun than (they, them).
11. May (we, us) boys go to the library to work on our history term papers?
12. (Who, Whom) do you think Sequoya was?
13. As soon as you know (who, whom) it was that wrote *Lord of the Flies,* raise your hand.
14. Besides Sharon and (I, me), there are no other candidates for the office.
15. (Him, His) winning the medal was a surprise to all of us.
16. Our teacher thought that Sue and (I, me) were not paying attention.
17. The title of valedictorian goes to (whoever, whomever) has the highest average for the four years.
18. You and (I, me) are now eligible for a National Merit Scholarship.
19. The gift that the class sent to (she, her) and her husband was a transistor radio.

20. Do you think Lynn and (she, her) would make good exchange students?

21. Jim Plunkett was the one (who, whom) I thought was most likely to succeed at a large university.

22. Since I haven't finished the book, please don't tell me (who, whom) the murderer is.

23. The Chamber of Commerce presented Mia and (he, him) with the awards for the best term papers on a local industry.

24. Should Cheryl and (she, her) wait for you?

25. The new neighbors are no more cooperative than (they, them).

# Chapter 8

# Correct Verb Usage

## Principal Parts; Tense, Voice, Mood

Verbs can be troublesome to many students. Most errors in the use of verbs stem basically from two sources: (1) unfamiliarity with the principal parts of verbs, and (2) misuse of the tense forms of verbs. To overcome such errors as *I seen, He brung, She knowed,* or *It busted,* both knowledge and practice are required. This chapter not only explains the verb, but it also provides extensive practice in correct verb usage.

## KINDS OF VERBS

A verb is a word that expresses an action or otherwise helps to make a statement.

EXAMPLES    Orlando Cepeda **hit** the ball for a base hit.

The student **thought** for several minutes before answering the question.

A verb that tells "what is" rather than "what is done" is called a *linking verb.* Such verbs act as a link or connection between the subject and a word or words in the predicate.

EXAMPLES    The weather **was** wet and cold.   [*Was* links *weather* to *wet* and *cold.*]

The gas **smelled** sickeningly sweet.   [*Smelled* links *gas* to *sweet.*]

Some verbs can be either action or linking verbs, depending upon the sentence:

ACTION   The sculptor Noguchi **felt** the smooth marble. [*Felt* expresses action.]

LINKING   The artist **felt** sick that day.  [*Felt* links the subject, *artist*, with *sick*, a word that describes the subject.]

You will find a list of the most common linking verbs on page 13. The verb used most often as a linking verb is the verb *be*, whose forms are *am, is, are, was, were*, and all verb phrases ending in *be, being, been: may be, could be, will be, has been, was being*, etc.

Besides being a linking verb, *be* can also be followed by an adverb or an adverb phrase.

They **will be here** soon.

The jewelry **is in the drawer**.

In this use, *be* is not generally classified as a linking verb. It does not link a word in the predicate to the subject.

# PRINCIPAL PARTS OF VERBS

Every verb has four basic forms called the four principal parts: the *infinitive*, the *present participle*, the *past*, and the *past participle*. All other forms of a verb are derived from these principal parts.

### *Principal Parts of the Verb* Push

| INFINITIVE | PRESENT PARTICIPLE | PAST | PAST PARTICIPLE |
|---|---|---|---|
| push | (is) pushing | pushed | (have) pushed |

Notice the words *is* and *have* before present and past participles. These words have been inserted to show that the participial forms are used with helping verbs, such as *have, has, had, is, are, am, has been, have been*, etc. (See pages 13–14 for a discussion of the helping verb and the verb phrase.)

## Regular Verbs

All verbs are described as either *regular* or *irregular,* according to the manner in which their principal parts are formed.

A regular verb is one that forms its past and past participle by adding *–d* or *–ed* to the infinitive form.[1]

| INFINITIVE | PAST | PAST PARTICIPLE |
|------------|------|-----------------|
| change | changed | (have) changed |
| surprise | surprised | (have) surprised |
| look | looked | (have) looked |
| print | printed | (have) printed |

## Irregular Verbs

An irregular verb is one that forms its past and past participle in some other way than does a regular verb, usually, but not always, by a vowel change within the verb.

| INFINITIVE | PAST | PAST PARTICIPLE | |
|------------|------|-----------------|--|
| drink | drank | (have) drunk | [vowel change] |
| lend | lent | (have) lent | [consonant change] |
| catch | caught | (have) caught | [vowel and consonant] |
| set | set | (have) set | [no change] |

Irregular verbs like the above cause the greatest single problem in standard verb usage because there is no single rule that applies to them. Students of our language must know the principal parts of every irregular verb that they use, and the only possible way to know them is to memorize them.

The following alphabetical list contains three principal parts of many common irregular verbs. Use this list for reference. Remember, however, that the list does not include every irregular verb. When in doubt about the principal parts of a verb, consult a dictionary, in which you will find any irregular forms listed.

[1] A very few regular verbs have an alternative past form ending in *–t:* *burn, burned* or *burnt,* (have) *burned* or *burnt;* see also *lean, leap.*

## *Principal Parts of Common Irregular Verbs*

| INFINITIVE | PAST | PAST PARTICIPLE |
|---|---|---|
| bear | bore | (have) borne |
| beat | beat | (have) beaten *or* beat |
| become | became | (have) become |
| begin | began | (have) begun |
| bite | bit | (have) bitten |
| blow | blew | (have) blown |
| break | broke | (have) broken |
| bring | brought | (have) brought |
| burst | burst | (have) burst |
| catch | caught | (have) caught |
| choose | chose | (have) chosen |
| come | came | (have) come |
| creep | crept | (have) crept |
| dive | dived *or* dove | (have) dived |
| do | did | (have) done |
| draw | drew | (have) drawn |
| drink | drank | (have) drunk |
| drive | drove | (have) driven |
| eat | ate | (have) eaten |
| fall | fell | (have) fallen |
| fight | fought | (have) fought |
| fling | flung | (have) flung |
| fly | flew | (have) flown |
| forget | forgot | (have) forgotten *or* forgot |
| freeze | froze | (have) frozen |
| get | got | (have) got *or* gotten |
| give | gave | (have) given |
| go | went | (have) gone |
| grow | grew | (have) grown |
| hang | hung | (have) hung |
| know | knew | (have) known |
| lay | laid | (have) laid |
| lead | led | (have) led |
| lend | lent | (have) lent |
| lie | lay | (have) lain |
| ride | rode | (have) ridden |
| ring | rang | (have) rung |
| rise | rose | (have) risen |

| INFINITIVE | PAST | PAST PARTICIPLE |
|---|---|---|
| run | ran | (have) run |
| see | saw | (have) seen |
| seek | sought | (have) sought |
| set | set | (have) set |
| shake | shook | (have) shaken |
| shine | shone *or* shined | (have) shone *or* shined |
| shrink | shrank *or* shrunk | (have) shrunk |
| sing | sang *or* sung | (have) sung |
| sink | sank *or* sunk | (have) sunk |
| slay | slew | (have) slain |
| speak | spoke | (have) spoken |
| spin | spun | (have) spun |
| spring | sprang *or* sprung | (have) sprung |
| steal | stole | (have) stolen |
| sting | stung | (have) stung |
| strive | strove | (have) striven |
| swear | swore | (have) sworn |
| swim | swam | (have) swum |
| swing | swung | (have) swung |
| take | took | (have) taken |
| tear | tore | (have) torn |
| throw | threw | (have) thrown |
| wear | wore | (have) worn |
| weave | wove | (have) woven |
| write | wrote | (have) written |

## 8a. Learn the principal parts of common irregular verbs.

On the following pages, the irregular verbs that are most frequently misused are presented in four groups. Memorize the principal parts of the verbs in each group; next, do the exercises. Concentrate on any verb that you have not used correctly and review its principal parts, repeating them over and over until the correct forms are fixed in your mind and the incorrect forms "hurt" your ears. In doing the exercises, remember that the past participle is always used with one or more helping, or auxiliary, verbs: *is, are, was, has, have, have been, could have, might have,* etc. To remind yourself of this fact, always use *have* before the past participle when you repeat the principal parts of a verb: thus, *bring, brought, have brought.*

## *Group 1*

| INFINITIVE | PAST | PAST PARTICIPLE |
|---|---|---|
| beat | beat | (have) beaten *or* beat |
| begin | began | (have) begun |
| blow | blew | (have) blown |
| break | broke | (have) broken |
| burst | burst | (have) burst |
| choose | chose | (have) chosen |
| come | came | (have) come |
| do | did | (have) done |

**EXERCISE 1.** Number your paper 1–20. After each number, write either the past or the past participle of the italicized verb at the beginning, whichever correctly fills the blank in the corresponding sentence.

1. *come*  My new car has —— at last.

2. *do*  We —— that assignment yesterday.

3. *begin*  Do not expect much sunshine once the rainy season has ——.

4. *beat*  Our basketball team —— every team in the league last season.

5. *choose*  The boy who was —— was the one who least expected to receive the honor.

6. *come*  Until our guest student, who had —— from Ghana, arrived, we had known little about her country.

7. *blow*  The wind —— for three days and nights.

8. *burst*  I jumped a mile when the balloon —— behind my back.

9. *break*  After the fire, the doll lay there charred and ——.

10. *do*  Mr. Tracy doesn't want to know who —— it; he wants to know who is going to fix it.

11. *blow*  Just before the accident, the right front tire ——.

12. *come*  I had almost given up hope when the answer —— to me.

13. *begin*  It had just —— to rain when we set out.

14. *break*  I am glad to know that your promise was not ——.

15. *beat*  Mother wants to know if you —— the rug yesterday.

16. *choose*   Couldn't you have —— a more recent edition to use than the one published in 1911?

17. *do*   Last term he —— an outstanding job on the school paper.

18. *blow*   A whistle was —— on the play.

19. *choose*   How many students were —— for the Honor Society?

20. *burst*   The subway was flooded when the water main ——.

## Group II

| INFINITIVE | PAST | PAST PARTICIPLE |
| --- | --- | --- |
| draw | drew | (have) drawn |
| drink | drank | (have) drunk *or* drank |
| drive | drove | (have) driven |
| fall | fell | (have) fallen |
| freeze | froze | (have) frozen |
| give | gave | (have) given |
| go | went | (have) gone |

**EXERCISE 2.** Number your paper 1–20. After each number, write either the past or the past participle of the verb at the beginning, whichever correctly fills the blank in the corresponding sentence.

1. *give*   How dare you break your promise once you have —— it?

2. *draw*   Yesterday at the Freshman Fair, our art teacher —— caricatures at fifty cents each.

3. *drink*   It was a dark day in the history of Greece when Socrates —— the potion of hemlock.

4. *drive*   The shrill notes of the off-key soprano have —— her neighbors to complain.

5. *fall*   We know that winter is on its way once the leaves have —— from the trees.

6. *drink*   Even before the sun rose, the dry ground —— up every drop of rain.

7. *go*   Although you deny it, I know that you have —— to great pains to help me.

8. *freeze*  The temperature was so low that the water in the pipes in the kitchen was ——.

9. *give*  The best gift my mother and father —— me was a love for books.

10. *drive*  Have you —— this car many miles?

11. *go*  Maio went to the University of Chicago, the same school to which her father had ——.

12. *drink*  The cow finally —— the bucket of water.

13. *go*  The whole gang has —— to the skating rink.

14. *freeze*  The combs on the chickens —— last winter.

15. *draw*  Has the last drop of water been —— from the well?

16. *give*  Have you —— him the present yet?

17. *drive*  How many times have you —— across the country?

18. *freeze*  Because of the early winter, all of my flowers were ——.

19. *fall*  How low had the temperature —— when you checked it last?

20. *drink*  My little brother —— all the soda.

**EXERCISE 3.** This exercise covers the verbs in Groups I and II. Number your paper 1–30. After each number, write a *C* if the italicized verb in the corresponding sentence is correct; if it is incorrect, write the correct form.

1. *Has* the lake *froze* over yet?
2. Before the bell rang, they *begun* to leave their desks.
3. The chair *was broke* before I sat on it.
4. The firecracker *bursted* the tin can.
5. Frank *blowed* the wrong note.
6. Kim *was chosen* to represent the school.
7. Since our school is new, many visitors *have come* to study it.
8. Under the circumstances, she *done* the best that she could.
9. About a week ago the trees *burst* into blossom.
10. In ten minutes the plant *drunk* all the water I gave it.
11. The sheep *were driven* to a higher pasture.
12. The holidays *have come* and *gone*, and we are back in school.
13. We dug up the bulbs before the ground *was froze*.

14. *Has* Mrs. Chung *given* out the test grades?
15. Bill and Joe *have went* ahead to start the fire.
16. *Have* you ever *gone* to the ballet?
17. Everyone in the class *done* the wrong assignment.
18. The ceiling in our bedroom *has fallen.*
19. When *will* the final exam *be given?*
20. The milk on the back porch *was frozen.*
21. They *have drove* day and night to get here on time.
22. *Have* you *drunk* your milk, Consuela?
23. *Was* that sketch *drawn* from a live model?
24. I *done* all the assigned work.
25. Ann was surprised when she *come* to the fourth problem.
26. Which essay *was chosen* for publication?
27. The test tube *must have broke* when you washed it.
28. The terms of the treaty *had been broke.*
29. The performance *began* at eight o'clock.
30. *Was* the rug *beat* or was it vacuumed?

## Group III

| INFINITIVE | PAST | PAST PARTICIPLE |
| --- | --- | --- |
| grow | grew | (have) grown |
| know | knew | (have) known |
| ride | rode | (have) ridden |
| ring | rang *or* rung | (have) rung |
| run | ran | (have) run |
| see | saw | (have) seen |
| sing | sang *or* sung | (have) sung |
| speak | spoke | (have) spoken |

**EXERCISE 4.** Number your paper 1–20. After each number, write either the past or past participle of the verb at the beginning, whichever correctly fills the blank in the corresponding sentence.

1. *ride*     I have never —— in a smoother-riding car.
2. *sing*     The chorus has seldom —— so well.
3. *know*    Fortunately, he never —— what hit him.

4. *grow*  How many inches have you —— this year?

5. *run*  I hoped she would win when she —— for president.

6. *ring*  The bell had already ——.

7. *see*  As we rounded the curve, we —— the accident occur.

8. *speak*  Has Ramón —— to you about going to the dance?

9. *ride*  When they looked at their watches, they realized how long they had ——.

10. *know*  Although he was accused of cheating, I have never —— him to do so.

11. *run*  How many people have —— a four-minute mile?

12. *sing*  That alley cat has —— its last serenade.

13. *see*  Have you ever —— a ghost?

14. *ring*  They have —— down the curtain for the last time.

15. *grow*  The crabgrass seems to have —— fast this year.

16. *speak*  Had anyone —— on that subject before I arrived?

17. *ring*  The telephone has —— at least a dozen times.

18. *ride*  If you've never —— a horse before, now is the time to start.

19. *run*  The mad dog —— in circles before it collapsed.

20. *speak*  "Do not speak until you are —— to."

## *Group IV*

| INFINITIVE | PAST | PAST PARTICIPLE |
|---|---|---|
| spring | sprang *or* sprung | (have) sprung |
| steal | stole | (have) stolen |
| swim | swam | (have) swum |
| swing | swung | (have) swung |
| take | took | (have) taken |
| tear | tore | (have) torn |
| throw | threw | (have) thrown |
| write | wrote | (have) written |

**EXERCISE 5.**  Number your paper 1–20. After each number, write either the past or past participle of the verb at the beginning, whichever correctly fills the blank in the corresponding sentence.

1. *tear*  Did you know that your jacket was ——?

2. *write*  About three hundred novels were —— in Alexander Dumas's "novel factory."

3. *steal*  Someone must have —— my sneakers while we were swimming.

4. *take*  All of the pictures needed for the yearbook have been ——.

5. *throw*  He realized there was no one to catch the pass after he had —— the ball.

6. *swim*  Shane Gould —— for Australia in 1972.

7. *write*  Has everyone —— a limerick for the contest?

8. *swing*  The fighter —— and missed.

9. *spring*  I don't like surprises to be —— on me like that.

10. *steal*  The night before the big game, our mascot was ——.

11. *throw*  That cowhand has —— a bull in fifteen seconds.

12. *swing*  All afternoon the batter —— and missed, —— and missed.

13. *swim*  Before he reached shore, the castaway had —— ten miles.

14. *take*  Which one of you —— my pen?

15. *write*  The statement, "I mourn over the loss of individuality," was —— by Maria Mitchell.

16. *tear*  When the new road was built, several lovely old houses were —— down.

17. *throw*  He just laughed as I —— him to the ground.

18. *swim*  Pam has —— since she was three years old.

19. *take*  I can recall the first time I was —— to the dentist.

20. *swing*  As the pendulum —— back and forth, I became very sleepy.

**EXERCISE 6.**  This exercise covers the verbs in Groups III and IV. Number your paper 1–33. After each number, write a *C* if the italicized verb in the corresponding sentence is correct. If it is incorrect, write the correct form.

1. We are short of school facilities because the population *has growed* so fast.

2. I *have* never *known* a more intelligent young woman.

3. *Have* you ever *ridden* a bronc?

4. The "lights out" bell *has rang*.

5. The red dye *has ran* onto the white clothes.

6. It was the largest fire I ever *seen*.

7. Until this year we *have* always *sung* the Alma Mater before every football game.

8. After the principal *had spoke* to the entire school, she introduced the new teachers.

9. The crocuses seem to *have sprang* up overnight.

10. The defendent claimed that he *had* not *stole* the car.

11. Before I *had swum* across the pool, I was breathless.

12. As the car hit the icy spot on the road, it *swang* around and headed in the opposite direction.

13. It *would have took* less time to do the job if we had done it my way.

14. *Has* Ted *tore* his jacket again?

15. We all agreed that she *had thrown* the longest pass we had ever seen.

16. The principal *has wrote* to my parents about my poor grade in English.

17. Did she lose her wallet, or *was* it *stole?*

18. She *has knowed* our family for many years.

19. Who *grew* those mammoth tomatoes?

20. The chorus *had sang* their opening number before we arrived.

21. During the past week, I *seen* fifteen movies on television.

22. *Has* he *run* into debt again?

23. I *have* never *spoken* into a microphone.

24. Writers of popular songs *have stole* many a melody from classical compositions.

25. The poet, Lord Byron, *swum* the Hellespont.

26. How many years *have* you *taken* piano lessons?

27. The branches *swung* gently in the breeze.

28. All books with pages that *have been tore* will be replaced.

29. Roberto's arm began to hurt after he *had thrown* for only five innings.

30. *Have*n't I always *spoke* up for you?

31. Richard *had tore* the most important part of the homework assignment out of his notebook.

32. *Have* you ever *written* to the girl that you met in camp last summer?

33. At the Olympics I *seen* him win a medal for this country.

**EXERCISE 7.** This exercise covers all the verbs in Groups I to IV. Number your paper 1–50. After each number, write either the past or past participle of the verb at the beginning, whichever correctly fills the blank in the corresponding sentence.

1. *come*    Did you say that they had —— home?

2. *freeze*    Ideas, like meat and vegetables, can be ——.

3. *run*    When a kangaroo and horse —— a race, the kangaroo won.

4. *swim*    At last year's meet, our team —— in three events.

5. *drink*    The little ones —— their orange juice.

6. *grow*    Developing one's own ideas is a sign that one has —— somewhat.

7. *see*    How many of you —— last night's program on Roberto Clemente?

8. *choose*    Ten tried out, but only two were ——.

9. *grow*    Our town has —— faster than ever in the last few years.

10. *ring*    When was the Liberty Bell last ——?

11. *steal*    How many bases were —— during the season?

12. *write*    If Gertrude Stein had not —— *Three Lives,* she would still be known for her salon.

13. *begin*    The track team has —— practice.

14. *sing*    What was that song you just ——?

15. *blow*    It must have been a hurricane that —— those trees down.

16. *burst*    The sun —— from behind the clouds.

17. *fall*    After he had —— on the ice three times, he gave up skating.

18. *ride*    Janet confessed that she had never —— a bicycle.

19. *go*    I've —— as far as I can go with this problem.

20. *throw*    Litterbugs had —— paper and other trash on the grass.

21. *choose*   Last year the judges —— Carol's painting.
22. *do*   Walter —— his term paper on Martina Arroyo.
23. *drive*   The President was —— in a bullet-proof car.
24. *blow*   When was this candle —— out?
25. *go*   This year the president and the vice-president of the Student Council have —— to the convention.
26. *know*   The actors should have —— their lines better.
27. *speak*   We had heard every word although he had —— quietly.
28. *tear*   The title page had been —— from the book.
29. *swim*   The salmon have —— up the river to spawn.
30. *ring*   The referee kept counting after the bell had ——.
31. *break*   When was the record ——?
32. *fall*   Has any rain —— in the valley yet?
33. *drink*   Although I hated the taste, I —— my medicine.
34. *grow*   The larva has —— into a stunning butterfly.
35. *sing*   The diva —— with clarity and spirit when I heard her.
36. *take*   All of the best seats have been ——.
37. *run*   Lorraine and Marlene have —— that store for twenty years.
38. *spring*   Mr. Carl has —— a test on his class.
39. *give*   Has Albert —— his ring to Frances?
40. *begin*   Everyone ran when it —— to rain.
41. *draw*   The troops have —— up in battle lines.
42. *go*   The seniors have —— to Washington, D.C.
43. *see*   Has anyone —— my notebook?
44. *swing*   As she —— around, the official called a foul.
45. *come*   The spring holiday has —— at last!
46. *throw*   Who has —— his coat on the couch?
47. *begin*   It wasn't until we reached Glenview that the road —— to climb.
48. *choose*   Each of us has —— a different color.
49. *do*   We —— what we could to help the dance committee.
50. *give*   Last week the telephone company —— us a new number.

## SIX TROUBLESOME VERBS

All of the verb problems in the preceding exercises were solved by the correct choice of a verb *form*. The *meanings* of the verbs were obvious. Verb problems arise, however, in which questions about both form and meaning must be answered. Such problems come up with verbs that are similar in sound but different in their meanings and principal parts. These verbs present special problems because you must, first, choose the correct verb and, then, the proper verb form. Six verbs of this kind have been selected for detailed study and drill. Taken in pairs, they are: *lie* and *lay, sit* and *set,* and *rise* and *raise.* The most troublesome pair is probably the first, *lie* and *lay.*

### Lie and Lay

The verb *lie* means "to rest" or "to stay, to recline, or to remain in a certain state or position." Its principal parts are *lie,* (is) *lying, lay,* (have) *lain.*[1]

The verb *lay* means "to put" or "to place" (something). Its principal parts are *lay,* (is) *laying, laid,* (have) *laid.*

It is necessary to understand the meanings of these verbs. Notice that the verb *lay* is transitive. It takes an object, indicated by the word *something* in parentheses after its definition. A person lays something down, or a chicken lays an egg. A person lays something in a specified place: Miguel laid the newspaper on the porch. On the other hand, the verb *lie* is intransitive. It takes no object. A person simply lies down (no object), or a thing lies there (no object): The eggs lie in the nest.

Memorize the principal parts of these two verbs:

| INFINITIVE | PRESENT PARTICIPLE | PAST | PAST PARTICIPLE |
|---|---|---|---|
| lie (*to rest*) | lying | lay | (have) lain |
| lay (*to put*) | laying | laid | (have) laid |

[1] Do not confuse *lie* (to rest) with *lie* (to tell a falsehood), a regular verb whose principal parts are *lie,* (is) *lying, lied,* (have) *lied.* Because the meanings of the two verbs are so different, this error is rare; but students occasionally confuse the two sets of principal parts.

   With the meanings and the principal parts clearly established in your mind, you can solve any *lie-lay* problem.
Work slowly and carefully, treating each of the two elements separately. A good way to attack the problem is to
ask yourself two questions—one to find the correct *verb*,
and the other to find the correct *form of the verb:*

*Question 1*   What is the meaning that I have in mind? Is it *to
             recline* or *rest*, or is it *to put* (something)?

You will know whether to use a form of the verb *lie* or a
form of the verb *lay* when you have answered this question.
Now ask yourself:

*Question 2*   What principal part expresses the time that I have
             in mind?

The answer to this question will tell you which verb form
to use.
   Now let us apply these two questions to some typical
*lie-lay* problems.

PROBLEM   Yesterday I (laid, lay) down but could not sleep.

*Question 1*   Meaning? The meaning here is *to recline;* the verb
             meaning *to recline* is *lie.*

*Question 2*   Principal part? Since the time is past, the verb must
             be in the past form; the past form of *lie* is *lay.*   [*lie,
             lay, (have) lain*]

SOLUTION   Yesterday I **lay** down but could not sleep.

PROBLEM   She (laid, lay) the car keys here before she left.

*Question 1*   Meaning? The meaning here is *to put;* the verb
             meaning *to put* is *lay.*

*Question 2*   Principal part? The time is past, and the verb must
             be in the past form; the past form of *lay* is *laid.*
             [*lay, laid, (have) laid*]

SOLUTION   She **laid** the car keys here before she left.

PROBLEM   The bulbs have (laid, lain) in the ground all winter.

*Question 1*   Meaning? The meaning here is *to remain in a certain
             position* or *to rest.* The verb meaning *to remain* or
             *rest* is *lie.*

*Question 2*   Principal part? The principal part required with the helping verb *have* is the past participle. The past participle of *lie* is *lain*. [*lie, lay, (have) lain*]

SOLUTION   The bulbs **have lain** in the ground all winter.

PROBLEM   Her car keys are still (laying, lying) on the table.

*Question 1*   Meaning? Again, the meaning is *to remain in a certain position*. The verb meaning *to remain* is *lie*.

*Question 2*   Principal part? Here the helping verb *are* requires the present participle. The present participle of *lie* is *lying*.

SOLUTION   Her car keys are still **lying** on the table.

This "two-question" method may seem slow at first, but it will pay you to use it. After a few trials the process will speed up, and you will be able to select both the correct verb and the proper verb form quickly. Eventually, when the meanings and the principal parts of *lie* and *lay* have become part of your mental "furniture," you should be able to discard the method entirely.

In addition to the two-question method, the following three hints should help you to use *lie* and *lay* correctly.

1. Most errors in the use of these verbs are made when the speaker should use a form of *lie*, meaning "to rest, recline," or "remain in a certain state or position." When this is the meaning you have in mind, be especially cautious.

2. Make use of the fact that *lay* usually takes an object while *lie* does not. Thus, if a sentence contains an object, always use a form of *lay*.

3. As a final check, substitute the verb *put* for the problem verb in a sentence. If the sentence makes sense after the substitution, use a form of *lay;* if it "sounds wrong," use a form of *lie*.

EXAMPLES   The book was (lying, laying) on my desk.   [*The book was "putting"* "sounds wrong," therefore:]

The book was **lying** on my desk.   [a form of *lie*]

The nurse (lay, laid) the baby in the crib.   [*The nurse "put" the baby* makes sense, therefore:]

The nurse **laid** the baby in the crib.   [a form of *lay*]

**EXERCISE 8.** *Oral Drill.* Read each of the following sentences aloud several times, stressing the italicized verbs. This is an ear-training exercise that is designed to fix the habit of using *lie* and *lay* correctly.

1. *Lay* the book on the desk.
2. Let the book *lie* on the desk.
3. The boat *lay* at anchor.
4. He *has lain* around the house all day.
5. We *laid* our plans carefully before leaving.
6. The snake *has been lying* in the sun.
7. *Have* they *laid* the new flooring yet?
8. When is she going to *lie* down and rest?
9. She said that she *has been lying* down all morning.
10. The joy *lies* in doing a good job.

**EXERCISE 9.** Number your paper 1–10. After each number, write the form of *lie* or *lay* that correctly fills the blank in the corresponding sentence. Use the two-question method of finding the proper verb and verb form.

1. How long has that carcass been —— there?
2. The lawyer —— the evidence before the jury yesterday.
3. When I saw him at the hospital, he was —— on the sundeck.
4. Why do you allow her to —— her bicycle down there?
5. The ironed shirts —— on my dresser for a week.
6. Who —— the flowers on my desk?
7. We —— in the sun on the beach all afternoon yesterday.
8. Too many magazines are —— on the table.
9. When I had a conference with my teacher, he —— great emphasis upon vocabulary development.
10. The cookies have been —— in the jar so long that they are stale.

**EXERCISE 10.** Number your paper 1–20. After each number, write the correct one of the two verb forms in parentheses. Use the two-question method in making your choice.

1. All of the paper (lying, laying) on the floor must be picked up.

2. The potatoes and carrots have (lain, laid) in the cold cellar for several months.
3. (Lie, Lay) the test tube on the counter.
4. The new housing development (lays, lies) west of town.
5. The snow shovel is (laying, lying) under the snow.
6. When was the linoleum (laid, lain)?
7. Dad and Steve (lay, laid) their coats on the bed.
8. Dense clouds have been (lying, laying) overhead all day.
9. That house still (lays, lies) empty after two years.
10. Comfortably filled with fresh young grass, the cows (laid, lay) in the field.
11. Mother has gone to (lie, lay) down for a short nap before the company arrives.
12. The key to the solution of the problem (lays, lies) here.
13. The new high school is (lain, laid) out in campus style.
14. The car had (laid, lain) unused in the garage all winter.
15. (Lie, Lay) here and relax before attacking the hill.
16. The plans for the siege had been (lain, laid) months before.
17. Her success in high school (laid, lay) the foundation for a brilliant career in college.
18. Let's try to discover where the fault (lays, lies).
19. The hen (lay, laid) her eggs on the uppermost bale of hay.
20. The shattered glass (lay, laid) on the living room floor.

## Sit and Set

The verb *sit* usually means "to assume or be in an upright sitting position." The principal parts of *sit* are *sit,* (is) *sitting, sat,* (have) *sat.*

The verb *set* usually means "to place or to put (something)." The principal parts of *set* are *set,* (is) *setting, set,* (have) *set.*

EXCEPTIONS The word "usually" in the definitions above indicates that these are the most common meanings and uses. On rare occasions, however, *sit* may be used with the meaning of *set* ("*Sit* the baby here"); in other rare uses, *sit* may take an object ("He *sits* a horse well"). The verb *set* has a few specialized meanings in which it does not take an object:

They set out at dawn.

The sun sets later every day now that it is spring.

Do not eat the pudding until it has set.

In studying the correct use of these verbs, you may find it helpful at first to use the two-question method outlined in the discussion of *lie* and *lay*.

Be sure that you have correctly memorized the principal parts of these verbs:

| INFINITIVE | PRESENT PARTICIPLE | PAST | PAST PARTICIPLE |
|---|---|---|---|
| sit (*to rest*) | sitting | sat | (have) sat |
| set (*to put*) | setting | set | (have) set |

In addition to the two-question method, these two hints should help you to use *sit* and *set* correctly:

1. Make use of the fact that *set* normally takes an object while *sit* does not. People simply *sit;* people *set* something. Thus, if the verb has an object (transitive), use a form of *set.*

2. As a final check, substitute the verb *place* for the problem verb in a sentence. If the sentence "sounds right" with the substitution, use a form of *set;* if it "sounds wrong," use a form of *sit.*

**EXERCISE 11.** Number your paper 1–10. After each number, write the form of *sit* or *set* that correctly fills the blank in the corresponding sentence. Use the two-question method of finding the verb and verb form.

1. My great-great-grandmother (set, sat) in this very chair that I am using.
2. Shall we try to find a place to (set, sit) down?
3. (Set, Sit) the trunk in the hall.
4. From where we were (sitting, setting) in the bleachers, it was difficult to judge the play at home plate.
5. That African violet plant has (set, sat) in the window for three years.
6. Since the vase is so large, why not (sit, set) it on the floor?
7. The Sphinx (sits, sets) and looks into the future.

8. Why don't you (sit, set) here in front of the fireplace?
9. Ms. Marshall will (sit, set) there.
10. There the dog (set, sat), guarding its owner's house.

## Rise and Raise

The verb *rise* means "to ascend" or "go up." The principal parts of *rise* are *rise,* (is) *rising, rose,* (have) *risen.*

The verb *raise* means "to cause (something) to move upward, to lift (something)." The principal parts of *raise* are *raise,* (is) *raising, raised,* (have) *raised.*

It is easy to apply the two-question method to a *rise-raise* problem. In meaning the two verbs are quite different. One *raises* something or somebody; like *lay* and *set, raise* may take an object (transitive). Like *lie* and *sit, rise* does not take an object (intransitive). In answering Question 1, then, remember that (1) one always *raises something* or *somebody;* (2) one cannot *"rise"* anything. Answering Question 2 is simplified by the fact that *raise* is a regular verb. Be sure that you know the principal parts of both verbs.

| INFINITIVE | PRESENT PARTICIPLE | PAST | PAST PARTICIPLE |
|---|---|---|---|
| rise (*to go up*) | rising | rose | (have) risen |
| raise (*to force up*) | raising | raised | (have) raised |

When the meaning that you have in mind is "to lift (something)," use *raise, raised,* or *raising* (regular principal parts). For other meanings, use *rise, rising, rose,* or *risen* (irregular principal parts).

**EXERCISE 12.** Number your paper 1–10. After each number, write a + if the italicized verb in the corresponding sentence is correct. Write a 0 if it is incorrect, and then write the sentence, using the correct form of the verb.

1. The river *has raised* to a threatening level.
2. One of the custodian's duties is to *raise* the flag every morning.
3. The temperature *has raised* to 85° every day this month.

4. He tried to *raise* from the couch, but his ankle was too painful.
5. Her blood pressure *rose* to a frightening degree.
6. As we left for the mountains, the sun was *rising*.
7. The person who *is rising* to express her views is Miss Mendoza.
8. The price of a quart of milk *was risen* by the retail stores.
9. The price of beef *has been raised* by the state agricultural committee.
10. The cost-of-living index *has risen* steadily during the past six months.

**EXERCISE 13.** This exercise covers the six special verbs discussed in this section. Number your paper 1–20. After each number, write the correct one of the two verb forms in parentheses. Work slowly and carefully; use the two-question method whenever you are in doubt about a choice.

1. The road (lay, laid) in a straight line for miles and miles.
2. Please do not let your dog (lie, lay) on our new slipcovers.
3. The class (set, sat) attentively while Adolfo recited a monologue from *Purlie Victorious*.
4. When will prices ever stop (rising, raising)?
5. After the windstorm, the clothes were (lying, laying) all over the yard.
6. The weather balloon (rose, raised) many miles into the atmosphere.
7. With great care the gardener (laid, lay) the seeds in the ground.
8. There we (set, sat) while the rain poured down outside.
9. The bread dough has been (raising, rising) for several hours.
10. The Caribbean Sea (lays, lies) north of the equator.
11. The tractor and combine have (laid, lain) in the open field all winter.
12. Shall we just (set, sit) around and talk?
13. The mountain (rises, raises) majestically above the plain.
14. Have you been (laying, lying) there all afternoon?
15. Please (sit, set) all the packages on the kitchen table.

16. The world seems to come alive once more as the sun (raises, rises).

17. Where have you (lain, laid) my new pinking shears?

18. A handsome black cat was (setting, sitting) on the window sill in the living room.

19. The victim (lay, laid) in the road until the ambulance arrived.

20. Where was the car (sitting, setting) when the truck skidded into it?

**EXERCISE 14.** The purpose of this exercise is to give you further practice in the use of the six troublesome verbs. Write four original sentences for both *lie* and *lay,* using the four principal parts of each. Write three sentences each for *sit, set, rise,* and *raise.* Do not use the same principal part twice for any one verb.

# TENSE

**8b. Learn the names of the six tenses and the way the tenses are formed.**

Verbs indicate the *time* of an action or a statement by changes in their form. Every form of a verb tells us something about the time of an action or statement; that is, it "places" the action or statement in the past, the present, or the future. These verb forms are called *tenses,* from the Latin word meaning "time." English verbs appear in six different tenses to indicate past, present, or future time. All six tenses are based upon the principal parts of a verb — the infinitive, the present participle, the past, and the past participle.

To learn the verb forms used in each of the six tenses, study the following *conjugations* of the verbs *see* and *be.*

### *Conjugation of the Verb* See

Present infinitive: *to see*     Perfect infinitive: *to have seen*

## Principal Parts

| INFINITIVE | PRESENT PARTICIPLE | PAST | PAST PARTICIPLE |
|---|---|---|---|
| see | seeing | saw | seen |

### Present Tense

| Singular | Plural |
|---|---|
| I see | we see |
| you see | you see |
| he, she, it sees | they see |

Present progressive: *I am seeing*, etc.

### Past Tense

| Singular | Plural |
|---|---|
| I saw | we saw |
| you saw | you saw |
| he, she, it saw | they saw |

Past progressive: *I was seeing*, etc.

### Future Tense

(*will* or *shall* + infinitive)

| Singular | Plural |
|---|---|
| I will (shall) see | we will (shall) see |
| you will see | you will see |
| he, she, it will see | they will see |

Future progressive: *I will (shall) be seeing*, etc.

### Present Perfect Tense

(*have* or *has* + past participle)

| Singular | Plural |
|---|---|
| I have seen | we have seen |
| you have seen | you have seen |
| he, she, it has seen | they have seen |

Present perfect progressive: *I have been seeing*, etc.

### Past Perfect Tense
(*had* + past participle)

| Singular | Plural |
|---|---|
| I had seen | we had seen |
| you had seen | you had seen |
| he, she, it had seen | they had seen |

Past perfect progressive: *I had been seeing,* etc.

### Future Perfect Tense
(*will have* or *shall have* + past participle)

| Singular | Plural |
|---|---|
| I will (shall) have seen | we will (shall) have seen |
| you will have seen | you will have seen |
| he, she, it will have seen | they will have seen |

Future perfect progressive: *I will have been seeing,* etc.

## Conjugation of the Verb Be

Present infinitive: *to be*      Perfect infinitive: *to have been*

### Principal Parts

| INFINITIVE | PRESENT PARTICIPLE | PAST | PAST PARTICIPLE |
|---|---|---|---|
| be | being | was | been |

### Present Tense

| Singular | Plural |
|---|---|
| I am | we are |
| you are | you are |
| he, she, it is | they are |

Present progressive: *I am being,* etc.

### Past Tense

| Singular | Plural |
|---|---|
| I was | we were |
| you were | you were |
| he, she, it was | they were |

Past progressive: *I was being,* etc.

### Future Tense

(*will* or *shall* + infinitive)

| Singular | Plural |
|---|---|
| I will (shall) be | we will (shall) be |
| you will be | you will be |
| he, she, it will be | they will be |

### Present Perfect Tense

(*have* or *has* + past participle)

| Singular | Plural |
|---|---|
| I have been | we have been |
| you have been | you have been |
| he, she, it has been | they have been |

### Past Perfect Tense

(*had* + past participle)

| Singular | Plural |
|---|---|
| I had been | we had been |
| you had been | you had been |
| he, she, it had been | they had been |

### Future Perfect Tense

(*will have* or *shall have* + past participle)

| Singular | Plural |
|---|---|
| I will (shall) have been | we will (shall) have been |
| you will have been | you will have been |
| he, she, it will have been | they will have been |

▶ **NOTE**   The progressive forms of the verb are not a separate tense. Progressive forms are made up of the various tenses of the verb *be* plus the present participle. Progressive forms are used to show continuing action.

## 8c. Learn the uses of each of the six tenses.

Each of the tenses has its own special uses. The names of the tenses do not in themselves explain the uses, nor does a conjugation alone tell us more than the forms taken by a verb in different tenses. Study the following detailed explanations of each of the six tenses. As you read, review the name of each tense and the correct verb forms by referring back to the conjugations of *see* and *be*. Learn the rules for the uses of each tense. Use these pages for reference whenever you meet a problem in tense that you cannot solve.

**(1) The *present tense* is used mainly to express an action (or to help make a statement about something) that is occurring now, at the present time.**

EXAMPLES   Ms. Taylor **teaches** English.

Ms. Taylor **does teach** here.   [emphatic form: the verb with *do* or *did* is called the emphatic form.]

Use the progressive form to express a continuing action, an action in progress.

She **is teaching** in our school now.   [progressive form]

The present tense has several minor uses in addition to its main one. Be sure that you understand all of the following uses.

In an idiomatic construction, the present tense may be used to express future time.

EXAMPLES   His leave of absence **starts** next semester.

He **leaves** in January.

The present tense may be used to express a customary or habitual action or state of being.

EXAMPLE   The classes **meet** in double periods.

The present tense is used to express a general truth, something that is true at all times.

EXAMPLES   The sun **is** at the center of our solar system.

Living things **are** interdependent with one another and with their environment.

The present tense is used to tell of things that happened in the past when the writer wants to make the past events seem alive and vivid. This use is called the *historical present*.

EXAMPLE In a totally unexpected move, Washington's army **crosses** the Delaware and **takes** the Hessians by surprise at Trenton.

**(2) The *past tense* is used to express an action (or to help make a statement about something) that occurred in the past and did not continue into the present.**

EXAMPLES She **hid** the treasure.

She **was hiding** the treasure when I spotted her.

▶ **NOTE** Past action may be shown in other ways.

I **used to live** in the city.

I **did live** there [emphatic form]

**(3) The *future tense* is used to express an action (or to help make a statement about something) that will occur in the future. The future tense is formed with *will* or *shall*.**

EXAMPLES She **will leave** tomorrow.

She **will be leaving** tomorrow.

▶ **NOTE** Future time may also be indicated in other ways.

She **leaves** tomorrow.

She **is going to leave** soon.

**(4) The *present perfect tense* is used mainly to express an action (or to help make a statement about something) that has been completed at some indefinite time in the past. It is formed with *have* or *has* and the past participle.**

They **have sold** their house.

Note the word *indefinite* in rule 4. The present perfect should not be used to express a *specific* time in the past.

NONSTANDARD They have sold their house last week.
STANDARD They have sold their house recently.
STANDARD They sold their house last week. [past tense]

The present perfect tense may also be used to express an action (or to help make a statement about something) that began in the past and is still going on.

EXAMPLES  We have waited a long time.

We have been waiting a long time.

**(5) The *past perfect tense* is used to express an action (or to help make a statement about something) that was completed in the past and preceded some other past action or event. It is formed with *had* and the past participle.**

EXAMPLES  The teacher said that she **had given** the assignment twice.  [The giving preceded the saying.]

By the time the police arrived, the disturbance **had been settled.**  [First the disturbance was settled, and then the police arrived.]

**(6) The *future perfect tense* is used to express an action (or to help make a statement about something) that will be completed in the future before some other future action or event. It is formed with *will have* or *shall have* and the past participle.**

EXAMPLES  The tourist season **will have begun** by the time we arrive in Florida.

By the end of June, she **will have been working** for thirty years.  [Thirty years of teaching will be completed by the future date.]

**EXERCISE 15.**  Number your paper 1–10. After each number, write the names of the tenses of the verbs in the corresponding pair of sentences. All the sentences are grammatically correct; they differ only in the tenses used. Be prepared to explain how these differences in tense alter the meanings of the sentences.

1. The president has left everything up to our committee.
   The president had left everything up to our committee.
2. I visited my aunt for several summers.
   I have visited my aunt for several summers.
3. We will take the first plane for Chicago.
   We will have taken the first plane for Chicago.
4. The school board has made its budget for the year.
   The school board had made its budget for the year.

5. Do you realize how fast I drove?
   Do you realize how fast I had driven?
6. We have set the date for the play.
   We had set the date for the play.
7. I will make an A in math next year.
   I will have made an A in math by this time next year.
8. I remember that I have promised to go.
   I remembered that I had promised to go.
9. What did the lecturer say?
   What has the lecturer said?
10. Ms. Ling was the principal for twenty years.
    Ms. Ling has been the principal for twenty years.

**EXERCISE 16.** This exercise will help you use the perfect tenses. Write original sentences as directed.

Three in the present perfect about literature
Three in the past perfect about movies and television
Four in the future perfect about animals

# SPECIAL PROBLEMS IN THE USE OF TENSES

Now that you have a knowledge of the six tenses and their uses, you are well on the way to avoiding errors in the use of verbs in speaking and writing. However, this knowledge, of itself, will not enable you to avoid all errors. Special problems must be solved by every writer. A few are discussed below.

## Sequence of Tenses

Normally the verbs in a compound or complex sentence follow the principle of sequence of tense. The sentence "The starting gate *opened,* and the horses *run* toward the finish line" is incorrect. It is not correct because the writer has needlessly switched from the past tense in the first clause to the present tense in the second clause. The entire sentence should have been written in either the present or the past tense: "The starting gate *opened,* and the horses *ran* toward the finish line" or "The starting gate *opens,* and the horses *run* toward the finish line."

Somewhat more difficult to handle are those sentences in which tense is deliberately and correctly changed to indicate a change in time. Study the following examples in which changes in tense are used to convey different meanings:

**I know** that **I like** her.   [The two present tenses agree.]

**I know** that **I liked** her.   [The change of the second verb to the past tense suggests that the person may be liked no longer.]

Marian **said** that she **went** to the party.   [The two past tenses agree.]

Marian said that she **would go** to the party.   [The change to *would go* tells us that Marian had not gone to the party at the time she made the remark.]

The relation between the tenses in the examples above is simple and clear. Other constructions and combinations, however, require special attention. Study the examples that follow:

NONSTANDARD   Since the new trainer took over the stable, our horse **won** all of its races.   [The new trainer took over at a definite, specific time; thus, the past tense is correct. The winning took place over a period of time, and the speaker has no specific race in mind; here the past tense is incorrect. The present perfect tense should be used.]

STANDARD   Since the new trainer took over the stable, our horse **has won** all of its races.

NONSTANDARD   He was now playing on the varsity team, but he **was playing** on the junior varsity earlier in the season.   [The meaning of the sentence is that the second action preceded the first; therefore, the second verb should be in the past perfect form.]

STANDARD   He was now playing on the varsity team, but he

had been playing on the junior varsity earlier in
the season.

**8d. Avoid the use of *would have* in "if" clauses expressing the earlier of two past actions. Use the past perfect tense.**

NONSTANDARD    If she would have run just a little faster, she
    would have won the race.

STANDARD    If she **had run** just a little faster, she would have
    won the race.

NONSTANDARD    I might not have said that I would attend if I
    would have known it was going to snow.

STANDARD    I might not have said that I would attend if I
    **had known** that it was going to snow.

NONSTANDARD    If Carmen would have sent her application in
    earlier, she probably would have been accepted.

STANDARD    If Carmen **had sent** her application in earlier,
    she probably would have been accepted.

**EXERCISE 17.**    Each of the following sentences contains an
error in the use of tenses. Decide how to correct the sentences, and then write the corrected verbs after the sentence numbers on your paper.

1. Francesca promised to show me the slacks she bought the
   day before.
2. The game will be played by that time.
3. My fifth-grade teacher was fond of saying, "Fools' names,
   like fools' faces, always appeared in public places."
4. The sale of book jackets improved since the new school
   store opened.
5. If he would have taken off his wet clothes, he might not
   have caught cold.
6. In August my parents will be married for twenty-five years.
7. After Pam saw the car skid, she rushed to see what happened.
8. Who has not heard that history repeated itself?
9. I would have brought my transistor radio if you would have
   suggested it.

10. Her family always showed that they have the utmost confidence in her.
11. I'd have helped you if you would have asked me to.
12. This report deals with conditions that have been corrected a long time ago.
13. Next month Ms. Bauer will be principal of this school for ten years.
14. If the judge would have known the background of the case, she might have reached a different decision.
15. Did you know that Election Day always fell on a Tuesday?
16. I have always been told that a stitch in time saved nine.
17. Photographers and reporters were waiting almost an hour by the time Governor Grasso arrived.
18. The concert will be given by then.
19. If all the tests have been corrected last Monday, why haven't they been handed back yet?
20. If he would have played the game correctly, he would have won.

## The Present and the Perfect Infinitives

### 8e. Use the present infinitive (*to push, to go,* etc.) to express an action that follows another action.

CONFUSING   Carrie said that she had hoped to have seen us at the reunion. [What did Carrie hope—*to see* us, or *to have seen* us? Surely she hoped to see us, since the action expressed by *see* follows the action expressed by *had hoped.*]

CLEAR   Carrie said that she had hoped **to see** us at the reunion.

### 8f. Use the perfect infinitive (*to have pushed, to have gone,* etc.) to express an action that took place before another action.

EXAMPLE   The explorers claimed to have found the lost city of Atlantis. [The perfect infinitive is correct because the action it expresses came before the time of the other verb *claimed.*]

**EXERCISE 18.** Each of the following sentences contains one or more errors in the use of verb forms. Rewrite the sentences, underlining each verb form that you change.

1. Carla would have been at the picnic if I would have remembered to have told her the date.

2. I tried to call Mrs. Weber at her office yesterday, but I found she just left.

3. How many adventurers have longed to have conquered Mt. Everest?

4. The building was evacuated before the fire company had arrived.

5. If she would have learned that to have a friend one must be a friend, she would not now be friendless.

6. We planned on seeing the Meads even before their letter had come.

7. Because she was a natural wit, Liza has been selected to play the lead in *The Skin of Our Teeth*.

8. My brother would have liked to have met you while you were here.

9. Alice Chan is pleased to see that the bowling team had done so well.

10. If it would have snowed another hour or so, we would not have had school today.

## ACTIVE AND PASSIVE VOICE

When a verb expresses an action performed *by* its subject, the verb is said to be in the *active* voice. A verb is in the *passive* voice when it expresses an action performed *upon* its subject or when the subject is the result of the action.

ACTIVE VOICE   The catcher threw the ball.   [subject acting]

PASSIVE VOICE   The ball was thrown by the catcher.   [subject acted upon.]

All verbs that take objects (transitive verbs) can be used in the passive voice.

<pre>
                       S        V        O
ACTIVE VOICE    The black horse threw Anne.
                       S        V
PASSIVE VOICE   Anne was thrown by the black horse.
                       S        V
                Anne was thrown.
</pre>

From these examples, you can see the formation of the passive construction and its relationship to the active. The object of the active sentence moves ahead of the verb to become the subject of the passive sentence, and the subject of the active sentence is either expressed in a prepositional phrase beginning with *by* or dropped completely.

Notice also that the verb from the active sentence has become a past participle preceded by the form of the verb *be* that indicates the proper tense.

ACTIVE   Many Americans **display** flags on the Fourth of July.

PASSIVE   Flags **are displayed** by many Americans on the Fourth of July.

ACTIVE   The burglar **opened** the door stealthily.

PASSIVE   The door **was opened** stealthily by the burglar.

## The Retained Object

Transitive verbs in the active voice often have indirect as well as direct objects. When they do, either object can become the subject of the passive sentence.

<pre>
                 S       V      IO          DO
ACTIVE    Mrs. Driscoll gave the child many presents.
</pre>

PASSIVE   The child was given many presents (by Mrs. Driscoll).

PASSIVE   Many presents were given the child (by Mrs. Driscoll).

In the passive sentences above, one of the objects becomes the subject and the other remains as a complement of the verb. In the first sentence the indirect object, *child,* becomes the subject, and the direct object, *presents,* is kept as a complement. In the second it is the indirect object that is retained. An object that continues to function as a complement in a passive construction is called a *retained object*.

## Use of the Passive Voice

Choosing between the active and passive voice in writing is a matter of style, not correctness. However, in most circumstances the passive voice is less forceful than the active voice and a string of passive verbs often produces an awkward paragraph.

AWKWARD PASSIVE   Last Saturday, the cooking was done by my sister, and the shopping was done by me.

ACTIVE   Last Saturday my sister did the cooking and I did the shopping.

AWKWARD PASSIVE   Our transportation problem was solved when the car was loaned to us by my parents.

ACTIVE   My parents solved our transportation problem by lending us the car.

SUCCESSION OF PASSIVES   When the invitation to do a guest lecture series *was received* by my mother, we were all delighted. No one in my family *had* ever *been asked* to do anything like this before. Since I was considered the most imaginative member of the family, I *was given* by my mother the delightful task of choosing subjects she would speak on to the eager young artists. Father *was elected* by mother to prepare the dinners for all of us every Wednesday night, the night the lectures *were to be given.* Formal invitations *were sent to us* by the university, to be in attendance at the lecture series. The first Wednesday night session finally arrived. My two brothers, my father, and I seated ourselves in the first row. The lecture *was begun* with a discussion of how art today *is influenced by* the abundance of crime stories on television and in magazines and newspapers. By the time the lecture *had been finished,* the rest of my family and I *were surprised* by the discovery of how much we had learned.

**8g. Use the passive voice sparingly. Avoid weak and awkward passives. In the interest of variety, avoid long passages in which all the verbs are passive.**

Although this rule is generally true, there are a few situations where the passive voice is particularly useful.

**(1) Use the passive voice to express an action in which the actor is unknown.**

An error **has been found** in your bank statement.

**(2) Use the passive voice to express an action in which it is desirable not to disclose the actor.**

The jewels **were stolen** last night.

Sometimes the passive voice is more convenient, and just as appropriate, as the active voice. In the following sentences the passive voice is completely acceptable and probably more natural.

Penicillin, like many breakthroughs in science, **was discovered** accidentally.

I **have been asked** to give the valedictory speech at commencement.

The fragile boat **was rocked** by the waves and **buffeted** by the strong winds.

**EXERCISE 19.** Revise the following sentences by changing the passive verbs to active verbs wherever you think the change is desirable. If you think that the passive is preferable, write *no change* after the number of the corresponding sentence.

1. When new taxes were proposed by the town council, a citizens' protest group was formed by my aunt.
2. Unfortunately, their objections were stated too late for anything to be done that year.
3. It was decided to wait until the next election, and then everything possible would be done to make sure that a new council was elected by the town.
4. After the play had been given the critics' award, the happy author was interviewed by the press and was asked how she felt about receiving the top prize.

5. By noon last Saturday the house had been cleaned, the lawn had been watered, the hedges had been trimmed, and the long, lazy afternoon awaited us.

6. The germ theory of disease was not proved conclusively by scientists until the end of the nineteenth century.

7. Many famous quotations from Churchill, Roosevelt, and Kennedy were used by the speaker in her talk on famous political orators.

8. The next day the speech was reviewed by the editor of our school paper and was highly praised by her.

9. The door was closed quietly, and then soft footsteps retreated down the hall.

10. Since the redecorating of the gym was finished so early, a surprise party was prepared for the work crew by the principal.

11. Although our team was penalized eighty yards in the last half, the game was finally won by us.

12. The first Thanksgiving was celebrated by the Pilgrims in Plymouth Colony, Massachusetts.

## THE SUBJUNCTIVE MOOD

Verbs may be in one of three moods: *indicative, imperative,* or *subjunctive.* Almost all the verbs you use in writing and speaking are in the *indicative mood,* which is used to make statements of fact. The *imperative mood* is used to express a request or command.

IMPERATIVE  Write the answers on your paper, not in your text-book.

Please close the window.

The only common uses of the subjunctive mood in modern English are to express a condition contrary to fact and to express a wish. These usages occur principally in written English and usually apply to only one verb form — *were.* The following partial conjugation of *be* will show how the subjunctive mood differs from the indicative.

| PRESENT INDICATIVE | | PRESENT SUBJUNCTIVE[1] | |
|---|---|---|---|
| *Singular* | *Plural* | *Singular* | *Plural* |
| I am | we are | (if) I be | (if) we be |
| you are | you are | (if) you be | (if) you be |
| he is | they are | (if) he be | (if) they be |

| PAST INDICATIVE | | PAST SUBJUNCTIVE | |
|---|---|---|---|
| *Singular* | *Plural* | *Singular* | *Plural* |
| I was | we were | (if) I were | (if) we were |
| you were | you were | (if) you were | (if) you were |
| he was | they were | (if) he were | (if) they were |

## 8h. The subjunctive *were* is used in contrary-to-fact statements (after *if* or *as though*) and in statements expressing a wish.

CONTRARY TO FACT  If I **were** you I'd try for the scholarship. [I am not you.]

If he **were** more conscientious, he'd be a better writer. [He is not conscientious.]

Whenever she criticized Judy's work, she sounded as though she **were** her enemy and not her friend. [She is not Judy's enemy.]

WISH  I wish it **were** true.

I wish she **were** not my roommate.

## REVIEW EXERCISE.  Some of the following sentences contain errors in the use of verbs. Others are correct. Number your paper 1–25. If the verbs in the sentence are correct, write *C* after the corresponding number on your paper. If you find a verb error, write the correct verb form after the proper number.

1. I wish you asked me before you took the car last night.

---

[1] The present subjunctive is used only in certain rather formal situations.

EXAMPLES  The presiding officer instructed that the delegates from the new nation *be* seated.

I move that the motion *be* tabled.

2. He would never make that wrong turn if he had studied the road map.

3. If she was less nervous about remembering her lines, she would be a good actress.

4. Martin says that he'd planned to have met us at the station when we arrived.

5. The first settlers in the Far West found that hunters and trappers had been there before them.

6. It seemed to me when the play was over that the audience witnessed a great performance by a great actor.

7. Did you think that she would accept my help if she were able to do it herself?

8. If they wouldn't have missed the bus, the picnic would have started on time.

9. It soon became apparent that the cast has not had enough rehearsals.

10. The garden tools should not have been left to lay on the damp ground all night.

11. Although the visitor thought she planned her trip down to the last detail, there was one thing she had forgotten.

12. If you would have remembered that haste makes waste, you wouldn't have burned the food.

13. The job would have been his, if he had been more reliable.

14. The hurtling cars raised clouds of dust, which laid over the track like a smoke screen.

15. A little boy as fair-skinned as Paul shouldn't be allowed to lay in the sun very long.

16. After he had refused the volunteer's request for a donation, he wished that he helped her.

17. Billions of seeds have been laying in the ground all winter waiting for spring to release them.

18. I regret that I forgot that fools and their money are soon parted.

19. The air conditioner turns on automatically every time the temperature raises more than five degrees.

20. If your candidate were more sure of her stand on foreign relations, I'd vote for her.

21. Once we rested, we were able to reach the top of the hill.

22. Mrs. Thompson, my mother's best friend, sometimes treats me as though I was her son.

23. If I had thought that the plane would be late, I would have sent you a telegram.

24. I am grateful to have graduated and to have an opportunity to go on with my education.

25. Although his sentences are long, the short story was effective.

# Chapter 9

# Correct Use of Modifiers

### Form of Adjectives and Adverbs; Comparison

Learning the definition and function of a part of speech does not mean that you will always know when to use a particular word in a sentence. For example, you have learned that an adjective modifies a noun or a pronoun, and that an adverb modifies a verb, an adjective, or another adverb, but you may have trouble deciding which to use after the verbs *taste, look, smell* or whether to say someone "sang good" or "sang well." These and other usage problems involving the use of adjectives and adverbs are discussed in this chapter.

## ADJECTIVE AND ADVERB FORMS

Before reviewing the usage of adjectives and adverbs, you should make sure that you are able to tell which is the adjective form of a word and which is the adverb form. The fact that most adverbs end in *–ly* (*clearly, happily, eagerly*) will be helpful if you understand that not *all* adverbs end in *–ly* and that a few common adjectives do end in *–ly*. Some words have the same form whether used as an adjective or as an adverb.

| ADJECTIVES | ADVERBS |
|---|---|
| a *fast* runner | She ran *fast*. |
| a *slow* boat | Go *slow*. |

| | |
|---|---|
| a *hard* mattress | He studies *hard*. |
| a *tight* shoe | Hold *tight*. |
| a *long* novel | She waited *long*. |
| a *late* meeting | He arrived *late*. |
| a *low* bridge | Sing *low*. |
| a *straight* ruler | Walk *straight*. |

ADJECTIVES ENDING IN −*ly*

*daily* exercise
*friendly* group
*early* bird
*kindly* stranger
*lively* band
*lovely* dress

**9a. Linking verbs, especially the verbs of sense (*taste, look, smell,* etc.), are often followed by an adjective. Action verbs are often followed by an adverb.**

EXAMPLES  The milk tasted **sour**. [The adjective *sour* is correct after the linking verb *tasted*. It modifies the subject *milk*.]

Her perfume smelled **strong**. [The adjective *strong* is correct after the linking verb *smelled*. It modifies the subject *perfume*.]

Some verbs may be used as either linking or action verbs. When they are used as action verbs, the modifier that follows modifies the verb rather than the subject and is, therefore, an adverb. For example, *looked* may be used as a linking verb and as an action verb.

EXAMPLES  The child looked **shy**. [After the linking verb *looked*, the adjective *shy* is correct. It modifies *child*.]

The child looked **shyly** at the clown. [After the action verb *looked*, the adverb *shyly* is correct. It modifies *looked*.]

When you are in doubt as to whether a verb is a linking verb or not, try substituting for it a form of *seem*, which is always a linking verb. If the substitution can be made without greatly changing the meaning of the sentence, the verb is a linking verb and should be followed by an adjective.

EXAMPLES    The dessert smelled strange.  [*The dessert seemed strange* gives about the same meaning; hence, *smelled* is a linking verb in this sentence.]

The dessert smelled strangely of pepper.  [*The dessert seemed strangely of pepper* makes no sense; therefore, *smelled* is not a linking verb in this sentence.]

**9b. In making a choice between an adjective and an adverb, ask yourself what the word modifies. If it modifies a noun or pronoun, choose the adjective. If it modifies a verb, choose the adverb.**

PROBLEM    The carpenters built the platform (sturdy, sturdily) enough to hold the entire choir.

SOLUTION    The carpenters built the platform **sturdy** enough to hold the entire choir.  [The adjective *sturdy* modifies the noun *platform*.]

PROBLEM    Has she been studying her lines (regular, regularly)?

SOLUTION    Has she been studying her lines **regularly**?  [The adverb *regularly* modifies the action verb *has been studying*.]

**EXERCISE 1.**    Number your paper 1–20. Select the correct one of the two words in parentheses in each sentence, and write it after the proper number. If the word modifies the subject, select the adjective; if it modifies the verb, select the adverb. Remember that a linking verb is followed by an adjective.

1. My old car still runs (smooth, smoothly).
2. After the Ohio River joins the Mississippi, the big river no longer moves so (swift, swiftly) to the sea.
3. As the results of the test show, Martin is still doing (poor, poorly) in science.
4. The new soprano did not seem to sing as (strong, strongly) as the famous tenor.
5. Do you think the leading man read that line (proper, properly)?
6. Why do vacations pass so (quick, quickly)?

7. To be good at tennis, you must practice (regular, regularly).

8. After our quarrel I felt (terrible, terribly) about some of the things I had said to my sister.

9. You don't have to speak out (bold, boldly) to be understood; speaking (clear, clearly) is much more important.

10. That engine was built (special, specially) for the Navy.

11. If Jack looks (anxious, anxiously) today, he is only worrying about finishing his research paper.

12. The woman looked (angry, angrily) at the man who had stepped on her foot.

13. When Gloria heard that her favorite team had lost again, she looked (miserable, miserably).

14. Even though the grocer said that the milk was fresh, I thought it tasted (sour, sourly).

15. Some people don't react as (rapid, rapidly) in emergencies as others.

16. If you would only shorten the sleeves one inch, that blouse would fit you (perfect, perfectly).

17. After playing in the yard for an hour, the baby went to sleep (peaceful, peacefully) in his crib.

18. As the night wore on, the wind howled (fierce, fiercely) like a hungry wolf.

19. If you cheer (energetic, energetically) enough, you might become a group leader.

20. By getting some more help, the builders finished the job (easy, easily) within three hours.

## Bad and Badly

*Bad* is an adjective, modifying nouns and pronouns. *Badly* is an adverb, modifying verbs, adjectives, and adverbs. Since the verbs of sense—*feel, smell, taste, sound*—are followed by an adjective (not an adverb) modifying their subjects, it is standard English to say *feel bad, smell bad,* etc.

I felt bad about receiving such poor marks in the examination.

The beach often smells bad after a storm.

► **USAGE NOTE** The expression *feel badly* has, through usage, become acceptable, though ungrammatical, English. However, *badly* used with other verbs of sense is not yet standard—*smell badly, taste badly,* etc.

## Well and Good

*Well* may be used as either an adjective or an adverb. As an adjective, *well* has three meanings.

1. *To be in good health:*

   He feels well. He seems well.

2. *To appear well-dressed or well-groomed:*

   She looks well in that dress.

3. *To be satisfactory:*

   All is well.

As an adverb, *well* means to perform an action capably.

   She sang very well.

*Good* is always an adjective. It should never be used to modify a verb.

NONSTANDARD   After practicing for weeks, the school orchestra finally played good.

STANDARD   After practicing for weeks, the orchestra finally played well.

## Slow and Slowly

*Slow* is used as both an adjective and an adverb. *Slowly* is an adverb. Except for the expressions *Drive slow* and *Go slow,* which have become acceptable because of their wide use on highway signs, you will be on the safe side if you use *slow* only as an adjective.

**EXERCISE 2.** Number your paper 1–20. If the italicized modifier in a sentence is correct, write *C* after the proper number on your paper. If it is incorrect, write the correct form, and after the correct form write the word it modifies.

1. They had known each other for years, and they got along *good* together.
2. It was only after my sophomore year that I began to take my studies *serious*.
3. When February is over, I look *eagerly* for spring.
4. Although she has been studying music for only two years, I thought Sophia played that sonata very *good*.
5. Don't feel *bad* if you don't make the team this year.
6. The juniors beat the seniors quite *easy* in the last game.
7. The seniors felt *bitterly* about losing.
8. If you don't feel *well*, please don't get up.
9. When you are talking to someone from another country, speak *slow* enough to be understood.
10. Even though we're twins, Elizabeth and I always dress *different*.
11. The cake I baked for the class picnic came out *good*.
12. Superstitious people always drive extra *careful* on Friday the thirteenth.
13. The music ended *sudden*, and the dancers stopped abruptly.
14. Drive *slowly* around this curve.
15. Don was not hurt *bad*, though he had fallen ten feet.
16. I always wanted to buy a red velvet dress until someone told me I didn't look *good* in that color.
17. You had better go home *quick*, if you want to avoid the storm.
18. The soldiers advanced *slow* against the still invisible enemy.
19. Four years ago she couldn't keep a tune, but now she sings very *good*.
20. Step by step, the quiet girl walked *steady* toward her goal.

## COMPARISON OF ADJECTIVES AND ADVERBS

**9c.** *Comparison* is the name given to the change in the form of adjectives and adverbs when they are used to compare the degree of the qualities they express. There are three degrees of comparison: *positive, comparative,* and *superlative.*

| POSITIVE | COMPARATIVE | SUPERLATIVE |
|---|---|---|
| loud | louder | loudest |
| eager | more eager | most eager |
| swiftly | more swiftly | most swiftly |
| fast | faster | fastest |
| softly | more softly | most softly |
| good | better | best |

## Comparative and Superlative Forms

**(1) Most adjectives and adverbs of one syllable form their comparative and superlative degrees by adding** *–er* **and** *–est.*

| POSITIVE | COMPARATIVE | SUPERLATIVE |
|---|---|---|
| short | shorter | shortest |
| late | later | latest |
| hard | harder | hardest |
| quick | quicker | quickest |

**(2) Some adjectives of two syllables form their comparative and superlative degrees by adding** *–er* **and** *–est;* **other adjectives of two syllables form their comparative and superlative degrees by means of** *more* **and** *most.*

| POSITIVE | COMPARATIVE | SUPERLATIVE |
|---|---|---|
| merry | merrier | merriest |
| anxious | more anxious | most anxious |

When you are in doubt as to how a word is compared, consult a dictionary.

**(3) Adjectives of more than two syllables and adverbs ending in** *–ly* **form their comparative and superlative degrees by means of** *more* **and** *most.*

| POSITIVE | COMPARATIVE | SUPERLATIVE |
|---|---|---|
| readable | more readable | most readable |
| cheerfully | more cheerfully | most cheerfully |

**(4) Comparison to indicate less or least of a quality is accomplished by using the words *less* and *least* before the adjective or adverb.**

| POSITIVE | COMPARATIVE | SUPERLATIVE |
|---|---|---|
| aware | less aware | least aware |
| tiresome | less tiresome | least tiresome |

## Irregular Comparison

Adjectives and adverbs that do not follow the regular methods of forming their comparative and superlative degrees are said to be compared irregularly.

| POSITIVE | COMPARATIVE | SUPERLATIVE |
|---|---|---|
| bad | worse | worst |
| good } well | better | best |
| little | less | least |
| many } much | more | most |

**EXERCISE 3.** Write the comparative and superlative forms of the following words. If you are in doubt about any of them, use a dictionary.

1. thick
2. handsome
3. happy
4. few
5. gracious
6. late
7. gladly
8. ill
9. much
10. far
11. thoughtless
12. well
13. cheap
14. quick
15. hopefully
16. bitter
17. satisfactorily
18. furious
19. little
20. early

## Use of Comparatives and Superlatives

**9d. In standard English the comparative degree is used when comparing two things, and the superlative degree when comparing more than two.**

COMPARISON OF TWO THINGS

Although Routes 17 and 611 both go to Scot Run, take the **longer** because it is more scenic.   [not *longest*]

After reading Poe's "The Masque of the Red Death" and "The Fall of the House of Usher," I decided that the first was the **more powerfully** written.   [not *most powerfully*]

COMPARISON OF MORE THAN TWO THINGS

I chose the bus trip because it was the **cheapest** way to get to Washington.   [not *cheaper*]

Of the four novels I read last year, I think that Mary Shelley's *Frankenstein* was the **most memorable.**   [not *more memorable*]

▶ **USAGE NOTE**   Rule 9d describes a practice generally observed by writers of formal English. In informal speech and writing, however, the superlative is often used for emphasis, even though only two things are being compared:

INFORMAL   Which book did you like best, *My Ántonia* or *Giant?* [formal: *better*]

Of the two recordings of *Hamlet,* Gielgud's interpretation is the most interesting to me. [formal: *more*]

## 9e. Include the word *other* or *else* when comparing one thing with a group of which it is a part.

NONSTANDARD   After exercising for six months, Kay was healthier than any girl in the class.   [This sentence says, illogically, that Kay was healthier than herself.]

STANDARD   After exercising for six months, Kay was healthier than any **other** girl in the class.

NONSTANDARD   The rookie outfielder hit more home runs last month than any member of the team.   [The rookie is a member of the team; he could not have hit more home runs than himself.]

STANDARD   The rookie outfielder hit more home runs last month than any **other** member of the team.

## 9f. Avoid double comparisons.

A double comparison is one in which the degree is formed incorrectly by both adding *-er* or *-est* and using *more* or *most*.

NONSTANDARD   This book has a more happier ending than the first one I read.

STANDARD   This book has a **happier** ending than the first one I read.

NONSTANDARD   The most farthest you can go on this road without running into heavy traffic is two miles.

STANDARD   The **farthest** you can go on this road without running into heavy traffic is two miles.

**REVIEW EXERCISE.** Number your paper 1–20. For each correct sentence, write *C* after the proper number; rewrite each incorrect sentence correctly.

1. One of my very favorite definitions of poetry is Marianne Moore's: poems are "imaginary gardens with real toads in them."
2. Which one of the new cars is the most fastest?
3. Angela felt bad about losing the golf match.
4. Does the United States give more in foreign aid than any country in the world?
5. The personnel manager decided that Alice was the best qualified of the two candidates for the job.
6. Whenever I see the Simpson twins, I can't decide which is the prettiest.
7. If you don't take your study of language serious enough, you will never do well on your College Boards.
8. Sarah chose to go to State College rather than City College because State suited her better.
9. The more even you divide the ice cream, the happier the children will be.
10. If you don't succeed at first, try more harder the next time.
11. The coach felt bad about our losing the final game, but he knew we had played as good as possible.
12. Doubtless they will question your statement that the old truck runs as efficient as a new one.

13. If you speak as clear as you can, your audience will know that you are interested in capturing their attention.

14. A comfortable chair should have sturdy legs and a reasonable wide seat.

15. In writing it is often wise to avoid the phrase that comes easy to mind—it is often a cliché.

16. Freshly brewed coffee smells temptingly in the morning.

17. If you don't work too slow, you should finish today.

18. Roberto, the oldest of the two brothers, plays tournament chess.

19. The water is much more deeper at this end of the pool than it is at that end.

20. Anyone who thinks carefully about it will say that Maria is a better dancer than anyone in her ballet class.

# Chapter 10

# Glossary
# of Usage

A glossary is a list of special terms or expressions, accompanied by brief comments and explanations. On the following pages you will find a short glossary of English usage, supplementing the material in Chapters 5 through 9.

This particular glossary contains solutions for two different types of usage problems. First, there is the problem in which a writer or speaker must choose between two words, one of which is less acceptable or appropriate than the other. Second, there is the problem of rejecting words and expressions that should not be used at all. You need merely look up any troublesome word in its alphabetical position in the glossary.

Problems of spelling, which are treated in Chapter 31, are not contained in the list. However, every word and problem discussed in this list is listed in the index, which begins on page 621. If the glossary does not contain the answer to a usage problem, consult the index.

To use the glossary properly, you will need to be familiar with the terms *formal* and *informal, standard* and *nonstandard.* If you are not sure of the terms after reading the brief description below, review Chapter 5, in which the terms are described in detail.

In doing the exercises in this chapter, as well as in the other parts of the book, use standard formal English.

## SUMMARY

### Standard English

Formal   The language of speakers who carefully observe all conventions of English usage; appropriate in any situation, but mostly found in serious writing and speaking.

Informal   The everyday language of people who observe most of the conventions of English usage, suitable for all but the most formal occasions.

### Nonstandard English

Variations in usage that are not acceptable in formal writing, and are best avoided in all but the most casual writing and speaking.

**accept, except**   *Accept* is a verb meaning "to take" or "to receive." *Except* may be used either as a verb or as a preposition: as a verb, it means "to leave out"; as a preposition, it means "excluding."

Please **accept** our sincere thanks.

Certain states **except** teachers from jury duty.   [verb]

They read all of the book **except** the last chapter.   [preposition]

**affect, effect**   *Affect* is a verb meaning "to act upon," "to influence." *Effect* may be used either as a verb or as a noun. As a verb, it means "to bring about" a desired result, "to accomplish"; as a noun, it means the "result" (of an action).

The release of atomic energy **affects** [influences] the destiny of the human race.

Atomic power may **effect** [bring about] crucial changes in industry.   [verb]

Its varying **effects** [results] are difficult to ascertain.   [noun]

**all the farther, all the faster**   Used informally in some parts of the country to mean *as far as, as fast as.*

NONSTANDARD  We told the troop leader that this was all the farther we were going before lunch.

STANDARD  We told the troop leader that this was **as far as** we were going before lunch.

**allusion, illusion**  An *allusion* is an intentional reference to something. An *illusion* is a false idea or a misleading appearance.

Flannery O'Connor makes numerous biblical **allusions** [references] in her stories.

**Illusions** [false ideas] of superiority characterize the egoist.

A mirage creates the **illusion** [misleading appearance] of water.

**alumni, alumnae**  *Alumni* (pronounced ə lum′nī) is the plural of *alumnus* (a male graduate). *Alumnae* (pronounced ə lum′ nē) is the plural of *alumna* (female graduate). The graduates of a coeducational school, considered as a single group, are referred to as *alumni*. Although in speech it is not considered incorrect to call a group of graduates from a women's college *alumni*, the distinction is still preserved in writing and formal speech.

The new dormitory was a gift from three **alumnae** who had been the first women to attain medical degrees from the school.

Each year the **alumni** provide two football scholarships.

Many of the mothers and fathers of our students are **alumni** of this school.

**among, between**  See, **between, among.**

**amount, number**  Use *amount* to refer to a singular word; use *number* to refer to a plural word.

NONSTANDARD  An unusual amount of students were absent on the first day of hunting season.

STANDARD  An unusual **number** of students [plural] were absent on the first day of hunting season.

STANDARD  A large **amount** of money [singular] was in the drawer.

STANDARD  A large **number** of coins [plural] were in the drawer.

**and etc.**  *Etc.* is an abbreviation of the Latin words *et cetera,* meaning "and other things"; thus, *and etc.* means "and and other things." There is no need to use *and* twice.

NONSTANDARD  Extracurricular activities include sports, clubs, the newspaper, yearbook, chorus, and etc.

STANDARD  Extracurricular activities include sports, clubs, the newspaper, yearbook, chorus, **etc.**

**anywheres, everywheres, nowheres**  Use these words and others like them (*somewhere*) without the final *s.*

I couldn't find it **anywhere** [not *anywheres*].

I searched for the book **everywhere** [not *everywheres*].
There was **nowhere** [not *nowheres*] else to look.

I didn't want to read it **anyway** [not *anyways*].

**as, like**  See **like, as.**

**at**  Avoid the nonstandard construction *where . . . at.*

NONSTANDARD  Where was he at when we needed him?
STANDARD  **Where** was he when we needed him?

**EXERCISE 1.**  The sentences in this exercise illustrate the usage problems presented in the preceding pages of the glossary. Number your paper 1–20. After each number, write the correct one of the two words in parentheses in the corresponding sentence.

1. Madame Chiang Kai-shek is an (alumna, alumnus) of Wellesley College.
2. If you have already (excepted, accepted) his invitation, you can't go to the play with me.
3. Did the operation on her knee (effect, affect) her game?
4. Has the (amount, number) of students in your school increased?

5. Did you recognize the (allusion, illusion) that he made to Emily Brontë's *Wuthering Heights?*

6. What reason did she give for not (accepting, excepting) the prize money?

7. Was that (as fast as, all the faster) he could run?

8. She realized that her speech was not having the proper (effect, affect) on the audience.

9. Students do not have to graduate from this school to be considered (alumni, alumnae).

10. Before selecting a career, he had to abandon some of his (allusions, illusions) about his own abilities.

11. Progress in medical science is often a side (affect, effect) of war.

12. The governor decided to (except, accept) the commission's recommendations.

13. A small (amount, number) of his friends remained loyal.

14. In this dispute management and labor should be able to (affect, effect) a compromise.

15. The lighting director had chosen certain colors to create an (allusion, illusion) of depth on the small stage.

16. What is the (amount, number) of steel ingots produced by this mill in a week?

17. The candidate was greeted by large crowds (everywheres, everywhere) she went.

18. A knowledge of mythology is necessary to understand many of the (allusions, illusions) found in poetry.

19. If you want to go to Richmond, you must choose another group, because Washington is (as far as, all the farther) this tour goes.

20. Lack of foresight can sometimes produce tragic (affects, effects).

**bad, badly** Strictly speaking, *bad* is an adjective, *badly* an adverb. The distinction between the two forms should be observed in standard formal usage.

The prospects for fair weather look **bad.** [The adjective *bad* modifies *prospects.*]

His ankle was sprained **badly.** [The adverb *badly* modifies *was sprained.*]

In informal usage, however, the expression "feel badly" has become acceptable, though ungrammatical, English.

INFORMAL    She felt badly about losing the contest.

FORMAL    She felt **bad** about losing the contest.

**because**    In informal spoken English, a sentence beginning *The reason is* is often completed by a clause introduced by *because*. In formal written English the use of *because* is avoided and *that* is used to introduce a clause giving the reason.

INFORMAL    The reason for the cold weather is **because** the Gulf Stream shifted its position.

FORMAL    The reason for the cold weather is **that** the Gulf Stream shifted its position.

**being as, being that**    Do not use these phrases as substitutes for *since* or *because*.

NONSTANDARD    Being that I don't have any homework, I'm going to the movies.

STANDARD    **Since** I don't have any homework, I'm going to the movies.

**beside, besides**    *Beside* means "by the side of" someone or something. *Besides* means "in addition to" or "moreover."

I sit **beside** [by the side of] Jack in every class.

What other idea, **besides** [in addition to] the one you gave, is important?

I have decided not to take Journalism I; **besides** [moreover], my schedule will not permit it.

**between, among**    The distinction in meaning between these words is usually observed in formal written English. Use *between* when you are thinking of two items or when you are comparing the items within a group.

What is the difference **between** greenish-blue and bluish-green?

Do you know the difference **between** a milkshake, a malted, and a frosted?

Use *among* when you are thinking of a group and are not comparing the items in the group.

The six boys found that they had only one dollar **among** them.

**bring, take** These two words are exactly opposite in meaning. Use *bring* to indicate motion toward the speaker; use *take* to indicate motion away from the speaker. Bring means "to *come* carrying something"; take means "to *go* carrying something."

Please **bring** your report cards tomorrow.
**Take** her away!
You may **take** the pie with you, but please **bring** the pan back tonight.
I will **bring** my records the next time I come.
She will **take** [not bring] the money to the bank when she goes downtown this afternoon.

**bust, busted** Avoid these words. Use a form of either *break* or *burst,* depending on the meaning you have in mind.

NONSTANDARD    The window is busted.
STANDARD    The window is **broken.**

NONSTANDARD    The water main has busted open.
STANDARD    The water main has **burst** open.

**can't hardly, can't scarcely** See *The Double Negative* (page 191).

**could of, should of, would of, might of** See *of.*

**done** This word is the past participle of *do.* Like all participles, *done* requires an auxiliary, or helping, verb (*is, have, had been, will be,* etc.) when used as a verb. Never use *done* as the past form of *do;* the past form is *did.*

NONSTANDARD    He done his best to improve his work.
STANDARD    He **did** his best to improve his work.

STANDARD He **has done** his best to improve his work.

**don't, doesn't** *Don't* is a contraction of *do not. Doesn't* is a contraction of *does not.* Never use *don't* after a singular noun or after *he, she,* or *it;* use *doesn't.* See page 96.

NONSTANDARD She don't like to read.
STANDARD She **doesn't** like to read.

**double negative** See page 191.

**effect, affect** See **affect, effect.**

**emigrate, immigrate** *Emigrate* is a verb meaning "to go away from a country" to settle elsewhere. *Immigrate* is a verb meaning "to come into a country" to settle there.

Thousands of Irish **emigrated** from Ireland during the 1840's. Most of the Irish refugees **immigrated** to the United States.

The nouns corresponding to these verbs are *emigrant* (one who goes away from a country) and *immigrant* (one who comes into a country).

**etc.** See **and etc.**

**except, accept** See **accept, except.**

**farther, faster** See **all the farther, all the faster.**

**fewer, less** Use *fewer* if the word it modifies is plural. Use *less* if the word it modifies is singular.

There are **fewer** boys than girls in the freshman class.
**Less** work seems to be the plea of many students.

**good, well** *Good* is an adjective; it should not be used to modify a verb; use the adverb *well.*

NONSTANDARD Pam pitches good. [The adjective *good* is incorrectly used to modify the verb *pitches.*]

STANDARD   Pam pitches **well**. [*Well* is correctly used as an adverb.]

*Well* may be used as either an adjective or an adverb. As an adjective, *well* has three different meanings: (1) to be in good health; (2) to appear well dressed or well groomed; and (3) to be satisfactory.

For an octogenarian, grandfather looks **well**.   [in good health]
Maria looks **well** [well dressed] in that simple style.
"Twelve o'clock and all is **well**," the guard cried.

As an adverb, *well* means "capably done or performed."

He argued so **well** that the other debaters conceded.

**EXERCISE 2.** This exercise covers the usage problems discussed in the glossary on pages 178–82. Number your paper 1–20. After each number, write the correct one of the two words in parentheses in the corresponding sentence.

1. Her horse jumped the fence (bad, badly) and stumbled.
2. An eight-cylinder car gets (less, fewer) miles to the gallon than a six-cylinder car.
3. I will (take, bring) the book back with me when I go.
4. During the Revolutionary War, many loyalists (emigrated, immigrated) from the United States.
5. The gardening chores were shared (among, between) the three roommates.
6. He did (good, well) on the entrance examinations.
7. (Don't, Doesn't) the manager approve of your work?
8. The reward money will be divided (among, between) all those who helped earn it.
9. Although he had little time to study, he (did, done) fairly well on the exam.
10. The season went (good, well), but we lost the championship.
11. While the West was expanding in the nineteenth century, many Orientals (emigrated, immigrated) into this country.
12. Although we lost the game by one point, the coach (doesn't, don't) seem unhappy.

13. (Beside, Besides) a Jersey cow, Chang owns a Holstein and a Guernsey.

14. Will you (take, bring) my letter to the post office?

15. My aunt has just bought the new house that was built (beside, besides) ours.

16. (Being that, Since) I am now seventeen, I can get my driver's license.

17. When she came home from the hospital, she still looked (bad, badly).

18. Problems do not become (fewer, less) as one grows older.

19. How many (beside, besides) you and me are going to try out for the class play?

20. The reward was divided (among, between) the four boys.

**EXERCISE 3.** This exercise covers all the usage problems discussed in the glossary so far. Number your paper 1–20. If a sentence is correct, write a *C* after the corresponding number. If a sentence contains usage errors, write the correct forms.

1. Don't he want us to write six book reports each semester?

2. The literature of many countries includes a large amount of myths and folk tales.

3. Do you use your free time badly?

4. Where was the police officer at when the accident occurred?

5. If you go to the beach, take your guitar.

6. The unseasonable frost affected the size of the orange crop.

7. More care usually assures less mistakes.

8. He played the piano so good that he won first prize.

9. When you go to the library, please bring back your overdue books.

10. You must persuade her to accept your help in her latest attempt to build a mousetrap.

11. Steve looked everywheres for his wallet, but it was nowheres to be found.

12. Who attended the conference besides you and Mrs. Rose?

13. During the French Revolution, many royalists abandoned their property but saved their lives by immigrating from France.

14. As an alumnus of Yale, he was pleased when his daughter was excepted by his alma mater.
15. Keep practicing, no matter how badly you seem to be doing.
16. This is all the farther the road will take us.
17. The speech contains several allusions to American history.
18. What language, beside English, will you be studying next year?
19. The five children divided the surplus candy between themselves.
20. I didn't guess until the last chapter that the maid, not the butler, done it.

**had of**   See **of.**

**had ought, hadn't ought**   Do not use *had* or *hadn't* with *ought.*

NONSTANDARD   Your application had ought to have been sent in earlier.

STANDARD   Your application **ought** to have been sent in earlier.

NONSTANDARD   She hadn't ought to answer so sharply.

STANDARD   She **ought not** to answer so sharply.

**hardly**   See *The Double Negative* (page 191).

**he, she, they,** etc.   Do not follow a noun with an unnecessary pronoun. This error is sometimes called the *double subject.*

NONSTANDARD   The puppy he cried all night.

STANDARD   The **puppy cried** all night.

**here, there**   See **this here, that there.**

**illusion, allusion**   See **allusion, illusion.**

**immigrate, emigrate**   See **emigrate, immigrate.**

**imply, infer**   *Imply* means "to suggest something." *Infer* means "to interpret" or "get a certain meaning" from a remark or action.

The lecturer's tone of voice **implied** that she found the question annoying.

I **inferred** from the lecturer's tone of voice that she found the question annoying.

**in, into**   In formal written English, observe the difference in meaning between these two words. *In* means "within"; *into* means "from the outside to the inside." In informal English the distinction is not always made, but careful speakers and writers always make sure to use these words with precision.

INFORMAL   The President himself walked in the room.

FORMAL   The President himself walked **into** the room.

**kind, sort, type**   In standard formal usage these nouns agree in number with a modifying adjective: thus, *this* or *that kind* (singular); *these* or *those kinds* (plural). In writing, do not commit the error of using a plural adjective with a singular noun, as in *those kind*.

**This kind** of medicine is tasty; **those kinds** are bitter.

**These types** of engines perform more economically.

**kind of a, sort of a**   The *a* is unnecessary.

INFORMAL   What kind of a teacher is he?

FORMAL   What **kind of** teacher is he?

**lay, lie**   See pages 136–38.

**leave, let**   Leave means "to go away." Its principal parts are *leave, leaving, left, (have) left. Let* means "to permit" or "to allow"; its principal parts are *let, letting, let, (have) let.*

NONSTANDARD   Leave them help if they want to.

STANDARD   **Let** them help if they want to.   [permit them to help]

NONSTANDARD The school nurse left Joan help in the Health Office.

STANDARD The school nurse **let** Joan help in the Health Office. [permitted her to help]

STANDARD We **let** the dog into the house. [permitted the dog to come into the house]

**less, fewer** See **fewer, less.**

**like, as** *Like* is a preposition and introduces a prepositional phrase containing an object. *As* is usually a conjunction and introduces a subordinate clause.

John looks **like** his father.
John looks **as** his father looked twenty years ago.

*Like* as a conjunction is commonly heard in informal speech, but it is still not acceptable in standard formal usage.

**like, as if** Phrases such as *as if, as though* are used as conjunctions to introduce a subordinate clause. In standard formal usage the substitution of *like* for one of these phrases is not acceptable, although *like* is often heard in informal speech.

INFORMAL The footsteps sounded like they were coming nearer.

FORMAL The footsteps sounded **as if** they were coming nearer.

**might of, must of** See **of.**

**myself, ourselves** See page 117.

**EXERCISE 4.** This exercise covers the usage problems discussed in the glossary on pages 184–86. Number your paper 1–20. After each number, write the correct one of the two words or groups of words in parentheses in the corresponding sentence.

1. The milk (hadn't ought, ought not) to have soured so quickly.

2. His words (implied, inferred) more than they said.

3. (That, Those) types of seed did not grow as well in our soil as (this, these) types.

4. That sort (of, of a) book doesn't appeal to me.

5. You ought not to have (left, let) him borrow your car.

6. What did you mean to (infer, imply) by that remark?

7. You seem to think that all movies (had ought, ought) to have a happy ending.

8. What kind (of, of a) sailboat did you build?

9. It looks (like, as if) it will rain.

10. Why won't your parents (leave, let) you go to camp this summer?

11. Since she cannot carry a tune, she (hadn't ought, ought not) to sing so loudly.

12. When in Rome, do (as, like) the Romans do.

13. (Those, That) kind of gloves will not do for heavy gardening.

14. I (implied, inferred) from Father's remarks about "spoiled children" that my sister and I had done something he didn't like.

15. Georgette raced up the stairs, ran (in, into) her room, and slammed the door.

16. Please follow the directions exactly (as, like) they appear on the box.

17. Why don't we (leave, let) Rosetta make the reservations?

18. We (hadn't ought, ought not) to swim so soon after eating.

19. Why did you (infer, imply) from the announcement that an unscheduled assembly had been called?

20. What sort (of, of a) personality does he have?

**none**  *None* may be singular or plural. See pages 86–87.

**nowheres**  See **anywheres, everywheres, nowheres.**

**number, amount**  See **amount, number.**

**of**  Watch for two common errors in the use of *of.* Do not write *of* in place of *have* in such phrases as *could have, should have, might have, must have,* etc. In everyday speech we often slur the word *have,* producing a sound that might be written *could've* or *could of*. Do not allow speech habits to lead you into spelling and usage errors.

| | |
|---|---|
| MISSPELLED | She could of had straight *A*'s if she had worked harder. |
| CORRECT | She **could have** had straight *A*'s if she had worked harder. |
| MISSPELLED | You ought to of mailed this letter. |
| CORRECT | You **ought to have** mailed this letter. |

Do not use *of* unnecessarily in such phrases as *had of* and *off of*.

| | |
|---|---|
| NONSTANDARD | If I had of known about the shortcut, I'd have been here sooner. |
| STANDARD | If I **had** known about the shortcut, I'd have been here sooner. |
| INFORMAL | The dog jumped off of the couch as soon as it heard its owner coming. |
| FORMAL | The dog jumped **off** the couch as soon as it heard its owner coming. |

**off, off of**  Do not use *off* or *off of* in place of *from*.

| | |
|---|---|
| NONSTANDARD | If you decide to read that book, you can borrow it off of Lucy. |
| STANDARD | If you decide to read that book, you can borrow it **from** Lucy. |

**or, nor**  Use *or* with *either;* use *nor* with *neither*.

The scholastic letter will be given by **either** the Student Council **or** the Honor Society.

I have often wondered why **neither** Robert Frost **nor** Ralph Ellison was given the Nobel Prize.

**ought**  See **had ought**.

**ought to of**  See **of**.

**raise, rise**  See page 142.

**reason is because**   See **because.**

**respectfully, respectively**   *Respectfully* means "with respect" or "full of respect." *Respectively* means "each in the order indicated."

Always act **respectfully** to your elders.
The answers to the questions are +, 0, +, **respectively.**

**rise, raise**   See page 142.

**scarcely**   See *The Double Negative* (page 191).

**shall, will**   The old distinction between these words is no longer observed by most Americans. *Shall,* which was once considered the only correct form for the expression of the simple future in the first person, has been replaced by *will* in most speech and writing.

STANDARD   **I shall** consider your offer.
     **I will** consider your offer.

**sit, set**   See pages 140–41.

**slow, slowly**   *Slow* is generally used as an adjective. *Slowly* is always used as an adverb. Although designers of highway signs use *slow* as an adverb in such expressions as *Go slow* and *Drive slow,* you will be on the safe side if you use only *slowly* as an adverb.

The Balinese dancer moved **slowly** and gracefully.
The **slow** movements of the young dancer captured the audience's attention.

**so**   Because this word is usually overworked, avoid it in your writing whenever you can. For example, do not use *so* in place of *therefore.*

POOR   The fog started to lift, so we began to drive a little faster.
BETTER   As the fog started to lift, we began to drive a little faster.

**some, somewhat** In standard formal usage, use *some-what* rather than *some* as an adverb.

> You seem **somewhat** [not *some*] happier today than you did yesterday.

**sort** See entries beginning **kind, sort, type.**

**take, bring** See **bring, take.**

**them** Never use *them* as an adjective. Use *these* or *those.*

> NONSTANDARD Are you going to give us one of them vocabulary tests tomorrow?
>
> STANDARD Are you going to give us one of **those** vocabulary tests tomorrow?

**these kind, those kind** See **kind, sort, type.**

**this here, that there** The words *here* and *there* are unnecessary and incorrect in these expressions.

> NONSTANDARD This here record is in the Top Ten.
> STANDARD **This** record is in the Top Ten.

**type, type of** In standard usage, do not make *type* an adjective rather than a noun by omitting a following *of.*

> What **type of** [not type] book is it?

See also **kind, sort, type.**

**ways** Use *way,* not *ways,* in referring to distance.

> INFORMAL San Francisco is a long ways from the Mexican border.
>
> FORMAL San Francisco is a long **way** from the Mexican border.

**well, good** See **good, well.**

**when, where** Do not use *when* or *where* as a substitute for a noun in writing a definition.

NONSTANDARD  A junior is when you are in the third year of high school or college.

STANDARD  A junior is a **student** in the third year of high school or college.

INFORMAL  A dictionary is where the words of a language are listed alphabetically and defined.

FORMAL  A dictionary is a **reference book** in which the words of a language are listed alphabetically and defined.

**where**  Do not use *where* in place of *that*.

I read in the *Death Valley News* **that** [not *where*] your sister was married.

**where . . . at**  See **at.**

**which, that, who**  *Which* should be used to refer to things only. *That* may be used to refer to either persons or things. *Who* should be used to refer to persons only.

Poe's first book, **which** was titled *Tamerlane,* is now worth thousands of dollars.
Is this the book **that** you wanted me to read?
Is Mr. Voss the man **that** you referred to in your letter?
Jane is a girl **who** [or **that**] can see humor in any situation.

**who, whom**  See page 113.

**would of**  See **of.**

## The Double Negative

A double negative is a construction in which two negative words are used where one is sufficient. Most double negatives are nonstandard English.

**can't hardly, can't scarcely**  The words *hardly* and *scarcely* convey a negative meaning. They should never be used with the negative *not*.

| NONSTANDARD | I can't hardly believe that the vacation is over. |
| STANDARD | I **can hardly** believe that the vacation is over. |
| NONSTANDARD | The fog was so thick that we couldn't scarcely see to drive. |
| STANDARD | The fog was so thick that we **could scarcely** see to drive. |

**can't help but** In standard formal English, avoid this double negative.

| INFORMAL | When the sun is shining, I can't help but feel very happy. |
| FORMAL | When the sun is shining, I **can't help** feeling very happy. |

**haven't but, haven't only** In certain uses, *but* and *only* convey a negative meaning. Avoid using them with *not* in formal writing.

| INFORMAL | I haven't but one excuse to offer. |
| FORMAL | I **have but one** excuse to offer. |
| | I **have only** one excuse to offer. |

**no, nothing, none** These words are clearly negative. Do not use them with another negative word.

| NONSTANDARD | I didn't have no time to eat lunch. |
| STANDARD | I **didn't have any** time to eat lunch. |
| STANDARD | I **had no** time to eat lunch. |
| NONSTANDARD | I didn't do nothing to make him angry. |
| STANDARD | I **did nothing** to make him angry. |
| STANDARD | I **didn't do anything** to make him angry. |
| NONSTANDARD | Can't none of them help with the cleanup? |
| STANDARD | **Can none** of them help with the cleanup? |
| STANDARD | **Can't any** of them help with the cleanup? |

**EXERCISE 5.** This exercise covers the usage problems discussed in the glossary on pages 187–92. Number your paper

1–20. After each number, write the correct one of the two words in the parentheses in the corresponding sentence. Some sentences contain more than one choice.

1. I read in a magazine (that, where) the testing of atomic bombs (has, hasn't) no effect on the weather.
2. Popular students generally treat not only adults, but also their peers, (respectfully, respectively).
3. My favorite math course was neither algebra (or, nor) trigonometry; instead, I liked geometry.
4. Haven't they (no, any) explanation for their missing (that, that there) bus?
5. Mother said that the storm must (of, have) started about midnight.
6. I listened carefully, and the teacher (says, said) that we were to read Chapter 10.
7. If you have neither ice-skated (or, nor) ski-jumped, you have missed a lot of excitement.
8. The book went very (slow, slowly) at first, but then the plot became more complex and, as a result, more interesting.
9. The first, second, and third American astronauts were Shepard, Grissom, and Glenn, (respectively, respectfully).
10. The acoustics in the auditorium were so poor that we (couldn't, could) hardly hear a word of the address.
11. As I left the Holland Tunnel in New Jersey and headed west, San Francisco seemed a long (way, ways) from home.
12. My bookshelves are so full that there (isn't, is) scarcely room for another volume.
13. Our new house is (some, somewhat) closer to town than the old one.
14. Whenever I have a usage problem I ask Ms. Phillips, (which, who) is the right person to go to for an answer.
15. "I'm afraid that there won't be (no, any) homework for the weekend," said the professor, smiling.
16. I am not sure that I can describe the (type, type of) person Wilma is.
17. Get (them, those) posters up before the weekend.
18. I read (where, that) you won a Merit Scholarship.

19. Don't leave your packages when you get (off, off of) the bus.
20. When asked about my job experience, I said I hadn't done (nothing, anything) yet.

**REVIEW EXERCISE.** This exercise covers the usage problems discussed in the entire glossary. Number your paper 1–25. If a sentence is correct, write a *C*. If a sentence contains an error, rewrite the sentence.

1. Egoism is when you have excessive love and thought of self.
2. Moving to a new town is going to effect many changes in my life.
3. The boys themselves admitted that they had played badly.
4. I have been reading the Brontës lately, beside Austen.
5. Everyone could of studied harder for the test.
6. This country owes a considerable debt to the many immigrants which helped it grow and prosper.
7. A default is when you lose a game through failure to take part in it.
8. We now have seven kittens in the barn, besides two cats.
9. A somewhat smaller amount of students than I had hoped for attended the concert series.
10. Keith is the type of young man that parents approve of.
11. After the party, there wasn't nothing left — not even a cookie.
12. Where is the reading room at in the Public Library?
13. I do not understand the allusions in Dickinson's poetry.
14. May I bring my books to my locker when I go there?
15. Now Sally is complaining that too many people excepted her invitations to the party.
16. This is all the farther I can go in solving the tenth problem.
17. Don and Leonard listened to the speaker respectively, although they didn't agree with anything that was said.
18. In baseball, a grand slam is where a home run is hit with the bases loaded.
19. If you leave people push you around, they will.
20. Didn't none of you club members go on the outing?
21. I prefer these kind of ice skates.
22. She had grown so tall that I couldn't hardly recognize her.

23. Are we to infer from your remarks that you approve of Stephen's behavior?

24. The far-reaching effects of Einstein's speculations could hardly have been predicted by Einstein himself.

25. Being that the rain never came, I didn't need my umbrella.

# Composition:
# Sentence Structure

PART THREE

# Chapter 11

# Complete
# Sentences

## Fragments and Run-on Sentences

Good English consists of clear, well-made, correct sentences. Writers may understand parts of speech, phrases, and clauses perfectly well,[1] yet have trouble with their sentences. Usually, the trouble arises from confusion in the writer's mind about what a sentence is and what it is not.

*A sentence is a group of words containing a subject and a verb and expressing a complete thought.* This définition is simple enough, but a definition cannot do our writing for us. Sentence errors are among the most common faults in the writing of young people. Fortunately, they are also easy to understand and avoid.

As you do more writing, you will develop a "feeling for sentences" or a "sentence sense," through which you will recognize almost at once whether a group of words is or is not a complete sentence. To a great extent, this sense can be developed consciously, by studying each of your sentences after you have written it, and by guarding against the carelessness which causes the majority of sentence errors. Above all, you must learn to watch for the two basic sentence errors: the *sentence fragment* and the *run-on sentence.*

---

[1] To understand this chapter, for example, you should know and understand the following terms: *prepositional phrase, participial phrase, gerund phrase, infinitive phrase, appositive, subordinate clause.* If you need to do so, look them up in Chapters 3 and 4.

A sentence fragment is a *part* of a sentence used as though it were a *whole* sentence. The fragment may be written with a capital letter at the beginning and an end mark (a period, question mark, or exclamation point) at the end; nevertheless, it is not a sentence because it does not express a complete thought. A run-on sentence, on the other hand, consists of two or more sentences which may be separated by a comma instead of a period or other end mark.

To test your ability to recognize complete sentences, take the following Diagnostic Test.

## Diagnostic Test

Some of the following groups of words are sentences; a few are fragments; others are run-on sentences. Number your paper 1–15. Place an *S* after the number corresponding to each complete sentence, an *F* for each sentence fragment, and an *R* for each run-on sentence.

1. Realizing that the best thing a college education has to offer.
2. An editorial board that is made up of outstanding authorities on vocational guidance.
3. I am sure that she did not know that she was lying.
4. State your case, and then wait for the decision of the judges.
5. Robert Frost won the Pulitzer Prize for poetry four times.
6. Realizing that you are busy with schoolwork and extracurricular activities.
7. Last summer I was a camp counselor, I enjoyed myself very much.
8. Did you know that gold is present in small quantities in sea water?
9. Tips for getting along on the job.
10. I will never forget the first time I saw the skyline of San Francisco, a view like that is a breathtaking sight.
11. What is the use of studying Latin it is a dead language.
12. High school students often develop their hobbies into careers.
13. Often being told to do things I don't like, such as getting out of bed.

14. I went to the country to visit my aunt, after that I stayed with an old friend for a few days.

15. Using important ideas as an aid to rapid reading.


## SENTENCE FRAGMENTS

**11a. A** *sentence fragment* **is a group of words that does not express a complete thought. Since it is part of a sentence, it must not be allowed to stand by itself, but should be kept in the sentence of which it is a part.**

Read the sentence below and compare it with the sentence fragment that follows it.

SENTENCE   High in the sky a silver plane swooped toward the horizon.

FRAGMENT   High in the sky a silver plane swooping toward the horizon

Because it lacks a verb, the sentence fragment does not express a complete thought. The lack of a verb is obvious. The word *swooping* may deceive you momentarily, but it is not a verb. Words ending in *–ing,* like *swooping,* are not verbs unless *helping verbs* are added to them to make a verb phrase. If you are uncertain about what a helping verb is and how it is used, turn to the discussion of verb phrases on page 13. Notice how *–ing* words are used in verb phrases in the following examples.

NO VERB   A blue haze settling over the rooftops

VERB PHRASE   A blue haze **was settling** over the rooftops.

NO VERB   Playing football on Saturday

VERB PHRASE   He **was playing** football on Saturday when he hurt his knee.

NO VERB   Writing novels for ten years

VERB PHRASE   She **had been writing** novels for ten years before she was recognized as a great author.

In these examples, the helping verbs round out the verb phrase in order to express a thought completely. Without a verb or verb phrase, we have only a part of a sentence, a fragment.

**EXERCISE 1.**  Some of the items in this exercise consist of one or more complete sentences; others contain sentence fragments. Number your paper 1–10. If an item contains *only* complete sentences, write *C* after its number. If an item contains a sentence fragment, rewrite it to eliminate the fragment.

1. Many great Americans had little or no formal education. Among these are political leaders, writers, artists, scientists, and business executives.

2. When Abraham Lincoln was a young man, he worked in a general store. And at the same time studied books on law.

3. Carl Sandburg is another example. Leaving school when he was thirteen years old but later going on to Lombard College after serving in the army during the Spanish-American War.

4. Our first President, George Washington, was a slow reader and a poor speller. Who struggled in later life to overcome his educational deficiencies.

5. Andrew Carnegie, who gave away many millions to charity, started to work at the age of thirteen. He attended school in Scotland but did not go to high school.

6. Eleanor Roosevelt had little formal education. Susan B. Anthony the equivalent of high school.

7. Gordon Parks attended high school. And later was named Magazine Photographer of the Year.

8. Booker T. Washington walked five hundred miles to attend school at Hampton Institute. And later founded Tuskegee Institute.

9. One of the great letter writers of all time, Abigail Adams, had no formal schooling. It was something she regretted.

10. On the other hand, many famous Americans had excellent educations. As a child, Willa Cather, for instance, was taught Greek and Latin by a Nebraska shopkeeper.

## The Phrase Fragment

A phrase is a group of words that is used as a single part

of speech but does not contain a verb and its subject. In Chapter 3, many different kinds of phrases are explained — prepositional, participial, gerund, infinitive, appositive. All phrases, however, have one important characteristic in common: they are *parts* of a sentence. A phrase should never stand alone; it must never be separated from the sentence in which it belongs. In the following examples, the italicized words are phrase fragments. Notice how the fragments are eliminated by attaching them to the sentences in which the phrases belong.

FRAGMENT    The cold wind made an eerie noise. *Like a screech owl's cry.* [The prepositional phrase in italic type acts as an adjective modifying the noun *noise*. Like any other adjective, the phrase belongs in the sentence that contains the word it modifies.]

FRAGMENT CORRECTED    The cold wind made an eerie noise like a screech owl's cry.

FRAGMENT    The haughty Estella denounced Pip. *Calling him a clumsy laboring boy.* [This participial phrase fragment modifies *denounced*. The fragment is corrected by joining it to the sentence in which it belongs.]

FRAGMENT CORRECTED    The haughty Estella denounced Pip, calling him a clumsy laboring boy.

FRAGMENT    Immediate aid was given to the stricken town. *Not only to feed the hungry but also to help the sick.* [Here two infinitive phrases have been separated from the verb phrase *was given*, which they explain. Both phrases must be joined with the verb they modify in order to complete the sentence.]

FRAGMENT CORRECTED    Immediate aid was given to the stricken town not only to feed the hungry but also to help the sick.

## The Appositive Fragment

An appositive is a word or group of words that closely follows a noun or pronoun and identifies or explains it. Such a word is "in apposition with" the word it explains. It cannot stand alone as a sentence; it is always part of the sentence containing the word it explains.

SENTENCE FRAGMENT    At nightfall the caravan wound into the fabled city of Kabaka. *A cluster of ruins.*   [The italicized words stand in apposition with the noun *city.* Within the appositive we find a main noun, *cluster,* modified by a prepositional phrase. The entire appositive must be included in the sentence of which it is a part.]

SENTENCE COMPLETED    At nightfall the caravan wound into the fabled city of Kabaka, a cluster of ruins.

## The Subordinate Clause Fragment

A clause is a group of words that contains a subject and a predicate and is used as a part of a sentence. A subordinate clause does not express a complete thought and cannot stand alone. Separated from the main clause on which it depends, the subordinate clause becomes a sentence fragment.

If you are not sure of the distinction between main clauses and subordinate clauses, refer to Chapter 4. It is necessary to understand the difference if you are to write complete sentences.

In the following examples, the subordinate clauses are printed in italics.

FRAGMENT    Everyone enjoyed the play. *Which was* Spreading the News *by Lady Gregory.*

FRAGMENT CORRECTED    Everyone enjoyed the play, which was *Spreading the News* by Lady Gregory.

FRAGMENT    The characters and events seemed humorous to the Chicago audience. *Although the play was written by an Irish woman in the early 1900's.*

FRAGMENT CORRECTED    The characters and events seemed humorous to the Chicago audience, although the play was written by an Irish woman in the early 1900's.

**11b. Do not separate a phrase, an appositive, or a subordinate clause from the sentence of which it is a part.**

Rules 11a and 11b are basic guides for building complete sentences. You may find, however, that, though you understand the rules perfectly, sentence fragments still occur in your writing. Almost always, carelessness is responsible for these errors. You can protect yourself against the use of sentence fragments by being certain that all your sentences contain complete thoughts. Reading your first draft aloud helps a great deal.

In checking over your work, you may find that two other constructions cause you trouble. They are items in a series and compound verbs.

FRAGMENT   Many reading lists for high school students include translations from Scandinavian writers. *Such as Lagerlöf, Undset, and Ibsen.* [Items in a series should never be separated from the sentence of which they are a part.]

FRAGMENT CORRECTED   Many reading lists for high school students include translations from Scandinavian writers such as Lagerlöf, Undset, and Ibsen.

FRAGMENT   When Pip moved to London, he lived with Herbert Pocket. *And was tutored by Matthew Pocket.* [The two verbs *lived* and *was tutored* have the same subject. They should be included in the same sentence.]

FRAGMENT CORRECTED   When Pip moved to London, he lived with Herbert Pocket and was tutored by Matthew Pocket.

**EXERCISE 2.** Some of the items in this exercise consist of one or two complete sentences; others contain sentence fragments. Number your paper 1–20. If an item contains *only* complete sentences, write *C* after its number. If an item contains a sentence fragment, rewrite the entire item with the fragment included in a complete sentence.

1. Logical thinking is a skill that can be developed. First by learning what it is and then by practicing it.
2. Most people, especially teen-agers, have problems. Which can be solved by thinking logically, not emotionally.
3. Many young people must face similar problems. Such as

choosing a career, going steady, and borrowing the family car.

4. I used to have a problem that made me miserable. My mother and father being my problem.

5. After I studied logical thinking, I realized that many of their requests were made in my interest. Now we are all happier than we had been.

6. Then the game began to move faster. Almost immediately after Ella's double, came Lill's homerun.

7. Federal budgets are difficult to understand. Especially when they contain so many items.

8. Few of those who left the discussion club had ever been members of our debating team. Frank Neilson, our former secretary, is the most important exception to the rule.

9. I could not go to his aid. Because, as luck would have it, we had not taken the precaution of bringing a spare paddle with us. I could only sit and look at him.

10. Beyond the high buildings, over the opposite bank of the river, the sun hung low. Its glow smothered by a haze.

11. Listen! It is midnight. Standing on this cliff over the town, you can hear the great bell in the church tower.

12. The ship in which Theseus returned from his victory over the Minotaur was preserved by the Athenians. Who removed the old planks as they decayed, putting new and stronger timbers in their place.

13. Treaties of peace are seldom observed for long periods. As history teaches us.

14. Sound trucks roamed through the city on election eve. Roaring the praises of the candidates. We heard them go by until nearly midnight.

15. As far as competition is concerned, the team has done well. Though they were generally smaller than their opponents, the boys have turned in a good record.

16. Whenever she went to the country, she went for long hikes. Then she would take a long bike ride into town. Realizing how healthy the fresh air and exercise made her feel.

17. The book tells the story of how a magazine publisher rose to power. Aided by a group of editors whom he alternately indulged and disciplined.

18. During the nineteenth century England was the center of a vast world trade. Ships going to England brought raw materials. On the outbound voyage the ships carried finished products for resale.

19. The choir sang choruses from the *Messiah* on Christmas Eve. For an audience that consisted mainly of relatives and friends.

20. A library catalogue card contains useful information. Including the author's name and the book's publication date.

## RUN-ON SENTENCES

Let us suppose that a writer has in mind a complete sentence. The rules of English usage tell how to indicate this fact. The sentence may be closed with a punctuation mark that indicates a full stop—a period, question mark, or exclamation point. If the writer wishes, the sentences may be linked by using a semicolon or a comma and a conjunction. The writer may *not* use any other kind of punctuation or part of speech to link two complete sentences.

When two complete sentences are separated by a comma or are not separated at all, the result is called a "run-on sentence." The first sentence "runs on" into the second. Of all sentence errors, the run-on sentence is probably the most common in high school writing.

The ordinary run-on sentence, in which a comma is misused to separate sentences or main clauses, is sometimes said to contain a "comma fault" or a "comma splice." The run-on sentence in which punctuation is completely omitted between main clauses is less common, probably because even the most casual inspection will show that something is wrong with such a sentence. Both errors are usually caused not by a lack of understanding but by carelessness—carelessness in punctuation, in writing, and in checking written material.

RUN-ON SENTENCE   The meeting seemed to last for hours, nothing was accomplished.

This run-on sentence consists of two independent clauses,

each capable of standing alone as a complete sentence. We can eliminate the error by *separating* the two sentences completely, using a period as punctuation:

> The meeting seemed to last for hours. Nothing was accomplished.

We can correct the sentence by using a semicolon:

> The meeting seemed to last for hours; nothing was accomplished.

We can link the two main clauses by using a comma and a *coordinating conjunction:*

> The meeting seemed to last for hours, **and** nothing was accomplished.

We can change one of the clauses to a subordinate clause, using a *subordinating conjunction:*

> The meeting seemed to last for hours **because** nothing was accomplished.

The last correction showed one possible relationship between the ideas of the two clauses: the second clause explained *why* the meeting seemed long. Using a semicolon and an adverb, we can bring out a different relationship between the two ideas:

> The meeting seemed to last for hours; **furthermore,** nothing was accomplished.

So far we have found five different ways in which a single run-on sentence can be corrected. Essentially, the reason for all of these corrections is simple: two complete sentences cannot be run together. The sentences should either be completely separated by a full stop or joined by a semicolon or a comma and a conjunction.

## 11c. Avoid run-on sentences. Do not use a comma between sentences. Do not omit punctuation at the end of a sentence.

**EXERCISE 3.** All items in this exercise are run-on sentences. Number your paper 1–10. After each number, copy the last word in any complete sentence of the corresponding item, and add the first word of the following sentence. As you fill in these words, indicate how you would correct the comma fault. You may use a period and a capital letter, a comma and a conjunction, a subordinating conjunction, or a semicolon, with or without an additional word. Do *not* be satisfied with using a period and a capital letter in every item; to make clear the relationship of ideas, some of the items should be corrected in other ways.

EXAMPLE  1. Jane's schedule allowed her only two days in Washington, she can hardly be said to know the city well.

 1. *Washington; consequently, she*

1. In the past a college education in America was a privilege for a few people, today, higher education has become a necessity for the many.

2. In the year 1295 Edward I of England gave the Dutch permission to fish in English waters later the English regretted this generosity when the Dutch became a wealthy and powerful competitive nation, as a result of the prosperity of their fishing industry.

3. One of the strangest trees in the world is the *Welwitschia mirabilis,* it lives for one hundred years and reaches a height of one foot.

4. Proper names, spelled with a capital letter, sometimes become common nouns, spelled with a small letter, that are used to name one of a class of things, an example of this kind of language evolution is the word *maverick.*

5. About three of every four Americans graduate from high school, many millions of young people every year have difficulty finding work in a society that places value on a high school diploma.

6. According to some, the mind of a newborn child is like a tablet upon which nothing has been written, then learning and experience begin to write upon the tablet and go on writing until life is done.

7. Under ordinary circumstances the meetings of the Student Disciplinary Committee are rather routine affairs, on Wed-

nesday the problem facing the committee was not an ordinary one.

8. Each week magazines by the million pour from the rotogravure presses, the quality of their color depends upon thin shells of copper deposited on the printing cylinders — shells that are only $\frac{1}{5000}$ of an inch thick.

9. In spoken English the voice usually drops at the end of a sentence and always pauses, in written English this full stop is indicated by punctuation.

10. The very room in which the Dramatic Society held its meetings always excited Nancy, it might look to a visitor like an ordinary classroom, smelling faintly of chalk and ink, to her it was a theater, with a theater's magic and mystery.

**REVIEW EXERCISE.** Each item in this exercise contains one or more sentence errors. Number your paper 1–20 and correct each item.

1. Some imaginative thinkers have proposed that Antarctica be used as a huge germ-free "refrigerator." Where all nations' surpluses of food can be stored against lean years. There is no doubt about the refrigeration, many an Antarctic traveler has used food left behind years before by a predecessor.

2. Handwriting analysis, called graphology, is a fascinating study that is supposed to reveal many traits of character. For example, shyness, secretiveness, and boldness.

3. Thanks to radar, ships and airplanes can "see" in fog as clearly as in broad daylight. But this does not mean that scientists have solved the problem of fog, fog-bound ships fall behind their schedules, airports close down during a fog.

4. Synonyms, which are words similar in meaning to another word, must be chosen with care. And used with considerable discretion because of fine distinctions in meaning.

5. Nonfiction is the presentation of factual material, fiction is storytelling.

6. Since its beginning, the United Nations has faced one crisis after another. Not a year has passed without moments of drama and decision. But the organization has always found measures that preserved the peace. Often in the nick of time.

7. Anyone who knows the early history of the United States can

understand the spirit of the new nations born since World War II. Nations which have freed themselves from the domination of another country. Led by patriots who have devoted their lives to bringing independence and self-government to their native lands.

8. The brakes of an automobile generate heat. Far more heat than most of us realize, for example, bringing a car to a full stop from 70 miles per hour generates enough heat to melt a pound of iron.

9. Lightning reaches our eyes at 186,000 miles per second through the air. While thunder, which occurs almost simultaneously, lazes along to our ears at 1,087 feet per second. So that we sense the same event twice, in different ways, at different times.

10. Hair derives its color from the varying ways in which light is reflected from the cells in a hair's medulla, or core. Since the cells are grouped in differing patterns with different shapes of air-space between them.

11. Bearing small white or pink flowers, and also thorns. The hawthorn is the state flower of Missouri.

12. Hawaii, Maui, and Oahu are only three of the major Hawaiian Islands. Honolulu, the capital, being on Oahu, right near Pearl Harbor.

13. Stravinsky was most widely praised for his energetic rhythmic effects, he seemed to have a special genius for creating a highly charged, restless, driving movement; but I like his harmonies, which he always worked out at the piano keyboard.

14. Movements of the human eye are made possible by seven muscles, which, functioning in conjunction with each other, make us able to shift the eyeball in all directions. And to see from almost any perspective we wish.

15. In 1969 the Pulitzer Prize for fiction was awarded to N. Scott Momaday. Who is of Kiowa and Cherokee descent. For his novel *House Made of Dawn.*

16. Jade Snow Wong's novel, *Fifth Chinese Daughter,* was published in 1945, it is a much-acclaimed story of a Chinese-American girl. However, the author, who is a ceramist, has never written another book.

17. The four major chemical elements of the human body, carbon,

oxygen, hydrogen, and nitrogen. These form the protein, fat, and carbohydrates which are the bulk of the body's materials.

18. Although it contains poetry, history, fables, and various forms of sophisticated writings. Western Scripture does tell, in the overall view, a single general story of human civilization.

19. Many people feel that the expression of a newspaper's opinions should be confined to its editorial page. So that readers can judge the news for themselves. "Slanted" news can be much more misleading than no news at all.

20. While the neutron does not carry a positive electric charge, the proton does. And is slightly lighter in weight. Despite their differences, at very high energies these particles act similarly.

# Chapter 12

# Coordination and Subordination

## Emphasis and Relationship of Ideas

## COORDINATE IDEAS

A single sentence frequently contains one or more ideas which may be equal or unequal in importance. Those that are equal are called *coordinate* ideas.

COORDINATE IDEAS    Mr. Jones teaches French. Mrs. Williams teaches English.

These sentences may be combined in a *compound* sentence that shows the relationship between the two ideas. When this is done so that the equality of the ideas is maintained, we call the clauses in the new sentence *coordinate* clauses.

EXAMPLES    Mr. Jones teaches French, **and** Mrs. Williams teaches English.   [ideas added together]

Mr. Jones teaches French, **but** Mrs. Williams teaches English.   [ideas contrasted]

In these examples, it is the connecting words *and* and *but* that make the sentences different in meaning. Conjunctions that connect ideas of equal importance are *coordinating conjunctions*.

Connectives may show other kinds of relationships between coordinate clauses.

EXAMPLES   Mr. Jones may teach French, **or** he may teach Spanish.  [alternative ideas expressed]

Mr. Jones speaks French fluently; **accordingly,** he has been appointed faculty adviser to the French Club. [result expressed]

Other connectives that may be used to link coordinate ideas are *yet, however, likewise, therefore, still, either . . . or, furthermore,* etc.[1]

## SUBORDINATE IDEAS

Often we wish to combine two unequal ideas in a single sentence. To do this, we introduce the secondary statement with a *subordinating conjunction.* Note, for example, the following sentences:

Maria and I often disagree.
I always respect her opinions.

If we wish to make the second sentence secondary to the first, or less important, we may place a subordinating conjunction in front of it and combine the two sentences:

Maria and I often disagree, **although** I always respect her opinions.

The position of the clauses may be changed without changing the relationship of the ideas:

**Although** I always respect her opinions, Maria and I often disagree.

Both these sentences focus attention on the fact that Maria and I often disagree, and "play down" or subordinate the fact that I always respect her opinions. If we wish to focus attention on my respect for Maria's opinions, that can be done in the same way. The same process is used. The statement to be made secondary or subordinate is introduced with the subordinating conjunction:

[1] For more information on the proper use of connectives, see Chapter 17.

**Although** Maria and I often disagree, I always respect her opinions.

I always respect Maria's opinions, **although** she and I often disagree.

In the sentences which follow, note how one idea is subordinated to the other.

Because no women were permitted on the Elizabethan stage, female roles were acted by boys.

When the coach finally announced tryouts for the varsity team, candidates crowded into the gym.

Marie, who is in bed with a bad cold, may have to cancel her party.

When the cattle were stranded on the mountain, a helicopter dropped fodder to them.

In your writing you should learn how to subordinate ideas by putting them into adverb or adjective clauses.

## Subordinate Adverb Clauses

As you may already have learned,[1] subordinate adverb clauses may tell *time, cause* or *reason, purpose* or *result, condition.*

These meanings are expressed in the subordinating conjunctions that introduce the clauses.

TIME **Before we could leave for the trip,** we had to obtain permission from our parents.

CAUSE Many new nations have economic difficulties **because they are not prepared for self-government.**

PURPOSE We had to gulp down the coffee **so that we could get to the station in time.**

CONDITION **Although wages are generally higher than they were ten years ago,** the cost of living has also gone up considerably.

You will find it easy to use subordinate adverb clauses effectively if you learn the following subordinating conjunctions that introduce them:

[1] See pages 63–64.

1. Subordinating conjunctions used to express **time:**

| | |
|---|---|
| after | until |
| as | when |
| before | whenever |
| since | while |

2. Subordinating conjunctions used to express **cause** or **reason:**

| | | | |
|---|---|---|---|
| as | because | since | whereas |

3. Subordinating conjunctions used to express **purpose** or **result:**

| | | |
|---|---|---|
| that | in order that | so that |

4. Subordinating conjunctions used to express **condition:**

| | | |
|---|---|---|
| although | even though | unless |
| if | provided that | while |

**12a.** **Make clear the relationship between subordinate adverb clauses and independent clauses by selecting subordinating conjunctions that express the relationship exactly.**

**EXERCISE 1.** Number your paper 1–25. From the preceding lists, choose an appropriate subordinating conjunction to fill the blank in each sentence, and write it after the proper number on your paper. Notice that when an adverb clause begins a sentence, it is followed by a comma.

1. —— New York City proved to be a central arena of the Revolutionary War, it actually remained in British hands from 1776 through 1783.

2. Washington arrived with little more than the Philadelphia light horse on April 13, 1776, —— General William Howe landed over 130 ships and more than 10,000 men off Sandy Hook on June 28.

3. Most of the spring and summer was spent in fruitless efforts at peaceful negotiation, —— war had not yet been fully declared.

4. —— these efforts ended, hostilities began in earnest at Brooklyn Heights on the night of August 26, 1776.

5. The colonials under Israel Putnam held Brooklyn Heights, —— the British and Hessian forces attacked the outer defense rings under Howe and Von Heister.

6. The imperial attack was executed without a flaw, —— by ten the following morning the colonials were confined to their immediate entrenchments on the Heights.

7. —— he arrived that afternoon, Washington found the troops on the Heights demoralized and pessimistic.

8. —— he knew it could not succeed in the face of any serious attempt to block it, Washington planned a surprise withdrawal from the position.

9. The surprise retreat would probably not have succeeded —— rain and impenetrable fog had not obscured the entire area.

10. —— Washington had withdrawn the troops under cover of the weather, the way to New York City lay open to the British.

11. —— he had tried once more to negotiate for terms of peace by sending his brother Richard to the Continental Congress at Philadelphia, Howe advanced across the bay and took New York City.

12. —— New York was little more than the southern tip of Manhattan Island at the time, now it extends well north of Harlem Heights, where Washington regrouped his forces.

13. —— their capture of the city had been effortless, Howe's troops were roundly defeated by the colonials the following day, September 16, at Harlem Heights.

14. Washington had sent Captain Nathan Hale behind the British lines —— Hale could relay advance plans to the American army.

15. —— he had denied the British charges when he was caught, Hale would have had more than an even chance of escaping punishment.

16. But he was executed by hanging at the gallows near the present corner of Third Avenue and Sixty-sixth Street, —— he confessed proudly and boldly to the charges of espionage.

17. —— their losses were far worse than those of the Americans, the British succeeded in capturing White Plains in the next few major battles.

18. —— military maneuvers continued in the upstate area during the next three years, these initial battles determined the fate of the city.

19. The bloody fighting continued inconclusively for another year until October 17, 1777, —— Saratoga was the scene of a major conflict which most historians regard as the turning point of the war and the beginning of the end for the imperial troops.

20. West Point, a pivotal position, would have been ceded to the British in the summer of 1779 —— Major Andre had not been captured with coded messages' from Benedict Arnold to a British commander.

21. —— this disaster was averted and Arnold had fled to the British lines, the major role of New York in the war was ended.

22. The treaty acknowledging American independence was signed on September 3, 1783, —— the British delayed their departure from New York until the end of November.

23. —— the formal evacuation was beginning, the American troops on parade at the Battery found that the flagpole bearing the English flag had been greased and its ropes removed.

24. —— an unknown sailor from the colonial troops had managed to climb the pole, he tore down the British flag and hoisted the Stars and Stripes.

25. The American cannons boomed out a thirteen-gun salute —— the British sailed out of the harbor to return home.

**EXERCISE 2.** Combine the statements in each group into one sentence, subordinating one statement by using a subordinate adverb clause. Be careful to select a suitable subordinating conjunction. If you put the subordinate clause first, you will need to separate it from the main clause by a comma.

EXAMPLE  1. Hand in your paper.
You should revise it carefully.

1. *Before you hand in your paper, you should revise it carefully.*

1. Robert F. Kennedy died in 1968.

He was at a high point in his political career.

2. You should eat vegetables.
   They are good for you.

3. Mrs. Murphy screamed.
   Her little daughter ran in front of the car.

4. The senator lost the election.
   He decided to write his memoirs.

5. Emily Dickinson wrote many poems.
   Most were not published until after her death.

6. I will prepare the report.
   You will do the research first.

7. The soldiers waited to make their attack.
   The full moon rose.

8. We had supper early.
   We would get to the theater on time.

9. S. I. Hayakawa wrote *Language in Thought and Action*.
   He wanted to explain the importance of semantics.

10. Beethoven wrote several symphonies in his later years.
    He was almost totally deaf.

11. Alvin Ailey starred as a high school athlete.
    He won international fame as a dancer and choreographer.

12. The new car models showed many improvements.
    Car sales went up considerably.

13. You may borrow six books.
    You have filled out the card properly.

14. The new drug may have unforeseen side effects.
    It must be thoroughly tested.

15. The curtain rises.
    We find ourselves in the Forest of Arden.

16. The applicants waited in the reception room.
    The personnel manager finally arrived.

17. The Incas had a highly developed civilization.
    It crumbled under Spanish attacks.

18. I will go to the concert.
    You will come along, too.

19. Poet Gwendolyn Brooks was born in Topeka, Kansas.
    Many of her poems are about Bronzeville, in Chicago.

20. The expedition lost their horses.
    They were forced to walk.

## Adjective Clauses

So far you have learned how to subordinate ideas in a sentence by means of an *adverb* clause. Another way in which a writer may indicate the relative importance of ideas is by using a subordinate *adjective* clause, which modifies a noun or a pronoun. Suppose you wish to combine in one sentence these ideas: *The Taj Mahal is located in India. It was built as a mausoleum for a maharanee.*

If you wish to emphasize the location in India, you will put the information in the first sentence in the main clause and that in the second sentence in the subordinate clause.

> **The Taj Mahal,** which was built as a mausoleum for a maharanee, **is located in India.**

On the other hand, if you wish to emphasize the purpose for which it was built, you will make that your main clause and place the location in the subordinate clause.

> **The Taj Mahal,** which is located in India, **was built as a mausoleum for a maharanee.**

Adjective clauses usually begin with *who, whom, whose, which, that, when,* or *where.*

In the following sentences, notice how the subordinate ideas are stated in subordinate clauses.

> The parade, **which began at noon,** ended at two.
> Everyone **who marched in it** went over to the rally.
> They raced toward the library, **where the noise came from.**

**12b. Make clear the relative emphasis of ideas in an independent clause and a subordinate adjective clause by placing the idea you wish to emphasize in the independent clause and subordinate ideas in subordinate clauses.**

**EXERCISE 3.** Combine the following paired sentences by subordinating one idea in an adjective clause.

EXAMPLE   1. The general greeted his former mess sergeant.
          He had not seen him in many years.

   1. *The general greeted his former mess sergeant,*
     *whom he had not seen in many years.*

1. Deep-sea divers know they must come to the surface slowly
   to avoid the "bends."
   They have had experience.

2. Emma Lazarus' sonnet is inscribed on the Statue of Liberty.
   It is called "The New Colossus."

3. My father used to be afraid of airplanes.
   He changed his mind after his first flight.

4. Mary Cassatt was an American artist.
   She participated in the movement called Impressionism.

5. Alice asked to see the red dress.
   It had been advertised in the newspaper.

6. The old glassworker shaped the molten ball into a beautiful
   vase.
   He had heated it red-hot.

7. The poem "Renascence" is by Edna St. Vincent Millay.
   It was written when she was nineteen years old.

8. Across the road lay a gigantic tree.
   The hurricane had blown it down.

9. He was an American artist.
   James McNeill Whistler was renowned throughout the world
   for his wit.

10. Rhododendrons are beautiful plants.
    They like an acid soil.

11. Many secrets were known to the ancient world.
    These secrets are still unknown to us.

12. James Earl Jones is a famous Shakespearean actor.
    He won the Obie Award in 1961.

13. In Paris we visited the Louvre Museum.
    Many famous paintings are hung there.

14. The word *centipede* is taken from Latin.
    It means "one hundred legs."

15. Can you remember the name of the town?
    Abraham Lincoln is buried there.

16. On her journey she saw a Roman villa.
    It was over two thousand years old.

17. Next week we are going to read about Lorraine Hansberry.
    She wrote *A Raisin in the Sun.*

18. Frances Perkins was Roosevelt's Secretary of Labor. She was the first woman cabinet member.
19. He coated the house with a new paint. This paint had a synthetic rubber base.
20. Marie Curie discovered radium and polonium. Polonium was named for her native Poland.

## Correcting Faulty Coordination

Faulty coordination occurs when two ideas of unequal importance are connected by a coordinate conjunction.

FAULTY COORDINATION  The white gulls almost hid the sun from view, and they circled over the water in a great cloud.

Faulty coordination may be corrected by subordinating one idea in a subordinate clause, a modifying phrase, or an appositive.

In the faulty sentence above, we may subordinate the second idea by revising the sentence in one of these ways:

SUBORDINATE CLAUSE  **As they circled over the water in a great cloud,** the white gulls almost hid the sun from view.

MODIFYING PHRASE  **Circling over the water in a great cloud,** the white gulls almost hid the sun from view.

Here is another example of faulty coordination, corrected by the use of an appositive:

FAULTY COORDINATION  The minister was a woman from Kentucky, and she administered a stinging rebuke to the city council.

APPOSITIVE  The minister, **a woman from Kentucky,** administered a stinging rebuke to the city council.

**12c. Correct faulty coordination by placing ideas of lesser emphasis in a subordinate position. An idea may be given less emphasis by being expressed in a subordinate clause, a modifying phrase, or an appositive.**

**EXERCISE 4.**  Correct the faulty coordination in the following sentences by placing the idea to which you wish to give less emphasis in a subordinate adverb or adjective clause. Choose appropriate subordinating conjunctions to introduce the adverb clauses.

1. Wanda Landowska was a famous harpsichordist, and she came to the United States after 1941.

2. *The Night Watch* is in the Rijksmuseum in Amsterdam and is one of Rembrandt's greatest paintings.

3. The math teacher explained the new proposition, and she made it look quite simple.

4. Many new drugs are tested each year, and not all of them are successful.

5. Paperbacks are now selling at the rate of hundreds of millions a year, and they can be bought practically everywhere.

6. The film won many awards, and the producers were pleased.

7. Bob won the speaking contest, and he is very shy.

8. My aunt is an actress, and she gave me the tickets.

9. Air conditioners have become popular in the last decade, and they are not very expensive.

10. A temple was discovered recently in Yucatán, and it is considered to be about 1,000 years old.

11. He reached for a book, and it was on the top shelf.

12. We drove to California, and we passed through the desert.

13. He painted a picture, and it showed roses in bloom.

14. Dr. Johnson went on a walking tour, and he traveled through the Hebrides Islands.

15. It was midwinter, and many children took a bus to school.

16. Judith Jamison interpreted the dance *Cry* on Alvin Ailey's tour of Europe in 1965, and it was the most successful European tour ever made by an American dance company.

17. The Cloisters is a branch of New York's Metropolitan Museum, and it is interesting to students of medieval art.

18. On the top of the Jungfrau is a flagstaff, and it flies the flag of Switzerland.

19. Harriet Tubman was a famous guide on the Underground Railroad, and she became known as "Moses."

20. Professor Richards delivered a lecture on poetry, and he spoke in Commonwealth Hall.

**EXERCISE 5.** Correct the faulty coordination in the following sentences by placing the idea to which you wish to give less emphasis in an appositive.

1. The opera *Aïda* is by Giuseppe Verdi, and he was an Italian composer.
2. The pirate scanned the sea for a Spanish ship, and he was an Englishman.
3. My aunt is a pianist, and she invited me to her concert.
4. Coleridge was a famous poet, and he had once wanted to establish a utopian community near Pittsburgh.
5. The rocket was the product of a long series of experiments, and set a record for the season.
6. Visit the Franklin Institute and you will find it one of the most remarkable scientific museums in America.
7. Shep Morrison was a newcomer on the team, and the fans roared with delight when he scored.
8. Georgia O'Keeffe is a well-known and very respected American painter, and she was influenced by the landscape of the Southwest.
9. Joan Crawford chairs the Board of Directors of Pepsi Cola, and she projected a new image of women in films.
10. When we were in Spain, we visited the Prado, and it was one of the most interesting museums we had seen.

## SUMMARY

1. Make clear the relationship between ideas in a sentence by using connectives that express the relationship exactly.
2. Correct faulty coordination by placing subordinate or secondary ideas in an adverb or adjective clause, a modifying phrase, or an appositive.

**REVIEW EXERCISE.** The relationship between ideas in the following sentences is not clear, either because the conjunctions used are not exact or because the sentences contain faulty coordination. Improve the sentences by rewriting them. Some can be improved in more than one way.

1. Wedgwood china is beautiful, and it is made in England.

2. The 1976 Winter Olympics were over, and skater Dorothy Hamill was a gold medal winner.

3. Vincent Van Gogh left his home, and he wanted to preach to the miners in the Borinage.

4. Lindbergh was the first to fly alone across the Atlantic, and he was acclaimed by all.

5. Cyrano thought no one could love him, and he had a very big nose.

6. Odysseus was a very clever man, and it took him ten years to reach home after the fall of Troy.

7. Franklin D. Roosevelt contracted polio as a mature man and later became President of the United States.

8. In *The Caine Mutiny* the captain was put on trial, and he was a bitter character.

9. Grandma Moses became a world-famous artist, and she didn't begin to paint until she was seventy-six.

10. We had had a severe drought, and it had begun in June.

11. The curtain parted to show a wild moor, and Macbeth would soon meet the weird sisters there.

12. She had washed the windows, and it had rained, and they were still spotted.

13. *A Wizard of Earthsea* was written by Ursula K. LeGuin, and she is the author of *The Left Hand of Darkness*, and it won the Nebula Award

14. She bought a hand-carved frame, and it was covered in gold leaf.

15. Roberta exhibited a bouquet of magnificent roses, and she had grown them in her own garden.

# Chapter 13

# Clear Reference

## Pronouns and Antecedents

One cause of ambiguity in writing is the use of pronouns without clear antecedents. A pronoun has no definite meaning in itself; its meaning is clear only when the reader knows what word it stands for. This word is called the *antecedent* of the pronoun. For instance, the pronoun *she* has no clear meaning in the sentence *The nurse told Mary that she had a fever.* Although the context suggests that it is Mary who has the fever, we cannot be sure. When we know that *she* stands for *Mary,* the pronoun has a definite meaning. We could revise the sentence to read: *The nurse said, "Mary, you have a fever"* or *The nurse said that Mary had a fever.*

In the following sentences arrows point from the pronouns to their antecedents.

The Pope asked Michelangelo to do the sculpture, but he refused.

The math teacher gave the students a problem which they couldn't solve.

After trying on the long blue dress, Mary said, "This fits perfectly."

**13a. A pronoun must refer clearly to the right antecedent. Avoid** *ambiguous reference, general reference,* **and** *weak reference.*

# AMBIGUOUS REFERENCE

**(1) Avoid** *ambiguous reference.* **Such reference occurs when a pronoun refers to two antecedents so that the reader does not know at once which antecedent is meant.**

AMBIGUOUS    Mrs. Smith smiled at Mrs. Jones when she was awarded the silver cup.

In this sentence we do not know whether Mrs. Smith or Mrs. Jones was awarded the silver cup. We can clarify the sentence by rearranging it.

CLEAR    When Mrs. Smith was awarded the silver cup, she smiled at Mrs. Jones.

AMBIGUOUS    The purser explained to the passenger the meaning of the regulation he had just read.   [Who read it?]

CLEAR    After reading the regulation, the **purser** explained its meaning to the passenger.

AMBIGUOUS    When the children brought the dusty rugs out to the garden, the maid beat them.   [the rugs or the children?]

CLEAR    The maid beat the dusty **rugs that** the children had brought out to the garden.

As you can see, ambiguous references may be corrected in several ways. The object is always to make your meaning clear.

**EXERCISE 1.** Find the ambiguous meanings in each of the following sentences. Make the sentence clear by revising it.

EXAMPLE   1. When the airplane struck the hangar, it burst into flames.   [airplane or hangar?]

      1. *When it struck the hangar, the airplane burst into flames.*

1. The loyal forces fought the guerillas until they were almost entirely destroyed.
2. The police officer told the sergeant that he had a button missing on his uniform.

3. The guide explained to the tourist the value of the stone she had found.

4. Marc informed Darrel that his social engagements would be more numerous when he went to college.

5. When Anna brought Lena to the conference, we asked her for her credentials.

6. Since the show was scheduled for the same night as the election, it had to be postponed.

7. The manager told the waiter that he would have to replace all broken dishes.

8. When the ambassador said goodbye to the foreign minister, reporters thought he looked confident.

9. When the truck hit the wall, it was hardly damaged.

10. Before the gate could fit the opening of the fence, it had to be made smaller.

# GENERAL REFERENCE

**(2) Avoid** *general reference.* **General reference occurs when a pronoun refers confusingly to an idea that is vaguely expressed. The antecedent is expressed in terms which are too general to be clear. Pronouns commonly used in this way are** *which, this, that,* **and** *it.*

GENERAL   More than twenty percent of those who enter college fail to graduate, *which* is a shame.

In this sentence the pronoun *which* refers to the fact that *more than twenty percent of those who enter college fail to graduate.* Since the pronoun *which* has no antecedent, the reader is confused. The sentence needs correction:

It is a shame that more than twenty percent of those who enter college fail to graduate.

In the following example, the pronoun *this* does not have a clear antecedent.

GENERAL   In the fall our school specializes in football, in the winter in basketball, and in the spring in baseball, tennis, and crew. *This* makes for a balanced athletic program.

CLEAR    Emphasizing all these sports makes for a balanced athletic program.

In the next example, the pronoun *it* does not have a clear antecedent. A definite noun makes the meaning clearer.

GENERAL    The ancient Romans conquered more of the world than they could reach readily with their troops. The troops themselves were frequently hired from a foreign power. Meanwhile, at home, the existence of slavery made honest labor no longer respectable. Eventually, *it* caused the great Roman Empire to collapse.

CLEAR    All these conditions eventually caused the great Roman Empire to collapse.

Sometimes general reference can best be corrected by revising the whole sentence.

GENERAL    The wind rose, the trees showed the pale undersides of their leaves, dark clouds appeared, and an ominous silver curtain moved in from the distant hills. *This* caused us to finish bringing in the hay as quickly as possible.

CLEAR    We brought in the hay as quickly as possible when we noticed how the wind rose, the trees showed the pale undersides of their leaves, dark clouds appeared, and an ominous silver curtain moved in from the distant hills.

**EXERCISE 2.** The following sentences contain examples of the general reference of pronouns. Revise the sentences or replace the unclear pronouns with nouns to make the meaning clear.

1. At the Uffizzi Gallery we saw the famous Botticelli *Primavera,* some Raphaels, a Titian, and a Michelangelo, which made the visit worthwhile.
2. A large number of young people have left Hastings Corners to work in the city, which is unfortunate for this town.

3. The guidance counselor asked me whether I wanted Latin, French, or Spanish, which was difficult to decide.

4. My parents bought a new rug and new curtains, and we hired a man to paint the walls and ceiling. That certainly improved the appearance of the room.

5. After the storm, the trail to the top of the mountain was washed out in some spots and was littered in many places with fallen branches. It made the ascent nerve-wracking.

6. The first part of the test was on chemistry, the second on mathematics, the third on physics. This made it very difficult.

7. Wolf Brothers' sale included household furniture, men's and women's clothing, automobile accessories, and sports goods. This was sure to bring in many customers.

8. Some of the eyewitnesses described the man as short, others said he was tall, and yet others said he was "about average." It confused the police investigators.

9. The principal said that the play would have to be given in the old auditorium unless by some miracle the new auditorium were to be completed ahead of schedule, which will be a blow to the Maude Adams Drama Club.

10. We walked up a long, dreary road, cut through a thicket of unpruned trees, and cautiously approached the lonely old house, which made us all tired and depressed.

11. I received a notice that two of my library books were overdue, which was a complete surprise.

12. The route to the top of the mountain led over deep chasms and vast sheets of ice. It made the ascent extremely difficult for the exploring party.

## WEAK REFERENCE

**(3) Avoid** *weak reference*. **Weak reference occurs when the antecedent has not been expressed but exists only in the writer's mind.**

WEAK   Every time a circus came to town, Alice wanted to join *them*.

In this sentence there is no antecedent for the pronoun *them*. *Them* refers to the people with the circuses, but these people are not specifically mentioned in the sentence.

CLEAR    Every time a circus came to town, Alice wanted to **become one of the troupe.**

In the following sentence, you will see that there is no clear antecedent for the pronoun *these*.

WEAK    He was a very superstitious person, and one of *these* was that walking under a ladder would bring bad luck.

In this sentence the antecedent for the pronoun *these* should be the noun *superstitions,* but the noun is only implied in the adjective *superstitious.* The error may be corrected by substituting a noun for the pronoun or re-writing the first part of the sentence.

CLEAR    He was a very superstitious person; **one** of his **superstitions** was that walking under a ladder would bring bad luck.

BETTER    He had many **superstitions,** one of **which** was that walking under a ladder would bring bad luck.

WEAK    Mother is very much interested in psychiatry, but doesn't believe *they* know all the answers.

CLEAR    Mother is very much interested in psychiatry, but doesn't believe that **psychiatrists** know all the answers.

Weak reference may be corrected by replacing the weak pronoun with a noun or by giving the pronoun a clear and sensible antecedent.

**EXERCISE 3.**  Correct the weak reference in each of the following sentences.

1. Arthur Conan Doyle began his career as a doctor and it explains his interest in careful observation.
2. The famous author has an enormous library, and she makes them available to her friends.
3. They planned to eat dinner outdoors by candlelight, but a strong wind blew them out.
4. For years after Mark Twain saw the steamboat in Hannibal, Missouri, he wanted to become one of them.

5. Even though it rained on the night of the concert, Ed went because his favorite ones were being played.

6. In Perugia the factory that made the world-famous candy was open, but we didn't buy any of them.

7. Although he is fond of poetry, he has never written one.

8. Tia's uncle has a huge vegetable garden, and he keeps them supplied with fresh vegetables all summer long.

9. In Central City, Colorado, opera is performed in the summer at the Teller Theater, but we did not see any of them.

10. Trout-fishing is not much sport unless you catch one.

## INDEFINITE USE OF PRONOUNS

**13b. In formal writing, avoid indefinite use of the pronouns *it*, *they*, and *you*.**

Although the indefinite use of these pronouns in sentences like the following may occur in ordinary conversation, such use is not acceptable in most writing.

INDEFINITE    On television *it* said that a new earthquake broke out in Italy.

BETTER    The television news reported a new earthquake in Italy.

INDEFINITE    In some histories *they* refer to the Civil War as the War Between the States.

BETTER    Some historians refer to the Civil War as the War Between the States.

INDEFINITE    In some nineteenth-century novels *you* are always meeting difficult words.

BETTER    In some nineteenth-century novels, the vocabulary is quite difficult.

In the first of each of these pairs of sentences, the pronouns *it, they, you* have no clear antecedents.

► NOTE Expressions such as *it is snowing, it is too early,* and *it seems* are, of course, entirely correct.

**EXERCISE 4.** The sentences in this exercise contain examples of the indefinite use of *it, they,* and *you.* Strengthen the sentences either by replacing the faulty pronoun with a noun, or by revising the entire sentence. Make the meaning unmistakably clear.

1. In *The Diary of Anne Frank* it shows a young girl's courage during two years of hiding.

2. Everyone is excited about graduation because you have worked so hard for it.

3. In South Africa they mine diamonds and sell them to jewelers to be cut.

4. In the sports sections of the daily newspapers, it tells all about the day's events in sports.

5. When grandfather was a child, you were supposed to be absolutely silent at the table.

6. In the Bible it states many truths that have inspired people for centuries.

7. Because modern artists have an idiom of their own, it leads to much misunderstanding.

8. On the book jacket they say that the author herself experienced these thrilling adventures.

9. They had whirled so fast it made them dizzy.

10. In his famous painting on the ceiling of the Sistine Chapel, they say that Michelangelo pictured his enemies among those being punished for their sins.

11. Among the attractions of the tour, they listed free admissions to all places of interest.

12. When Katharine Hepburn's play came to town, they sold out all the tickets far in advance.

**REVIEW EXERCISE.** The sentences in this exercise contain examples of ambiguous, general, weak, and indefinite reference. Correct the errors by using a noun instead of the faulty pronoun or by rephrasing the sentence.

1. For days after he saw a baseball game, Tim wanted to be one.

2. I heard the owl hoot from a tree nearby, but I couldn't see it.

3. Whenever Ruthie went to the library for something interesting to read, she couldn't find one.

4. My mother told my aunt that she did not remember that child-hood episode correctly.

5. In small print on the insurance policy, it said that they were not responsible for damage caused by floods.

6. We hiked almost twelve miles to the campsite, erected our tents, arranged our sleeping bags, and then made our supper. This so exhausted us that we immediately went to sleep.

7. Just as they were about to go to bed, Jane told her mother that it was her turn to wind the clock.

8. The motorist passed the red light, for which the police officer gave him a ticket.

9. They worked very hard, but it made them neither rich nor comfortable.

10. Many of our presidents began their political careers as minor public officials, which is a good thing.

11. Jane Austen was one of the greatest English novelists of the nineteenth century, and I like them very much.

12. In *Mama's Bank Account,* it tells how a Norwegian-American family lives in San Francisco.

13. At the Air Force Academy at Colorado Springs, they teach foreign languages to the cadets in a few months.

14. The boys toured the North Shore Boat Club but did not go aboard any of them.

15. When we saw the flock of geese, they told us that they had flown all the way from northern Canada.

16. After the barbers had cut the children's hair, some of them looked as if they had been scalped.

17. The shipwrecked men paddled their raft with their hands day after day, but this brought them no closer to land.

18. When the mirror crashed to the floor, it shattered it into a thousand pieces.

19. Out in the country, far away from city lights, they say you can frequently see the aurora borealis.

20. Our safety man tackled their halfback just as he was about to fall.

Chapter **14**

# Placement
# of Modifiers

## Misplaced and Dangling Modifiers

Many young writers become unconscious humorists through carelessness in their use of modifiers. In the sentence, *The tense hunter watched the raging lion come charging at him with a bow and arrow,* the lion is made to appear the owner of the bow and arrow. Successful writers make their meaning clear at first reading. If your readers are puzzled by what you write and have to read the sentence several times, they waste time, become confused, and may lose interest in what you have written. A *misplaced modifier,* like the one just mentioned, is an obstacle to understanding.

## MISPLACED MODIFIERS

**14a. Place phrase and clause modifiers as near as possible to the words they modify.**

Sentences like the following may be clear at first glance; yet, because of a misplaced word or group of words, they may mislead the reader or force a second look.

CONFUSING   We listened breathlessly to the stories told by Scheherazade in *The Arabian Nights* munching peanuts and crackers.

As the sentence reads, the storyteller, Scheherazade, is munching peanuts and crackers. That was obviously not intended and either makes us laugh or stop and reread. It would be better to place the participial phrase closer to the word it modifies, which is *we*.

CLEAR    Munching peanuts and crackers, we listened breathlessly to the stories told by Scheherazade in *The Arabian Nights*.

CONFUSING    Lenny spied a dog gnawing a bone on his way to school.

According to this sentence, the dog was on his way to school.

CLEAR    On his way to school, Lenny spied a dog gnawing a bone.

CONFUSING    They were delighted to see a field of daffodils climbing up the hill.

CLEAR    Climbing up the hill, they were delighted to see a field of daffodils.

In all the examples so far, the meaning was made clearer when the modifier was placed near the word it modifies.

**EXERCISE 1.** The following sentences are not entirely clear because they contain misplaced modifiers. Place the modifiers near the words they modify.

1. My uncle wore the brilliant red scarf around his neck, which he had just bought in London.
2. The presiding judge reprimanded the hesitant witness quoting from the statutes.
3. The principal enjoyed taking the visitors to the new cafeteria, glowing with understandable pride.
4. The small shopkeeper finds it difficult to compete with the large corporations having limited funds.
5. Many of our grandparents came to this country from other lands filled with a desire for a better life.
6. The orator thanked her listeners for applauding her speech with sincerity and tact.
7. The manager tried hard to sell us the new car with glowing words of praise.

8. On this July night, the composer played his composition for piano and orchestra, dripping with perspiration.

9. There is an Egyptian bracelet in a local museum that is four thousand years old.

10. The bookseller discovered a valuable manuscript in her storeroom by Anne Bradstreet with three missing pages.

11. Rushing out into the street he caught the puppy, clad only in his pajamas and bathrobe.

12. The crowd listened to what the mayor said without believing a word of it.

13. Mary rushed to the airport as the Los Angeles plane arrived and grabbed a malted milk.

14. She photographed a bear crossing the road with her camera.

15. The book collector examined the first edition which he had just bought through his gold-rimmed glasses.

16. My aunt lost her pet dog, which answers to the name of Roger, walking through the park.

17. The investigators spied the wreckage of the plane peering through the binoculars.

18. The President pinned the medal with words that were few and appropriate on the soldier.

19. We saw Shelley Winters take a bow from the balcony.

20. In the dictionary she studied the definition of *solecism* which she had bought secondhand.

## DANGLING MODIFIERS

**14b.** **A modifying phrase or clause must clearly and sensibly modify a word in the sentence. When there is no word that the phrase or clause can modify, the modifier is said to dangle.**

EXAMPLE   Eating my dinner quietly, the explosion made me jump up.

It is clear that the *explosion* could not be eating my dinner. Here is one way in which the sentence may be corrected:

Eating my dinner quietly, I jumped up when I heard the explosion.

In this instance a word has been added (*I*) which is modified by the participial phrase. You may also correct the dangling modifier this way:

While I was eating my dinner quietly, the explosion made me jump up.

Here the participial phrase has been changed to an adverb clause.

Study the following examples of dangling modifiers and the ways in which they have been corrected. You will note that usually there is more than one way to eliminate such an error.

DANGLING MODIFIER   While correcting papers, the message came from the principal.

CORRECTED   While correcting papers, we received the message from the principal.

CORRECTED   While we were correcting papers, the message came from the principal.

DANGLING MODIFIER   Dashing madly for the train, Mary's books and papers fell out of her arms and scattered.

CORRECTED   While she was dashing madly for the train, Mary's books and papers fell out of her arms and scattered.

CORRECTED   Dashing madly for the train, Mary dropped her books and papers.

A few dangling modifiers have become accepted in idiomatic expressions.

**Generally speaking,** Americans are living longer.

**To get the best results,** the recipe must be followed exactly.

However, you should avoid making your sentences sound absurd or impossible because of dangling modifiers.

**EXERCISE 2.** Each of the following sentences is confusing because of a dangling modifier. Remove the danglers by revising the sentences.

1. Fastened to the tree stump, rage and despair filled the heart of the captive.
2. Ailing and near starvation, both fame and fortune had abandoned the once-celebrated poet.
3. All bundled up in a new blanket, the baby's first outing was a brief one.
4. After eating his usual breakfast, two unexpected visitors arrived at the door.
5. While doing her daily homework, Jane's mother read the newspaper.
6. Tying the scarf tightly around her neck, the wind blew violently.
7. Living in Nantucket every summer, the fishing vessels were familiar to her.
8. While digging for change, his car hit the toll booth.
9. After drinking many toasts to the happy couple, the reception lasted for hours.
10. After administering the anesthetic, the patient fell into a deep slumber.

## TWO–WAY MODIFIERS

When a modifier may refer to more than one person or thing, it is difficult to understand what the writer means. For example:

> The Prime Minister said in the press interview her opponent spoke honestly.

This may be interpreted in two ways. Did the Prime Minister hold the press interview? Or did her opponent? The two-way modifier fails to clarify the question.

Study the following examples of modifiers that modify two words.[1]

NOT CLEAR     Joan of Arc declared after considerable pressure she would maintain her convictions.

    CLEAR     After considerable pressure, Joan of Arc declared she would maintain her convictions.

---

[1] Some grammar books call these "squinting modifiers."

NOT CLEAR    The mayor said when the city council met he would discuss the proposed budget.

       CLEAR    When the city council met, the mayor said he would discuss the proposed budget.

       CLEAR    The mayor said that, when the city council met, he would discuss the proposed budget.

NOT CLEAR    The manager told the rookie after the game had begun to report to the dugout.

       CLEAR    After the game had begun, the manager told the rookie to report to the dugout.

       CLEAR    The manager told the rookie to report to the dugout after the game had begun.

**REVIEW EXERCISE.** The following sentences contain errors in the use of modifiers. Revise each sentence so that on first reading there will be no doubt about the meaning.

1. Having eaten the remains of the zebra, we watched the lion lick its chops.
2. After making many discoveries, the scientific acumen of the chemist was appreciated.
3. The girls counted twelve shooting stars sitting on the porch last night.
4. After practicing for twenty years, the piano was closed with a bang.
5. While cleaning his eyeglasses, his car skidded dangerously into the curb.
6. She had long wanted a pet pony with the acute yearning of a young child.
7. Playing her own composition, the melody soothed her guest.
8. He regarded Helen Hayes after twenty years of playgoing with respectful admiration.
9. The leader of the safari promised in the morning we would see a herd of eland.
10. While running for the bus, my wallet must have dropped out of my pocket.
11. Always threatening rain, we glared at the leaden sky.

12. Catching the pop fly with her usual accuracy, the inning was completed.
13. She came to Paris espccially to see the *Venus de Milo* in her new car.
14. After crumbling for a hundred years, we found the castle quite dilapidated.
15. Eyes flashing hatred, we drew back in fear from the magnificent animal.

# Chapter 15

# Parallel Structure

## Matching Idea to Form

Good writing is not only clear to the reader, but also correct in form. People appreciate things stated in such a way as to reveal a mind that is well organized and trained in appropriate habits of thinking. The careful writer or speaker expresses ideas of equal importance in parallel form.

### 15a. Express parallel ideas in the same grammatical form.

You should be able to use three kinds of parallel structure: coordinate, compared or contrasted, and correlative.

Coordinated ideas are of equal rank and are connected by *and, but, or, nor,* which are called coordinate conjunctions (or coordinate connectives). For proper coordination, a noun is paired with another noun, a phrase with a phrase, a clause with a clause, an infinitive with an infinitive, a word ending in *–ing* with another word ending in *–ing.* In parallel constructions, observe this principle of pairing one part of speech with another, or one kind of construction with another.

POOR   In the winter I usually like skiing and to skate.  [gerund paired with an infinitive]

BETTER   In the winter I usually like **skiing** and **skating**.  [gerund paired with a gerund]

BETTER   In the winter I usually like **to ski** and **to skate.** [infinitive paired with an infinitive]

POOR   The company guaranteed increases of salary and that the working day would be shortened. [noun paired with a noun clause]

BETTER   The company guaranteed **that the salaries would be increased** and **that the working day would be shortened.** [noun clause paired with noun clause]

Ideas that are compared or contrasted are parallel.

POOR   Einstein liked mathematical research more than to supervise a large laboratory. [noun contrasted with an infinitive]

BETTER   Einstein liked mathematical **research** more than **supervision** of a large laboratory. [noun contrasted with a noun]

POOR   To chew carefully is as necessary for a good digestion as eating slowly. [infinitive contrasted with a gerund]

BETTER   **Chewing** carefully is as necessary for a good digestion as **eating** slowly. [gerund contrasted with a gerund]

Correlative constructions are formed with the correlative conjunctions *both . . . and, either . . . or, neither . . . nor, not only . . . but (also).* They should be expressed in parallel form.

POOR   With *Ship of Fools,* Katherine Anne Porter proved she was talented not only as a short story writer but also in writing novels.

BETTER   With *Ship of Fools,* Katherine Anne Porter proved she was talented not only as a short story writer but also as a novelist.

## 15b. Place correlative conjunctions immediately before the parallel terms.

POOR   A President of the United States must not only represent his own political party but also the entire American people. [*Not only . . . but also* should directly precede the parallel terms *his own political party* and *the entire American people.*]

BETTER A President of the United States must represent **not only** his own political party **but also** the entire American people.

POOR Washington both experienced the gloom of Valley Forge and the joy of Yorktown.

BETTER Washington experienced **both** the gloom of Valley Forge **and** the joy of Yorktown.

# EXERCISE 1. Revise the following sentences by putting parallel ideas into the same grammatical form. Correct any errors in the placement of correlatives.

1. Dentists advise brushing the teeth after each meal and to avoid too much sugar in the diet.
2. Lady Bird Johnson spoke with warmth and in a humorous vein.
3. Eudora Welty's short stories have good plots, good characterization, and their style is interesting.
4. In John Steinbeck's "The Leader of the People," the old grandfather delighted in telling his grandson how he had led the wagon train across hostile territory and his final success.
5. Swimming in a lake is more fun for my family than to swim at the seashore.
6. Margaret Bourke-White not only photographed men in frontline trenches but also notable figures such as Gandhi.
7. My grandmother neither enjoyed modern music nor modern art.
8. A modern physician in a small town must not only be proficient in general medicine but surgery as well.
9. Mathematics has opened many avenues of research in improving communications and in how to live better.
10. Unfortunately, Aristotle not only relied on his own firsthand investigations but also on hearsay reports.
11. Many poets at some time in their careers began painting and then to write.
12. Mary Renault is both a novelist and does amateur archeology.
13. Listen to Judith Anderson's recording of Lady Macbeth not only to get the meaning but also the speech patterns.

14. When Mark Twain went to Oxford for his honorary degree, he was cheered wildly by admirers, wined and dined by prominent people, and gave many coveted interviews to the press.

15. In order to absorb what a lecturer says, to have a clear mind and taking good notes is necessary.

16. Francis Bacon, the first great inductive thinker, neither had scientific equipment nor knowledge of experimentation.

17. In her commencement address the famous author spoke sincerely and in a simple manner about the role of the educated woman in modern American society.

18. Iris Murdoch is both a philosophy don at Oxford and she writes best-selling novels.

19. The great writer Ruskin used to say that he could tell a person's character by observing the things that made him laugh and what he cried about.

20. King Ferdinand and Queen Isabella indicated to Columbus not only that they had faith in him but also would supply funds for the trip.

21. Toward the end of her career, the once-successful lecturer lost popularity because of her difficult topics and the fact that she spoke poorly.

22. Soil conservation should not only be studied by rural students but by urbanites as well.

23. Tschaikowsky's *1812 Overture* makes you imagine the thunder of cannon, the marching of soldiers, and how they celebrated the victory.

24. Dorothy Sayers' short stories have suspense, style, and they are well constructed.

25. The murals in Santa Fe depict the past glory of the Aztec ancestors of the artists and how the artists hope for the future.

## 15c. In parallel constructions repeat an article, a preposition, or a pronoun whenever necessary to make the meaning clear.

AMBIGUOUS   After the celebration we were introduced to the president and master of ceremonies. [Does this mean that the same person held both jobs?]

CLEAR   After the celebration we were introduced to the

president and **to the** master of ceremonies. [These are two individuals.]

AMBIGUOUS   Winning the Westinghouse Scholarship was as great a pleasure to the teacher as the student. [This means that the student was as great a pleasure as the scholarship.]

CLEAR   Winning the Westinghouse Scholarship was as great a pleasure to the teacher as **to** the student.

AMBIGUOUS   The mansion of the Duke of Suffolk was as magnificent as the Duke of Bedford.

CLEAR   The mansion of the Duke of Suffolk was as magnificent as **that of** the Duke of Bedford.

**EXERCISE 2.**   Correct the parallelism in each of the following sentences by supplying the omitted words.

1. The paintings in the Kansas City Museum of Art are probably as famous as the Buffalo Museum.
2. Mahalia Jackson's style is different from Billie Holiday.
3. In the Folger Library in Washington you will find more first folios of Shakespeare than the Bodleian Library in Oxford.
4. The Nancy Drew books are similar to the Hardy boys.
5. The award she received for the painting was much smaller than the collection of prints.
6. You will discover that the facts in the latest edition of an encyclopedia are more up-to-date than an old edition.
7. The reaction of the amoeba to the stimulus was similar to the paramecium.
8. Seats in the balcony are always cheaper than the orchestra.
9. The howling of the dogs was louder than the wolves.
10. While traveling in England, my friend preferred the food in the little wayside inns to the cafeterias at home.

**REVIEW EXERCISE.**   The following sentences are weak because of faulty parallelism. Correct each so that the meaning is clear.

1. Riding on the roller coaster and to spin the Wheel of Luck were her two greatest pleasures at the carnival.

2. In college you will be both required to study on your own and to take good notes.

3. Many immigrants came to America to seek their fortune or because they desired freedom of worship.

4. The new baby-sitter was very strict about having children get to bed early and brushing their teeth themselves.

5. The budget discussion centered on the large appropriations for defense and paying the bills promptly.

6. The frightened private did not know whether he had been ordered to stand trial for disorderly conduct or because he had disobeyed.

7. The writing of a research paper is a much greater challenge than an ordinary essay.

8. Recent historians attribute events to the acts of leaders of nations as well as wishes of the people.

9. Virginia Woolf's success as a novelist was as great a tribute to her style as her plots.

10. To milk a goat is more difficult than a cow.

11. Advertising executives place great emphasis on arousing needs for a product, making the product attractive, and that the product be fairly inexpensive.

12. In Elizabethan days many playgoers preferred the plays of Ben Jonson to Shakespeare.

13. Dentists advise us to cut down on sweets and brushing our teeth after each meal.

14. If you listen intently enough you will be able to distinguish the singing of Leontyne Price from Marilyn Horne.

15. Playing lacrosse can sometimes be more dangerous than to play football.

# Chapter 16

# Sentence Variety

## Interest and Emphasis

Good writing means more than putting down the first words that come to your mind. It means careful revising and rewriting until you have expressed yourself in the best possible way. One of the great writers of the nineteenth century, Robert Louis Stevenson, never stopped learning. Read the statement that follows. Notice particularly not only *what* he says, but *how* he says it. Observe the ways in which he varies the beginnings of his sentences, and his sentence length and structure. Some sentences begin with adverb clauses, some with adverb phrases. Other sentences begin with the subject and follow the usual pattern of subject, verb, complement. There are both long and short sentences. In this way, Stevenson has achieved variety, adding the pleasure of a fortunate arrangement of words to the pleasure of their meaning.

All through my boyhood and youth I was known and pointed out for the pattern of an idler; and yet I was always busy on my own private end, which was to learn to write. I kept always two books in my pocket, one to read, one to write in. As I walked, my mind was busy fitting what I saw with appropriate words. When I sat by the roadside, I would either read, or a pencil and a penny-version book would be in my hand, to note down the features of the scene or commemorate some halting stanzas. Thus I lived with words. And what I thus wrote was for no ulterior use, it was written consciously for practice. It was not so much that I wished to be an author (although I wished that too) as that I had vowed that I would learn to write.[1]

## VARYING SENTENCE OPENINGS

**16a. Give variety to your sentence structure by varying the beginnings. Begin some of your sentences with a transposed appositive or with a modifier.**

### Appositives

SUBJECT FIRST   Easter Island, the outpost of Polynesia, has always been a land of mystery.

TRANSPOSED APPOSITIVE FIRST   **The outpost of Polynesia,** Easter Island has always been a land of mystery.

### Single-word Modifiers

SUBJECT FIRST   Emily Dickinson was shy and retiring and did not enjoy social activities.

SINGLE-WORD MODIFIERS FIRST   **Shy and retiring,** Emily Dickinson did not enjoy social activities.

SUBJECT FIRST   Many of the committee's suggestions have been rejected lately.

SINGLE-WORD MODIFIERS FIRST   **Lately,** many of the committee's suggestions have been rejected.

### Phrase Modifiers

SUBJECT FIRST   Alicia de Larrocha was incomparable on the concert platform.

PREPOSITIONAL PHRASE FIRST   **On the concert platform** Alicia de Larrocha was incomparable.

SUBJECT FIRST   The examiners worked around the clock to finish correcting all the papers in one week.

INFINITIVE PHRASE FIRST   **To finish correcting all the papers in one week,** the examiners worked around the clock.

[1] Robert Louis Stevenson, *Memories and Portraits.*

SUBJECT FIRST    The engineer examined the blueprint carefully and then said that the bridge could never be constructed that way.

PARTICIPIAL PHRASE FIRST    **Examining the blueprint carefully,** the engineer said that the bridge could never be constructed that way.

## Clause Modifiers

SUBJECT FIRST    The chemists analyzed the sodium compounds after they had analyzed the potassium.

CLAUSE FIRST    **After they had analyzed the potassium,** the chemists analyzed the sodium compounds.

SUBJECT FIRST    Edna St. Vincent Millay moved to New York City and soon became a leading literary figure.

CLAUSE FIRST    **Soon after she moved to New York City,** Edna St. Vincent Millay became a leading literary figure.

## EXERCISE 1.  In this exercise you will be asked to revise the sentences in one of several ways. Follow the instructions carefully.

1. Madame Curie, after completing the experiments, decided to publish an account of them. [Begin with a prepositional phrase containing a gerund phrase.]
2. Dr. Jonas Salk was convinced that his vaccine would prevent polio and asked the American Medical Association to test it. [Begin with an adverb clause.]
3. The human body can protect itself against mild infections through its own antibodies. [Begin with a prepositional phrase.]
4. The prize winner, happy and smiling, embraced his mother and kissed her. [Begin with single-word modifiers.]
5. Narcissa Whitman traveled across the Continental Divide in 1836 along with Eliza Spalding. [Begin with a prepositional phrase.]
6. The shopkeeper accepted my traveler's check after she had verified my signature. [Begin with an adverb clause.]
7. Many newly independent nations have become full members

of the United Nations recently.  [Begin with a single-word modifier.]

8. The English poet Keats was weak and consumptive and died at the age of twenty-six.  [Begin with single-word modifiers.]

9. School will open right after Labor Day, as usual, unless circumstances compel a postponement.  [Begin with an adverb clause.]

10. Bolivar, an idol among his contemporaries, has been the inspiration for many modern revolutions.  [Begin with an appositive.]

11. The newly formed symphony orchestra will perform nightly during the winter season.  [Begin with a prepositional phrase.]

12. The old soldier, thin and haggard, could barely drag along with the rest.  [Begin with single-word modifiers.]

13. Lila Acheson Wallace, a cofounder of the *Reader's Digest,* is also a patron of the arts.  [Begin with an appositive.]

14. Amy Lowell worked tirelessly on behalf of the Imagist poets and developed a reputation for eccentricity.  [Begin with a prepositional phrase containing a gerund phrase.]

15. Constant research has brought color television to a high level of efficiency, and more people are buying color sets.  [Begin with an adverb clause.]

16. Birds fly south in the winter through an instinct not completely understood by scientists.  [Begin with a prepositional phrase.]

**EXERCISE 2.**  Rewrite each of the following sentences so that it will begin with an appositive or a modifier. You may have to change the wording slightly in some sentences.

1. Football players frequently take on strenuous jobs in the summer to get into good physical condition.

2. The Prime Minister, harassed and weary, closed the session of the Cabinet.

3. The summer visitors, eager for news, clustered around the drugstore.

4. The audience sang along with the chorus while the conductor beat out the rhythm.

5. The Portuguese sailors, expert navigators, often went out to sea in threatening weather.

6. Mt. Rushmore National Memorial, towering seven hundred feet above the valley floor, is an impressive sight.

7. Child specialists now feel that too much leniency may be harmful to children, although the evidence on the matter is not yet complete.

8. Cervantes wrote his great comedy, *Don Quixote,* while he was in prison.

9. Rodgers and Hammerstein produced many famous musical comedies over a period of years.

10. Shinichi Suzuki is seen as one of the world's great violin teachers as a result of his method for early music education.

11. The Pulitzer Prize for drama, awarded each year, is coveted by every professional playwright.

12. This statue of solid marble should endure for centuries.

13. Pelé scored an incredible 1,220 goals in 1,253 games in his 18 years of professional soccer in Brazil.

14. Homer, in his description of the Aegean, calls it the "wine-dark sea."

15. Some people from the eastern states have difficulty breathing when they come to the high mountain areas.

## VARYING SENTENCE LENGTH

**16b. Using subordination, vary the structure and length of sentences. Avoid the exclusive use of simple and compound sentences.**[1]

Too many short, simple sentences result in a monotonous, choppy style. You can add interest to your style by writing sentences of different length and different structure. Short, simple sentences can often be effectively combined by proper subordination into longer, complex sentences, as in these examples:

SIMPLE SENTENCES  Eddie Rickenbacker was a distinguished pilot in World War I. He entered the air transportation business at the close of the war. He later became president of a commercial airline.

[1] For a review of subordination, see pages 58–64. For an explanation of the kinds of sentences, see pages 66–69.

COMPLEX SENTENCE. After he had distinguished himself as a pilot in World War I, Eddie Rickenbacker entered the air transportation business, later becoming president of a commercial airline. [In this example, ideas in the first and third sentences were subordinated by means of an adverb clause and a participial phrase, respectively.]

SIMPLE SENTENCES The *Tale of Genji* is a novel. It is the greatest work of Japanese literature. It was completed by Lady Shikibu Murasaki in 1008.

COMPLEX SENTENCE The *Tale of Genji,* the greatest work of Japanese literature, is a novel which was completed by Lady Shikibu Murasaki in 1008. [In this example subordination was achieved by an adjective clause and an appositive.]

**EXERCISE 3.** By using various means of subordination (participial phrase, appositive, subordinate clause, etc.) combine the short sentences in each group into one long, smooth sentence. You may find it necessary to change the emphasis or the meaning slightly, but you should not change or omit any of the ideas given.

1. Red Grange played for the University of Illinois. He was considered one of the greatest football players of all time. He was called the Galloping Ghost.
2. Countee Cullen is an American lyric poet. He was a member of Phi Beta Kappa. He received a master's degree from Harvard University.
3. Reading improvement is now taught in many colleges. Students take the course to speed up their reading. It also improves their comprehension.
4. In the borough of Brooklyn, New York, there are streets named after Lafayette, Pulaski, Kosciusko, and Von Steuben. These were all foreign generals who aided America in the Revolutionary War.
5. The Statue of Liberty was presented to us by the French government. Frederic Bartholdi was the artist. It is one of the first sights to greet newcomers to America.
6. There are now many kinds of dictionaries. One such is a dictionary of synonyms and antonyms. Another is a bio-

graphical dictionary. A third is a geographical dictionary with pronunciations given.

7. A symphony orchestra has many sections. One consists of the strings. Another consists of the woodwinds. The third is the brass. Then there is the percussion section.

8. Neon lighting works on a unique principle. The tube is filled with a rare gas called neon. An electric current causes this gas to become fluorescent.

9. *Roget's Thesaurus* was written over a hundred years ago. The author was Peter Mark Roget. He was a physician by profession. He lived in England.

10. You can review your mythology by reading about today's spacecraft. There is one called Jupiter. Another is called Gemini. A third is called Atlas.

# USING SUBORDINATION

**16c. Give variety to your writing by avoiding the "stringy" style which results from the overuse of *and* and *so*.**

In your daily conversation you may have noticed how many people use *and* and *so* over and over again when they are telling a story. Such a practice soon makes conversation and writing monotonous. Here are some ways of overcoming this tendency.

**(1) Correct a stringy sentence by subordination of ideas.**

STRINGY Jane went to Cornell University to study hotel management and she liked it very much and urged her friends to take it also.

IMPROVED At Cornell University, Jane studied hotel management which she liked so much that she urged her friends to take it also.

STRINGY The smaller cars are less expensive and they are more maneuverable in parking and travel more miles on the gallon.

IMPROVED The smaller cars, which are less expensive and more maneuverable in parking, travel more miles on the gallon.

STRINGY   The mayor was an astute politician, so she refused to commit herself on the issue until after election.

IMPROVED   Because the mayor was an astute politician, she refused to commit herself on the issue until after election.

STRINGY   Vermeer used a special kind of blue paint and was the only one to use it, so it has become known as "Vermeer blue."

IMPROVED   The blue paint, which Vermeer was the only one to use, has become known as "Vermeer blue."

**(2) Correct a stringy sentence by dividing it into two sentences.**

STRINGY   The representatives visited several locations for a permanent site of the United Nations and they were turned down by the communities so they decided to come to New York.

IMPROVED   The representatives who were visiting several locations for a permanent site of the United Nations were turned down by several communities. They then decided to come to New York.   [stringiness corrected by subordination and division into two sentences]

STRINGY   Dr. Fleming was studying a colony of bacteria and he noticed that a substance in the dish was impeding the growth of bacteria and so he continued his investigations and discovered penicillin.

IMPROVED   While Dr. Fleming was studying a colony of bacteria, he noticed a substance impeding its growth. After further study he discovered penicillin.   [stringiness corrected by subordination and by division into two sentences]

**(3) Correct a stringy sentence by reducing coordinate clauses to a compound predicate.**

STRINGY   Henry David Thoreau built a hut on Walden Pond and he furnished it simply and settled down for a life of contemplation and writing.

IMPROVED  Henry David Thoreau built a hut on Walden Pond, furnished it simply, and settled down for a life of contemplation and writing.

**EXERCISE 4.** This exercise consists of stringy sentences, which you are to revise by one or more of these methods: subordination, division into more than one sentence, reduction of coordinate clauses to a compound predicate. Avoid excessive use of *and* and *so*.

1. Isabella Stewart Gardner built a palace on a Boston dump, and she filled it with art treasures, and then in her will she said that each item must stay forever where she placed it.

2. It is easy to complain of our petty discomforts and forget that people all over the world may be so much worse off and so perhaps we should really be grateful.

3. Jessica Mitford wrote *The American Way of Death* and this best-selling book led eventually to an official investigation of the funeral industry.

4. In studying an assignment it is wise to read it over quickly at first and then to see the major points and finally to outline the material.

5. During the past two decades motels have sprung up everywhere and they have encouraged travel by car so that more Americans are seeing the country.

6. In *Silas Marner* Eppie is discovered by Silas asleep on the hearth, and he takes care of the little girl, and he becomes very fond of her.

7. Suburban life has made many commuters into clock-watchers and train-watchers, and this development has not helped either their peace of mind or their digestions.

8. Many museums offer special services to schools and these include lectures and guided tours.

9. Willa Cather was a high school teacher, and it is believed that her short story "Paul's Case" was based on an experience in her school, and it is a very moving story.

10. A great tragedy in Beethoven's life is that he became deaf, and he could not hear his *Ninth Symphony* and when he conducted it, he did not even hear the applause.

# Composition:
# Paragraphs and
# Longer Papers

# PART FOUR

Chapter **17**

# The Paragraph

## Structure and Development of Paragraphs

The word paragraph is a combination of two Greek words: *para* (beside) and *graph* (write). It originally referred to the symbol ¶, which early printers placed in the margin of a page of writing to indicate units of thought. We still use the same mark as a correction symbol to indicate an error in paragraphing.

The paragraph mark, as well as the indention or extra spacing that we now use to set off paragraphs in writing, may be considered a form of punctuation marking a unit of thought that is generally longer than a single sentence and shorter than the whole composition in which it appears. The indention, however, doesn't make the paragraph any more than a period makes a sentence. Unless a group of sentences is a unit of thought, setting it off as a paragraph is as misleading as any other error in punctuation. Paragraphs should include the ideas that writers want their readers to think of together.

**17a. A paragraph is a series of sentences developing one main idea or topic.**

The length and content of paragraphs vary according to the nature of the writing in which they appear. In exceptional cases, a paragraph may consist of a single sentence. One-sentence paragraphs are sometimes used to give added emphasis to a statement or to make a transition between two longer paragraphs. In general, however, paragraphs in a short piece of writing are likely to consist of a number of sentences and to average between 100 and 150 words in length. Except in narrative writing, paragraphs usually make a general statement and then give a number of specific details or reasons in support of that statement.

## THE TOPIC SENTENCE

**17b. The topic of a paragraph should be stated in a single sentence somewhere in the paragraph. This sentence is called the *topic sentence*.**

Writers may state topics and then give details to back them up, or they may give the details first and lead up to their general statements. Although there are advantages to both methods, the inexperienced writer usually finds the paragraph that begins with the topic sentence easier to handle. In this position, the topic sentence tells the reader the direction the thought is taking, and it also helps the writer to keep on the track. One detail can lead to another that may be interesting but irrelevant to the idea of the whole paragraph. Stating the topic at the beginning decreases the possibility of such digressions.

> **Machines and tools have always been created in the image of man.** The hammer grew from the balled fist, the rake from the hand with fingers outstretched for scratching, the shovel from the hand hollowed to scoop. As machines became more than simple tools, outstripping their creators in performance, demanding and obtaining increasing amounts of power, and acquiring superhuman speed and accuracies, their outward resemblance to the natural model disappeared; only the names of the machines' parts show vestiges of their human origin. The highly complex machinery of the industrial age has arms that swing, fingers that fold, legs that support, and teeth that grind. Machines feed on material, run when things go well, and spit and cough when they don't.[1]

[1] From "The Thinking of Men and Machines" by John H. Troll, from *The Atlantic Monthly,* July 1954. Copyright © 1954, by The Atlantic Monthly Company, Boston, Mass. Reprinted by permission of the author.

Occasionally, the topic sentence will appear in or near the middle as in the following paragraph. In the following example the topic sentence links two related but different observations: the unusual fact that American literature began with a letter written by an Italian who never set foot on this continent, and the fact that travelers like to tell their stay-at-home friends about their experiences:

Most of the literature of the United States is written in the English language, much of it by men and women whose forebears came from the British Isles; yet the first man from Western Europe to write home about his adventures in the New World was not an Englishman, nor was the land he discovered a part of the continental United States. **Even so, the famous Columbus letter (1493) sets the form and the point of view of the earliest American literature.** In a far country, man's immediate impulse is to tell his distant friends of what he finds and how he fares. Columbus, a Genoese in the service of the Spanish King Ferdinand, wrote to the Royal Treasurer, "Because my undertakings have attained success, I know that it will be pleasing to you." Here was the beginning of the written record of the American adventure.[1]

In the following example, the topic sentence concludes the paragraph, giving its general meaning.

The shores of Hawaii were soon far behind us, as we steamed ever northward toward the Bering Strait and to an entirely different world from the one we had left four weeks before. Our reactor, the powerful source of energy that drove us, gave us light, cooked for us, and shaved us, performed silently and majestically. Watch-standers scanned networks of instruments, each of which had a vital story to tell about how our magnificent ship was performing. **Ours was a world of supreme faith—faith in instruments, faith in the laws of physics, faith in each other and in Him who guided our destiny in the unknown seas ahead.**[2]

[1] From *The Cycle of American Literature* by Robert F. Spiller. Copyright 1955, 1956 by Macmillan Publishing Co., Inc. Reprinted by permission of the publishers.
[2] From *Nautilus 90 North* by William R. Anderson and Clay Claire, Jr., Copyright © 1959 by William Anderson and Clay Claire, Jr. Reprinted by permission of Thomas Y. Crowell Company, Inc., publisher.

In your reading, you will notice that not all paragraphs have topic sentences. Sometimes the idea of a paragraph can be made clear without being explicitly stated. Once again, however, inexperienced writers should remember that a topic sentence is a help to their readers and to themselves. Your paragraphs are likely to be better if you make it a habit to state the topic in a single sentence.

## THE CONCLUDING SENTENCE

Sometimes, to make the point of the paragraph emphatic, there is a summarizing statement at the end in addition to the topic sentence. This *concluding sentence* often restates the idea expressed in the topic sentence, relating to the specific details given in the paragraph.

> Our fascination with the technique of bullfighting is something shared by all the Spanish youngsters — all the poor ones at any rate. They all dream of becoming bullfighters. It's a way of getting off bleak, rocky farms, out of jammed city hovels and into the world of economic royalty. Almost as important, in a land of rigid social stratification, success with the capes can lift a boy from the wrong side of the tracks onto a level with the titled set of Spain. A peasant, or bootblack, is an artist if he can master the rituals of the *corridas* regardless of whether or not he chooses the right fork or splits his infinitives correctly. When a bullfighter stands in the sand-packed arena facing a charging half-ton of fury, no one is likely to be concerned about the inadequacy of his grammar, schooling or family background. **For all these reasons the bullring has been a magnet to the youngsters of Spain.**[1]

**EXERCISE 1.** The following subjects lend themselves to development into paragraphs. Select five of them and write a topic sentence for each.

[1] From *Mention My Name in Mombasa* by Maureen and William McGivern. Copyright © 1958 by William P. McGivern and Maureen Daly McGivern. Reprinted by permission of Lurton Blassingame, the authors' agent, and Dodd, Mead & Company.

1. Our newest frontier
2. Unfair criticisms
   of adolescents
3. Television commercials
4. Chemistry in the kitchen
5. Testing, testing, testing!
6. Pay television
7. Current fads
8. The world of 1999
9. The politician
10. Small colleges vs.
    large colleges

## DEVELOPING A PARAGRAPH

**17c. A paragraph is usually developed by means of additional, detailed information that supports the idea stated in the topic sentence.**

Topic sentences are usually general statements — the kind that express attitudes or opinions or make generalizations about things. For example:

> People who are accused of crimes should have a fair trial.
> Every language suits the needs of the people who speak it.

General statements of this kind are important; they tell us what is important and worth knowing. However, to be significant, general statements should be backed up by specific details. Before we can judge whether or not an accused person should have a fair trial, we have to know what a fair trial is. Before the second statement above can mean much, we need to know specific ways in which particular languages fit the needs of their speakers. The various methods of developing paragraphs differ mainly in the kinds of details given in support of the topic sentence.

**(1) A topic sentence may be developed by facts.**

You will often find paragraphs developed this way in social studies and science textbooks. In the following paragraph, notice how details are supplied to clarify the topic sentence:

> **Between the sunlit surface waters of the open sea and the hidden hills and valleys of the ocean floor lies the least-known**

**region of the sea.** These deep, dark waters, with all their mysteries and their unsolved problems, cover a very considerable part of the earth. The whole world ocean extends over about three-fourths of the surface of the globe. If we subtract the shallow areas of the continental shelves and the scattered banks and shoals, where at least the pale ghost of sunlight moves over the underlying bottom, there still remains about half the earth that is covered by miles-deep, lightless water that has been dark since the world began.[1]

## (2) A topic sentence may be developed by examples.

In our conversations and in our reading we frequently hear or read paragraphs which contain several examples of the truth stated in the topic sentences. In the following paragraph the writer gives three examples to support his opening statement.

**Much of the early work on television consisted of developing systems that would not work successfully.** Scientists ran up many a blind alley and had to turn back to try another path; but step by step, they kept moving toward success. In 1880 Ayrton and Perry in England, and Carey, in the United States, proposed very complicated devices that were patterned somewhat after the human eye. Tiny electric cells took the place of the rods and cones and sent electrical impulses through wires as varying amounts of light fell on them. The electrical impulses then operated electromagnets in the receiver, and these moved a series of vanes, which made up the viewing screen. This device was very complicated and did not work successfully. Later a German, Paul Nipkow, suggested a "scanning" disk, with a series of small holes in it. When the disk was rotated, the holes broke up the scene into a series of tiny spots of light. But here, again, great mechanical difficulty prevented success. Then, in 1907, a Russian, Boris Rosing, suggested that, in place of cumbersome mechanical devices, electrons could be used to scan the scene. Dr. Vladimir Zworykin, another Russian, who moved to the United States in 1919, proposed a method of accomplishing

---

[1] From *The Sea Around Us* by Rachel L. Carson. Copyright © 1950, 1951 by Rachel L. Carson. Published by Oxford University Press, New York; and by Staples Press Ltd., London. Reprinted by permission of Marie Rodell, Literary Agent.

this. His proposal was the basis of our modern television system.[1]

**(3)  A topic sentence may be developed by an incident.**

This method of development relies on a brief story or anecdote to illustrate the meaning of a general statement. An incident used in this way is really only an elaborate example.

> **Self-pity is the root of many of our worries.** When I was practicing medicine in London, one of my patients, a young married woman, was stricken with infantile paralysis. She was sent to a good hospital, where it soon became apparent that she was responding to treatment and would eventually recover. Some weeks later I received a visit from her husband. In a state of intense nervous upset, he complained of sleeplessness and inability to concentrate. After a checkup, I found nothing whatever the matter with him. But when I suggested that he get back to his job he turned on me furiously. "My wife is seriously ill. And you expect me to go on as though nothing had happened. Haven't you any feeling *for me?*" The basic cause of his worry was self-pity, masquerading as concern for his wife.[2]

**(4)  A topic sentence may be developed by comparisons or contrasts.**

In this type of paragraph, the topic sentence states that two things are similar or different, as the case may be. The succeeding sentences tell specifically what the similarities or differences are.

The following paragraph considers the various elements that two plays have in common.

> **Shakespeare's** *Hamlet* **and Maxwell Anderson's** *Winterset* **are linked not only by the revenge theme and by a rich, life-like verse but also by common pleas for balance, individual**

---

[1] From *Understanding Science* by William H. Crouse. Copyright © 1956 by William H. Crouse. Reprinted by permission of McGraw-Hill Book Company.

[2] From "How to Stop Worrying," by A. J. Cronin, from *Reader's Digest,* May 1954. Reprinted by permission of the author.

**strength, and careful judgment.** Both Hamlet and Mio show a tragic loss of balance in the face of overpowering emotions, while Claudius and Garth, Gertrude and Esdras reveal and suffer from fear to face and right a known wrong. The misfortunes suffered by Laertes and Gaunt and the pain they cause others are results of indiscriminate judgments. Both plays, by exposing these human shortcomings, enable a reader to gain insight into his own problems.[1]

Paragraphs may also be developed effectively through contrasts.

**The way of the desert and the way of the jungle represent the two opposite methods of reaching stability at two extremes of density.** In the jungle there is plenty of everything life needs except more space, and it is not for the want of anything else that individuals die or that races have any limit set to their proliferation. Everything is on top of everything else; there is no cranny which is not both occupied and disputed. At every moment, war to the death rages fiercely. The place left vacant by any creature that dies is seized almost instantly by another, and life seems to suffer from nothing except too favorable an environment. In the desert, on the other hand, it is the environment itself which serves as the limiting factor. To some extent the struggle of creature against creature is mitigated, though it is of course not abolished even in the vegetable kingdom. For the plant which in the one place would be strangled to death by its neighbor dies a thirsty seedling in the desert because that same neighbor has drawn the scant moisture from the spot of earth out of which it was attempting to spring.[2]

### (5) A topic sentence may be developed by reasons.

The topic sentence in an argumentative paragraph is developed by reasons which will "prove" the writer's point or argument.

[1] From "Pleas for Balance, Responsibility and Judgment." by Jeffrey Goodman, from The Atlantic contest booklet, 1961–62. Copyright © 1962 by The Atlantic Monthly Company. Reprinted with permission of the publisher.

[2] From *The Desert Year* by Joseph Wood Krutch. Copyright 1951, 1952 by Joseph Wood Krutch. Reprinted by permission of William Morrow & Co., Inc.

**First of all, then, get into the habit of reading carefully and, whenever you can, slowly.** Take your time. The purpose of a journey is to arrive, but the pleasures of travel lie in the journey itself. The purpose of reading is not to finish the short story, the poem, the essay, the play, the novel, but to enjoy it and in all other ways to profit by it as one reads and when one has read it. Read at leisure, savouring as you go; and savour it again when you have finished. Don't lock the door on it, don't put it away in a cupboard and forget all about it: store it in your memory, so that you may think of it again, enjoy it again. And you'll do so the more easily, indeed you'll do it inevitably, if you read without haste, without strain. Never read feverishly, never read as though you were racing against time — unless you wish to derive neither pleasure nor profit from your reading. Expressed thus, the statement sounds so obvious as to be silly. Yet there are many, young and old, who read as though reading were either a form of athletics or a sort of penance. I should not care to say that, on such people, reading is wasted, but I do say that when people read a book, a magazine, a newspaper in that way, they are wasting their time and paying a mighty poor compliment both to what they are reading — and to themselves.[1]

## (6)  A topic sentence may be developed by definition.

Sometimes a paragraph may be developed around the meaning of a key word or concept.

**Plot is essentially the account of human activity, of significant changes from one state of human affairs to another.** It is, in other words, the element in the work of fiction which is representative of men and women in *action*. Action, of course, need not be of an overt, physical kind. In fiction of an adult sort, indeed, action more often than not consists of the reflections, discoveries, decisions, and responses — the changes in knowledge and attitude and circumstances — which for most of us go to make up the shifting pattern of life itself.[2]

[1] From *English: A Course for Human Beings* by Eric Partridge, published by Winchester Publications Ltd., London. Reprinted by permission of Macdonald & Company Limited, publishers.
[2] From *What Happens in Literature* by Edward W. Rosenheim, Jr. Reprinted by permission of the University of Chicago Press.

**(7) A topic sentence may be developed by a combination of methods.**

It is not always wise to develop a topic exclusively by fact, examples, etc. Various combinations are possible.

The face of the earth is a graveyard, and so it has always been. To earth each living thing restores when it dies that which has been borrowed to give form and substance to its brief day in the sun. From earth, in due course, each new living being receives back again a loan of that which sustains life. What is lent by earth has been used by countless generations of plants and animals now dead and will be required by countless others in the future. In the case of an element such as phosphorus, so limited is the supply that if it were not constantly being returned to the soil a single century would be sufficient to produce a disastrous reduction in the amount of life. No plant or animal . . . can establish permanent right of possession to the materials which compose its physical body.[1]

*comparison*

*facts*

*example*

*topic sentence*

**EXERCISE 2.** Write the topic sentence from the following paragraphs on your paper. After each, indicate by the rule number the method used in developing the paragraph.

[1] From *Deserts on the March,* by Paul B. Sears. Copyright 1935, 1947 by the University of Oklahoma Press. Reprinted by permission of the publisher.

(1) facts
(2) examples
(3) incident or anecdote

(4) comparisons or contrasts
(5) reasons
(6) definition

1

. . . If we are to be guided by experience in the natural and biological sciences, techniques tend to be more persistent than the theories that originally called them into play. Alchemists, for example, appear to our minds to have had rather misguided ideas about the nature of matter, but the experimental techniques which they evolved in pursuit of their goal of transmutation, and the incidental knowledge which they gained of the behavior of matter, are still of great importance to chemistry. Modern chemical techniques have been enormously refined and elaborated, but they are still recognizably the offspring of alchemy.[1]

2

Blank verse may be said to consist of unrhymed lines of ten syllables each, the second, fourth, sixth, eighth, and tenth syllables bearing the accents (iambic pentameter). This form has generally been accepted as that best adapted to dramatic verse in England and is commonly used for long poems whether dramatic, philosophic, or narrative. Because of its freedom it appears easy to write, but good blank verse probably demands more artistry and genius than any other verse form. The freedom gained through lack of rhyme is offset by the demands for richness to be secured through its privileges. This richness may be obtained by the skillful poet through a variety of means: the shifting of the caesura, or pause, from place to place within the line; the shifting of the stress among syllables; the use of the run-on line, which permits of thought-grouping in large or small blocks (these thought-groups being variously termed verse "paragraphs" or verse "stanzas"); variation in tonal qualities by changing diction from passage to passage; and, finally, the adaptation of the form to reproduction of differences in the speech of characters in dramatic and narrative verse and to differences of emotional expression.[2]

[1] From *The Tools of Social Science* by John Madge, published by Longmans Group Limited. Reprinted by permission of the publishers.
[2] From *A Handbook to Literature* by C. Hugh Holman, based on the original by William Flint Thrall and Addison Hibbard. Copyright © 1936, 1960 by The Odyssey Press, Inc., 1972 by the Bobbs-Merrill Company, Inc. Reprinted by permission of the publisher.

3

It is impossible for Mexicans to produce the humblest thing without form and design. A donkey wears a load of palm leaves arranged on either flank in great green sunbursts. Merchants hang candles by their wicks to make patterns in both line and color. Market coconuts show white new moonstrips above the dark, fibrous mass. Serapes are thrown with just the right line over the shoulders of ragged peons, muffling them to the eyes. Merchants in the market will compose their tomatoes, oranges, red seeds and even peanuts into little geometric piles. Bundles of husks will be tied in a manner suitable for suspension in an artist's studio. To the traveller from the north, used to the treatment of cold, dead produce as cold, dead produce, this is a matter of perpetual wonder and delight.[1]

4

A simple experiment will distinguish two types of human nature. Gather a throng of people and pour them into a ferryboat. By the time the boat has swung into the river you will find that a certain proportion have taken the trouble to climb upstairs, in order to be out on deck and see what is to be seen as they cross over. The rest have settled indoors, to think what they will do upon reaching the other side, or perhaps lose themselves in apathy and tobacco smoke. But leaving out those apathetic or addicted to a single enjoyment, we may divide all the alert passengers on the boat into two classes—those who are interested in crossing the river, and those who are merely interested in getting across.[2]

5

The course of history is determined by the faith that men are guided by. If they misread the lessons of expanding knowledge and in their brazen egotism believe that all things are known or knowable, then they will see nothing but an endlessly repeating pattern of sordid strife, the ascendancy of ruthlessness and cunning, man damned to exist a little time on an earth where there is nothing higher than to seize and kill and dominate. If they see beyond this they will see by faith, and not by reading instruments or combining numbers. They may look beyond by religious

[1] From *Mexico* by Stuart Chase. Copyright 1931 by Stuart Chase, renewed 1959 by Stuart Chase. Reprinted by permission of Macmillan Publishing Co., Inc.

[2] From *The Enjoyment of Poetry* by Max Eastman. Reprinted by permission of Charles Scribner's Sons.

faith, or they may look merely because they feel validity in the heart's desire and conviction that good will is not a delusion. If they have faith they will build, and they will grow strong that their buildings may endure.[1]

**EXERCISE 3.** Number your paper 1–20. After the proper number indicate by the rule numbers — (1), (2), (3), (4), (5), (6) — the method you would use to develop a paragraph from each of the following sentences. With most sentences, more than one choice is possible.

1. To Abigail Adams, the word *liberty* had a specific meaning.
2. You don't have to travel far to find adventure.
3. Good manners begin at home.
4. Hemingway and Faulkner, who died only a year apart, had little in common as writers.
5. Sometimes opportunity knocks more than once.
6. Automation has created new kinds of jobs for people.
7. Vertical flight will soon change our ideas about travel.
8. Nicknames can be cruel.
9. Nothing succeeds like a good slogan.
10. The average American today is (is not) a pioneer.
11. You don't have to join a team to practice good sportsmanship.
12. Democracy does not have the same meaning for us that it had for the ancient Greeks.
13. At least once a year everyone should try some gardening.
14. Comedy and tragedy are simply different ways of looking at life.
15. Fashions in slang are quick to change.
16. The principles of flight are quite simple.
17. Many important discoveries have come about because of lucky accidents.
18. There is nothing like television when an important news story breaks.
19. Culture has many meanings for twentieth-century Americans.
20. Most highway accidents could have been prevented.

[1] Vannevar Bush, *Modern Arms and Free Men.*

**EXERCISE 4.** From the following topics, select one which can be developed by facts and one which can be developed by examples. For each topic, formulate a statement which can serve as the topic sentence of a paragraph. Then write the two paragraphs fully developed (about 150 words). At the end of each paragraph write "facts" or "examples" to indicate how you developed it.

1. Qualities of a good baby-sitter
2. The perfect highway
3. If I were a teacher
4. Household chores
5. How not to get lost in the woods
6. The family car
7. A typical vacation
8. Things someone should invent
9. The best day of the week
10. The value of a college education

**EXERCISE 5.** Select one of the following topics and compose a general statement about it that will serve as a topic sentence. Then write a paragraph (100–150 words) beginning with this statement and developed by an incident which illustrates its truth.

1. The best way to make an enemy
2. The importance of hunches
3. Good neighbors
4. Learning the hard way
5. A lucky accident

**EXERCISE 6.** The following topics may be developed by comparison or contrast. Write a topic sentence for one of them and develop it into a paragraph (100–150 words), supplying the details needed to make the similarities or differences clear.

1. Supermarkets and neighborhood groceries
2. Saturday and Monday

3. Pioneers today and yesterday
4. Small colleges vs. large colleges
5. Two magazines
6. Reading for fun and assigned reading
7. People and machines
8. Two kinds of music
9. Two ways of preparing for a test
10. Two kinds of teachers

**EXERCISE 7.** Using facts, examples, or any other appropriate means, clarify the meaning of one of the following terms in a paragraph of 100–150 words.

1. Sportsmanship
2. Snobbishness
3. Sense of humor
4. School spirit
5. Courage
6. The honor system
7. Fair play
8. A similar word of your choice

## UNITY IN THE PARAGRAPH

**17d. A paragraph should be unified, that is, concerned with a single topic.**

A paragraph possesses *unity* when it has one central idea which is clarified, explained, or reinforced by all the other statements in the paragraph. Skillful writers, once they formulate an idea and state it in a topic sentence, will then develop the idea by any one of the methods already mentioned in this chapter, keeping in mind that whatever they write must deal with only this idea.

Suppose you are writing about rocket engines. You happen to know something about earth satellites as well and are interested in space stations. But will you display all this knowledge in a single paragraph? In a paragraph about rocket engines, the last two topics will be irrelevant, unless you show how they are connected to your main topic. The unity of your idea will be destroyed if you introduce anything that does not have direct bearing on your main idea, even though the second subject may be related in a general way.

Remember that the ideas you put into a paragraph should be those that you want your reader to think about together. If you have a good idea that is only vaguely related to the topic of your paragraph, save it. You will only confuse your reader if you mix your ideas indiscriminately in one paragraph.

**EXERCISE 8.** The following paragraphs fail to achieve unity because certain sentences in them are unrelated to the topic. The topic sentence has been printed in bold-faced type. Study each paragraph and point out which sentences you would eliminate.

### 1

**Today's. teen-agers have more educational opportunities than their grandparents had.** More and better schools are being built all over the country. Scholarships are available in much greater number for thousands of deserving students. Radio and television bring some of the finest plays and players to almost every home. The modern college serves better food in its students' cafeteria. Books are more readily obtainable now because of the many good paperbacks. Compared to the adolescent of sixty years ago, today's adolescent has a much better chance to get a well-rounded education.

### 2

**People are reading more and more every day.** There is hardly a drugstore in the United States which doesn't sell a line of paperback books. Today the best books in fiction, science, travel, biography, and drama can be purchased for a fraction of their original cost. Magazines of ten million readers per issue are not uncommon. Unfortunately some magazines, in spite of their increased circulation, have had to suspend publication because of high production costs. Library circulations reach new records each month. It is a far cry from the "good old days" when few people could afford a home library because of the expense.

3

**You don't need to be rich to become a collector.** Today you can purchase books, art, china, furniture, and many other things at reasonable prices and start a private collection. Begin in a small way and concentrate in a limited field. You may want to collect first editions of Ernest Hemingway, Edith Wharton, or some other novelist. Or your interests may run to reproductions of great paintings, or to illustrated books on natural history. You will find that by carefully studying catalogues and watching for sales, you may pick up some rare items at no great expense. The Morgan Library has one of the largest collections of illuminated medieval manuscripts. The Huntington Library in California has served many scholars because of its valuable collections of first editions.

4

**The high school sports program today is both intramural and extramural.** No longer does a mere handful of boys or girls represent the school in a few sports. Today hundreds of teen-agers may participate in such varied sports as badminton, volleyball, tennis, hockey, baseball, track, basketball, football, and swimming. Coaches are getting better salaries than they did twenty years ago. Greater participation in school sports is one of the aspects of our high school life most noticed by foreign visitors.

**EXERCISE 9.** Select one of the topic sentences that follow or a sentence of your own, and develop it into a paragraph of about 150 words. Be sure that everything you include relates to the topic sentence. If you select a sentence that really appeals to you and about which you have done some thinking, you should produce a paragraph with some interesting facts or conclusions.

1. There is more to good teaching than simply knowing the subject matter.
2. There is too much emphasis on getting into the "right" college these days.
3. Can television commercials annoy us and still make us buy?

4. Eventually, television and tape recorders will be as common as textbooks in the classroom.

5. Science and technology have advanced too quickly for the good of all people.

## COHERENCE IN THE PARAGRAPH

**17e. A paragraph should be coherent, that is, arranged according to some definite plan.**

In addition to relating to the topic sentence, the sentences in a paragraph should stand in a clear and logical relation to each other. When the ideas in a paragraph flow from one to the other in logical order, the paragraph has *coherence*. To achieve this quality, you must plan what you are going to write. Sometimes you will have to rearrange or rewrite several times before you arrive at the best possible order for your ideas.

Among several methods of ordering ideas are chronological order, spatial order, and order of importance.

### Chronological Order

One method that you have long been acquainted with is *chronological order*—the order in which things happen. In addition to narratives, an explanation of the steps in a process often follows chronological order.

In English it will usually be found that the so-called learned words are of foreign origin. Most of them are derived from French or Latin, and a considerable number from Greek. The reason is obvious. The development of English literature has not been isolated, but has taken place in close connection with the earnest study of foreign literatures. Thus, in the fourteenth century, when our language was assuming substantially the shape which it now bears, the literary exponent of English life and thought, Geoffrey Chaucer, the first of our great poets, was profoundly influenced by Latin literature as well as by that of France and Italy. In the sixteenth and seventeenth centuries the Greek and Latin classics were

vigorously studied by almost every English writer of any consequence, and the great authors of antiquity were regarded
as models, not merely of general literary form, but of expression in all its details. These foreign influences have varied
much in character and intensity. But it is safe to say that
there has been no time since 1350 when English writers of
the highest class have not looked to Latin, French, and Italian authors for guidance and inspiration. From 1600 to the
present day the direct influence of Greek literature and philosophy has also been enormous — affecting as it has the finest
spirits in a peculiarly pervasive way — and its indirect influence is quite beyond calculation. Greek civilization, we should
remember, has acted upon us, not merely through Greek literature and art, but also through the medium of Latin, since
the Romans borrowed their higher culture from Greece.[1]

## Spatial Order

A paragraph developed by concrete details, such as the
description of a place, may follow *spatial order*. The rest
will follow in an orderly way, as from near to far, etc.

These trade winds, always warm, but nevertheless re-
freshing sea breezes, blow mostly from the east or the northeast. Thus one side of every island is windward, and the other
side is leeward. The third great geographical fact about these
islands is that most of them are mountainous, giving to the
windward sides much more rain than the leeward sides receive. This makes great differences in climate within short
distances, a thing quite unknown in the eastern half of the
United States, where our slowly whirling cyclonic winds blow
in quick succession from all directions upon every spot of
territory. Thus both sides of the Appalachian Mountains are
nearly alike in their rainfall, forest growth, and productive
possibilities. On the contrary, the West Indian mountains have
different worlds on their different slopes. The eastern or windward side, cloud-bathed and eternally showered upon, is damp
and dripping. There are jungles with velvety green ferns, and
forests with huge trees. The rainbow is a prominent feature of

[1] From *Words and Their Ways in English Speech* by J. B. Greenough
and G. L. Kitteridge, The Macmillan Company, 1901. Reprinted by
permission of the publishers.

the tropic landscape. On the windward side one receives a striking impression of lush vegetation. On the leeward side of the very same ridge and only a few miles distant there is another kind of world, the world of scanty rainfall, with all its devastating consequences to vegetation. A fourth great geographic fact is the division of these islands into two great arcs, an outer arc of limestone and an inner arc of volcanic islands. The limestone areas are low. The volcanic areas are from moderately high to very high. Some islands have both the limestone and the volcanic features.[1]

## Order of Importance

A paragraph developed by reasons is often organized according to the *order of importance* of the ideas. The usual procedure is to begin with the least important reasons and build up to the most important.

The building should be thoroughly fumigated. Nothing but fumigation offers any secure hope of rooting out the roaches at the source. Minor sprays and traps would only attack the appearances. They would not hit at the nests within the walls. A fully professional extermination job would not only destroy the nests and rid us of the present population; it would also serve as an effective guard against future reinfestation. Finally, it would be the only way of preventing the pests from overrunning the public areas of the building and beginning to infiltrate the apartments and offices themselves.

There are of course many other ways of organizing the details in paragraphs. A paragraph developed by contrast or comparison may, for example, describe topic A fully before moving on to B. Or, it may alternate between them, describing one aspect of A, then one of B, and so on. The main point is that details should be presented in a logical and orderly way.

**EXERCISE 10.** The following topics can be developed into

[1] From *North America* by J. Russell Smith and M. Ogden Phillips. Reprinted by permission of Harcourt Brace Jovanovich, Inc.

paragraphs in which the details are organized chronologically, spatially, or by order of importance. Choose three topics, one to be developed in each of these three ways, and write a good topic sentence for each. Then write the three paragraphs.

1. Automobile design in the last five years
2. Preparing for a test
3. The danger of indifference to public affairs
4. Preparing for a career
5. Why I like classical music
6. The layout of a shopping center
7. What the past can teach us
8. The ideal school building (or house, workshop, or kitchen)
9. A simple experiment
10. What I like (or don't like) about suburbs
11. Changing ideas about distance
12. An airport terminal during the holidays
13. Humor on television
14. Backstage on opening night
15. How to cover and write a news story

# LINKING EXPRESSIONS AND CONNECTIVES

**17f. Strengthen the coherence of a paragraph by using linking expressions and connectives.**

If you have been successful in eliminating all ideas that do not bear on the topic sentence and if your sentences are arranged in a logical order, your reader should have little trouble in following your train of thought. Remember, however, that your reader will not be as familiar with the ideas in the paragraph as you, the writer, are. Connections that are clear to you may not occur to your reader at once. For this reason it is a good idea to supply, occasionally, clues to help your reader see the direction in which the thought is moving. By making the organization obvious, these clues, or direction signals, will give your paragraph an added feeling of coherence.

The usual ways of showing the connection between ideas in a paragraph are by using pronouns that refer to an idea already mentioned, by repeating a key word from a previous sentence, and by using connecting words that express the relation in thought between two sentences.

## Use of Pronouns

In the following example, the bold-faced pronouns tie the sentences in the paragraph together and give the sense of a continuing explanation.

> Sometimes when you face a multiple-choice question on a test, you realize that you do not know the correct answer. You may, however, be able to determine **it** by a process of elimination. In this process, you consider all the choices one by one, questioning their reasonableness. **Some** of **them** will be obviously absurd and may be eliminated. **That** which is left may be a fairly safe guess.

## Repetition

In the paragraph that follows, the repetition of the phrase *reading a book* (*reading books*) and the word *pleasure* helps to show the relation of a number of different ideas, as well as to give emphasis to the central idea of the paragraph.

> I suppose that most of you in the book trade assume that the product you sell is associated with **pleasure.** You would say that **reading a book** is a **pleasure,** whereas, in contrast, a pharmacist's product is associated with **displeasure:** taking medicine is not a **pleasure.** I use this sharp contrast to empha-size a point that is easy to forget, namely that **reading books** is not a **pleasure** to a great many people. There is little doubt that **reading books** is hard intellectual labor for the majority of people, and that the **pleasure** component only outweighs the hard work component by a little bit for a large additional

group of the population. **Reading a book** is sheer **pleasure** alone for a very small minority of people.[1]

## Transitional Expressions

In addition to the use of pronouns and the repetition of key words, the choice of an appropriate connective often provides a useful clue to the relationship of ideas. These transitional words and expressions can be conveniently grouped according to the kind of relations they express.

(1) Connectives that link similar ideas:

| | | |
|---|---|---|
| again | for example | likewise |
| also | for instance | moreover |
| and | furthermore | of course |
| another | in addition | similarly |
| besides | in a like manner | too |

(2) Connectives that link ideas that are dissimilar or apparently contradictory:

| | |
|---|---|
| although | nevertheless |
| as if | on the contrary |
| but | on the other hand |
| conversely | otherwise |
| even if | provided that |
| however | still |
| in spite of | yet |
| instead | |

(3) Connectives that indicate cause, purpose, or result:

| | |
|---|---|
| as | hence |
| as a result | since |
| because | so |
| consequently | then |
| for | therefore |
| for this reason | thus |

[1] From "Roadblocks to Bookbuying" by Elmo Roper, *Publishers Weekly,* June 16, 1958. Copyright © 1958 by R. R. Bowker Company. Reprinted by permission of *Publishers Weekly.*

(4) Connectives that indicate time or position:

| | |
|---|---|
| above | finally |
| across | first |
| afterward | here |
| around | meanwhile |
| at once | next |
| at the present time | presently |
| before | thereafter |
| beyond | thereupon |
| eventually | |

Of course the connectives listed above and others like them can help the reader only when they are appropriately used. Transitional devices are like road signs: one that points in the wrong direction is worse than no sign at all.

Notice in the paragraph that follows how connectives have been used to tie the ideas together, to show their relative importance, and generally to enable the reader to follow the writer's thought easily.

> Stevenson's choice of telling a large part of *Treasure Island* from Jim's point of view has obvious advantages. **First,** the boy hero's account gives the illusion that we are reading an authentic document—a report of exciting events by someone who participated in them. **Second,** we are spared in Jim's narrative many details which an impersonal description of the action would have to include but which would probably contribute little to the unfolding of the story. **In other words,** Jim's adventurous young mind filters out incidents and data that a more mature narration would include in favor of the high points of excitement and suspense. **Finally,** since Jim's own discoveries play such an important part in the plot, his account enables us to share the ignorance and curiosity that precedes them and the surprise, fear, or delight which they produce.

**EXERCISE 11.** Select a topic that appeals to you from the list below. Write a topic sentence and develop it into a paragraph of about 150 words. Evaluate your paragraph by asking yourself the questions in the checklist on page 283.

1. A person (student, adult, historical figure, etc.) typical of a particular era
2. How one can help fight against pollution
3. Politics and television
4. Sports on television
5. Keeping a scrapbook
6. Problems of an autograph collector
7. The zone defense
8. A car is more than transportation.
9. The plays of Lorraine Hansberry
10. The day nothing happened
11. Efforts being made to save an endangered species
12. Finding your way in the *Readers' Guide* (or another reference book)
13. Who's superstitious?
14. Witnessing history on television
15. What to see in the Far West (South, Midwest, East, etc.)
16. Organizing a scavenger hunt
17. Part-time jobs
18. A simple experiment
19. The art of getting a whole meal ready at once
20. Making up your own mind

## CHECKLIST FOR PARAGRAPH REVISION

1. Does the topic sentence clearly state the main idea of the paragraph?
2. Is the topic sentence adequately supported by specific details?
3. Do all of the ideas in the paragraph have a clear relation to the topic sentence?
4. Are the ideas arranged in an understandable order?
5. Are transitional devices used where they are needed? Do the transitional words accurately express the relations between ideas?

# Chapter 18

# The Whole Composition

## Selecting a Subject; Planning and Writing the Composition

Like most other complicated tasks, the writing of a composition is best approached as a series of steps that can be taken one at a time. Considered altogether, the business of choosing a subject to write about, gathering material, and writing and revising seems a long and difficult process. The task may never be easy, but if taken step by step, it is at least manageable. In this chapter, the writing of a composition is divided into seven separate steps, beginning with the selection of the subject and ending with the final draft. The letters designating these steps in the list below correspond to the rules in this chapter.

a. Choosing and limiting the subject
b. Assembling materials
c. Organizing materials
d. Outlining
e. Writing the first draft
f. Revising
g. Writing the final draft

For short compositions and for those that you are asked to write in class, you will sometimes be able to combine several of these steps into one. As a rule, however, you will find it helpful to take each of these steps separately and in order, solving the problems of one before moving on to the next.

Inexperienced writers facing an assignment of 500 to 1,000 words may understandably think that the larger the subject, the easier it will be to fill the required number of pages. Even if writing were just a matter of putting a certain number of words on paper, this reasoning would be faulty. On a broad subject like "Science" or "The Causes of Wars," most writers would be able to make only a few general statements before they ran out of ideas. Good general statements are an important part of writing, but they must always be backed up with specific details that make them meaningful. A piece of writing is judged not by the impressiveness of the subject but by what the writer has to say about it.

In choosing a subject to write about, it is quite natural for you to think of large ones first. The point is not to stop there, but to focus on successively smaller aspects of the subject until you arrive at one that you can handle. A traveler journeying from outer space might first see North America as a whole, then the part of it that the United States occupies, then the east coast, New York City, and finally a destination—say, Kennedy Airport. In much the same way, writers limit their subjects by moving in and narrowing their views.

Starting with the unlimited subject "Science," the process works like this:

| | |
|---|---|
| UNLIMITED | Science |
| SLIGHTLY LIMITED | Modern Science |
| LIMITED FOR 2,000-WORD TREATMENT | The Work of Modern Scientists |
| LIMITED FOR 1,000-WORD TREATMENT | Careers in Science |
| LIMITED FOR 500-WORD TREATMENT | Preparing for a Career in Science |

## THE SUBJECT

**18a. Select a subject that interests you and that can be adequately treated within the limits of your composition.**

Many of the composition assignments you do in school will be on an assigned topic. In this case, you will not have to worry much about Step One. You are then in the situation of someone in business who has a letter to answer or a scientist who has a particular piece of information to report about an experiment — your subject is determined by the occasion. At other times, the choice of subject will be yours. When you are choosing the subject, you have the chance to write about something that really interests you — something you have thought about and upon which you have definite opinions or special information. Since your choice of a subject is your most important decision, allow yourself the time you need to think about it.

**(1) Choose a subject that interests you.**

Writers who are bored by their own subjects will bore their readers. But how can you be sure that your own interest in a subject is deep enough to sustain a whole composition? One simple test is to ask yourself the following questions: Do I know the subject well enough to talk about it at some length? If not, am I curious enough about the subject to want more information than I have, and do I know where to get that information? If your answer to any of these questions is *Yes,* you probably have enough interest in the subject to make a worthwhile composition.

**(2) Limit the subject so that you can treat it adequately within the assigned space.**

**EXERCISE 1.**  Within each of the following broad subjects, select three narrower subjects suitable for a composition of 500 words.

| | |
|---|---|
| 1. Education in America | 6. Astronomy |
| 2. Family Life | 7. Medicine |
| 3. Systems of Government | 8. Recreation |
| 4. Automobiles | 9. Modern Literature |
| 5. Electronics | 10. Conservation |

**(3) Determine the purpose of your composition.**

As you select and limit your subject, you will see more and more clearly exactly what you will try to do in the composition itself. You may decide that you will try to give certain information to your readers as clearly and simply as you can. You may want to tell a story or prove a point or explain your attitude on a specific issue. Whatever your purpose, write it down now, as soon as you have it clearly in focus. A one-sentence statement for your subject might be: *My purpose in this composition is to make clear the requirements for a career in science.*

The statement of your purpose is not the same thing as your title, which will usually be only a few words. This statement usually will not appear in the composition itself. Its purpose is to help you remember exactly what it is that you are trying to accomplish in this piece of writing. Keep it before you during all stages of the planning and writing. It will help you to eliminate all ideas that do not bear directly on the accomplishment of your purpose.

**EXERCISE 2.** Choose three topics that interest you from the list of suggestions on pages 307–12. (You may substitute one or more of your own choosing if you wish.) For each, write a title that would be appropriate for a paper of approximately 500 words and a statement of purpose that you would follow if you were writing the paper.

EXAMPLE  *Tennis* [general topic], *Sport for Everyone*

*My purpose in this composition is to show that tennis is an ideal sport for people of all ages.*

## ORGANIZING AND ARRANGING MATERIAL

Having chosen your subject, limited it, and decided upon your basic purpose, you are ready to begin the second stage of composition: the collection and organization of your facts and ideas. For some subjects, you may feel that all the material you need is already in your possession, though specific points may have to be checked against reference books or other sources. Other subjects may involve background reading or library research. (For assistance in the preparation of such subjects, see Chapter 21.)

**18b. List all the ideas you can think of that bear upon the subject and purpose of your composition.**

With your summary statement before you, jot down any ideas that it suggests to you. Make this part of the job as free and simple as you can. We all know that ideas tend to flow through our minds at random; at this stage, do not try to impose any order upon this random flow of your ideas. Do not worry, either, about phrasing or style. The first list of ideas might look something like this (ignore the asterisks for the moment):

TITLE   Preparing for a Career in Science

PURPOSE   My purpose in this composition is to make clear the requirements for a career in science.

Good grades
Curiosity about science
*Chance to help humanity
Solid background and skill in mathematics
*Science concerns everything we do.
*Different fields of scientific work
*Basic subjects
Student should be enthusiastic about a field.
*Changes in scientific training
Work in pure science and work in applied science
High school courses
College training
Hobbies and extracurricular activities
Check on all courses required for a scientific career.
*Describe requirements for different scientific careers.
Personality of a good science student
Teaching science
*Rewards of a scientific career

Once your ideas are down on paper, study them carefully, evaluate them, and prepare to arrange them in a logical order. For the time being, do not concern yourself with matters of phrasing or form. In the list above, for example, some items consist of short phrases; others, of complete sentences; still others, of notes or reminders which the writer wishes to include here. At this stage of composition, these differences in form are not important. What *is* important is whether each item contributes to the purpose of the composition and can be handled within the limited space assigned.

Examine the items on the list that are marked by an asterisk. Each of these items should be eliminated at this point in the planning stage. Some items have little or nothing to do with the *purpose* of the composition: "chance to help humanity"; "science concerns everything we do"; "different fields of scientific work"; "rewards of a scientific career." Other items cannot possibly be covered adequately in a composition of 500 words; thus, a wise writer will eliminate "changes in scientific training" and "requirements for different scientific careers." One item, "basic subjects," should be eliminated for an obvious reason: it could only duplicate the discussions you have already included under such heads as "high school courses," "check on all courses required for a scientific career," and "solid background and skill in mathematics."

Removing irrelevant and unmanageable material is only one part of the job of evaluation. In your list of ideas, some items will be borderline cases. You may feel, for example, that a brief discussion of the nature of a scientific career would benefit the composition as a whole. On this ground, you may decide to retain the item on "work in pure science and work in applied science." On the other hand, you may find that as your composition begins to take shape in your mind, the item on the teaching of science does not fit under any of the principal points that you plan to make. The matter of "good grades" will undoubtedly be covered in the discussion of high school and science courses. In reaching these decisions, you are moving on to the next step in the preparation of the composition: the arrangement of your material in a logical order.

## 18c. Group related ideas together and arrange the groups in a logical order.

Now that you have eliminated the ideas that do not belong in your composition, your next job is to group similar ideas together and to find the best order in which to present them in your paper. As you go over your list of ideas once again, certain items begin to stand out as major points. For example, the "personality of a good science student" is an important concept, which includes such other items as "curiosity about science" and "enthusiasm for a scientific field." Other items on your list of ideas stand out because they are closely related: "high school courses," "college training," and "extracurricular activities" clearly belong together as parts of the academic training of a prospective scientist. Finally, there is the decision previously made to include a brief discussion of the nature of a scientific career. To round out this discussion, you may decide to split one of your items into "pure science" and "applied science."

Three main headings—personality, academic training, and scientific careers—are now available, a good number for a 500-word composition.

The last problem to be solved is the *order* of the three main headings. Planners of compositions must introduce and develop their ideas logically. When their ideas are fairly independent of one another, they may choose simply to work from the less important to the more important, or from simple ideas to complex ones. Usually, however, they will find that some topics depend upon other topics for their full meaning. If a reader must understand Point A before Point B can be understood, then Point A must come before Point B in the finished composition.

Let us apply this principle to our three main headings. Clearly, prospective students of science should know something about their objectives before they commit themselves to long years of rigorous training; thus, the brief discussion of scientific careers makes a logical opening for all the other material. A student who lacks the aptitudes and personality traits of a scientist probably should not consider taking a scientific course in high school or college; thus, the discussion of "personality" logically precedes that of "academic training." Within this new order of ideas, the subtopics fall naturally into place:

1. *Scientific careers:* pure science; applied science
2. *Personality:* scholarship (general aptitude, special skills); curiosity about science; enthusiasm for a scientific field
3. *Academic training:* high school courses; college training; extracurricular activities

**EXERCISE 3.** Copy the statement of purpose and list of ideas that follow. With the purpose in mind, cross out all ideas that you think do not belong. Group the ideas that remain in whatever way you think would be effective.

PURPOSE  My purpose is to show that tennis is an ideal sport for people of all ages.

equipment less expensive than many sports
only need one other player
can be played at all ages
good exercise
courts easy to find
grass courts are hard for beginners
strategy is important part of game
unusual method of scoring
good form as important as strength
indoor courts available in many places
game invented in France

## OUTLINING

### 18d. Observe rules for form in making a topic outline.

Having grouped your ideas and put the groups in proper order, you are ready to make an outline — a plan for writing that shows at a glance the order, relationship, and relative importance of the ideas you will be writing about.

There are two main kinds of outlines: the *topic outline,* in which the ideas are stated in words or brief phrases (not in sentences), each with a number or letter to show order and relative importance; and the *sentence outline,* in which the ideas are expressed in complete sentences. The topic outline is easier to make and quite sufficient for most purposes.

**(1) Place the title above the outline. It is not one of the topics within the outline itself.**

**(2) Do not use the terms "Introduction," "Body," and "Conclusion" in the outline. These are not topics to be discussed in the composition; they are organizational units in the writer's mind.**

**(3) Number main headings with Roman numerals; letter the subtopics under each main heading with capital letters. Divisions of subtopics, in descending order of importance, are given numbers and letters as follows: Arabic numerals, small letters, Arabic numerals in parentheses, small letters in parentheses.**

**(4) Indent subtopics so that all corresponding letters or numbers are in a vertical line.**

NUMBERS, LETTERS, AND INDENTIONS IN OUTLINE FORM

I.
   A.
   B.
      1.
      2.
         a.
         b.
            (1)
            (2)
               (a)
               (b)
II. (*etc.*)

**(5) Never allow a subtopic to stand alone; use two or more subtopics, or none at all. Subtopics are divisions of the**

topic above them, and a topic cannot be divided into fewer than two parts.

(6) Begin each topic and subtopic with a capital letter; otherwise, capitalize only proper nouns and adjectives. In a topic outline, do not follow topics with a period.

(7) All main topics should be parallel in form; each group of subtopics should be parallel in form. For example, if the first main topic is a noun, the other main topics must also be nouns; if the first subtopic under this main topic is an adjective, the corresponding subtopics must also be adjectives.

In the following example, both main topics and subtopics arc incorrectly worded.

I. There are two kinds of science. [sentence]
   A. Working in pure science [gerund phrase]
   B. Applied science [noun and modifier]
II. Personality [noun]
   A. A good scholar [noun and modifiers]
      1. General aptitude [noun and modifier]
      2. Has special skills [verb, noun, and modifier]
   B. Curiosity [noun]
   C. Enthusiastic [adjective]

Now study the first two sections in the complete outline given below. Notice that the main topics I and II have been made parallel in form, and that they match III. Each group of subtopics consists either of a single noun or a noun and modifier.

### Preparing for a Career in Science

I. Basic types of science careers
   A. Pure science
   B. Applied science
II. Personal characteristics of the science student
   A. Scholarship
      1. General aptitude
      2. Special skills
   B. Curiosity
   C. Enthusiasm

III. Academic training of the science student
    A. High school courses
    B. College courses
    C. Extracurricular activities

**EXERCISE 4.** The following list contains all the material needed for a complete topic outline—a title, a group of main topics, and several groups of subtopics. Each item is correct in form. Draw up a topic outline from the list, using every item, and numbering and lettering them properly as main topics and subtopics. Place the title of the composition at the head of the outline.

| | |
|---|---|
| Enforcement | Driver's-license laws |
| Highway engineering | In high schools |
| In the armed forces | Traffic engineering |
| Engineering | The courts |
| The police | The three big "E's" of traffic |
| Traffic laws |   safety |
| In adult driver-training courses | The laws |
| Automotive engineering | Education |

**EXERCISE 5.** Correct the following outline, keeping the following points in mind: (1) Every topic and subtopic must contribute to the purpose of the composition. (2) Organizational terms should not be used in an outline. (3) Complete sentences should not be used in a topic outline. (4) Main topics should be parallel in form; each group of subtopics should be parallel in form. (5) A single subtopic should never be allowed to stand alone.

### *Learning to Live with Nature*

  I. Introduction: Natural forces often cause great destruction
 II. Nature against people
    A. Earthquakes
    B. Volcanoes
    C. Storms
       1. The violent storms called hurricanes
       2. Tornadoes
    D. The damage caused by floods

E. Erosion is a natural force
F. Droughts
G. Other natural forces
    1. Forest fires
III. What people can do and have done
    A. Taming the floods
    B. Protecting the soil
    C. Conservation
    D. Saving the forests: How people fight forest fires
    E. Preparedness: Guarding against dry years
IV. Working with nature
 V. Conclusion: People can learn to live with nature

**EXERCISE 6.** Several topics are listed below. In each group, only one topic is a main topic and the others are subordinate. Choose the main topic in each group and be able to explain your choice.

    1. The discovery of America
       The first moonshot
       The search for a new horizon
    2. Fiction
       Autobiography
       Literature
       Literary criticism
    3. The condition of the grass
       The house at a distance
       The number of windows
       The size of the backyard

## WRITING THE COMPOSITION

The completion of the topic outline marks the end of the planning stage. You have settled on what you want to say; it remains to find the right way of saying it. Once again, as with the whole process of writing the composition, it is best to proceed one step at a time.

**18e. With your topic outline before you, write the first draft of your composition.**

Begin writing as soon as you have your ideas in order. Starting to write is something that comes hard to most people, and as a result they can find countless reasons for putting it off. Some prolong the planning stage too long; others wait for inspiration to strike. Beyond a certain point, planning can become an excuse for not starting the job. If you wait for inspiration, you are likely only to add the pressure of a tight deadline to your worries.

It is not essential, on the other hand, that you begin at the beginning. The introduction of a composition is important—it must tell readers your purpose and make them want to read on. If you aren't able to think of a strong opening sentence or paragraph right away, begin with the first main topic of your outline and come back to the introduction later.

Wherever you start, write as rapidly and freely as you can. Do not try now for perfection in word choice, sentence structure, and punctuation. The correction of errors is a slow process, requiring deliberation and care that will only interrupt your flow of ideas at this point. There will be time in the revision stage for corrections and improvements.

Your completed first draft will consist of three parts: an introduction, a body, and a conclusion. Each of them presents its own special problems.

## The Introduction

The introduction may consist of a single sentence or a whole paragraph, depending on your subject and the length of the paper. Long or short, the introduction should catch the reader's interest and get the composition moving. There are many different ways of beginning a composition. Among the most effective are (1) a general statement showing the writer's point of view and purpose; (2) a striking fact or example; (3) a challenging question. The introduction may, but need not, contain an explicit statement of your purpose; but stated or not, your purpose should be clear to all who read your introduction.

The following examples illustrate the kinds of introduction mentioned above:

GENERAL STATEMENT

I read Hermann Hesse's *Siddhartha* immediately after finishing *The Glass Bead Game*. Despite the fact that both works are written by the same author, there is an enormous difference between them, not only in their subjects but also in their styles of writing and their points of view. That the same man's thinking had gone into the creation of each was intriguing. It was then that the notion of comparing the two works first came to mind.

IMPORTANT FACT

The atomic age began at exactly 5:30 mountain war time on the morning of July 16, 1945, on a stretch of semi-desert land about fifty air miles from Alamogordo, New Mexico, just a few minutes before the dawn of a new day on that part of the earth. At that great moment in history, ranking with the moment when man first put fire to work for him, the vast energy locked within the heart of the atoms of matter was released for the first time.[1]

QUESTION

What colors can animals see? Is the world more brightly colored or duller to animals than it is to us? To find the answers to these questions, scientists have used a method of training the animals to come to the different colors, which is similar in principle to the method used in studying the sense of hearing in animals.[2]

## The Body

The body or main part of a composition fulfills the purpose expressed in the introduction. It may consist of only a few paragraphs in a short composition or it may consist of many. (As a rough guide, you may think of the body as being about three-fourths the length of your whole composition.)

[1] From *Dawn Over Zero*, The Story of the Atomic Bomb, by William L. Laurence, Alfred A. Knopf, New York, 1946. Reprinted by permission of the author.
[2] From *The Personality of Animals* by H. Munro Fox. Reprinted by permission of Penguin Books, Ltd., publishers.

Your outline is the blueprint for the body of your composition. You may devote a paragraph to each main topic in your outline, or you may at times use a whole paragraph to develop an important subtopic. In any case, each paragraph should bear a clear relationship to an item on your outline.

Each paragraph should be developed according to the principles of unity and coherence discussed in Chapter 17. Remember that a paragraph is not merely a physical division of a page — it is also a stage in your thinking. A good paragraph develops a single idea, and this idea should have a clear and direct bearing on the subject of the whole composition. Remember also that a paragraph must contain enough details to develop its idea fully. Be lavish with details in your first draft. It is much easier to cut when you are revising than it is to hunt for new material with which to fill out sparse paragraphs.

## The Conclusion

The conclusion of a composition has two main functions: it rounds out your treatment of your subject and tells your reader that you have finished. It may be a single sentence at the end of a longer paragraph or it may be a separate paragraph, but in either case the conclusion should sound like an ending. It should make the reader think that you have *finished,* not given up. Since the conclusion is your last word to the reader, it is important that it emphasize the main point that your paper is supposed to make. There are several good ways of doing this: (1) by summarizing the main idea of the paper; (2) by repeating in different words the main idea stated in the introduction; (3) by making a significant proposal.

In the first example that follows, the writer restates in summary form the argument that he has been making in the body of his essay:

The great pleasure of ignorance is, after all, the pleasure of asking questions. The man who has lost this pleasure or exchanged it for the pleasure of dogma, which is the pleasure of answering, is already beginning to stiffen. One envies so inquisitive a man as Jowett, who sat down to the study of psychology in his sixties. Most of us have lost the sense of our ignorance long before that age. We even become vain of our squirrel's hoard of knowledge and regard increasing age itself as a school of omniscience. We forget that Socrates was famed for wisdom not because he was omniscient but because he realized at the age of seventy that he still knew nothing.[1]

The following example consists of two excerpts from an essay. The first is taken from the opening paragraph, the second from the end of the essay. Notice how neatly the restatement ties the conclusion to the beginning.

By the carefully repeated definition of men who stand to make money out of its acceptance, baseball is the Great American Game. The expression was invented long ago and it has been rammed home by talented press agents ever since. . . .

. . . It is a rough, tough game, encased by rules that were made to be broken if the breaking can be accomplished smoothly enough, a game that never quite became entirely respectable, a game in which nobody wants to do anything but win. It will undoubtedly be around for a good time to come, and it will continue, in spite of its own press agents, to be in truth the great American game.

Or so, at least, believes one old-time fan.[2]

A composition intended to persuade the reader to think or act in a particular way will probably conclude with a specific proposal or suggestion of action, as in this example:

. . . The scientist must learn to teach science in the spirit of wisdom and in the light of the history of human thought and human effort, rather than as the geography of a universe uninhabited by mankind. Our colleagues in the nonscientific faculties must understand that if their teachings ignore the

[1] Robert Lynd, "The Pleasure of Ignorance."
[2] From "The Great American Game" by Bruce Catton, *American Heritage,* April 1959. Reprinted by permission of American Heritage Publishing Co., Inc.

great scientific tradition and its accomplishments, their words, however eloquent and elegant, will lose meaning for this generation and be barren of fruit.

Only with a united effort of science and the humanities can we hope to succeed in discovering a community of thought which can lead us out of the darkness and the confusion which oppresses all mankind.[1]

# REVISING THE COMPOSITION

## 18f. Revise the first draft carefully. Make this draft perfect in every detail before writing the final draft.

One of the best arguments for getting an early start on your first draft is that you will then be able to lay your paper aside for at least a short while before starting the revision. Most writers find it hard to improve on the expression of ideas they have just put down on paper. A few hours or a few days later, however, these writers can view their work more objectively and find ways of improving on it. If you are going to put off something, let it be the revision.

Your job in revising is to make every change and every correction that you can think of to improve your first draft. Some of the changes will probably be major ones. The following rules cover matters to keep in mind as you revise.

### (1) Check content.

Ask yourself whether your first draft contains the right kind of facts and examples and enough of each to accomplish the purpose you had in mind. Are there any places where more or better details would improve your presentation? Are there any details which distract from your main idea and should be eliminated?

### (2) Check organization.

Although your first draft follows your outline, there is

---

[1] From "Scientist and Humanist" by I. I. Rabi, from *The Atlantic Monthly*, January 1956. Reprinted by permission of the author.

always a possibility that you can improve upon the order in which you present your ideas. Sometimes imperfections in logic or organization show up in the first draft that are not obvious in outline form. Your outline is subject to change at any time. Do not hesitate to add new ideas, eliminate or switch around paragraphs, or rewrite.

### (3) Check paragraphing.

Does your paragraphing show a systematic development of your ideas? Are there any sentences that sound as though they should be starting a new paragraph? Does the thought flow naturally from one sentence to another within your paragraphs?

### (4) Check transitions between paragraphs.

The opening of a new paragraph tells readers that a new idea is about to be introduced. It should also tell them how this new idea is related to the one they just read about. To accomplish this, the writer must provide a smooth transition from one paragraph to the next.

Four main types of transitional devices are explained and illustrated in the following pages in an order of increasing subtlety. In general, they work by (1) referring to the preceding paragraph, or (2) using a linking expression which shows the reader a connection between the ideas of the preceding paragraph and those in the new paragraph.

1. *Refer to the preceding paragraph.*

    a. *Repeat the last idea in the preceding paragraph word for word.*

        EXAMPLE ... The beauty of its verse, the vividness of its language, and the power of its thought—all these make the *Odyssey* a great poem.

        **While the *Odyssey* is a great poem,** it is also, in a way, the world's first great novel. . . .

    b. *Repeat one or more key words from the preceding paragraph.*

EXAMPLE ... Worst of all, architects have made a custom of never putting the entrance to a public building at the street level, so that a person can walk in; instead, they perch it at the top of a flight of steps, so that no one can get in without climbing.

The **architects'** defense of the **custom** is that the **entrance** looks better that way. Perhaps it does—to **architects** and to tourists, who never go into the building. ...

2. *Use a connective or linking expression.*

Of all transitional devices, connectives are perhaps the most effective and the most common. Without repetition or waste of space, connectives both refer the reader to what has gone before and indicate what is coming. Like every literary device, they can be misused or overused, but in the hands of a skillful writer they are invaluable tools.

Study the lists of connectives on pages 281–82.

EXAMPLES ... These figures show that the boasts of Soviet leaders are not always exaggerated.

The cost of Soviet expansion, **however**, has been enormous.

... On a hot summer evening you can almost see the cornstalks stretch and swell, and almost hear the thick roots pushing the damp earth aside.

Autumn, **too**, is a good season in our country, with its ripeness, its rising mists, its sudden frosts, and its far-off honk of birds flying south.

**EXERCISE 7.** In a current newspaper or magazine, find five examples of the transitional devices used by professional writers to link paragraphs together. Clip these out or copy the paragraph endings and beginnings. Underline the transitional devices.

**(5) Check style and sentence structure.**

Is your style smooth and effective, without wordiness or trite expressions? Is your language clear and accurate?

Read your paper aloud, listening for awkward repetitions, overly involved sentences, sentence fragments and run-on sentences. If you have used any words whose meanings you are not sure of, this is the time to look them up.

**(6) Check capitalization, punctuation, and spelling.**

The checklists for capitalization and punctuation on pages 420–21 and 441–42, respectively, provide guidance in many common problems. You may also find it worthwhile to scan the list of spelling demons on pages 564–66 — many of these words are bound to turn up in your first draft.

**18g. After completing the revision, copy the composition neatly according to standard practice.**

If every previous step in planning and writing your composition has been correctly followed, you need be concerned at this point only with the accuracy and appearance of your manuscript. Copy your revised draft carefully, using a typewriter if possible. For discussions of detailed questions of manuscript form and special manuscript problems, see Chapter 26.

The final draft of the composition on careers in science is given below. Read this model as an example of a final draft. The subheadings in the right-hand margin will serve as helpful guides in following the general outline of the composition (pages 291–94), the introduction and development of main topics (pages 296–98), and the style and placement of transitions (pages 301–02).

## PREPARING FOR A CAREER
## IN SCIENCE

In an Age of Science — and no period in history merits that name better than our own — trained scientists are fortunate people. Their training is a matter of national concern, for our nation badly needs more scientists than it has. Their futures are boundless; they can advance as fast and as far in science as their ambitions and talents permit. Most important, they stand at the very center of the forces which are conquering and remaking the world around us. It is small wonder that young people everywhere dream of entering one or another scientific profession. In this composition, I shall describe some basic requirements for a career in science.

`introduction`

`purpose`

Aside from the differences between the sciences themselves, there are two main types of scientific careers. On the one hand, there is the "pure scientist," who specializes in research. On the other, there is the "applied scientist," who finds practical applications for the researcher's discoveries. To a certain extent, these two types of careers lead in different directions and appeal to different talents and dispositions. The dreamer and thinker will choose pure science, looking toward a career in a university or industrial laboratory. The practical person, who enjoys the excitement and activity of actual production, will choose a career as an engineer or technologist.

`— main topic I`

Both pure and applied science, however, have certain requirements in com-

`transition`

mon. Both, for example, make stern demands upon a student. Science is no career for the merely average student. It demands that a student be of better than average aptitude, with a high school record good enough to justify further training. Within that good record, certain grades should stand out. Thus, engineering and the physical sciences (such as astronomy, physics, and chemistry) depend upon mathematics; a student who finds algebra and geometry puzzling or boring should look elsewhere for a career.

— main topic II

Yet academic grades alone do not make a scientist. "Born scientists" are people of endless curiosity — curiosity about nature. They want to know how things are put together and how they work; they are driven to understand natural processes and their causes. To sustain this curiosity, scientists must have enthusiasm. Once their attention is focused upon a problem, they will want to know all there is to know about it as they search for answers. They must be prepared for disappointments, discouragement, and doubts. Without enthusiasm, their training may be worthless.

transition

Scholarship, curiosity, enthusiasm — these qualities, then, distinguish even the youngest "scientists-to-be." With this foundation, students can under-

transition

take their academic training with confidence. In high school they should try to study the science of their choice, at least one related science, as much mathematics as possible, and a foreign language. They will then go on to four years of study at a college or university, leading to either a Bachelor of Science or an engineering degree. At this point the paths of the pure scientist and the applied scientist are likely to diverge. For teaching or for research, additional years of formal study and a graduate degree may very well be required; an engineer or technician, on the other hand, will probably go directly to a job in industry.

—main topic III

Both kinds of scientists, however, really spend a lifetime of constant learning. Even during their years at school, they participate in extracurricular projects, such as science fairs and science clubs. In later years they go on learning, in the laboratory or on the job.

transition

Clearly, the road to success in science is not an easy one. Yet, as I pointed out at the beginning of this composition, the rewards are great. Those who love science, who have the basic qualities of the scientist, and who can master college work have the ability and the opportunity to prepare themselves for a career in science.

transition

conclusion

## SUMMARY OF THE STAGES OF COMPOSITION

### The Subject

18a. Choose a subject that interests you. Limit the subject, so that you can treat it adequately within the assigned space. Decide upon and state the purpose of the composition.

### Preparation

18b. List all the ideas you can think of that bear upon the subject and purpose of the composition.

18c. Group related ideas together under summary headings. Arrange the groups of ideas in a logical order.

18d. Observe rules for form in making a topic outline.

### Writing

18e. With the topic outline before you, write the first draft of your composition. Include an introduction and a conclusion. Divide your text into paragraphs, and pay careful attention to the transitions between paragraphs.

18f. Revise the first draft carefully. Make this draft perfect in every detail before writing the final draft.

(1) Check content.
(2) Check organization.
(3) Check paragraphing.
(4) Check transitions between paragraphs.
(5) Check style and sentence structure.
(6) Check capitalization, punctuation, and spelling.

18g. After completing the revision, copy the composition neatly according to standard practice.

# TOPICS FOR COMPOSITION

The topics in the following lists are all suitable for development according to the techniques described in this chapter. Whenever your teacher asks you to choose a subject for composition, study these lists for suggestions. Remember that these topics are no more than suggestions; you are completely free to change their wording, to limit their scope, or to write on any other subjects which these topics suggest to you.

### The Arts

1. How to read a poem
2. Modern trends in drama
3. Designing and building a stage set
4. The wisdom of folk music
5. Today's "top ten" records
6. How to plan a concert
7. A career in music (art)
8. Formula for a TV variety show
9. What to listen for in music
10. The movies vs. the stage
11. My favorite novel (poem, play, etc.)
12. Decorating a room
13. Modern vs. traditional houses
14. Jazz — America's music
15. Art in advertising
16. At the ballet
17. Moving-picture ratings
18. Book illustrations
19. Should foreign opera be sung in English?
20. What an abstract painting "shows"
21. Planning a record collection
22. Color in the home
23. Fads in popular music

### Science

1. The importance of oceanography
2. The pesticide menace
3. The risks of smoking
4. Air (water) pollution
5. Types of rockets
6. Inventions I'd like to see
7. Problems of space travel
8. A science research project
9. Recent trends in automobile design
10. Biological aspects of space travel
11. Scientific farming
12. Conservation: wildlife
13. Weather forecasting
14. The science of soils
15. This age of antibiotics
16. Nuclear power: fusion vs. fission
17. A hero of science
18. Synthetic fabrics
19. How an "atom smasher" works
20. Records in the earth
21. Kitchen chemistry
22. The plastics revolution
23. Modern computing machines
24. Building a hi-fi set
25. Traveling to the stars
26. Science aids the homemaker
27. A science field trip
28. Why scientists study eclipses
29. Conservation: soil erosion
30. Conservation: flood control
31. Conservation: forests
32. Artificial satellites

33. The principle of crop rotation
34. How a vaccine is made
35. Making aviation safer
36. The search for oil substitutes
37. Lengthening the life span
38. "Pure" vs. "applied" science

## Social Studies

1. The threat of unemployment
2. Beyond nationhood: world government?
3. Principles of democracy
4. The war on poverty
5. Difficulties of a new nation
6. The Monroe Doctrine today
7. Foreign aid
8. A conservative's creed
9. A liberal's creed
10. Society's responsibility for the aged
11. Urban renewal
12. Our changing population
13. Threats to our freedom
14. Why a two-party system?
15. Causes of labor disputes
16. A workable disarmament plan
17. Flaws in the U.N.
18. A turning point in American history
19. How a bill becomes a law
20. Organization of the judicial system
21. The meaning of —— (a recent news event)

22. Telling America's story to the world
23. The case for (or against) welfare
24. Changing our constitution
25. Installment buying— blessing or curse?
26. The cause and cure of inflation
27. A worthwhile project in current affairs
28. How not to read an advertisement
29. The Bill of Rights today
30. Helping the "have-not" nations
31. Dangers of drug addiction
32. Merit system vs. spoils system
33. What all Americans share
34. The geography of my town
35. Two important government services
36. Obligations of the citizen
37. Causes of the increase in crime
38. Traffic in our cities
39. Causes of juvenile delinquency
40. Taxes— fair and unfair

## School

1. Why we have dropouts
2. Lesson saboteurs
3. Do we want more federal aid to education?
4. Are standardized tests fair?
5. Who should go to college?
6. Educational TV at home
7. Advice to a sophomore

8. Preparing for an exam
9. A teacher's worst problem
10. Comprehensive vs. vocational high schools
11. A democratic student government
12. Learning from a machine
13. Building school spirit
14. A good school newspaper
15. How a school can help the community
16. The ideal high school
17. The value of vocational guidance
18. How to prepare for college
19. Movies (TV) in the classroom
20. High school heroes
21. Does the honor system work?
22. Improving my study habits
23. How much homework?
24. Cafeteria manners
25. The lateness habit
26. One year to go
27. School clothes
28. Fruitful assignments — and wasteful ones
29. Are extracurricular activities taking too much of our time?
30. Planning a field trip

## Sports

1. How to keep physically fit
2. Should professional boxing be outlawed?
3. Why —— is my favorite sport
4. The Olympics
5. Our winter sports boom
6. Soccer or football?
7. Skin diving
8. Camping out
9. Record-breaking performances
10. The good referee
11. When sportsmanship counts
12. How to watch football or any other sport
13. The cheerleader's job
14. Is football a dangerous sport?
15. Coaches' nightmares
16. Team sports vs. individual sports
17. Teamwork in basketball
18. On not making the team
19. My favorite sports figure
20. Why practice?
21. Swimming safely
22. What the varsity stands for
23. A well-equipped gym
24. Great sports stories
25. "Rolling with the punches"

## Social Life

1. Popular dances
2. Planning a party
3. Handling the "life of the party"
4. Social maturity and immaturity
5. The social life of adults
6. An ideal recreation center
7. Is "going steady" wise or foolish?
8. *Do*'s and *Don't*'s in getting acquainted

9. The art of conversation

## People

1. My grandfather (or grand-mother)
2. Mr. (or Miss) Know-it-all
3. My favorite singer
4. Our doctor
5. My dentist
6. A person I'll never forget
7. My brother (or sister)
8. The politician
9. The teacher who has most influenced me
10. My closest friend
11. The typical high school student
12. A person I would like to meet

## Family Life

1. Allowances or wages?
2. Should teen-agers be treated as adults?
3. Sharing household chores
4. My family's favorite anec-dote
5. Family reunions
6. Two working parents
7. How to handle parents
8. Thanksgiving dinner
9. The breakfast rush
10. Moving day
11. Bringing up a baby
12. My family plans a vacation
13. An evening at home
14. Sunday morning
15. The elastic family budget

16. When parents disagree
17. Traffic in our living room
18. If I were running our household
19. Is "keeping up with the Joneses" worth the trouble?

## Personal Affairs

1. What is security?
2. Myself ten years from now
3. Economical shopping
4. The company you keep
5. Living on a budget
6. My debts (not financial)
7. On keeping a diary
8. A young person's hopes and fears
9. How to be popular
10. An adequate wardrobe
11. An ideal day
12. A childhood experience
13. Earning my own money
14. My biggest problem
15. If I could pick my own name
16. The dangers of self-pity
17. Where do I go from here?
18. Can I use my time more efficiently?
19. On appearance
20. On being bored
21. My first performance
22. When I was *glad* to be sick
23. A teen-ager views his (or her) elders
24. Finding and using my strong points
25. Why I would like to be a ——

26. "That doesn't interest me any more."
27. A fear I have conquered
28. "Puppy love"
29. My frenzied finances
30. The values I live by

### General

1. Profitable use of leisure
2. Adjusting to a new school (community)
3. TV commercials
4. Trading stamps
5. On getting away from it all
6. Ghosts I'd like to meet
7. Current humor
8. Buying a used car
9. The teen-age driver
10. On rainy days
11. Building your sales resistance
12. The latest slang
13. America as Hollywood sees it
14. Telephone manners
15. Exploring in a supermarket
16. Summer joys
17. The Age of the Atom
18. Some unusual careers
19. Advice to a younger brother or sister
20. Do gadgets rule our lives?
21. Superstitions and their effects
22. City vs. country living
23. On comic books
24. Our town, yesterday and today
25. Preventing highway accidents
26. If the people in advertisements were real
27. Adult and childish television
28. Do "good fences make good neighbors"?
29. A baby-sitter's handbook
30. Why join the Scouts?
31. "Success" can be empty.
32. The endless job of growing up

# Chapter 19

# Clear Thinking

Writing down your ideas for someone else to read is always an excellent test of the clarity of your thinking. Fuzzy thinking is much more noticeable in writing than in speech. When readers are confused or unconvinced by what you have written, they have the opportunity that listeners do not have to go back over your words and inspect carefully the logic of what you have said. For this reason, if you are to write well, you must constantly challenge the logic of your statements.

An important aid in testing the thinking behind your statements is an understanding of some of the common errors in logic, of which almost everyone has been guilty at one time or another. Errors in logic are called fallacies. Awareness of these fallacies will help you to think more clearly and write more convincingly. It will also help you to evaluate the thinking behind everything you hear and read. This ability is extremely important in the age of the powerful mass media — magazines, newspapers, books, radio, and television — constantly battering the individual.

## THE FALLACY OF OVERGENERALIZING

How often have you heard people state conclusions that they had reached on the basis of very little real evidence? For example, you invite a friend to go to a movie in which the leading role is played by Rock Salt. She reacts explosively.

"No, thanks. I wouldn't cross the street to see that fink!"

"Why?" you ask in surprise.

"Oh, because he always acts so conceited and thinks he's so smart and everything."

"How many of his pictures have you seen?"

"Well, I saw one of them, and that was one too many!"

The thinking fallacy your friend has committed is the fallacy of overgeneralizing. Having disliked Rock Salt in one movie, she generalizes that she will dislike him in all other movies. You could point out to her that judging an actor for all time on the basis of only one performance is unfair and unsound reasoning. "One swallow doesn't make a summer." Of course, there is no reason why a person should go to a Rock Salt movie if the desire to see it is lacking; but, in this instance, your friend should realize that her reasoning is hardly sound.

Judgments based on one instance, or too few instances, are examples of the fallacy of overgeneralizing. *The soundness of any generalization depends on the number of instances on which it is based.* The greater the number, the greater the likelihood that the generalization is sound.

The following statements are probably examples of overgeneralizing:

1. We no longer stop at Motor Gorge restaurants. Their food is poor, and their service is terrible. (Based on how many stops?)
2. Beaver Lake is not good for fishing. My friend went fishing there last year and didn't catch a thing. (How often? Why?)
3. My parents don't want me to go to Ajax University because, they say, the students there are not law-abiding. They read in the paper about a student who was arrested for disorderly conduct.

The use of such words as *all, always, never, none, everyone,* and *only* in a generalization is dangerous because it may result in overgeneralizing. When a family on tour has had unsatisfactory experiences at as few as three Motor Gorge restaurants, they would probably be justified in deciding not to stop at any more restaurants in the Motor

Gorge restaurant chain. Nevertheless, they should not declare on the basis of just three experiences that *all* of the sixty-five restaurants in the chain have poor food and terrible service. They may possibly come upon a Motor Gorge restaurant where the food is delicious and the service excellent. Not until they had tested all the restaurants would the generalization about *all* of them be true.

Usually we cannot wait to exhaust all possibilities before we fashion a generalization, and so we naturally generalize on less than total experience. If we have a large number of instances behind our generalization, we are probably wise to guide our behavior accordingly. Even the most dependable generalizations express only a probability, not an absolute certainty.

A common type of overgeneralizing is represented by the familiar expression "I know someone who. . . ." What the speaker is doing here very likely is basing a generalization on the experience, or the opinion, of one person. Frequently, if we know people well and trust their judgment, we are wise to pattern our actions on their opinions, but we must not commit the error of thinking that one person's experience is everyone's. The following are examples of the "I know someone who . . ." kind of overgeneralizing.

> The parks of this city are unsafe after dark. I know a man who was robbed while walking through Paine Park one night.

> Teachers are doing very well these days. My mother knows a teacher who drives a Cadillac and has bought a yacht.

Not only must the cases cited in support of a generalization be numerous enough to justify generalizing, but they must also be typical of their group. A teacher who drives a Cadillac and buys a new yacht is hardly typical of teachers in general.

## Generalization and the Scientific Hypothesis

Probably no one is more aware of the dangers of overgeneralizing than scientists, yet scientists in the course of their work must overgeneralize. When they begin to suspect that a certain generalization may be true, they put it down, but because they have not proved it, they call it a hypothesis. A hypothesis is really an overgeneralization; that is, it is based on too few observations to be dependable. Scientists regard it as only tentative until they have been able to test it a great many times. If, during long experimentation, they encounter no exceptions to a hypothesis, they then state it as a principle that can be relied on. The overgeneralization in the form of a hypothesis is an essential element in scientific work. Scientists do not accept a generalization as true until they have tested it, and they are always ready, in the face of facts that weaken the hypothesis, to admit that the hypothesis was wrong, that it was indeed an overgeneralization.

## Overgeneralizing and Prejudice

One kind of overgeneralization that does a vast amount of harm is the kind that fosters prejudice. Having encountered two or three Scots who displayed a quick temper, we must not let ourselves be prejudiced against *all* Scots on the grounds that the Scottish people are quick-tempered. Such a prejudice would obviously be an example of the fallacy of overgeneralizing. We must always recognize the difference between "*Some* Scots are quick-tempered" and "*All* Scots are quick-tempered." It is the overgeneralization that produces the unfair prejudice.

**EXERCISE 1.** Each of the following is either a generalization or a statement based on a generalization. Examine the items critically and state which ones you consider sound thinking and which ones examples of the fallacy of overgeneralizing.

1. This pencil will drop if I let go of it.
2. Don't wander from the path, for, if you do, you will get poison ivy.
3. If I take some aspirin, this headache will go away.

4. German shepherd dogs have mean dispositions.

5. I don't want to go to —— College because only dopes go there.

6. My grandmother says savings belong in a savings bank, not in stocks.

7. Nobody has much fun at school dances.

8. Cigarette smoking is hazardous to your health.

9. Avoid ——— Airlines. Their planes are always late.

10. Never trust the French. All they care about is your money.

## THE FALLACY IN SOME CAUSE-AND-EFFECT REASONING

You have a stomach ache. Naturally you think back over what you have eaten today to find something that may have caused your indigestion. You remember that the tuna fish salad sandwich you had for lunch in the cafeteria did not taste as good as usual. You conclude: "That sandwich was the cause of my stomach ache." Of course your conclusion could be sound, but to accept it at once as the cause would be poor thinking because a stomach ache could be the result of a number of other causes: overeating, fatigue, worry about a test, eating too fast, a virus. If several other students who ate tuna fish salad sandwiches also suffered stomach aches, you would have a good reason for your conclusion, but if the only reason you have for attributing your pain to the sandwich is that the eating of the sandwich preceded the pain, you would be committing the reasoning fallacy of assuming that because an event preceded a second event, it caused the second event. The Latin phrase used to name this fallacy is *Post hoc, ergo propter hoc,* meaning "After this, therefore because of this." This kind of reasoning is referred to as *post hoc* reasoning.

*Post hoc* reasoning is responsible for much poor thinking. A classic example was the belief in the eighteenth and nineteenth centuries that malaria was caused by night air. In fact, the word *malaria* means literally "bad air." The disease was given this name because of the observation that people who contracted the disease were people who had exposed themselves to the night air, which was considered unhealthful. People in malaria-infested regions, believing that night air was a cause of the disease, did not go out at night and kept their windows closed. Medical science, however, eventually traced the cause of malaria to the bite of a mosquito. The fact that mosquitoes attack most effectively in the dark — when you can't see them — led to the conclusion that it was the dark night air itself that caused the disease.

From the simple belief that a black cat's crossing your path was the cause of subsequent bad luck, to the track coach's conclusion that Nancy lost the race because she had broken training, *post hoc* reasoning is with us all the time.

Like overgeneralizing, attributing an effect to a cause simply because the "cause" came before the effect is a major concern of the scientific method. Just as true scientists do not generalize a principle from only one or two observations, so they do not attribute an effect to a cause until they have exhaustively investigated all other possible causes. One of the best-known examples of this in recent years is the research that has finally established cigarette smoking as an important cause of lung cancer. Although it was well known that lung cancer was much more common among cigarette smokers than among nonsmokers, scientists did not accept cigarette smoking as a cause until they had, through research, ruled out many other possible causes.

## THE FALLACY OF THE FALSE ANALOGY

A student who wants to get out of an honors course presents her case by comparing the student in an honors course with a person who is forced to eat and eat until becoming ill. "In an honors course," she says, "you are fed so much knowledge that it's like being forced to eat three full-course dinners every day. Pretty soon, you lose your appetite, and then you suffer severe indigestion. In an honors course, you have to absorb so much knowledge that you get tired of studying, sick of books, and pained by mental indigestion."

Arguing in this way by drawing a comparison is called arguing by analogy. It is a common form of argument but not a very good one. For instance, what is your opinion of this student's analogy? On the surface you may find some similarities between being overfed with food and overfed with knowledge. As you examine the analogy further, however, you will undoubtedly find more dissimilarities than similarities between the compared experiences. How similar, for example, are learning and eating? Does acquisition of knowledge, like eating, destroy the appetite for more knowledge or increase it? Is the mind, like the stomach, limited in its capacity? What, after all, is mental indigestion?

Many analogies, like this one, grow weaker the more carefully you examine them. The analogy which does not stand up under inspection is a false analogy.

Still the analogy is often useful in clarifying a point of view, even though it never proves anything. It is convincing only when the similarities between the things being compared greatly outnumber the differences. An analogy says, in effect, that if two things are alike in a number of ways, they will be alike in the way being discussed. An analogy is an attempt to explain one situation in terms of another. As Stuart Chase says, "The fallacy comes in when we use an analogy instead of proof, read more into it than the facts warrant, and note only similarities while ignoring differences."[1]

**EXERCISE 2.** Evaluate the analogy in the following passage. What two things are compared? Although readers today may find the language to be sexist, does the analogy help to clarify the point the author is making?

[1] *Guides to Straight Thinking* by Stuart Chase. Copyright © 1956 by Stuart Chase. Reprinted by permission of Harper & Row, Publishers, Inc., and A. Watkins, Inc.

In the old whaling days a man did not get to be master of the ship unless he was by all odds the best sailor aboard. When the going was rough, the crew expected to see him standing on deck in the storm, handling the ship himself. He knew every star in the heavens, and when the gale struck he did not need to ask from which direction the wind was blowing. He felt it directly in his face.

The counterpart of this is not true in American industry today, and this may be what is wrong with it. The men at the top of our great corporations, those who direct the vast enterprises that mean so much both to our economy and to our social welfare, so live their lives that they no longer take the wind directly in their faces.

Responsibility breeds isolation. As a man's authority increases, so do the barriers that cut him off from direct contact with the world about him. This may not be his nature, nor his wish, but the manner of life he feels compelled to follow causes him steadily to withdraw into the shelter of his own intimate circle. After he reaches the very top, he is seldom seen in public, and seldom heard. He becomes a myth. An aura of mystery surrounds him which is unwholesome both for the man and for his company. The consequence is that when the great storm comes, as it does sooner or later to every large corporation, and he is driven out into the turbulence of public opinion, he may not be ready to go on deck. He may still be the best sailor on the ship, but something vital, something essential to leadership, has gone out of his life.[1]

**EXERCISE 3.** Evaluate each of the following analogies. How effective do you think each is? Compare the similarities that support and the differences that weaken the analogies.

1

A parent explains the necessity for strict discipline: A household is like a ship. The parent is captain; the children are crew. There can be only one captain, and a captain's orders must be carried out by the crew; divided authority and crew failure al-

[1] From "Business, Too, Has Its Ivory Towers" by Clarence Randall, from the *New York Times Magazine.* July 8, 1962, © 1962 by The New York Times Company. Reprinted by permission of the publisher.

ways imperil a ship. Hence strict discipline is as essential in a family as it is on a ship.

### 2

Ms. Fong calls the mechanic who keeps her car in condition "doctor." She explains that the mechanic makes a sick car healthy just as a medical doctor makes a sick person well. She says furthermore that, since her medical doctor sets bones and performs surgery, she is just as much a mechanic as is her "car doctor."

### 3

My guidance counselor said I should think of my college career in the same way that I think of my future career in business. He pointed out that success depends on rising above the competition; that the rewards are in the form of grades rather than money; that my goal should be to turn out a better product—myself—so that future buyers—corporations—will want to hire, or buy, me.

### 4

Society should treat the scientists who developed the atom bomb in the same way that it treats a person who supplies guns to criminals.

**EXERCISE 4.** Number on your paper from 1 to 7. Evaluate the reasoning in each of the following examples. If you consider the reasoning fallacious, write after the proper number the name of the fallacy: overgeneralizing, *post hoc,* or false analogy. If you think the reasoning is sound, write O.K. after the proper number. Be prepared to explain your answers. (Note: *Post hoc* is one kind of overgeneralization. Nevertheless, if you find an example of it, write *post hoc,* not "overgeneralization.")

1. Don't invite the Smith twins. They live on Blane Street, where those awful Jones boys come from.
2. Students are not paid to attend this university; they pay to come here to ready themselves for a useful future. In effect, they employ the university to educate them. Just as the administration gives orders to the faculty it employs, so the students should have a voice in how the university conducts their education.

3. The plane that crashed at London Airport last night had just been completely overhauled. Obviously some mechanic had not done the job properly.

4. Water freezes at 0° C.

5. Jerry, who was arrested by the police for breaking into a supermarket, admitted under questioning that his favorite TV programs are crime movies.

6. I will not vote for a Democrat for President because I do not want our country to go to war. The country went to war under Franklin Roosevelt, Truman, and Johnson—all Democrats.

7. Try to get Ms. Rivera for English. She gave my sister an *A*.

# THE FALLACY OF ATTACKING THE MAN INSTEAD OF THE ISSUES

Two closely related kinds of poor reasoning, more common in heated oral arguments than in writing, are those which attack the person presenting a point of view rather than the point of view itself. Of course, before we accept a person's views, we are justified in considering the person as well as the person's views. Is the person competent? Does the person's experience give weight to what is being said? Are there any selfish motives behind the opinions? When we attack people for actions and personal qualities that have no bearing on the opinions they hold, we are guilty of fallacious reasoning.

Senator A asks Senator B for an opinion of Senator C's proposal for lower tariffs. Senator B's reply is, "I hear he's been campaigning too much lately and staying away from the office."

Obviously, Senator B has completely ignored the issue. He has attacked Senator C, not the proposal. We should always remember that if an argument is sound, it is sound regardless of who presents it. (A Latin expression used to name this kind of thinking is *ad hominem*—to the man. Instead of responding to the issue we respond "to the man.")

A related kind of personal "argument" is that which is best expressed as "you're another." We are guilty of "you're another" arguing when, being criticized, instead of discussing the criticisms leveled at us, we in turn criticize our opponent for the same weaknesses.

Sally spends a large part of the money she has made baby-sitting recently on a new bathing suit that she does not really need. When her parents scold her for wasting her money, Sally replies, "Well, you didn't *need* that new car you bought last week either."

"You're another" arguing is natural but childish. It is characterized by the common phrases, "Put your own house in order," and "People in glass houses shouldn't throw stones." When people from other countries criticize Americans for their treatment of poor people, a common "defense" is "What about the treatment accorded poor people in your own country?" While this reaction may be natural, it is not really a defense of American practices at all. It is a clear example of serious and dangerous "you're another" reasoning. Like attacking the person rather than the issue, it accomplishes nothing.

## THE FALLACY OF RATIONALIZING

Rationalizing is giving plausible but untrue reasons for our behavior. *Ad hominem* and "you're another" thinking are forms of rationalizing because they are means of avoiding the issue. The girl who justified buying a bathing suit she did not need is not only arguing by "you're another" reasoning, but she is also rationalizing her purchase by giving a false reason for it. The real reason for her buying the suit was that she thought she would look attractive in it and it gave her pleasure to buy it.

When actually pinned down, most of us admit our rationalizing. The danger point comes when we rationalize unconsciously and believe our own rationalized reasons or motives. Persons who neglect family and business to play golf several times a week may rationalize such behavior by saying that golf is necessary to preserve their health. One of them might say, "What good would I be to anyone if I were sick all the time? The exercise golf provides is what keeps me well." The truth is that they would rather play golf than work and are simply indulging themselves at the expense of their families.

## THE FALLACY OF "EITHER–OR"

We all have a natural tendency to think in terms of alternatives: right and wrong; good and bad; yes and no; black and white. Thinking of a problem or a solution as having only two sides is either–or thinking, and it is responsible for much poor reasoning. Just as we often ignore exceptions when we generalize, we frequently ignore the in-between positions — the many other choices — when we think in terms of alternatives. Either–or thinkers who sincerely believe that their opinions are right may reason that all other opinions must therefore be wrong. If they cling stubbornly to this either–or thinking, they will not be willing to negotiate or to compromise, but it is through negotiation and compromise that human beings and institutions manage to live peacefully together. Except in an imaginary world, people are not all good or all bad. In life, people are partly good and partly bad. Pure black and pure white are imaginary concepts. What we actually have to deal with are the various shades of gray in between.

Senator M is a very outspoken, hard-working anti-conservationist. Senator J disagrees with Senator M on many issues. Following the either–or kind of thinking, Senator M says, "J is refusing me her support on this tax bill. If she's not for me, she must be against me. J is surely a conservationist and wants to help the conservationists."

We can, through another simple example, see how unfortunate this kind of reasoning can be. A friend has a business that fails. I say to myself that business failure is due *either* to stupidity *or* to laziness. I know that my friend is not stupid. I must conclude, therefore, that my friend is lazy. Having set up the either–or premise, I have allowed only two possibilities. Anyone, of course, can give other possible reasons for a business failure.

# THE FALLACY OF CIRCULAR THINKING— BEGGING THE QUESTION

Circular thinking occurs when people *appear* to be presenting arguments in favor of a point, but, in reality, present no arguments at all. What they say, in effect, is that a statement is true because it is true. For example, a friend declares that Mrs. Wise's history test was unfair. You ask her what she means by an unfair test, and she replies that she means the kind of test Mrs. Wise gave. Here nothing has been explained; no evidence has been offered. The discussion has simply gone in a circle.

A patent medicine salesman tries to sell his product by claiming that it is effective because it contains a number of effective ingredients. "How do you know," asks a skeptic, "that these ingredients are effective?" "Because," says the salesman, "they are in this drug." A similar example of circular thinking is the reasoning of the woman who quotes a book on Asian politics because, she says, the author is an authority. Then, when asked why she thinks the author is an authority on Asian politics, she replies, "She wrote a book on it, didn't she?"

A common kind of circular thinking is called "begging the question." Used in this sense, the word *beg* means "to assume that something is established or proved." The trouble arises when someone expects you to accept as proved the idea that needs to be proved. For example, the subject for a debate may be so worded that what has to be proved is simply assumed to be true.

Suppose that you are confronted with the following statement as a question for argument: The poor school spirit of our student body is disgraceful. The point that must be established in the argument is that the school spirit actually is poor, but when the framers of the question slip "poor" into it, they assume as true what, in fact, they are supposed to prove. They beg the question and, in so doing, take for granted that everyone will agree with them that the school spirit is poor. The statement should be "The school spirit of our student body is disgraceful."

**EXERCISE 5.** Each of the following is an example of one of the reasoning fallacies described on the preceding pages. On your paper write after the proper number the fallacy the example illustrates. In some cases more than one may apply. Be prepared to explain your answers.

FALLACIES

overgeneralizing
false cause and effect—*post hoc*
false analogy
attacking the man—*ad hominem*

rationalizing
either–or thinking
circular thinking—begging
   the question

1. When my parents talk to me about how important it is that I take piano lessons, I remind them that they did not take piano lessons.

2. You can't beat a team that has the referee on its side.

3. I wondered what had gone wrong with our TV until I remembered that I had seen Jo fiddling with it earlier.

4. This grossly unfair tax should be repealed.

5. The police in this town are carrying their efforts to the extreme. One driver got three traffic tickets in one week.

6. Because freedom to express one's opinions is a basic human right, freedom of speech should not be denied to anyone.

7. "Theology teaches that the sun has been created in order to illuminate the earth. But one moves the torch to illuminate the house, and not the house in order to be illuminated by the torch. Hence it is the sun which revolves around the earth, and not the earth which revolves around the sun." Besian Array, 1671.

8. Either Joyce earned the money she's been spending lately or she inherited it. I know she hasn't had a job for months, so she must have inherited it.

9. The kids that go to Mitchell Academy are all snobs. Look at the Perez twins!

10. The price level takes care of itself. Price controls, subsidies, and other interferences are just monkey wrenches in the economic machine. The machine will work if you let it alone.

**EXERCISE 6.** Read the editorials and letters to the editor in several issues of a daily newspaper. Bring to class any examples you find of fallacies in reasoning.

# Chapter 20

# Exercises
# in Writing Prose

## The Essay, the Book Review,
## the Précis

This chapter contains a number of assignments which will give you practice in planning and writing four different kinds of compositions: the informal personal essay, the serious essay of opinion, the book review, and the précis, or brief summary of an article. In writing essays, you will draw upon your own experiences and ideas. In writing précis and book reviews, you will be working with the writing of others. During the year you will probably be expected to write several compositions of each kind.

## THE ESSAY

Our daily conversation is, in general, concerned with two things—events and opinions. We are usually engaged in telling what happened or in telling what we think about a subject—giving an opinion. In composition, when we tell what happened, we are writing a story. When we express our opinion, we are writing an essay. Editorials, letters to the editor, and the writings of columnists are examples of essays. To be sure, they are based on events, but their purpose is to express attitudes of the writer about the events.

In other words, an essay is a composition that analyzes or interprets a particular subject. Its style may be chatty and entertaining or it may be very formal; its viewpoint may be limited or broad; its aim may be to amuse readers or to convince or to inform them.

## The Informal (Personal) Essay

This kind of essay may be written on any subject, provided the writer's attitude is informal and personal. Being personal, the essay reveals its author's personality and draws heavily upon the author's own experiences. Usually a large part of a personal essay is narrative — using incidents and anecdotes to maintain interest and to support the writer's opinions.

The unforgivable sin in an informal essay is dullness. To sustain interest, the writer begins with an idea that is fresh and unusual, then develops it in a stimulating, perhaps even a surprising fashion. The development may appear to be unsystematic, but this apparent lack of careful planning is usually deceiving. The essay sticks to its central idea in spite of frequent digressions, and overall it follows a distinct plan. A writer who merely rambles is likely to be irritating, not interesting.

As you read J. B. Priestley's essay on "Cooking Picnics," note the following:

1. The abrupt, interest-arousing opening statement of a strong opinion.
2. The frequent citing of specific examples explaining the opinion: salads, sandwiches, jam, sour apples.
3. The description of a typical "cooking picnic." This could have been effectively handled by telling a story about one particular picnic, but Priestley chose to characterize the "typical" directly.
4. The breezy tone and the tendency to exaggerate.
5. The final statement summarizing his opinion.

## COOKING PICNICS

Like most people, I detest picnics. One reason is that I am

usually very hungry out in the open and I dislike the kind of food provided by picnics. Thus, there are few things to eat better than a properly dressed salad in a fine salad bowl, but there are few things less appetizing than an undressed salad out of a paper bag or cardboard box. Then, except for thick slices of ham between thin slices of bread, I have a growing distaste for the whole sandwich family, especially paste, egg, or cheese sandwiches. Again, anything with jam in it or on it is a curse on a summer's day. Finally, there is a peculiarly hard, green, sour little apple that must be grown specially for picnic boxes.

Nevertheless, I have delighted in my time — and am not yet past it — in one kind of picnic, namely, the cooking picnic. This is for great souls. The instrumental basis of it is the frying pan. Sausages will do, though steak of course is better. Fried potatoes are essential, and persons whose stomachs shrink from a greasy chip rather underdone should stay at home and nibble health foods. Coffee, which stands up to wood smoke better than tea, is the beverage.

The cooking picnic is, I will admit, a smoky job, at least in this damp climate of ours. I have superintended cooking picnics — with inflamed and streaming eyes and every sinus wrecked, spluttering and coughing and choking, glaring at would-be helpful children until they ran away and howled. I have stoked and fried and stewed and dished out portions until there was nothing left for me but a few bits of greasy muck and a half cup of coffee grounds. And even my pipe has tasted all wrong in the inferno of wood smoke. Yet I would not have missed a moment of it for a five-pound lunch in a private room on somebody else's expense sheet. Somewhere among the damp obstinate sticks, the dwindling sausages, the vanishing fat, the potatoes that would not brown and the water that would not boil, the billowing smoke on the hillside, the monstrous appetites of the company, there has been delight like a crumb of gold.[1]

**EXERCISE 1.** Write an informal essay of 300–500 words on any of the topics listed below. Your essay need not be a humorous one, like J. B. Priestley's, though you may, if you

---

[1] "Cooking Picnics" from *Delight* by J. B. Priestley. Copyright 1949 by J. B. Priestley. Reprinted by permission of Harold Matson Company, Inc. and A. D. Peters & Co.

wish, use that essay as a guide in tone and style. If none of the topics below appeal to you, take your subject from the longer list on pages 307–12.

| | |
|---|---|
| 1. On greeting cards | 6. Getting up in the morning |
| 2. Daydreams | 7. On the road |
| 3. The interview | 8. On opera lovers |
| 4. Books for a rainy day | 9. Movies I could do without |
| 5. On cafeteria manners | 10. My best time-wasters |

## The Essay of Opinion

An essay of opinion aims to *convince* or *persuade* its reader. By a logical arrangement of facts and considerations, using the tone and style of formal discussion, the essayist seeks to prove the validity of one point of view and to show the weakness of opposing positions. Thus, we are dealing here with a formal essay, based upon formal literary devices of argument and exposition.

Like the informal personal essay, the essay of opinion may already be more familiar to you than you realize. Whenever you pick up the editorial page of a newspaper, read through a "Letters to the Editor" column, or listen to a political speech on a specific issue, you are in a position to judge a writer's attempt to persuade readers or listeners. You yourself may have engaged in a formal debate or prepared compositions giving your evaluations of a set of facts.

### Choosing an Arguable Subject

Conclusions and opinions alone, however, do not make an essay of opinion. The basic subject matter is equally important. It may seem unnecessary to point out that a debate, whether written or spoken, should be on a "debatable" subject, yet young writers often forget this obvious fact. Never write an essay of opinion without choosing and limiting a truly controversial subject—that is, a subject which has more than one clear side, which is still unsettled, and which can be covered adequately with the facts available. Remember that a statement or proposition which cannot be proved or disproved is a subject for speculation, not debate. Similarly, a question so general or complex that it cannot be fully explored is not a suitable subject for a short essay of opinion.

## Gathering Your Material

Once you have chosen a debatable subject you are ready to assemble the evidence that will support your opinion. However reasonable your view of things may be, you cannot expect people to adopt it unless you give them good reasons for doing so. In general, you will want to look for two kinds of evidence in support of your opinion:

1. *Factual evidence.* Nothing provides a sounder basis for argument than facts. If you can give a number of definite, provable facts to back up your argument, it should be quite easy for you to make a persuasive statement of your opinion. You must be sure, however, to choose facts that can be verified and that are relevant to the issue under discussion.

2. *Testimony of authorities.* Next to facts, the opinions of authorities on a subject make the most convincing evidence. Law courts accept the testimony of such expert witnesses as doctors, handwriting specialists, and fingerprint experts, and your readers will likewise be impressed with sound, professional opinion. Before you can cite authorities, however, be certain that they are competent and unbiased as far as the particular question is concerned. A minister may be an authority on matters of religion but not on the advisability of putting seatbelts in automobiles; a scientist in the employ of a cigarette company may not be in a position to make disinterested statements about the dangers of smoking.

## Organizing Your Material

Always important in writing, organization assumes special importance in the essay of opinion where you are attempting to persuade your reader through ordered arguments.

Be sure that your introduction enlists the reader's interest, states the proposition and issues fairly, and indicates clearly where you stand on the question. In addition, the introduction may define key terms and take up briefly the history and significance of the question.

In ordering the main part of the essay — your direct arguments — it is usually wise to begin and end with your strongest arguments. Be sure that your arguments are fully and logically developed, supported by sufficient evidence and authoritative testimony.

Should you bother in this essay to anticipate and refute the opposing arguments? The answer to this question depends on a great many things. To begin with, in a very short essay you probably are better off spending all your time developing your own arguments. In a longer essay the decision will be based on how you assess the following factors: how widely known are the opposing arguments (Would failure to deal with them be construed as weakness on your part? Would dealing with them only make others more aware of them?); how effectively can you refute the opposing arguments (a strong refutation helps your positive arguments; a weak refutation will not).

If you decide to include refutation or rebuttal in your essay, you have three ways of placing it: you may deal with each refuted issue as you raise a positive argument; you may place the refutation before your direct arguments; or you may place it after the direct arguments.

In a short essay, conclude with your most effective point; in a longer essay, conclude with a brief summary of your main arguments or with suggestions as to a future course of action.

## Style and Tone

As you write your essay, be conscious of word choice and style. Strive to achieve a style characterized by:

1. *Clarity.* Be sure that all difficult terms have been defined and that there are no ambiguous statements.

2. *Persuasiveness.* Your chief object is to convince and persuade the reader. Think of the composition as an attempt to sell an idea.

3. *Honesty.* Do not sacrifice honesty for the sake of winning a point. Don't hold back evidence or "load the deck." Avoid name-calling. Deal with issues, not personalities.

## LET'S KEEP VARSITY FOOTBALL

1   We hear these days mounting cries that public high schools should cease playing interscholastic varsity football. True, the protests are nothing new; they have been with us since the extremists of progressive education maintained that football was harmful to the character. Now the arguments come from those who would make our school academically tougher by eliminating all extracurricular activities. But whether coming from the followers of John Dewey, liberal, or Admiral Rickover, conservative, the arguments fail to convince anyone who examines the issues objectively.

2   The drawbacks of varsity football are merely abuses of excess and can be eliminated by sensible control; the advantages of varsity football are significant and can be offered by no other curricular or extracurricular activity.

3   The drawbacks, of course, are real and must not be ignored. Players do get injured — and injured seriously. Fans do get riotous and cause damage. Coaches do get obsessed with winning and sometimes lose sight of larger objectives. All these, however, are not arguments *against* varsity football, merely arguments *for* sensible control and moderation on the part of all — students, coaches, players, and adult rooters.

4   With sensible controls imposed on participants, coaches, and spectators, the advantages of the sport to both the players and the school at large would become even more obvious.

5   The players themselves benefit in many ways. Supreme Court Justice Byron "Whizzer" White has said on many occasions that the competitive spirit he developed in playing football stood him in good stead both on the battlefield and in his profession. A study conducted last year by our own principal indicated that the grades of football players were higher during the season than they were during any other period. Var-

sity players to whom I have talked tell me that the rigorous physical demands of both practice and games keep them in top condition. And last year three of our varsity players who would otherwise not have been able to afford college were able to attend outstanding institutions by virtue of athletic scholarships and grants.

6    I do not suggest, of course, that the fact that thirty varsity players benefit in these ways is in itself sufficient justification for continuing varsity football. More importantly, this activity should be continued because the entire school benefits.

7    First, the school benefits financially. A study published recently indicated that in 85% of the high schools throughout the nation, the proceeds from varsity football were used to subsidize so-called "minor" sports with less spectator interest but with just as much appeal to the participant. Our school board cannot see its way clear to support the wrestling team, the rifle squad, the girls' hockey team. Since these sports cannot attract sufficient fee-paying spectators to support themselves, they must rely on football receipts.

8    There is, however, a more significant advantage that varsity football brings to the school—it serves to crystallize, marshal, and increase school spirit. I don't mean just the crazed excitement of screaming students at pep rallies or the fanatic loyalty of adults at the game. I mean the spirit of cohesiveness and oneness that come about only when we can identify with "our team," playing its heart out on the football field for a school that means a lot to them. Such a spirit does not depend on a winning team; it develops with any varsity football team that does its best in the name of the school. And such a spirit can never be developed by any such spurious substitutes as assemblies, homeroom competitions, or even intramural sports.

9    We cannot close our eyes to the excesses of varsity football. It would, however, be even more dangerous to listen to those who would destroy it.

## Questions for analysis:

1. What is the proposition? What are the issues? Where are they stated?

2. What is the purpose of the first paragraph? What does the last sentence of that paragraph try to accomplish? Would the com-

position be just as effective if it went from the first sentence of paragraph 1 to the first sentence of paragraph 2?

3. What is the purpose of paragraph 3? Do you feel this paragraph is sufficiently developed? Would the composition be more effective with this paragraph omitted?

4. What is the function of paragraph 4? What is the effect if it is omitted?

5. Where do the direct arguments in support of varsity football begin? Would it be a better composition if it were limited to the direct arguments, or if the refutation came at the end?

6. Paragraphs 7 and 8 both relate to the second major advantage of varsity sports. Why are two paragraphs used here, when one sufficed for the first major advantage?

7. The essential test of this essay of opinion, of course, is, *does it persuade you and convince you?* If it has convinced you, how has it managed to do so? If it failed, why did it fail?

**EXERCISE 2.** Choose one of the topics given below and write an essay of opinion (300–500 words) in the form suggested.

1. Select a controversial school issue that interests you. Find out all you can about it by talking with teachers, administrators, and other students. Take a stand on the issue and write your essay of opinion as a letter to the editor of your school paper. Some possibilities to investigate: cafeteria regulations, honor system, library procedures, new courses that should be added, homework policies, school publication censorship, powers of student government, appropriate dress, the marking system.

2. Investigate a controversial community issue. Review all published research, talk to influential citizens, consult with local officials. Write an essay of opinion in the form of a letter to the editor of your local paper, in which you state your position. Some possibilities: teen-age curfew, zoning laws, parks and playgrounds, local taxes, pollution, school budget.

3. Investigate the background and qualifications of the candidates for a local, state, or national election; choose the one who you think best deserves your vote. Write a campaign article in which you try to convince your audience why they should vote for your candidate.

# THE BOOK REVIEW

The book review is an important type of essay. You will read many reviews in school and college, and you have probably written and will continue to write many of them as school assignments. Despite its familiarity, many students find it a difficult assignment; the suggestions below should help you do a better job with it. These suggestions relate specifically to the review of a work of fiction since this is the type most commonly assigned; you will probably find, however, that they will be of general help with any review.

## Before You Read

Your first job—and one of the most important—must be done even before you start to read: you have to decide on the standards you will use in judging the book. What makes a good historical novel? What are the criteria or standards to be used in judging science fiction? To a certain extent the criteria will vary with the specific kind of novel, but there are some general suggestions which apply to most works of fiction.

   **1.** *Plot.* Since the essence of fiction is story or plot, you should have many questions to ask about the plot.

a. Do the events of the story seem to grow out of the nature of the characters? Is there sufficient conflict to arouse your interest? Do the events of the story move along swiftly enough to sustain your interest?

b. Are the incidents of the story believable within the context and framework of the novel?

c. Is there any kind of pattern or structure to the events of the plot that may have some larger significance? (Better writers, for example, will often use plot incidents to contrast with or to reinforce each other.)

d. And what of the ending? Does the ending seem to grow naturally out of the rest of the book, or does it seem too contrived? Does it leave you with a sense of satisfaction, or do you feel cheated in some way?

**2.** *Characters.* The most important criterion here is development that is complete and satisfactory.

a. Do you feel that you really know the main characters and understand them fully, or do they seem merely to have been sketched in with broad strokes? Are the characters convincing in the way they behave, in the faults and virtues they display?

b. Are the principal characters people with whom you can sympathize and identify so that you really feel gripped by their problems and their conflicts? Do the characters change and develop in any way, and are the reasons for change clear and convincing?

c. Is the dialogue realistic and true to life? Does the dialogue accurately reflect character? Is this the way you would expect a character of this type to speak?

**3.** *Setting.* The importance of the setting will vary from book to book, but it is an element that you should judge.

a. Is the setting real or imaginary? If real, how accurately is it depicted?

b. How important is the setting? What effect does it have on plot or characters?

**4.** *Style.* You may feel that you are too inexperienced to criticize an author's style, but your taste and sensitivity can be developed by applying the following questions to any book.

a. Are words used effectively and precisely? Do sentences read smoothly, with the meaning always clear?

b. Is there original use of figurative language, especially in descriptive portions?

c. Do you feel that in any way the writing itself is memorable?

**5.** *Theme.* Not every book has a message or moral lesson added to its basic story, but almost every serious work of fiction has levels of meaning that run beneath the surface.

a. Is there a recurring theme or pattern to the book? Is it concerned with a significant aspect of life? Does it try to help us understand something about ourselves, or our purpose in life?

b. If there is such a theme, how clearly is it shown throughout the book? To what extent can we accept the answers the author has given us? What is the author's view of life and people?

## As You Read

As you read, keep in mind the following points:

1. Try to determine the author's intent or purpose in writing the book. The book can be judged fairly only on the basis of author's purpose. For example, we should not criticize science fiction because it deals with improbable events. Sometimes you will find the writer's purpose clearly stated in a preface or foreword, but most often you will have to discover the author's intent by careful reading. Is the chief purpose to amuse, to re-create a period of our history, to help us understand a social problem, to excite us with a story of adventure?

2. Form tentative evaluations as you read. This doesn't mean that you should judge a book on the basis of the first chapter; it merely means that you carry your critical awareness all through the book, reaching a final conclusion only when you have finished.

3. Note evidence as you read. Develop the habit of making notes to yourself as you read. Jot down the specific evidence that will support your judgments—important scenes, key passages. If you own the book you are reading, you may wish to underline or make notes in the margins; if it is a borrowed book, make your notes on 3 × 5-inch cards.

## Writing the Review

Before you begin writing, ask yourself the following questions:

1. Who will read the review—and for what purpose? The answers to these questions will greatly influence the content of your review. If you are writing to interest a friend in reading the book, you will want to reveal just enough of the content to arouse interest, and your critical

comments will tend to be brief. If you are writing it as an assignment, to indicate that you have appreciated and understood the book, you will probably want to include more factual detail about the plot and characters and include more criticism and interpretation.

2. How should the review begin? Two essential kinds of information should appear near the beginning of the review. First, it is essential that the book be completely identified by title, author, and type of book. (Sometimes the publishing information can be given in parentheses after the title.) Second, you should make some general statement evaluating the book as a whole. You may then tell about the author or other books the author has written; you may give some background information about the writing of the novel or the times or events with which it deals. You may even point out how other writers have handled similar ideas.

3. How much of the plot should be told? Again, the answer to this question depends on your audience and your purpose. Many students do too much reporting of content, sometimes devoting almost the entire review to retelling the plot. On the other hand, you have an obligation to readers to tell them what the book is about, but such summarizing should not account for more than one third of the whole review. A point to watch for: in summarizing the plot, you may use either the past or present tense of the verb — but be consistent.

4. What should be criticized and in how much detail? Unless you are writing a very long review, you cannot deal successfully with all the questions and all the aspects discussed in the section above on critical standards. It makes more sense to deal only with those aspects of the novel that are remarkable either for their strengths or weaknesses. If, for example, the author has done a very routine job of handling characterization, you may wish merely to make a comment such as: "The characterization is neither much better nor much worse than that found in most science fiction stories."

5. How can the reader be convinced of the soundness of

the judgment? Support every major judgment or criticism you make of the novel with specific reference to the book itself. This is where your notes should prove to be useful. If, for example, you feel a character has acted inconsistently, cite scenes where behavior seems at odds with previous actions; if you feel dialogue has been handled poorly, quote portions of it that will prove your point.

6. How can the readers be helped to understand the meaning of the novel? The best review is more than a summary and an evaluation; it goes beyond these first two objectives and tries to arrive at an interpretation of the meaning and significance of the book. There will be times when you will be unsure about an underlying theme or meaning. While you can legitimately admit such uncertainty, you still have an obligation to your readers to help them see what the author was trying to say.

7. How should the review conclude? On the basis of your interpretation and evaluation, conclude by coming to a balanced judgment about how and where the work succeeds and fails — for in most cases it will do both. Finally, you may wish to make a general recommendation to readers about whether the book will be worth their time.

When you have finished writing your first draft, read your paper carefully to see that you have made none of the mistakes commonly made by beginning reviewers. Do not devote too much space to summary of content. Review the whole book, not parts of it. Avoid digressions; be sure to stick to the work at hand. Beware of sweeping generalizations going beyond the limits of your own experience. You cannot really say, "This is Muriel Spark's best novel," for example, unless you have read all her novels. Finally, do not make too many unfounded and unsupported evaluations like, "It was a wonderful book."

**EXERCISE 3.** List the standards you would use in judging the types of novels indicated below. Do not repeat any of the general criteria given above, but indicate only how they would have to be modified or extended.

1. The historical novel
2. The biographical novel
3. The science fiction novel
4. The detective story
5. The novel of fantasy
6. The sports story
7. The "career" novel
8. The adventure novel
9. The romantic novel
10. The political novel

**EXERCISE 4.** Using the general and specific standards developed in Exercise 3, write a 350–500-word review of a novel that you have recently read.

**EXERCISE 5.** As an alternative to Exercise 4, you may wish to try one of the following assignments instead of writing a regular review.

1. Design an original book jacket for a book you enjoyed, including a favorable summary of the contents similar to those on many commercial jackets.
2. Write a letter to a friend in which you try to persuade him or her to read the book.
3. Write a letter to the author of the book stating how you liked the book.
4. Dramatize one of the important scenes in the book.

## THE PRÉCIS

The need for making accurate and concise summaries is a constant one in daily life. Newscasters on radio and television make such summaries daily. Law students summarize hundreds of cases in the course of their legal studies. Reporters must learn how to get the gist of the news and present it to their readers in the most effective manner. Scholars share the knowledge gained from wide reading by making abstracts of what they have read.

In your studies, you will be practicing the art of extracting and expressing in your own words the principal ideas from what you read. This skill can be one of the most valuable you will ever learn.

A brief summary of the main points of an article is called a *précis*. In such a composition, which should be not more than one third as long as the original, you express the central idea of the original writer in clear, concise language of your own. All illustrations, amplifications, or embellishments are omitted from the précis, which includes only bare essentials.

There are a few simple rules for making a précis:

1. Read the original paragraph or selection through attentively, to learn the general idea. Do not take notes.

2. Read it a second time, this time looking up all unfamiliar words, phrases, or allusions. You now judge the selection more carefully, noting what appear to be important ideas and what are details.

3. List in your own words what you judge to be the essential point or points made by the author.

4. In your own words, write the first draft of the précis. Omit examples, illustrations, conversations, or repetitions.

5. Read your first draft and compare it with the original for accuracy and emphasis.

6. Eliminate all unnecessary words and change words until you have expressed concisely and clearly the main point of the selection. The précis should be no more than one third the length of the original.

With sufficient practice you will be able to skip certain steps, until you acquire the facility of making a précis in a few minutes. At first, you should revise repeatedly until you have just the right words and order.

Study the following example of précis writing.

What are the real aims of study? The object of study is, in the first place, to get fast and firm possession of facts—facts of spelling, reading, mathematics, composition, history, language, geography, and the like. It is highly desirable that we should know how to spell *Chicago* and *business; Boston* and *brains;* and that we should know for all time. We want to know once for all that seven times nine is sixty-three; that Abraham Lincoln signed the Emancipation Proclamation; that an island is a body of land completely surrounded by water; and that a proper name should begin with a capital letter. Many, many minute facts, as well as certain connected bodies of truth, should be embedded in one's memory as deeply and securely as a bullet that has lodged in the heart of a growing tree. And one should master certain processes of thought, and grip a few great underlying and unchanging principles of life and conduct.[1]                     [160 words]

The first reading will tell you that the paragraph is about the aims of study. There are few if any words which you have to look up, and you undoubtedly know the Emancipation Proclamation. In your second, more careful, reading, you note that the following ideas are expressed, and you jot them down:

1. The first aim of study is to acquire facts (there are several examples given of such facts).
2. The second aim is to master processes of thought.
3. The third aim is to learn certain principles of conduct and of life.

You notice that while several illustrations of the first aim have been given by the author, none are given for the other two. In the précis you omit *all* illustrations and stick to the main ideas. The next step is to combine the three ideas you have jotted down into a single sentence, if possible.

> There are three aims of studying: to learn certain necessary facts in many areas; to learn how to think; and to learn the great rules about life and the conduct of it.          [32 words]

Examining your first draft, and rereading the original, you see that you have accurately expressed the writer's ideas, but that your statement of the first and third ideas can be made more concise. In length, your précis is much

---

[1] Frances C. Lockwood, *The Freshman and His College.*

shorter than one third of the original; this is because the original consists largely of examples which expand the first idea. Your final version might be:

> The aims of study are three: to acquire needed facts; to learn how to think; to learn the universal principles of life and conduct. [24 words]

**EXERCISE 6.** Write a précis for each of these passages.

1

An alert and curious man goes through the world taking note of all that passes under his eyes, and collects a great mass of information, which is in no sense incorporated into his own mind, but remains a definite territory outside his own nature, which he has annexed. A man of receptive mind and heart, on the other hand, meditating on what he sees, and getting at its meaning by the divining-rod of the imagination, discovers the law behind the phenomena, the truth behind the fact, the vital force which flows through all things, and gives them their significance. The first man gains information; the second gains culture. The pedant pours out an endless succession of facts with a monotonous uniformity of emphasis, and exhausts while he instructs; the man of culture gives us a few facts, luminous in their relation to one another, and freshens and stimulates by bringing us into contact with ideas and life.[1] [157 words]

2

The problem of finding a common system of weights and measures, like the problem of finding a common language, is only gradually being solved. Its solution is the gradual adoption throughout the world of the metric system. This was the brainchild of an obscure seventeenth-century vicar of Lyons, Gabriel Mouton. Originally proposed in 1670, its attractive simplicity and logic led to the founding of the International Bureau of Weights and Measures in 1875, and it is now either permitted or obligatory in almost every nation on earth. It is an orderly decimal system, based now upon the wavelength of light and the volume of water, both under specified conditions. The meter is 39.37 inches, the kilogram is 2.2046 pounds, and the liter is 1.0567

[1] Hamilton Wright Mabie, *Books and Culture.*

quarts. Although the standards and the terminology of the old British Imperial and American Customary systems are delightfully ancient, they are devilish for practical purposes when compared with those of the metric system. The multiples and subdivisions of the metric system are named in accordance with similar prefixes, which makes them easier both to grasp and to manipulate. Thus, a *deca*gram is ten grams, a *deca*meter ten meters, and a *deca*liter ten liters; a *deci*gram, *deci*meter, and *deci*liter are each *one tenth* of the respective unit. The prefix *hecto-* means one hun*dred,* and the prefix *centi-* one hun*dredth,* of the given unit. Similarly, the prefix *kilo-* means one thous*and,* and the prefix *milli-* one thous*andth.* The old systems, despite their being colorful, are chaotic; the simplicity of the metric system's basic standards — light and water — and the efficiency of its vocabulary make it a welcome improvement.                [270 words]

## 3

That man, I think, has had a liberal education, who has been so trained in youth that his body is the ready servant of his will, and does with ease and pleasure all the work that, as a mechanism, it is capable of, whose intellect is a clear, cold, logic engine, with all its parts of equal strength, and in smooth working order; ready, like a steam engine, to be turned to any kind of work, and spin the gossamers as well as forge the anchors of the mind; whose mind is stored with a knowledge of the great and fundamental truths of Nature and of the laws of her operations; one who, no stunted ascetic, is full of life and fire, but whose passions are trained to come to heel by a vigorous will, the servant of a tender conscience; who has learned to love all beauty, whether of Nature or of art, to hate all vileness, and to respect others as himself.

Such a one, and no other, I conceive, has had a liberal education; for he is, as completely as a man can be, in harmony with Nature. He will make the best of her, and she of him. They will get on together rarely; she as his ever-beneficent mother; he as her mouthpiece, her conscious self, her minister and interpreter.[1]

                                                    [224 words]

## 4

In any scientific inquiry the first step is to get at the facts, and this requires precision, patience, impartiality, watchfulness

[1] T. H. Huxley, *Selected Essays.*

against the illusions of the senses and the mind, and carefulness to keep inferences from mingling with observations. The second step is accurate registration of the data. In most cases science begins with measurement. As Lord Kelvin said, "Nearly all the grandest discoveries of science have been but the rewards of accurate measurement and patient, long-continued labor in the minute sifting of numerical results." There is a certain quality of character here, and it is very significant that Clark Maxwell should have spoken in one sentence of "those aspirations after accuracy of measurement, and justice in action, which we reckon among our noblest attributes as men."

A third step is arranging the data in workable form—a simple illustration being a plotted-out curve which shows at a glance the general outcome of a multitude of measurements, e.g., the range of variability in a particular specific character in a plant or animal. The data may have to be expressed in its simplest terms, reduced perhaps to a common denominator with other sets of facts with which they have to be compared. There is a danger here of losing sight of something in the process of reduction. Thus in reducing a fact of animal behavior to a chain of reflex actions we may be losing sight of "mind"; or, in reducing a physiological fact to a series of chemical and physical facts we may be losing sight of "life."

The fourth step is [made] when a whole series of occurrences is seen to have a uniformity, which is called their law. A formula is found that fits—the finding being sometimes due to a flash of insight and sometimes the outcome of many tentatives. Newton's "passage from a falling apple to a falling moon" was a stupendous leap of the scientific imagination; the modern science of the atom is the outcome of the testing of many approximate formulations.[1]                                     [335 words]

## 5

In the three hundred years of the life of the American nation, the best art that has been produced has been chiefly in imitation of European styles, as in architecture and furniture, or work so close to that of contemporary European movements, in painting especially, that there is very little to differentiate it. This was the situation down to c. 1900. With an unprecedented development of resources and material prosperity, why is this so? Three reasons,

[1] From *The Outline of Science* by J. Arthur Thomson, G. P. Putnam's Sons, 1937. Reprinted by permission of the publishers.

at least, stand out clearly. First, the unfortunate conditions, artistically, into which the nation was born; second, the youth of the nation; and third, the diversion of all energy into the development of the natural resources of the country. The American nation happened to be born into an age in which art production everywhere was at low ebb, and in which art was rapidly being segregated from the affairs of life chiefly because of the industrial revolution. England was entering upon that age of bad taste and mediocre imitation against which the Pre-Raphaelites protested. France, under the domination of the Academy, had also reached the low level of emptiness and artificiality against which the naturalists and impressionists revolted. Lifeless imitation of Italian art everywhere stifled natural creative expression. It was inevitable that these traditions should develop, perhaps with provincial mediocrity, to their logical end—empty copying—unless some vitalizing force should evolve new ones. But the youth of the nation has operated against this. The heterogeneous elements found among the American people have not yet fused into a unity—political, social, religious, and intellectual—to create fundamental traditions, to establish capacity for appreciation on the part of the mass of the people, and thus to create a demand for the real artist. The energies of the nation have gone into the development of the country—again the inevitable condition of a colonizing people—which has led into an age of great mechanical and scientific industrialism, with a materialism frequently preponderant at the cost of the spiritual, ethical, and intellectual. The creative impulse, under these conditions, has found comparatively little encouragement.[1]          [365 words]

[1] From *Art Through the Ages* by Helen Gardner. Reprinted by permission of Harcourt Brace Jovanovich, Inc.

# Chapter 21

# The Research Paper

## Research Techniques;
## The Formal Composition

A research paper is an extended formal composition based on information gathered from a number of sources and on the thinking and judgment of the writer. Since the preparation of such a paper involves the use of reference books, the search for suitable source material in books and periodicals relating to the subject, as well as the skills of planning and writing you studied in connection with shorter compositions, the research paper presents few problems that are altogether new. Because it is a more ambitious undertaking, however, each step of the planning, research, and actual writing assumes special importance. A poor choice of subject or faulty organization is a flaw in a composition of any length. In a research paper that may take weeks in the writing, such faults loom larger and become harder to correct. Therefore, this chapter deals with some of the procedures you studied in connection with the whole composition as well as some new ones that apply mainly to the longer paper.

One important difference between the research paper and other compositions is the time it takes to write. The preparation of a thorough research paper takes weeks to complete. If you are to use this time wisely, you will want to plan your time carefully as soon as your teacher makes the assignment. Work out a definite schedule, with your teacher's guidance, that will permit you to work through each stage in a thorough and unhurried way.

Each research paper is different, but all research papers have certain things in common. From the experiences of others facing the same problems, a standard procedure and form has been developed.

### *Seven Steps in Writing a Research Paper*

1. Selecting and limiting the subject
2. Preparing a working bibliography
3. Preparing a preliminary outline
4. Reading and taking notes
5. Assembling notes and writing the final outline
6. Writing the first draft
7. Writing the final draft with footnotes and a final bibliography

## PREPARING THE RESEARCH PAPER

**21a. Select a subject suitable for research, in which you have a genuine interest.**

Finding the right subject is one of the most crucial steps in the whole process. If you make a poor choice of subject, you will find it almost impossible to write a good paper. Some teachers consider the choice of subject so important that they will assign a subject that they know is manageable. If you are given a choice, these suggestions will help.

1. *Choose a subject that interests you.* You will be spending a great deal of time and effort on the paper; it is important that the subject you choose is one that you want to learn more about.

2. *Choose a subject for which research materials are readily available.* Make sure you choose a subject about which your own library has materials. In general, it is wise to avoid subjects that are too technical in nature or too recent in development. Your school librarian can often be

of assistance here in helping you avoid subjects on which the library has very little information.

3. *Avoid straight biography.* Although it is sometimes possible to write a successful research paper on a person's life, this kind of subject presents problems that you will do well to avoid. If the person is well known, full-scale biographies are likely to exist and you will find it hard to avoid rehashing a book or encyclopedia article; if the person is not well known, or if there happen to be no good biographies, the problems of assembling enough material to document the person's life and accomplishments will be difficult. Biographies are usually based on extensive research involving interviews, letters, and other unpublished material; only in exceptional cases will you be able to avail yourself of such sources.

4. *Choose a subject of significance.* The hours you spend in research on a subject should add to your stock of knowledge as well as provide the important material for your paper. Avoid topics that do not seem to be of lasting importance.

5. *Choose a subject that can be presented objectively.* A research paper is not the place for arguments and persuasion. Select a subject that can be treated objectively. "Why the United States Should (or Should Not) Have Socialized Medicine," for example, may be the right topic for a debate but it is the wrong one for a research paper. On the other hand, "The Development of Group Medical Plans in the United States" may be suitable.

**21b. Limit your subject so that it can be handled within the length of your paper.**

Many students err initially by choosing too broad a subject and soon run into serious problems. Either they must spend endless hours producing a paper much too long, or else they do a very superficial job.

Suppose you are interested in modern American music and have a vague idea that you would like to do a paper in this field. You can successively limit the topic as follows:

1. Modern American music
2. Jazz
3. History of jazz

To stop here and attempt a 2,000–word history of jazz is an almost impossible task. To get a better paper we must carry the limiting at least one more step.

4. History of New Orleans jazz
5. New Orleans jazz in the 1920's
6. King Oliver's Creole Jazz Band

Having reduced your topic as far as steps 5 and 6 above, you must consider whether you have carried the narrowing process too far. Unless you have available several books on the history of jazz and a promising supply of articles on the subject, you may find it difficult to find enough material on a topic as limited as the influence of a particular jazz band. You may find on reflection that topic 4 is about the right size for your paper.

Let's consider another specific example. Suppose you are interested in the works of Ernest Hemingway and feel you would like to do a term paper on this author. Successive limitations of the topic may go something like this:

1. Ernest Hemingway
2. The works of Hemingway
3. The novels of Hemingway
4. *A Farewell to Arms, For Whom the Bell Tolls, The Old Man and the Sea*

Now you have reached an intermediate stage; you have focused on three of Hemingway's novels which you have read and know well. The topic, however, is still too broad, for very much could be said about each of these novels. You can now focus more sharply on any one of a number of specific aspects of these novels—theme, style, symbol, autobiographical element, and so on. You choose then your final limitation of the topic:

The progress of the hero in three of Hemingway's novels

Now you have a term paper topic which meets all the criteria listed above and which is limited enough to be manageable.

**EXERCISE 1.** Listed below are several topics for research papers. Some are suitable, while others are too broad or too limited. Indicate with each faulty subject the nature of the weakness and revise it accordingly.

1. The works of Doris Lessing
2. Water skiing
3. Experiments with the fruit fly
4. Punting techniques and their use in professional football
5. Careers in science
6. Will we ever reach Mars?
7. Life of Willa Cather
8. The Pulitzer Prize
9. The contributions of Asian-Americans
10. The concept of evil in modern American literature
11. The first year of World War II
12. Union cavalry in the Battle of Gettysburg and its effectiveness
13. Birds of America
14. Black Elk of the Sioux
15. Elizabethan theater
16. The manufacture of transistors
17. Problems of urban growth
18. Atomic energy for industrial power
19. The changing role of women
20. American land booms

**EXERCISE 2.** Bring to class three topics of interest which you think would make suitable subjects for research papers. Be sure that each is properly limited and that it can be adequately researched.

## 21c. Prepare a working bibliography.

Once you have settled on a subject and discussed your choice with your teacher, your next step is to begin your search for source material. Before you go to the *Readers' Guide* and specialized reference books, however, you will do well to turn to a good encyclopedia.

You will not find an encyclopedia article on your specific subject—at least you won't if you have limited your subject properly. What you will find is a general article on the larger subject of which yours is a part. Such an article will give you a broad view of the whole subject and may suggest related ideas that you will want to bear in mind as your idea gradually takes shape. This introductory article may also suggest a modification in your original subject. It is still not too late to shift the subject of your paper, but if the change you have in mind is a major one you should consult your teacher once again.

Your search for specific sources will involve the research aids explained in Chapters 27 and 28. Unless you can tell at a glance that you know the information in these chapters, now might be a good time to look through them. Whatever the nature of your paper, you will want to consult the following:

1. *The card catalogue.* You will miss some useful books listed in the card catalogue if you limit your search to books that obviously relate to your specific topic. Look as well under the broad general subjects of which yours is a part. For example, if your paper is to be about Virginia Woolf, don't content yourself with only the books that have her name for a subject label. Major biographies and works of criticism mainly concerned with Woolf will be found there; however, many books that may have informative chapters on Woolf may not be entered. Try "British Literature," "Twentieth Century Literature," "Literary Criticism," "the Novel," and any other general subjects that may yield sources for you. A book about modern British literature would be certain to have something on Virginia Woolf. The description of the book on the card will tell you whether the book is worth investigating.

**2.** *The* **Readers' Guide.** This source will give you current articles on your subject. Remember that your library has cumulative bound volumes of the *Readers' Guide* for past years. For most topics, past volumes of the *Readers' Guide* will be as useful as present ones.

**3.** *Specialized reference books.* In addition to useful material on your subject, specialized reference books often suggest titles of additional books that may be useful. Turn to the list of reference books on pages 501–02 of Chapter 28 and consult those in your library that bear on your subject.

Your objective at this point is to locate as many books and articles as possible that may prove useful. You will not always be able to tell from the information given on the catalogue card, in the *Readers' Guide,* or in a bibliography, whether the book or article will be helpful. In general, however, it is wise to include in your working bibliography even items you are doubtful about. If such items turn out to be of little use, you can simply drop them from your bibliography later.

The following will help you to decide which titles may be promising as far as your subject is concerned:

**1.** *Is the author an authority on the subject?* At the beginning, you won't be able to know about this in most cases. However, an author who has written several books or articles on a subject may turn out to be an authority — particularly if the author's work is often referred to in other books on your subject. As you read, be on the watch for writers whose opinions are quoted or otherwise mentioned.

**2.** *Is the book or article listed in any of the bibliographies you have consulted?* The first bibliographies you will look at are those in reference books. However, many of the books on your working bibliography are likely to contain bibliographies of their own. When you find one of these, check your own list of possible sources against it. Books and authors that keep cropping up on such bibliographies are worth investigating.

3. *If a magazine article, what kind of magazine did it appear in?* In general, articles appearing in popular general interest magazines, such as those you see on the newsstand, will not be suitable sources for research papers. You can usually afford to ignore such articles unless they turn up in one of the bibliographies you encounter.

4. *If a book, for what audience is it intended?* There are many interesting books on a variety of subjects that are intended for younger readers. Such books will usually not do for source material.

Use a separate 3 × 5-inch card or slip for each bibliographical reference. As you find books and magazine articles that look promising, you may be tempted merely to jot down title and author in a rough list. However, the pains you take now will ultimately save you a great deal of time. Your bibliography cards should contain this information:

BOOKS

1. Call number in upper left-hand corner
2. Author or editor, last name first for alphabetizing later. (Indicate editor by placing *ed.* after the name.) If a book has two or more authors, only the name of the first author is given, last name first. The names of the others are given first name first.
3. Title (volume, if necessary) underlined. Pamphlets only: series and number, if any, in parentheses
4. Place of publication
5. Publisher
6. Year of publication (or date for some pamphlets)

MAGAZINE, NEWSPAPER, AND ENCYCLOPEDIA ARTICLES

1. Author (unless article is unsigned)
2. Title of article, enclosed in quotation marks
3. Name of magazine, newspaper, or encyclopedia
4. For magazines: volume and page numbers as in *Readers' Guide.* For newspapers: page number. For encyclopedias: volume and page numbers.
5. For magazines and newspapers: date. For encyclopedias: place of publication, publisher, year of publication.

As you go on to the steps that follow, the importance of making out a full record of the bibliographical data for each source will become clear. For the present, make special note of the importance of giving each card a number (the circled number at the upper right-hand corner of the models on this page). During the next three steps of composition, in which you will complete the planning of your paper and do most of the actual writing, your card numbers will be invaluable. By jotting down the number you will free yourself from the boring task of copying details about your sources to identify every note and quotation.

808.3
W                                                                ②

West, Ray B., Jr., *The Art of Modern Fiction*, N.Y.,
        Holt, Rinehart and Winston, 1949.

                                                                ③

Schorer, Mark, "With Grace Under Pressure,"
        *New Republic*,          127 : 19-20
        October 6, 1962

**Typical Cards in a Working Bibliography**

**EXERCISE 3.** On the page following you will find a reproduction of part of a page from the *Readers' Guide to Periodical Literature*. Suppose you are writing on the hero in three novels of Hemingway—the same topic as in Exercise 4. Answer the following questions by giving the key letters for the appropriate entries.

**HEMINGWAY, Ernest**

A Letter from Hemingway to Bernard Kalb.
  por Sat R 35:11 S 6 '52

B Old man and the sea; novel. por Life 33:
  34-54 S 1 '52

C Tribute to mamma from papa Hemingway.
  Life 33:92 Ag 18 '52

*about*

D Achievement of Ernest Hemingway. L.
  Gurko. Engl J 41:291-8 Je '52

E Clean and straight. por Time 60:114 S 8 '52

F Cuban looks at Hemingway. L. Novás Calvo.
  Américas 4:37-8 N '52

G Great American storyteller. por(cover) Life
  33:20 S 1 '52

H Hemingway in Hollywood. il N Y Times Mag
  p58-9 S 14 '52

I Hemingway's gimmick. por Newsweek 40:102-
  3 S 8 '52

J Hemingway's Old man. H. Breit. Nation 175:
  194 S 6 '52

K Hemingway's wastelanders. C. Baker. Va Q
  R 28 no3:373-92 [Jl] '52

L Lifesize Hemingway. Time 60:48 S 1 '52

M Male-ism and moralism. W. Phillips. Am
  Mercury 75:93-8 O '52

N Measure of Hemingway; review of Hemingway, by C. Baker. P. F. Quinn. Commonweal 57:73-5 O 24 '52

O Momentary scoop. L. Z. Hobson. Sat R 35:4
  Ag 23 '52

P Mountain and the plain. C. Baker. Va Q R
  27 no3:410-18 [Jl] '51

Q Old man and society. J. A. Portuondo. il pors
  Américas 4:6-8+ D '52

R "The old man" and the book. Pub W 162:1011
  S 13 '52

S Portrait
  1   Sat R Lit 34:7 Je 2 '51
  2   Sat R Lit 34:64 O 13 '51
  3   Sat R 35:7 Ag 23 '52
  4   Sat R 35:8 D 27 '52
      Time 60:112 D 15 '52

T Prodigy into peer; review of Hemingway, by
  C. Baker. A. Mizener. Sat R 35:25 O 18
  '52

U Religion of art. V. Brooks. il por Sat R Lit
  34:13-14+ D 1 '51

V Truth and poetry; review of Hemingway, by
  C. Baker. New Repub 127:21 O 13 '52

W Valor and defeat; review of Old man and the
  sea. S. Krim. Commonweal 56:584-6 S 19
  '52

X With grace under pressure. M. Schorer. New
  Repub 127:19-20 O 6 '52

From *Readers' Guide to Periodical Literature*, April 1951 – March 1953, Vol. 18. Reprinted by
permission of The H. W. Wilson Company.

1. Which articles are by Hemingway?

2. Which articles are reviews of a Hemingway book?

3. Which articles are likely to be useless for your paper?

4. Which Hemingway novel is discussed in several of these articles?

5. Which articles contain pictures of Hemingway?

6. Where would you find an article about how a Cuban views Hemingway?

7. Which article seems to contain a publishing history of one of his novels?
8. Which articles would probably give the best biographical information about Hemingway?
9. Which articles are illustrated?
10. Which articles are likely to contain useful discussions of Hemingway's heroes?

**EXERCISE 4.** Listed below are several books by and about Ernest Hemingway. Suppose you are doing a term paper on the Hemingway hero as seen in three of his novels. Indicate which of these books sound as if they would be quite helpful, which you would be doubtful about, and which you could probably ignore safely.

Aronowitz, Alfred C., and Peter Hamill, *Ernest Hemingway: The Life and Death of a Man*
Baker, Carlos, *Hemingway and His Critics*
Baker, Carlos, *Hemingway: The Writer as Artist*
Fenton, Charles A., *The Apprenticeship of Ernest Hemingway*
Hemingway, Ernest, *The Wild Years*
Hemingway, Leicester, *My Brother, Ernest Hemingway*
Lania, Leo, *Hemingway: A Pictorial Biography*
McCaffery, John K. M., *Ernest Hemingway: The Man and His Work*
Ross, Lillian, *Portrait of Hemingway*
Sanford, Marcelline H., *At the Hemingways: A Family Portrait*
Singer, Kurt, *The Life and Death of a Giant*
Young, Philip, *Ernest Hemingway*

## 21d. Bring your subject into focus by stating your purpose.

Once you have thought through your general subject and have done some background reading, you are ready to bring your subject into sharper focus. Try to state in one sentence the thesis, or purpose, of your paper. The thesis is a statement of your purpose—what you intend to show in the paper. In a more formal sense it is a proposition to be proved—and the proof is in the rest of your paper. The thesis, or statement of purpose, is to the longer paper what the topic sentence is to the paragraph.

Later on as you work through the paper you may wish to revise your thesis; stating it as sharply as you can at this stage, however, will direct your thinking and make your note-taking more efficient and productive. Remember that material that does not relate directly to your purpose does not belong in your paper and consequently has no place in your notes.

Returning to the Hemingway paper mentioned on page 351, you will recall that the decision was made to write on the subject of the progress of the hero in three of Hemingway's novels. This may be suitable as a title, but it is not a statement of purpose. It must still be recast into the form of a declarative statement which is to be proved. The purpose may be stated as follows:

> "In the Hemingway novels *A Farewell to Arms, For Whom the Bell Tolls,* and *The Old Man and the Sea,* the hero moves from hopeless resignation to meaningful retreat."

## 21e. Prepare a preliminary outline as a guide for reading and taking notes.

At this stage in your work you have a stack of cards — your working bibliography — and a clear statement of the purpose of your paper. Your next step is to prepare a rough outline that will suggest the general heading under which you will be taking notes.

Begin by thinking through your subject to see what major divisions and subdivisions suggest themselves. Using these as outline topics, make your preliminary outline. Do not worry about matters of style or about the final organization of the topics. As your reading progresses, you will find that some topics turn out to be irrelevant or inadequately covered in the sources. These topics will be eliminated. On the other hand, your reading will suggest new topics that you will want to include.

When you are ready to draw up your preliminary outline, follow these suggestions:

1. Put the title of your paper at the top.
2. Immediately below the title, write the word *purpose* followed by a statement of your purpose.
3. Follow standard outline form. (See pages 291–93.)
4. Do not include too much detail in your preliminary outline. A three-step outline should be sufficient; more detail will be added as you go along.

The preliminary outline below shows how the topic and thesis of the Hemingway paper have been expanded into a plan of action for a long paper.

Title: The Progress of the Hero in Three of Hemingway's Novels

Purpose: In the Hemingway novels *A Farewell to Arms, For Whom the Bell Tolls,* and *The Old Man and the Sea,* the hero moves from hopeless resignation to meaningful retreat.

   I. Hemingway's influence
     A. The influence of his works in general
     B. The influence of his hero
  II. The hero of *A Farewell to Arms*
     A. Frederick Henry's disillusionment
     B. Henry's code
     C. Meaning in retreat
 III. The hero of *For Whom the Bell Tolls*
     A. Disillusionment with the cause
     B. Integrity as a part of the code
     C. Meaning in death and loss
 IV. The hero of *The Old Man and the Sea*
     A. The old man as hero
     B. Courage as part of the code
     C. Meaning through loss
  V. The hero's progress
     A. The changing code
     B. The changing meaning

## 21f. Take notes on your reading. Enter your notes on cards, classified by topics in the preliminary outline.

With your working bibliography and preliminary outline before you, you are ready to continue your reading. Now you have a clear idea of exactly what you are looking for. *Never read sources for a research paper without taking notes on your reading.* Even for the main points in a paper, your memory is an unreliable guide. When it comes to detailed references and quotations, you *must* have a full and accurate record of the material you have accumulated.

Take all notes on 4 × 6-inch index cards. Using the larger size will enable you to keep your note cards from getting mixed up with your bibliography cards. Follow the form and style of the model note card below. The various entries on the same note card are explained below. Note that the explanations are numbered to correspond to the key numbers in the illustration.

1. *The "slug."* The line at the upper left, called a "slug," is simply a topic or subtopic copied from your preliminary outline. Include on a card only notes pertaining to the slug: use a different card for each source. Ideally, every note you take would fall naturally under one or another of the outline's topics and subtopics. Actually, as you know, the preliminary outline is subject to constant revision. If you find yourself frequently taking notes that do not fit any topic or subtopic, stop to revise or add to the outline and enter the

1. slug — from preliminary outline

2. number of working bibliography card

Old Man as Hero　　③

The old man's Franciscan qualities support the idea of Christian martyrdom. His humility without sentimentality, his love of fish, birds, porpoises, his sense of the independence of all things separate from his own character are all parts of this Franciscan quality.

3. note

page 19

4. page reference

**A Sample Note Card**

new slug on your cards. You may delete part of the outline if your sources clearly do not contain usable material on a topic or group of topics. If you decide, during your reading, that two topics should be combined, remember to change both the outline and the slugs on appropriate cards.

2. *Bibliographical reference.* At the upper right-hand corner of each note card, enter the source from which the note is taken. To save time, use the card number for that source which you find on the working bibliography card. For example, the number on the model note card is the number of the working-bibliography card for an article entitled "With Grace Under Pressure" by Mark Schorer. By referring to the card in the working bibliography, you can check the title, the author, the name of the magazine, and the issue and page number whenever you wish.

QUOTATION

Discovery through loss ③

"In this isolation [his going out into the deep water] he wins a ... victory, which means his destruction and triumph. We permit his martyrdom because he has earned it. His sigh is 'just a noise such as a man might make involuntarily, feeling the nail go through his hands and into the wood.'"

page 20

3. *The note.* The notes you take should generally be in your own words. Read a passage carefully and then paraphrase it in your own words. This will save you unnecessary copying and prevent you from committing unconscious plagiarism. Occasionally, you will want to copy down an author's exact words. Do so when the author's

statement of a point is so well expressed that you will want to quote it in your paper or when paraphrasing might tend to distort the meaning of the passage. Sometimes it may be desirable to combine paraphrase and quotation on the same card. The sample note card on page 361 illustrates paraphrase. The two note cards on these pages are examples of quotation and combined quotation and paraphrase, respectively.

There are some special points of punctuation to note on the index card on page 362. First, the double quotation marks are used to indicate a verbatim quotation. Next, observe that the note-taker has added the words *his going out into the deep water* to the quoted material in order to clarify the nature of the isolation. Brackets are placed around these words to indicate that they did not appear in

COMBINED PARAPHRASE AND QUOTATION

Old Man as Hero ③

There is no dramatic falseness in the book. He is an old man alone at sea, and his talking aloud, his dialogues with himself, advance the story. "... almost a running drama between that which is only possible and that which is real."

page 20

the original. Third, the ellipsis (. . .) is used to indicate that some words have been omitted from the original.

Finally, single quotation marks are used to indicate a quotation from the novel.

A research paper should not be a collection of quotations from various authors on one subject. However, it is outright dishonesty to pass off another person's words as though they were your own. Summarize and paraphrase, but do not copy unless you intend to use the quoted material within quotation marks in your paper.

4. *Page reference.* Beneath the note, jot down the number of the page on which you found the material. This page reference serves two purposes. First, you may wish to return to that page to clarify a point during one of the later stages of composition; and second, you will need exact page references when you write the footnotes for your final draft.

## 21g. Assemble and organize your note cards and decide upon the final outline.

Obviously, the outline of a long research paper must be more complex than that of a short composition – yet it should not be so complex that a reader has difficulty in following the organization. Once again, the standard methods of preparing the paper will help you to simplify your material. Whether you realize it or not, you have already done a large part of the job of simplifying and writing your final outline.

Each of your note cards is headed by a slug. Shuffling through your cards, assemble every card bearing the same slug into a single pile. You now have before you a number of piles of cards, each pile covering one of the major or minor divisions of your preliminary outline. Study these piles of cards in terms of the information that each pile contains and the extent to which the piles conform to your tentative outline. To some extent, the very size of a pile is significant, for it tells you whether you found a good deal of information on the subject, or only a little. If you find that you have little or no information on one of the subdivisions, you will either have to do more looking or revise your outline so that that particular subdivision is eliminated. As you read through the notes in a pile, some topics will emerge as main divisions of your subject, some as subdivisions, some as more minor subdivisions (we might call them "sub-subdivisions"). Do not be afraid to reject some cards and piles of cards entirely; all researchers pick up some material which has no proper place in their papers. Finally, when you have chosen your main topics and sub-topics, and tested every note card for its relevancy to your subject, begin to prepare your final outline. This is the time to concern yourself with such matters as the order of topics within the outline and the logical organization of all your material. You may find yourself moving an entire main topic from one place to another, or shifting note cards to different positions. Every wise change and decision you make at this stage will help you in the actual writing of your paper.

Essentially, the process you are completing is the last stage of writing a topic outline, as described on pages 291–93. The main difference is in the larger body of information you must handle and the corresponding complexity of the outline itself. Do not, however, permit your outline to get out of hand. The fact that this research paper will be three times as long as a composition does not mean that its outline should be three times as elaborate. Usually your material, however rich and varied, can be organized under no more than five main headings. If you find that you have more than this number, recheck your organization and coverage. Have you mistaken subtopics for main topics, or tried to include too much information?

## WRITING THE RESEARCH PAPER

### 21h. Write the first draft from your final outline.

With your final outline as complete as possible and your note cards sorted to conform to that outline, you can put your information and ideas down on paper. The rules and suggestions for writing a first draft (pages 295–300) will help you here. Above all, remember that this draft is meant for your eyes alone. Matters of style and form, the mechanics of punctuation, even the full transcription of your material from the note cards — all these can be ignored. Simply set your ideas down fully and freely, in a form that you will be able to follow when the time comes for polishing and revision.

Be sure to keep your note cards before you as you write, and to take advantage of all the information that they contain. Make constant use, particularly, of the bibliographical and page references on the cards. A research paper is not the place for speculation or unsupported opinions, but for solid information drawn from your reading. Whenever you set down a fact or idea, write after it the number of the source in your working bibliography and the page reference.[1] Use these references, also, to save yourself time. For example, if you plan to use an extended quotation at some point, there is no need to copy it carefully into both the first and final drafts. For the first draft, simply write down the first few words of the quotation along with the identifying reference numbers; then, when you write the final draft, pick up the entire quotation from your note card. Another way of saving time is to clip the note card you intend to copy onto the page of the rough draft on which it will appear.

## 21i. Write the final draft.

Except for the inclusion of footnotes and the preparation of the final bibliography, the final draft of a research paper presents the same problems as the final draft of any composition. The techniques of revision discussed on pages 300–02 are appropriate here and should be reviewed. Because the research paper represents a great deal of work, you will want to take special pains with the appearance of your manuscript. Follow the recommendations concerning manuscript form in Chapter 26.

[1] This rule need not apply with a fact so generally known that it has become public property; for example, the fact that Hemingway was a famous American writer. Do not, however, assume too much knowledge on the part of your readers. If you are uncertain whether a specific fact is a matter of general or special knowledge, give its source.

## Footnotes

The important facts and ideas in your research paper should be supported by detailed references to the original sources. In your first draft these references took the form of numbers keyed to your note cards and working bibliography. In the final draft these references must be spelled out in footnotes.

To indicate the addition of a footnote to your text, write or type a number above and to the right of the last word in the quotation that you wish to credit. There are two common ways of numbering footnotes; be sure that you know which method your teacher wants you to follow. In the first, the numbering begins over on each successive page. That is, two footnotes on page one will be numbered 1 and 2, and the first footnote on page two will be numbered 1. In the second method, footnotes are numbered consecutively throughout the paper, without regard to the page on which they appear. Thus, in a paper with a total of twenty footnotes, the last one will be number 20.

The footnotes themselves are added at the bottom of a page. By noticing where footnotes are called for in the first draft, you can determine how many will fall on a single page and allow enough space for them. Plan each page so that there will be enough space for all the necessary footnotes.

Check the form and style of your footnotes carefully. Be sure, first, that you have numbered the footnotes correctly, so that each footnote reference in the body of the text has an identically numbered footnote at the bottom of the page. Within the footnotes themselves, be sure that you include all necessary items in their correct order. The correct items and order are given in the lists below. (A footnote for an anonymous work begins with the title.) In footnotes, all items are separated by commas.

You will occasionally see footnotes containing bibliographical data (publisher, date of publication, etc.); since a research paper is followed by a detailed bibliography, these data should be omitted from your own footnotes. For a list of abbreviations commonly used in footnotes, see pages 373–74.

| BOOK OR PAMPHLET | MAGAZINE OR NEWSPAPER ARTICLE |
|---|---|
| 1. Author's name (first name first) | 1. Author's name (first name first) |
| 2. Book or pamphlet title (underlined) | 2. Title of article (in quotation marks) |
| 3. Page number | 3. Name of magazine or newspaper (underlined) |
| | 4. Volume number (if any) of magazine |
| | 5. Date |
| | 6. Page number |

EXAMPLES

¹ George R. Stewart, Names on the Land, p. 121. [book]

² Bergen Evans, "But What's a Dictionary For?" Atlantic, 209, May, 1962, p. 58. [magazine article]

³ "Webster's Way Out Dictionary," Business Week, September 16, 1961, p. 89. [anonymous magazine article]

If your footnotes make several references to the same source, you need not repeat the title and the full name of the author in each footnote. If the references occur in consecutive footnotes, you may use the abbreviation *ibid.* (for the Latin word *ibidem,* meaning "in the same place"). Give the page number only if you are referring to a different page from the one cited in the previous footnote.

EXAMPLE

¹ Lewis Leary, Mark Twain, p. 113.

² Ibid., p. 204.

When a footnote reference to another source comes between references to the same source, *ibid.*, which always refers to the footnote immediately preceding, cannot be used. In this case, you use the last name of the author and follow it with the page number.

EXAMPLE

¹ Lewis Leary, <u>Mark</u> <u>Twain</u>, p. 113.

² Kenneth S. Lynn, <u>Mark</u> <u>Twain</u> and <u>Southwest-</u><u>ern</u> <u>Humor</u>, p. 112.

³ Leary, p. 204.

**EXERCISE 5.** The following lists contain all the information needed to number and write a group of footnotes. Assign footnote numbers and write the six footnotes in the order given below.

*Footnotes on page 7 of manuscript:*

1. A book entitled Mark Twain and Southwestern Humor written by Kenneth S. Lynn. Reference to page 112.
2. An article entitled Mark Twain and J. D. Salinger: A Study in Literary Continuity, by Edgar M. Branch, in American Quarterly, Volume 9 (1957). Reference to page 151.
3. A book entitled Sam Clemens of Hannibal, by Dixon Wecter. Reference to page 27.
4. A second reference to Wecter's book. Reference to page 44.

*Footnotes on page 8 of manuscript:*

5. A book entitled The Adventures of Tom Sawyer, by Mark Twain. Reference to page 54.
6. An article entitled Mark Twain, by Dixon Wecter, published in Literary History of the United States. Reference to page 931.

## The Bibliography

You are now ready to put your rough bibliography into final form.

All the information you need is already present on your working bibliography cards. Your tasks in the revision are those of selection and styling. The final bibliography should include only those books and articles that you actually used; that is, the sources referred to in your footnotes plus any additional sources which played an important part in the preparation of your paper. In style and form, your final bibliography will differ from the working bibliography only in certain details, but these details are important. Remember that the bibliography is your best support for every statement in your paper.

Give the following items of information, in the order shown, for each bibliographical entry. All items should be separated by commas; use a period at the end of each entry.

### BOOK
Author (last name first)
Title (underlined)
Place of publication (city)
Name of publisher
Year of publication

### MAGAZINE ARTICLE
Author (last name first)
Title of article (in quotation marks)
Name of magazine (underlined)
Volume and page numbers
Date

### PAMPHLET
Author (last name first)
Title (underlined)
Name of pamphlet series, if any (in quotation marks), followed by series number (Place this entire item in parentheses.)
Date (if given)

### NEWSPAPER ARTICLE
Title of article (in quotation marks)
Name of newspaper (underlined)
Date
Page number

In arranging bibliographical entries, observe the following formal requirements:

1. Alphabetize items according to the last names of authors or, for anonymous articles, the first important word in titles. (The job of alphabetizing can be simplified by arranging cards from the working bibliography in alphabetical order.) Do *not* number entries.

2. When a bibliography includes more than one work by an author, do not repeat the author's name after its first appearance. Instead, substitute a long dash for the author's name in the second and subsequent entries.

3. When an entry takes more than one line, indent all lines after the first.

EXAMPLES

Hinton, Norman D., The Language of Jazz Musicians ("Publications of the American Dialect Society," No. 30), November, 1958. [pamphlet]

"On New Words and New Meanings," St. Louis Post Dispatch, December 17, 1961, p. 5. [newspaper article]

Reed, Carroll E., American Dialects, Seattle, University of Washington Press, 1958. [book]

———— "The Pronunciation of English in the Pacific Northwest," Language, 37:559-64, 1961. [magazine article by Carroll E. Reed, author of the previous entry]

## Charts, Diagrams, and Illustrations

Include such material whenever you believe it will help your paper, being careful to indicate the source. It is usually best to copy or trace these items.

**EXERCISE 6.**  The following list contains information about a number of bibliography items in a research paper on Hemingway. Arrange the items for a bibliography in accordance with the principles that you have just learned in this chapter.

1. A book by Carlos Baker entitled *Hemingway: The Writer as Artist,* published in Princeton, New Jersey, by Princeton University Press in 1956.

2. Joseph Warren Beach's article "How Do You Like It Now, Gentlemen?" in the *Sewanee Review,* Volume 59, pages 311–28, Spring, 1951.

3. An anonymous article in *Time* magazine entitled "Life-size Hemingway," Volume 60, page 48, published on September 1, 1952.

4. A book by Philip Young, entitled *Ernest Hemingway,* published in New York by Rinehart and Company in 1952.

5. A book edited by John K. M. McCaffery, published by the World Publishing Company in Cleveland in 1950. The book is entitled *Ernest Hemingway: The Man and His Work.*

6. An anonymous article in *Publishers' Weekly* for September 13, 1952, Volume 162:1011. The article was entitled, " 'The Old Man' and the Book."

7. A book of articles edited by Carlos Baker, entitled *Ernest Hemingway: Critiques of Four Major Novels,* published in 1962 in New York by Charles Scribner's Sons.

# THE COMPLETE PAPER

Assemble the following parts of a complete research paper in the order shown below.

**1. *Cover.*** Using staples, metal clasps, or other fastening, bind your paper in a stiff cover. Give the title of the paper on the outside; make the cover simple but attractive.

**2. *Title page.*** Use a separate page as a title page; on it, type or write the title of the paper, your name, the name and number (if any) of the course, and the date on which the paper is to be submitted. The name of the paper and your own name should appear at the center of the title page; the other information belongs near the bottom of the page, either centered or flush with the right-hand margin used in the text.

**3. *Final outline.*** Copy your final revision of the topic outline neatly, and insert it directly after the title page. In this position, the outline will serve as a kind of table of contents.

**4. *The paper itself.*** Begin your page numbering with the first page of the paper proper. Number all pages of the paper, including those containing only charts or diagrams.

**5. *The bibliography.*** Use as many pages as you need for the bibliography, allowing the same margins as those on the pages of the paper itself. Do not number the pages of the bibliography.

## *Abbreviations in Sources and Research Papers*

In your reading for the research paper, you will encounter

a number of scholarly abbreviations, established by long usage. A short checklist of the most common abbreviations is given below. Learn to recognize these abbreviations, but use them sparingly in your own work.

**c or** ©    *copyright;* used before a date to indicate the year in which copyright was obtained: © 1958. If a date appears on the *title page* of a publication, use that date in your bibliographical references; otherwise, use the copyright date on the *back* of the title page.

**c., ca.**    *about* (from the Latin *circa, circum*); used with dates: *c.* 1000; *ca.* 500 A.D.

**cf.**    *compare* (from the Latin *confer*); always printed in italics or underlined: *cf.* Declaration of Independence ["Compare (this statement, etc.) with the Declaration of Independence"].

**ch.**    *chapter, chapters*

**ed.**    *editor, edited, edition*

**e.g.**    *for example* (from the Latin *exempli gratia*); always printed in italics or underlined.

**et al.**    *and others* (from the Latin *et alii*); also, *and elsewhere* (from the Latin *et alibi*); always printed in italics or underlined.

**f., ff.**    *following page, pages;* p. 51f. ("page 51 and the following page"); pp. 51ff. ("page 51 and the following pages").

**ibid.**    *in the same place* (from the Latin *ibidem*); always italicized or underlined.

► NOTE   You should learn to use this abbreviation freely in the footnotes of research papers. Whenever two or more successive footnotes refer to the same source, the abbreviation *ibid.* is a valuable time- and space-saver. Be careful, however, to use it only in the second, third, etc., footnotes of a series of *successive* footnotes on the same source. For other footnote usage see *op. cit.*

**i.e.**    *that is* (from the Latin *id est*); always italicized or underlined.

**l., ll.**    *line, lines*

**loc. cit.**    *in the place* (*source*) *previously cited* (from the Latin *loco citato*); always italicized or underlined.

**ms., mss.**   *manuscript, manuscripts*

**N.B.**   *note well* (from the Latin *nota bene*); always italicized or underlined.

**n.d.**   *no date;* an abbreviation used in bibliographies when a source contains no indication of a publication or copyright date.

**op. cit.**   *in the work previously cited* (from the Latin *opere citato*); always italicized or underlined; see also *ibid.*

▶ **NOTE**   This abbreviation is sometimes used in the footnotes of research papers to avoid repeating a reference in full; do not use it in your own work unless your teacher advises you to do so. When used, it has a meaning similar to *ibid.* above; it is used in addition to the author's last name.

**p., pp.**   *page, pages*

**q.v.**   *which see, whom see* (from the Latin *quod vide* or *quem vide*); always italicized or underlined.

**sic**   *thus* (from the Latin); always italicized or underlined. This abbreviation is used (in brackets) in direct quotations from a source, particularly when the quotation contains an error, to indicate that a specific fact or statistic is correctly copied.

**vide**   *see* (from the Latin)

THE PROGRESS OF THE HERO IN THREE NOVELS
OF ERNEST HEMINGWAY

Thomas Cooley

[The following are sample pages from a
high school student's research paper. Use them
as a model in preparing your own paper.]

English XI
Mr. Brodsky
May 4

# The Progress of the Hero in Three Novels
## of Ernest Hemingway

Contemporary critics are sharply divided in
their final judgments of the literary achievement of Ernest Hemingway: some consider him one
of the great novelists of our century; others
consider him merely a skilled craftsman who often
failed in his craft. There is, however, una-
nimity about the influence Hemingway has had both
on his readers and on contemporary writers. His
sparse, lean prose produced a flood of imitators
and set a new standard for twentieth-century
prose writing. And the "Hemingway hero" made
such an impact on the readers of the novels that
the term became almost a part of contemporary
American folklore.

The singular nature of that term, the
"Hemingway hero," indicates something significant:
no matter how much the locale or subject matter
of the novel varied, the hero and his life showed
the same characteristics from novel to novel.
While such a broad generalization cannot obviously hold true for all of Hemingway's fiction,
a close examination of three novels--A Farewell
to Arms, For Whom the Bell Tolls, and The Old
Man and the Sea--will show that in each case we
are confronted with a wounded hero who begins

with failure or disillusion, tries to live according to a strict code, and finds insight and salvation through retreat, loss, or failure. [purpose]

Certainly these characteristics of the Hemingway hero are manifestly clear in A Farewell to Arms, Hemingway's first commercial success. In this novel of the American ambulance driver and the British nurse who fall in love and live the way they sought, we have a work whose wounded hero fits almost exactly this archetypal pattern of knowing disillusionment, living by the code, and finding meaning in retreat.

There is disillusionment with life in general, a disillusionment that has sent him to Italy in what Edgar Johnson calls a "flight from responsibility."[1] [direct quotation] This general disillusionment turns into a disgust with war, expressed in the memorable lines:

> I was always embarrassed by the words
> sacred, glorious, and sacrifice, and the
> expression in vain....I had seen noth-
> ing sacred, and the things that were glo-
> rious had no glory and the sacrifices
> were like the stockyards at Chicago... [2]
> [extended quotation]

---

[1] Edgar Johnson, "Farewell the Separate Peace," Sewanee Review, 48, July, 1940, p. 112.

[2] Ernest Hemingway, A Farewell to Arms, p. 191.

## 3

It seems somewhat clear that Henry has come to
Italy to try to find meaning in a life without
meaning; the disillusionment that war brings to
him forces him to turn to love for meaning.

Confronted with this disillusionment in a
meaningless world, Henry tries to find order by
living according to his code, always an important
part of the hero-pattern. Ray B. West, Jr., sees
Henry as a "strong man giving odds to his weaker
opponent...the strong man aware that the only
order in the universe is that which he himself
can supply...."[1] To this quality of strength
H. K. Russell would add gentleness: "The peculiar
combination of toughness and gentleness, a sort
of depreciated gallantry is the familiar characteristic of many of Hemingway's people."[2]
There is a tenderness with Catherine, of course,
but there is also much tenderness with Rinaldi
and the priest.

A third part of the Hemingway code is faith-
fulness to those who share the code--the in-
itiated. Russell makes clear the importance of
this initiation: "They [Hemingway's people] are
the initiates, those who know what it is to be

---

[1] Ray B. West, Jr., The Art of Modern Fiction, p. 626.

[2] H. K. Russell, "The Catharsis in A Farewell
to Arms," Modern Fiction Studies, 1, August, 1955,
p. 29.

broken and have learned to be careful....They are
inclined to be snobbish toward those who have not
felt the vicious power of the system."[1]

[*The paper goes on to discuss the rest of the code and the way in
which Henry finds meaning in withdrawal and retreat. The part of
the paper that follows shows how a transition paragraph makes
for a smooth movement into the next major section of the paper.*]

It seems rather clear, then, that Frederic
Henry is almost a prototype of the Hemingway
hero: he begins feeling a pervasive bitterness
about life in general and war in particular,
lives according to a rigid code, and finds even
in the loss of love that love is the only thing
that can give life meaning. Even though the
second book to be considered, <u>For Whom the Bell
Tolls</u>, seems imbued with a more positive tone, we
can still see the same general pattern.

In this latter work the disillusionment stems
not so much from the central figure as it does
from the nature of the cause, a point made very
strongly by Burton Rascoe.[2] Although Jordan has
a positive belief in the war, the cause is a lost
one and any noble thoughts, Rascoe notes, are
ironical in tone.

---

[1] <u>Ibid.</u>

[2] Burton Rascoe, "Wolfe, Farrell, and Hemingway," <u>American Mercury</u>, 51, December, 1940,
p. 493.

[*The paper goes on to discuss the nature of disillusionment in* For Whom the Bell Tolls, *the code of its hero, and his discovery of meaning. The final major section takes up the book* The Old Man and the Sea, *discussing the sense of failure with which it opens, the nature of the code here, and the meaning of the book. The paper concludes as follows:*]

Even in his physical position, then, we see clearly that the old man has achieved victory even as he has failed: by going out too far, by losing the fish, he has found his true place in a hostile world.

It would seem finally that these three novels are all of a piece, at least in so far as they focus on one heroic pattern. The nature of the initial bitterness and disillusionment varies slightly from work to work. In all three, however, we see a man trying to be a man by living according to the same tight code. Most important, we see in the three books a hero who paradoxically yet convincingly finds victory, meaning, and commitment in defeat and withdrawal. And perhaps this tragic victory has something important to say about the body of Hemingway's works.

[*The bibliography follows on a separate page.*]

# BIBLIOGRAPHY

Baker, Carlos, Hemingway: The Writer as Artist, Princeton, N.J., Princeton University Press, 1956.

Burhans, Clinton S., Jr., "The Old Man and the Sea: Hemingway's Tragic Vision," American Literature, 31:446-55, January, 1960.

Frankenberg, Lloyd, "Themes and Characters in Hemingway's Latest Period," Southern Review, 7:776-88, Winter, 1942.

Hemingway, Ernest, A Farewell to Arms, New York, Charles Scribner's Sons, 1949.

———— For Whom the Bell Tolls, New York, Charles Scribner's Sons, 1940.

———— The Old Man and the Sea, New York, Charles Scribner's Sons, 1952.

Johnson, Edgar, "Farewell the Separate Peace," Sewanee Review, 48:110-14, July, 1940.

Rascoe, Burton, "Wolfe, Farrell, and Hemingway," American Mercury, 51:493-95, December, 1940.

Russell, H. K., "The Catharsis in A Farewell to Arms," Modern Fiction Studies, 1:29-35, August, 1955.

West, Ray B., Jr., The Art of Modern Fiction, New York, Rinehart, 1949.

# The Business Letter

## Standard Practice in Business Correspondence

During the next few years you will have many occasions to write business letters. When you write to a college, order merchandise or tickets by mail, apply for a job through the mail, or let a newspaper editor or senator know how you feel about an issue, you will have to know how to write a good business letter that will do an effective job of speaking for you.

### Form in a Business Letter

Unlike friendly letters and social notes, business letters are always written according to standard practice. The body of a business letter may be formal or informal in tone, but conventions should always be followed in the form and in the placement of parts. Since the rules governing business letters are both elaborate and rather precise, you should study the following pages with special care.

**22a. Observe standard practice in writing business letters.**

**(1) Use appropriate stationery.**

Business stationery is cut in two standard sizes: $8\frac{1}{2} \times 11$ inches and $5\frac{1}{2} \times 8\frac{1}{2}$ inches.

**(2) Make an attractive "letter picture."**

Most of us know that a business letter should be typed, not handwritten; but typing is only the beginning of a readable, attractive business letter. Business executives and their assistants think of letters as tools for earning their living, and know that a letter which makes a poor impression can be worse than no letter at all. Before a single word of a letter is read, the person who receives it forms an impression of the writer – an impression based upon the over-all "picture" presented by the letter at a first glance. You can make your "letter pictures" attractive by checking every letter you finish for each of the items on the following list.

1. *Regular margins.* Think of the margins as a frame enclosing the letter picture. A good frame is balanced. The left margin should be about as wide as the right margin, the top margin about as deep as the bottom margin.

2. *Placement.* Few business letters cover an entire page. Determine in advance whether a letter is short, medium, or long, and begin the inside address at a point that will produce nearly identical top and bottom margins. A letter that is not centered on the page should be retyped.

3. *Indention.* Adopt a single indention style for your business letters (see detailed explanation below and models on page 384), and follow it consistently in each letter.

4. *Paragraphing.* Do not use too many short paragraphs; avoid writing a paragraph that consists of a single line. Similarly, do not make your paragraphs too lengthy; avoid writing a single paragraph that covers more than half a page. A short letter, however, may well consist of a single paragraph.

5. *Correct spacing.* Space the letter parts carefully and consistently, following the directions given in subrule (5), page 386.

6. *Typing standards.* Only an experienced typist can be expected to combine speed with accuracy. Type carefully, and avoid the following common errors: uneven typing, strikeovers, messy erasures, heavily struck punctuation marks.

**(3) Follow a standard form of indention.**

Standard forms or styles have been worked out for business

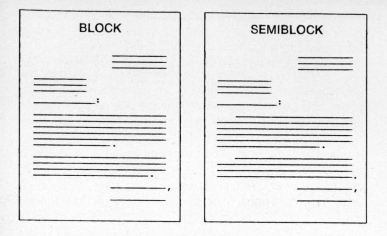

**Model Business Letter Forms**

letters, differing in certain respects from the style of the personal letter. The models shown above illustrate three of the styles. Any one of these is acceptable and presents an attractive letter picture.

1. *Block style.* Every line, except for the heading, complimentary close, and signature, begins at the left-hand

margin. Since it eliminates indentions for the openings of paragraphs, the block style also saves some time and does not seem quite so unbalanced as the full block.

**2.** *Semiblock,* or *block indented style* is similar to block style, except that the opening line of each paragraph is indented either five or ten spaces. This is the most common of all business-letter styles, and may be used in any situation.

**3.** *Full block style.* Every line begins at the left-hand margin. Since it eliminates all indentions, the full block style is often used by those who are concerned with saving typing time. Some object to the appearance of the full block because it seems unbalanced to the left.

**(4) Follow standard practice when a second page is needed.**

Whenever possible, a business letter should be completed on one side of a single page. If this cannot be done without crowding (a margin of at least one inch should follow the last line of the letter), go on to a second page. The second page should be the same size as the first, but it should always be plain paper, without a letterhead.

The letter picture presented by a second page has its own distinctive characteristics. One inch (about six typewriter lines) from the top of the page, prepare a one-line heading, with the name of the addressee at the left, the page number at the center, and the date of the letter at the right, as shown below. The continuation of the letter itself

```
        Mr. R. H. Dodd        2        April 4, 1976
```

begins four spaces below this heading. It should be long enough to avoid looking "lost" on the page. Never carry over fewer than three lines of the body of a letter to a second page; never begin a second page with the last line of a paragraph. Use the same right- and left-hand margins on both the first and second pages.

**(5) Learn the six parts of a business letter.**

Each of the six parts discussed below is illustrated in the model letter on the next page. Study this model carefully, and refer to it frequently as you read.

## The Heading

Almost all business firms use stationery imprinted with a letterhead containing the firm name and address. On such stationery only the date need be added to complete the heading. The date may be centered or typed flush with the right-hand margin; it should always be at least four spaces below the bottom of the letterhead.

A business letter typed on plain paper begins with a full three-line heading arranged in block form, giving your street address on the first line, the city and state (with a comma between them) and the zip code number on the second line, and the date (with a comma between the day and year) on the third line.

## The Inside Address

The inside address, an essential part of a business letter, is typed in block form flush with the left-hand margin. It generally begins four spaces below the date. It consists of the addressee's name (this may be the name of a firm, an individual, or both) and full address. The style of abbreviation and punctuation should be identical with that of the heading.

## The Salutation

Type the salutation flush with the left-hand margin, two spaces below the last line of the inside address. The salutation of a business letter is always followed by a colon: in

```
                        24 Hudson Road
                        Ogden, Utah 84401        ——— heading
                        July 9, 1976


Dunning and Watts, Inc.
210 Hiller Building                              ——— inside
Salt Lake City, Utah 84101                           address

Gentlemen:                                       ——— salutation

     Mr. Ralph Gray, who has applied for a position
with your firm, has requested me to send you exam-
ples of the work he has performed under my direction
at the High School of Printing Trades.  I am enclosing
four color reproductions prepared by Mr. Gray during
the past semester.                               ——— body

     The quality of Mr. Gray's work will, I believe,
speak for itself.  Let me add that he has been an ex-
ceptionally cooperative and enthusiastic student in
both his classwork and extracurricular printing
activities.

                        Truly yours,             ——— closing

                        Charles Haskell          ——— signature

                        Charles Haskell
                        Instructor in Printing

CH:ge
Enclosures (4)
```

**Model Business Letter**

all other respects, its form depends upon the form of the first line of the inside address. In the examples below, a variety of inside addresses is given, with the salutation appropriate to each address. As you study these examples, compare the first line of each address with the corresponding salutation.

1. *Inside address to a firm or group.* The first line of the address is the name of the firm or group; the traditional salutation is *Gentlemen* followed by a colon. In such an instance, it is understood that the group you are writing to may be composed of both men and women.

EXAMPLE     Western Electric Company
            195 Broadway
            New York, New York 10007

            Gentlemen:

2. *Inside address to an individual by title rather than name.*
When you are writing to a specific official but do not know his
or her name, use the correct official title as the first line of the
inside address; the correct salutation is *Dear Sir:* or *Dear Madam:*
(do *not* use *Dear Miss:*).

EXAMPLES    Sales Manager
            Corning Silver Company
            1790 Shattuck Avenue
            Berkeley, California 94704

            Dear Sir:

            Fashion Consultant
            Bon Marche Shops
            292 Rose Boulevard
            Chicago, Illinois 60607

            Dear Madam:

3. *Inside address to an individual whose name is used.* The
first line of the address is the name of the individual, preceded
by a title and followed, if possible, by an official position; the
correct salutation is *Dear Mr. ——:* The abbreviations *Mr., Mrs.,
Ms.,* and *Dr.* may be used for the titles preceding the individual's
name; all other titles, such as *Professor, Captain, Reverend,* etc.,
should be spelled out. If you do not know whether a woman is
married or unmarried, address her as *Ms.* The official title following a name in the inside address should never be abbreviated;
if it is a long title, type it in full on a second line.

EXAMPLES    Mrs. Elinor S. Clark, President
            Clark Electronic Corporation
            26 Bowdoin Street
            Boston, Massachusetts 02109

            Dear Mrs. Clark:

Ms. Dorothy Adams
Mutual Fidelity Company
710 Roanoke Building
Milwaukee, Wisconsin 53202

Dear Ms. Adams:


Professor Bruce Cunningham
Department of Mathematics
University of New Hampshire
Durham, New Hampshire 03824

Dear Professor Cunningham:


Dr. Irene Sosa
Dean, School of Education
Doremus University
Orlando, Florida 32802

Dear Dr. Sosa:


4. *Special forms of address and salutation.* Occasionally, you may wish to write a letter to a high government official, a religious dignitary, or the like. The addresses and salutations of such letters follow certain standard forms established by custom.

PRESIDENT OF THE UNITED STATES

The President
The White House
Washington, D.C. 20013

Dear Mr. President:
          *or*
Dear President _____:


UNITED STATES SENATOR

The Honorable Edward W. Brooke
Senate Office Building
Washington, D.C. 20013

Dear Senator Brooke:

UNITED STATES REPRESENTATIVE
> The Honorable Shirley Chisholm
> House Office Building
> Washington, D.C. 20013
>
> Dear Ms. Chisholm

GOVERNOR OF A STATE
> The Honorable Ella Grasso
> Governor of Connecticut
> Hartford, Connecticut 06115
>
> Dear Madam:
> > *or*
> Dear Governor Grasso:

MAYOR OF A CITY
> The Honorable Abraham Beame
> Mayor, City of New York
> New York, New York 10007
>
> Dear Sir:
> > *or*
> Dear Mayor Beame:

PRIEST OF A ROMAN CATHOLIC CHURCH
> Reverend Joseph R. Murphy
> St. Patrick's Church
> Lancaster, Pennsylvania 17601
>
> Dear Father Murphy:
> > *or*
> Reverend and dear Father Murphy:

RABBI
> Rabbi David S. Josephson
> Temple Israel
> Lancaster, Pennsylvania 17601
>
> Dear Rabbi Josephson:

MINISTER OF A PROTESTANT CHURCH

The Reverend John R. Jones
Lancaster Community Church
Lancaster, Pennsylvania 17601

Dear Mr. Jones:
*or*
Dear Father Jones:

## The Body

Begin the body of a business letter two lines below the salutation. In the majority of letters, the body is typed single space, with a double space between paragraphs.

Business, as the word suggests, is conducted by busy people. Your business letters should be as short and clear as you can make them. Decide in advance just what you want to say, preparing notes or a first draft if necessary. Decide upon the order of the points to be covered, and never try to develop two topics at once. Devote a single paragraph to each important point.

The brevity and clarity of a good business letter do not free the writer from the basic requirements of good manners — courtesy, tact, and friendliness. Writers of good business letters get their points across by simplicity and directness of language, not by curtness or rudeness of tone.

Study and restudy the phrasing of every business letter you write. Have you used wordy phrases for simple words — *at an early date,* when you mean *soon;* or *at the present time,* when you mean *now* — in a mistaken attempt to give an effect of dignity? Even worse, have you used trite and meaningless expressions because you hoped they sounded businesslike? A student of English usage once called the business letter "the great warehouse of clichés." Do not muddy your language with stilted, old-fashioned phrases such as *as per your inquiry, yours of the 15th received, we beg to reply, contents carefully noted, enclosed please find, wish to state, please be advised, thanking you in advance.*

## The Closing

Type the closing two spaces below the last line of the body of the letter, beginning at a point just to the right of the middle of the page. Capitalize the first word only, and follow the entire closing with a comma.

The phrase *Yours truly* and its variations — *Very truly yours, Yours very truly, Truly yours* — are acceptable closings for any business letter. When the writer and receiver of a letter have a close personal or business relationship, a more informal closing, such as *Sincerely yours* or *Cordially yours,* may be used. For extremely formal letters, such as those opening with the addresses and salutations listed on pages 389–91, the phrase *Respectfully yours* is appropriate.

## The Signature

Your name should be typed at least four spaces below the closing; your written signature is placed in the space between the closing and the typed signature. The typed signature is not preceded by a title unless a woman chooses to identify herself as *Miss.* The typed signature may be followed by an official title.

A married woman may give her full married name in the form she prefers.

EXAMPLES

| Very truly yours, | Yours truly, |
|---|---|
| *Donald Kennedy* | *Judith Hyde* |
| Donald Kennedy | (Miss) Judith Hyde |
| | |
| Yours truly, | Very truly yours, |
| *Ann Howland* | *Joanne Spencer* |
| (Mrs.) Ann Howland | Joanne Spencer |
| *or* (Mrs. Robert M. Howland) | Manager, Track Team |

**(6) Follow standard practice when addressing the envelope.**

Always be sure that the name and address on the envelope are identical in form with the inside address on the letter itself.

```
Joan Cooper
122 King Street
Waco, Texas   76701


                    Miss Nancy Wilson
                    2447 Park Avenue
                    Seattle, Washington   98101
```

## A Model Envelope

**(7) Learn how to fold a letter according to the procedure described.**

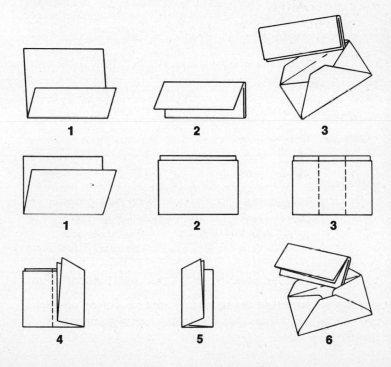

1

2

3

1

2

3

4

5

6

If the sheet is the same width as the envelope, fold the sheet about one third of the way up from the bottom, then down from the top about one third. If the sheet is wider than the envelope, fold it up from the bottom to within a quarter of an inch of the top; then fold the right side over a third of the way, and fold the left side over that. Always insert the letter into the envelope along the folded edge.

**EXERCISE 1.** This exercise is designed to test your knowledge of the inside address and salutation. Each of the following examples contains all the information necessary for these two parts of a business letter. Write or type each inside address in block form; beneath it, in the correct position, add the appropriate salutation.

1. The Director of Personnel, Erica Wilson, at the Alting Aircraft Corporation, located in zip code area 92104 in San Diego, California, at 4297 Lake Road.

2. N.O.M.A., or the National Office Management Association, located at Number 12 on East Chelten Avenue, in Philadelphia, Pennsylvania, zip code area 19144.

3. Either of the two United States senators from your state. Address the senator by name.

4. The city of Granville in the state of Ohio is the home of Denison University. Write to the Director of Admissions there, zip code area 43023.

5. The University of Michigan is in the city of Ann Arbor. Write to the Dean of Students, zip code area 48103.

**EXERCISE 2.** Write appropriate closings and signatures for each of the letters described below. Type or print the lines that would be typed in a business letter; write out any line that would be written.

1. A letter of application which you have written in response to an advertisement that appeared in your local newspaper.

2. A formal letter from George Maclaren, a physician, to his representative in Congress.

3. A business letter written by Professor Maria Trabert to a personal friend.

## 22b. Learn to write various types of business letters.

The business letter you write will conform to the rules of style, format, and content suggested on the previous pages. You can probably write an effective business letter of any type merely by using the proper form and by applying what you already know about good writing. Some of the types of letters you will write most often, however, do pose special problems of content, arrangement, and emphasis.

## The Letter of Inquiry or Request

Almost every person must occasionally write letters that ask for information. If you are interested in college, you will have to write to request a catalogue or to arrange for an interview. Travelers may write ahead for maps, folders, or other information about regions they plan to visit. In business, letters of inquiry are constantly sent out for samples, price quotations, terms of payment, etc.

A special word of caution is needed here about writing for assistance with a research or class project. Authors and other public figures have frequently protested in print about the letters they receive from students which ask, "Please write and tell me all about yourself as I am doing a term paper on you," or, "Please write and tell me all you know about New Mexico."

Before you write to such people, check to be sure that the information you seek is not available in published form. If you feel you must write, follow these suggestions: be very courteous; check form and appearance of the letter carefully; make your request very specific; and enclose a self-addressed, stamped envelope.

All letters of inquiry must be clear and should be short. If you are asking a question, you must phrase it so that the recipient cannot possibly misunderstand what you want to know or give you less information than you need. If you ask for printed matter, make clear what you want, then stop. Avoid the cliché *Thanking you in advance.* . . . Usually the information or material you seek will be given as

22 Roosevelt Avenue
Hightstown, New Jersey 08520
January 3, 1976

Director of Admissions
Douglass College
Rutgers University
New Brunswick, New Jersey 08901

Dear Sir:

    Please send me your catalogue of courses and an application form for admission to Douglass College. Although I shall not complete my high school courses at North High School until June of next year, I am already attempting to choose the college and program most suitable for me. Can you tell me, specifically, whether your institution has different requirements for the admission of liberal arts students, on the one hand, and students seeking a teaching certificate, on the other?

               Very truly yours,

               *June L. Proctor*

               June L. Proctor

a public service, and no thanks are necessary. If the recipient of your letter has made a special effort for your benefit, you may, and certainly should, write a letter of appreciation afterward.

    Students who are planning to attend college will have to write two special letters of request: one asking for a catalogue and application forms; the other, requesting an interview.

22 Roosevelt Avenue
Hightstown, New Jersey 08520
March 16, 1976

Director of Admissions
Douglass College
Rutgers University
New Brunswick, New Jersey 08901

Dear Sir:

Since I have had the chance to examine the catalogue which you so kindly sent me and have had the opportunity to talk with my counselor, I have become even more interested in applying for admission to Douglass College. In order to gain some first-hand knowledge of your campus and facilities and to talk personally with someone from the admissions office, I would like very much to arrange for a visit and an interview.

North High School, which I attend, will be on vacation from April 10 to April 17; and I understand that classes at Douglass will be in session then. That week, then, would be an ideal time for me to visit, and I would be very happy to come on any day and at any time you would suggest.

Will you please let me know when such an interview could be arranged? I look forward very much to this opportunity of visiting your college.

Very truly yours,

*June L. Proctor*

June L. Proctor

## The Letter of Adjustment or Complaint

Errors are bound to occur in business transactions; the letter of adjustment or complaint calls attention to such errors.

1. *What exactly is wrong?* Go as far back into the history of the transaction as you need to do in order to explain the error.

2. *What do you want the company to do about it?* Never

write a letter of complaint without indicating clearly the way in which you would like the error corrected. If you do not know the best method of making the adjustment, say so, and tell the recipient of your letter that you will wait for suggestions.

3. *Courtesy.* No one in business deliberately antagonizes customers by errors in service. Always remember, when you write a letter calling for an adjustment, that the error which gave rise to your complaint was unintentional. A courteous, restrained tone,

---

278 Ellsworth Road
Springfield, Illinois 62714
October 26, 1976

The Hiller Store, Inc.
1905 Grant Avenue
Springfield, Illinois 62702

Gentlemen:

On October 18 I bought a green wool skirt at your Sport and Travel Shop for $19.95 and had it charged to the account of my mother, Mrs. Henry R. Benson. When the skirt was delivered to my home on October 25, I found that the package had burst open and that the skirt itself was badly torn. I cannot judge whether the skirt was poorly packed or whether the damage was the fault of your parcel delivery service. Whatever the cause, I am returning the skirt, and would like to have its cost credited to my mother's account. You will receive the package containing the skirt by parcel post.

Very truly yours,

*Shirley Benson*

Shirley Benson

---

**Model Letter of Adjustment or Complaint**

which implies that the firms with which you deal are honest, will get the best results.

## The Letter of Application

Of all the types of business letters discussed in this section, the letter of application requires and justifies most care in preparation. The reason is obvious. In the other letters, an error in tone or in form, though unfortunate, would probably not prevent the letter from achieving its objective. In a letter of application, on the other hand, every detail — of wording, letter form, neatness, grammar, spelling, etc. — *must* be faultless. A prospective employer frequently makes the decision for or against an applicant on the basis of just such details. A good position attracts many applicants. Many letters of application must be discarded after a single hasty reading. If you are too careless to check a spelling, or too lazy to recopy a letter to improve its balance or appearance, your application may be tossed aside without serious consideration.

Whenever you write a letter of application, check its contents against the following list:

**1.** *Opening.* Begin by naming the position for which you are applying and explaining how you heard of the vacancy.

**2.** *Personal information.* In your own letters, this section will be brief. State your age. You may also give details on your health, physical appearance, etc., *if* they are relevant to the position you seek.

**3.** *Education.* Name your school, and list any courses which you feel make you especially qualified for the position. This is the place to mention any special training you may have had which may interest your prospective employer.

**4.** *Experience and personal qualifications.* At this point in your career, you may have little or no previous experience in the field of work in which you are applying for a position. Do not let this fact show up as a weak point in your letter of application. Describe the experience you do have, if any; then go on at once to give your reasons for feeling qualified to do the job well. Your interest in the field, your familiarity with its requirements, and

588 Beverly Drive
Reading, Pennsylvania 19606
June 2, 1976

Mr. Morton Miller
Baker and Miller, Inc.
710 Raleigh Building
Reading, Pennsylvania 19601

Dear Mr. Miller:

    I have learned from Mrs. Grace Thomas, your associate,
that a vacancy exists in your stenographic staff for
the summer months. Please consider me as an applicant
for this position.

    I am seventeen years old and a student in the Junior
Class at West Falls High School in this city. My course
of study has been a commercial one; during the past two
years I have had classes in shorthand, typing, bookkeeping, business English, and office practice. I can take dictation at the rate of ninety words a minute, and can type
either from shorthand notes or dictograph recordings at a
rate of about fifty words a minute. For over a year, I have
spent part of my weekends assisting my father, Mr. Frank
Stacy, president of the Imperial Welding Company, 28
Field Boulevard, as a stenographer and typist. In addition,
I have been employed at various times since last December as a part-time typist at the Reading office of the
Hartford Fidelity Company. My interest in this work and
the fact that I shall return to school for my senior year in
September make me especially suited, I feel, for the full-
time summer position with your company.

your confidence in your ability to meet these requirements — all
these will help you to "sell yourself" in your letter.

    **5.** *References.* Never give fewer than two references in a let-
ter of application; three is the usual number. The people you
name as references should be able to give a prospective employer
information about both your ability and your general character.
You should never give names as references before you have secured permission from the persons involved. You may choose
among a former employer, a teacher, a minister, an adult friend

Mr. Morton Miller        2        June 2, 1976

My father can, of course, give you information about the work I have done under his supervision. I also have permission to refer you to the following men:

Mr. Frederick Tuttle, Office Manager, Hartford Fidelity Company, 211 Hilton Building, Reading, Pennsylvania.

Mr. James Hess, principal of West Falls High School, Reading, Pennsylvania.

Reverend Francis McGinnis, rector of St. Ann's Church, 400 Manchester Drive, Reading, Pennsylvania.

May I have a personal interview at your convenience? My telephone number is Reading 9-6454.

Very truly yours,

*Helen Stacy*

Helen Stacy

of yours or your family, or a leader in your community.

**6.** *Closing.* End a letter of application with a direct request for an interview at the employer's convenience. Be sure to explain clearly where and when you may be reached by telephone.

Your letters of application should follow standard business letter form, as illustrated in the model on pages 400–01. (Notice that this letter follows the organization of material shown above.)

## The Personal Résumé

Sometimes, instead of including all information about your qualifications and background in the body of the application letter, it is better to submit this information in the form of a personal résumé.

The personal résumé — sometimes called a personal profile — is a brief summary of your education, experience, and relevant personal characteristics. This kind of presentation has several advantages: it is easier to read than a lengthy letter; several copies can be made and used for many purposes; it has an efficient and businesslike appearance.

Some suggestions about its form might be helpful. One possible model is shown on page 403. Although some people in personnel work recommend a résumé in sentence and paragraph form, the outline form shown is simpler to write and easier to read. If at all possible, keep your résumé to a single page; later on, when you have had more experience and more education, additional pages might be necessary.

In deciding what to include and what to omit in the résumé, keep in mind its essential function: to interest an employer in interviewing you by presenting in brief form the highlights of your qualifications. The résumé is not a substitute for an interview or a job application; consequently, you should not feel obliged to include every minor detail about your background. Nothing, in fact, should be included unless it gives the potential employer an additional reason for hiring you. Remember that you want most of all to create a favorable impression; be sure that both form and content create the effect you want.

If you include a résumé with your letter of application, you should not repeat any of the résumé information in the letter itself. Your letter — or "cover letter" as it is sometimes called — will be much briefer than the model shown on pages 400–01. Like that model, it will begin with a brief statement of the position for which you are applying and indicate how you learned of the vacancy. Instead of discussing your qualifications, however, a simple reference to the résumé will be enough; for example, "I am enclosing

John R. Jones

Address: 1632 Esther Drive     Telephone: BY-6-1234
         Glenside, Pennsylvania 17109
Personal: Date of birth: April 3, 1959
          Place of birth: Glenside, Pennsylvania
          Marital status: Single
          Height: 5'8"    Weight: 150
          Health: Excellent
          Selective Service Classification: Class IH
          Social Security Number: 194-12-2818
Education:
    High school: Abington Senior High School, Abington,
        Pennsylvania, June, 1977, business course.
Skill achievements: Shorthand: 120 words a minute
                    Typing: 70 words a minute
                    Business machines: dictating,
                        calculating, and duplicating
                        machines.
    Extra curricular activities: Vice President, Future
        Business Leaders of America; member, National
        Honor Society.
Experience:
    Abington Memorial Hospital, 1200 Old York Road,
        Abington, Pennsylvania--volunteer secretarial
        work after school, 1976.
    Camp Holiday, Beaver Lake, Pennsylvania--camp
        counselor, summers of 1975 and 1976.
References:
    Dr. Walter A. Smith, Principal, Abington Senior High
        School, Abington, Pennsylvania.
    Mrs. Esther A. Jones, Supervisor of Volunteers,
        Abington Memorial Hospital, Abington, Pennsyl-
        vania.
    Mr. Walter A. Bruce, Director, Camp Holiday,
        Beaver Lake, Pennsylvania.

along with this letter a résumé of my experience and education." The letter can then close with a request for an
interview.

**EXERCISE 3.** Write the following letters observing standard practice for business letters.

1. Write a letter of adjustment or complaint. Inform the credit
   department of a local store that certain items (name the items)

which you ordered were returned to the store but not credited to your account; ask that your account be adjusted to the correct balance.

2. Write a letter ordering two tickets for a performance of *Candide* which is to be given at the Watermill Summer Theater, Saugus, Massachusetts 09106, on the evening of July 10; the tickets you want cost $3.00 apiece.

3. Write a letter of application answering a help-wanted advertisement in your local newspaper for a position that you think you can fill. Cut the advertisement out of the paper and hand it in with your letter.

4. Write a letter to your representative in Congress or state senator about a piece of proposed legislation. Make sure that it is something about which you have definite convictions as well as specific information.

5. Write a letter to the editor of your school paper, taking a stand on some controversial issue affecting your school.

6. Write a letter to a local television station expressing your opinion about a show you have seen recently.

# Mechanics

# Capitalization

## Rules of Standard Usage

Correct capitalization is part of good usage. Writing *The City of washington, D.C. is the capital of the United states* is as incorrect, in its own way, as writing *He don't live hear* or *Theirs the teams skedual.* The *meaning* of these sentences is perfectly clear; but in each instance, rules of standard usage are violated. Each sentence shows a lack of understanding and control of the written language; each is unacceptable to those who follow the conventions of standard English usage.

This chapter contains the basic rules for capitalization. In your reading of books, magazines, and newspapers, you may very well find examples of capitalization or cases of a lack of capitalization that do not agree with the rules stated here. This is because capitalization practices change. For example, a word like *king* or *communist* may be capitalized in some cases and not in others. This is often a matter of the style of the piece in which the word appears. Fortunately, most writers follow the basic rules that are given here; it is only occasionally that one encounters variations. Therefore, by understanding and learning the rules, by developing the habit of applying them correctly, and by taking pride in your own writing, you can avoid capitalization errors.

Capital letters do at least three useful jobs in written English. First, they indicate the beginnings of sentences. Readers do not have the rise and fall of a speaker's voice to show them where one sentence ends and another begins. Second, capital letters distinguish proper names and titles from the other words in a sentence so that readers can grasp the meaning quickly. Third, capital letters show respect in such sentences as *The Lord is my shepherd* or *Mother Earth.*

## 23a. Capitalize the first word in every sentence.

Most students know this rule and follow it automatically. If it is not followed, the reason is usually either carelessness or the inability to recognize the end of one sentence and the beginning of the next. If you find the latter fault in your writing, review Chapter 11, "Complete Sentences," especially the pages dealing with run-on sentences.

EXAMPLES    The nominee for the state legislature was a dark horse. No one had expected her to be chosen.

"How much is she paying you?" my mother asked.

► NOTE    Although each line of poetry does not necessarily begin a new sentence, it is traditional to capitalize the first word.

EXAMPLE    Let me not to the marriage of true minds
Admit impediments. Love is not love
Which alters when it alteration finds,
Or bends with the remover to remove.

SHAKESPEARE, *Sonnet 116*

## 23b. Capitalize the pronoun *I* and the interjection *O.*

The pronoun *I* is always capitalized. The interjection *O* is used mainly as an invocation in solemn or poetic language. It should not be confused with the common interjection *oh. Oh* is capitalized only when it appears at the beginning of a sentence and is always followed by punctuation. *O* is always capitalized and never followed by punctuation.

EXAMPLES    Bowing his head, he prayed, "O Lord, hear our plea."

I think that I've read all of her books—oh, no, not the first one.

## 23c. Capitalize proper nouns and adjectives.

A *proper noun* is the name of a particular person, place, thing, or idea. Its opposite, a *common noun,* does not name any particular person or thing, but refers to any and all members of a class or type. For example, *Patsy Mink* (proper noun) is a particular *woman* (common noun); *Asia* (proper noun) is a particular *continent* (common noun); the *White House* (proper noun) is a particular *building* (common noun). As the preceding illustrations show, proper nouns are capitalized in standard usage, while common nouns are not.

| COMMON NOUN | PROPER NOUN |
|---|---|
| cat | Mittens |
| airplane | *Spirit of St. Louis* |
| automobile | Ferrari |
| novel | *The Pearl* |

A *proper adjective* is an adjective formed from a proper noun.

| PROPER NOUN | PROPER ADJECTIVE |
|---|---|
| Russia | Russian |
| Peru | Peruvian |
| India | Indian |

Proper nouns have many forms and name a great variety of persons, places, and things. Study the classification of these nouns and learn the rules that govern their capitalization.

### (1) Capitalize the names of individual persons.

Always capitalize the first letters of given names (*Leland, Mary*) and surnames (*Proctor, Taylor*).

In some surnames another letter besides the first should be capitalized. For instance, in names beginning *O'* or *Mc,* the following letter should be capitalized:

| | |
|---|---|
| O'Brien | McLean |
| O'Donahue | McCullen |
| O'Hara | McWilliams |

Usage varies in names beginning with *Mac:*

| | |
|---|---|
| MacMillan | Macmillan |
| MacLean | Maclean |

Usage also varies in the capitalization of *van, von, de, du,* and other parts of foreign names. Whenever possible, check such names against a reference source, such as a dictionary, or determine the personal preference of their owners.

Always capitalize the abbreviations *Sr., Jr.,* and *Esq.* when they follow a name:

EXAMPLES  George Hammond, Sr.    Martin Luther King, Jr.
 H. M. Pulham, Esq.

## (2) Capitalize geographical names.

POLITICAL UNITS: *Countries, states, counties, townships, cities*
 United States of America, Germany, Iran, South Carolina, Hunterdon County, Bucks County, Alexandria Township, Laramie, San Diego

LAND MASSES AND LAND FORMS: *Continents, islands, peninsulas, etc.*  North America, Europe, Iceland, Long Island, Malay Peninsula, Cape May, Cape of Good Hope, Lookout Point, Isthmus of Corinth

TOPOGRAPHICAL AND OTHER LAND FEATURES: *Mountains, canyons, plains, forests, parks, dams, etc.*  Rocky Mountains, Mount Rainier, Bryce Canyon, Plains of Abraham, Gobi Desert, Guiana Forest, Petrified Forest, Yosemite National Park, Prospect Park, Hoover Dam, Frenchtown Reservoir, Crystal Cave, Delaware Valley

*Bodies of water*  Indian Ocean, Red Sea, Persian Gulf, San Francisco Bay, Lake Michigan, Budd Lake, Bering Strait, Hudson River, Boston Harbor, Walden Pond

*Streets and roads*  River Road, Riverside Drive, Michigan Boulevard, New York Thruway, King's Highway, Route 22, Fifty-seventh Street  [Notice that in a hyphenated street number, the second word begins with a small letter.]

## (3) Capitalize compass directions when they are used as the names of definite sections of a country or of the world.

**Do not capitalize them when they merely indicate direction.**

EXAMPLES    the Far West       west of Broadway
the Southwest     heading southwest
the North           north of Philadelphia

Do not capitalize an adjective indicating direction unless it is a part of the name of a political unit or a recognized region: southern Iowa, but Southern Hemisphere; a northern climate, but Northern Ireland.

**(4) When a common noun or adjective is part of a name, it becomes a proper noun or adjective and should be capitalized. Do not capitalize such a word unless it is part of a name.**

EXAMPLES    Suez Canal        that canal
Long Island       an island in New York
Pike's Peak       a peak in the Rockies
Delta of the Nile    a delta formed by the Nile

This rule also covers nouns and adjectives used in names other than those of places. Thus, a high school, Hunterdon High School; the eve of a holiday, New Year's Eve.

▶ NOTE   An opposite process, by which proper nouns and adjectives lose their initial capital letter, goes on constantly as English grows and changes. Over a long period of time, a proper noun or a word derived from it may acquire a special meaning and become part of the common vocabulary.

EXAMPLES    sandwich     from fourth Earl of Sandwich
tuxedo       from a country club at Tuxedo Park, New York
china        from China

The change from a capital letter to a small letter does not take place all at once. In the English of our own time, many words are apparently undergoing such a change, and in these words either a capital or a small letter is acceptable — thus, india (or India) rubber, turkish (or Turkish) towel, etc. Whenever you are in doubt, consult your dictionary.

**EXERCISE 1.** Copy the following sentences and phrases, using capital letters wherever they are required. If two versions are possible, give both.

1. the near east
2. a town south of chicago
3. the mississippi delta
4. around cape horn
5. flannery o'connor
6. boulder dam
7. northern wisconsin
8. stop the presses!
9. mohave desert
10. move to the northwest
11. gulf of mexico
12. mary mcleod bethune
13. an island culture
14. vine deloria, jr.
15. stokes state park
16. a famous south american diplomat
17. delaware bay
18. swimming in the ocean
19. Turn south at the next light.
20. a persian cat
21. canadian big game
22. the rio grande
23. west indian food
24. sutton place south
25. thirty-fourth street
26. new nations of the african continent
27. the hollywood freeway
28. a river in the south
29. somerset county, new jersey
30. the dead sea
31. an english toy spaniel
32. peter m. mcdaniel, esq.
33. the woods of maine
34. the himalayan mountains of tibet
35. in the florida swamplands
36. riverside drive
37. a spanish dance
38. san pedro, california
39. a desert island
40. paris fashions
41. pennsylvania dutch
42. anchored in a nearby harbor
43. on the eve of a new life
44. along memorial drive
45. thoreau's pond
46. greek city-states
47. visit the british isles
48. countries of south america
49. macadam is named for john l. mcadam.
50. an egyptian queen

**(5) Capitalize all important words in the names of organizations, institutions, government bodies, business firms, brand names of business products, buildings, ships, planes, trains, special events, historical events and periods, items on the calendar, races, religions, tribes, and nationalities.**

► **NOTE** Throughout this section of the chapter, keep Rule 23c (4) clearly in mind: a common noun or adjective is not capitalized unless it is part of a proper name.

| | |
|---|---|
| Cornell University | a university in New York |
| Erasmus Hall High School | a high school in Brooklyn |
| Georgia State Legislature | a state legislature |

*Organizations and institutions*   United States Coast Guard, Young Men's Hebrew Association, Baltimore County Board of Education, Actors Studio, History Department, University of New Mexico, Wellesley College, New Hope High School, Junior Class

*Government bodies*   United Nations, United States House of Representatives, Department of the Interior, Tennessee Valley Authority, Court of Domestic Relations, House of Lords, Veterans' Administration

*Business firms, brand names of business products*   Harcourt Brace Jovanovich, Inc., Nevada Savings & Loan Association, Southern Railway System, General Electric, The Associated Press, Kodachrome II, Chevron Supreme, Tide

► **NOTE**   Except in advertising displays, a common noun or adjective following a brand name is *not* capitalized: Gleem toothpaste, Sweetheart soap, Rambler station wagon.

*Buildings, ships, trains, planes*   Madison Square Garden, Chrysler Building, Pasadena Playhouse, Booth Theater, *U.S.S. Nautilus* (ship), *Musketeer* (plane), *Twentieth Century Limited* (train), Mark Hopkins Hotel

*Special events*   Olympic Games, National Open Golf Championship, Junior-Senior Prom, Republican National Convention

*Historical events and periods*   Battle of Gettysburg, War Between the States, Pan American Conference, Dark Ages, Age of Reason, the Jazz Age, the Restoration

*Calendar items*   Monday, July, Memorial Day, Christmas, World Peace Week

► **NOTE**   Do not capitalize the name of a season unless it is personified.

**EXAMPLES**   the first day of winter
Old Man Winter

*Races, religions, nationalities, tribes*   Italian, Caucasian, Methodist, Roman Catholic, Boër, Brazilian, Cherokee

**(6) Do not capitalize the names of school subjects, except for proper nouns and adjectives. Course names followed by a number are usually capitalized.**

EXAMPLES    Russian, English, Greek, Sanskrit

Advanced Mathematics 301, Bookkeeping II

mathematics, bookkeeping, American history, classical literature

► **USAGE NOTE**    The name of a class may be capitalized when it specifies a particular event, e.g., Senior Prom, Freshman Picnic.

**EXERCISE 2.**    Copy the following words and phrases, using capital letters wherever they are required.

1. a revlon lipstick
2. the latin department
3. the league of nations
4. the first church of christ, scientist
5. williams college
6. the *chief* (train)
7. the securities and exchange commission
8. an off-broadway theater
9. the war of the roses
10. taking courses in applied physics
11. the world series
12. chinese cooking
13. french history
14. states' rights
15. empire state building
16. barrett & browne, inc.
17. 118 twenty-fifth street
18. on labor day
19. the government printing office
20. *queen elizabeth 2* of the cunard line
21. the hotel savoy
22. the new york world's fair
23. indian summer
24. maxwell house coffee
25. an asian history course

**EXERCISE 3.**    This exercise covers all capitalization rules presented up to this point. Each of the sentences below contains words that should be capitalized. Write these words in a list opposite the number corresponding to each sentence. When two or more words belong in a single capitalized phrase, write them as a phrase: *Grant's Tomb; Washington, D.C.; United States Military Academy;* etc.

EXAMPLE    1. An excellent novel is *national velvet* by enid bagnold. The story deals with a british girl who wants her horse to run in england's greatest race.

1. *National Velvet*
   *Enid Bagnold*
   *British*
   *England's*

1. The airedale, a large breed of dog of the terrier class, was named for the aire valley in northern england.

2. Apelles was born in colophon, ionia, a greek colony in asia minor. He became a friend of alexander the great and was alexander's court painter.

3. The constitution gives congress the power to provide for the territories of the united states. Territories that have become states are alaska and hawaii.

4. Modern universities developed from the european monastery schools of the middle ages. The oldest university in this country, founded in 1636, is harvard university in cambridge, massachusetts.

5. San francisco, california, is a city built on hills. For this reason, it often reminds visitors of rome. The ancient city of rome was built on seven hills, of which the palatine and capitoline hills are perhaps the best known.

6. Our biology II teacher, mrs. o'donnel, took us to new york city to visit the museum of natural history.

7. The european renaissance started in italy during the thirteenth century and lasted until the reformation in the 1500's. Several outstanding events of the renaissance were the end of feudalism, the beginning of modern science, the invention of movable type, and the revival of greek and roman culture.

8. Many of today's electronics engineers began as "hams." A ham who wishes to set up a transmitting station must obtain a license from the federal communications commission. The radio amateur civil emergency service is an organization that stands ready at all times to give assistance in cases of disaster. The united states army and navy both have ham organizations to give radio service in emergency situations.

9. My friend, pam jones, was born on a chicken farm on mcquinn road in a little town called maryville, about thirty miles from new york city. Today, thirty years later, the farm is the center of a bustling city. Where the chickens ranged, there are a rexall drugstore, a shell service station, the maryville high school, and the new general motors building, where small parts are manufactured.

10. The congress of the united states has the power not only to pass new laws but also to repeal old ones. Sometimes a new law repeals "by implication" an old law. The kansas-nebraska bill, for instance, had the effect of repealing the missouri compromise.

11. The longest river in the western hemisphere is the amazon in south america; the longest in the eastern hemisphere is the nile in africa.

12. In the united states, sunday is the only holiday recognized by common law. Each state has the authority to designate the holidays it will observe. The federal government designates the holidays to be observed in the district of columbia and by federal employees throughout the country.

### 23d. Capitalize titles.

**(1) Capitalize a title belonging to a particular person if it precedes the person's name. If a title stands alone or follows a person's name, capitalize it only if it refers to a high official or to someone to whom you wish to show special respect.**

EXAMPLES   Professor Webster; Joan Webster, professor of philosophy; the professor; a professor

Superintendent Chase; Dr. Chase, superintendent of schools; the superintendent; a superintendent

President Lee; Stanley F. Lee, president of Caravans, Inc.; the president; a president

General Clark; General Charles C. Clark, Chief of Staff; a general

Secretary of State Russell; B. L. Russell, Secretary of State; the Secretary of State

Queen Elizabeth II; Elizabeth II, Queen of England; the Queen of England; the Queen or queen; a queen

the Secretary of Labor; the Prime Minister; the Chief Justice of the Supreme Court; the Princess of York; the Shah of Iran; the Governor of South Dakota

Some titles are capitalized when they refer to a particular person or are used in place of a person's name. This is often true when used in sentences of direct address.

EXAMPLES  The Bishop left for England this morning.
A bishop has many administrative duties.
May I leave the hospital tomorrow, Doctor?
My doctor is a graduate of the Yale School of
Medicine.

► **NOTE** The word *president* is always capitalized when it
refers to the head of a nation; the compound word *vice-president*
is capitalized (with two capital letters) when it refers to the Vice-
President of a nation.

► **NOTE** Do not capitalize *ex-, -elect, former,* or *late* when
they are used with a title: ex-Congressman Hartley, the Governor-
elect, former President Nixon; the late President Kennedy.

The rules governing titles of honor or position also apply, in general, to words indicating family relationships,
such as *mother, father, grandmother, sister, brother, aunt.*
Such words are capitalized when they precede a name:
Uncle Norman, Cousin Elizabeth. They may be capitalized
when they are used in place of a person's name, especially
in direct address: "Did you call me, Mother?" When used
alone, they are usually not capitalized: Sara has two
sisters.

► **NOTE** Do not capitalize a word indicating relationship when
it follows a possessive noun or pronoun unless it is considered a
part of the name: Mrs. Fuller's son, my sister Ruth, but my
Aunt Jane.

**(2) Capitalize the first word and all important words in the
titles of books, magazines, newspapers, articles, historical
documents, laws, works of art, movies, and television programs.**

EXAMPLES  *Main Street, Newsweek,* the *Daily Herald,* Articles of
Confederation, Selective Service Act, Bill of Rights,
Fifth Amendment, Marshall Plan

► **NOTE** Capitalize *a, an,* or *the* in a title only when it is the
first word of the title. When used in a sentence before the names
of magazines and newspapers, these words are normally not capitalized. Long prepositions (five or more letters) are often capitalized.

EXAMPLES *The Bridge of San Luis Rey,* "A String of Beads" [*The* and *A* are part of these titles.]

the *Canterbury Tales* of Chaucer [The word *the* is not part of the title.]

the *English Journal,* the *New York Times*
*Alice's Adventures in Wonderland*

## 23e. Capitalize words referring to the Deity.

EXAMPLES God, Jehovah, the Father, the Son, the Messiah, the Almighty, the Lord

Pronouns referring to God (*he, him,* and, rarely, *who, whom,* etc.) are often capitalized.

Faith in God rests on belief in His goodness.

For He cometh, He cometh to judge the earth.

► **NOTE** Do not capitalize *god* when referring to the gods of ancient mythology.

EXAMPLE The names of ancient gods and goddesses live on in such terms as the *Titans,* an *atlas,* and *January.*

**EXERCISE 4.** Copy the following items, using capital letters wherever they are required. If an item does not require any capitals, write *C* for correct after the number.

1. the *easton express*
2. president-elect Truman
3. w. h. taft, chief justice of the supreme court
4. president of the club
5. ex-senator margaret chase smith
6. the *mona lisa* (painting)
7. a captain in the air force
8. the privileges of a senator
9. the duke of bedford
10. aunt rosa
11. the constitution of the united states
12. *the edge of night* (television program)
13. congresswoman jordan of texas
14. cocaptains of the basketball team
15. the mckinley tariff
16. the interstate commerce commission
17. the *tv guide*
18. thus saith the Lord, who bringeth everlasting life.
19. the senator's speech
20. mayor hinkle

21. the late bessie smith
22. "don't forget, mother."
23. zeus, the ruler of the gods.
24. the president of our company
25. the duchess of windsor

## 23f. Capitalize the parts of a compound word as if each part stood alone.

EXAMPLES   French-speaking students, God-given rights [Only the first parts of these compound words would be capitalized if they stood alone.]

pro-Chinese feelings, un-American sentiment, non-Hellenic culture, pre-Victorian [The prefixes are not normally capitalized; the proper adjectives are always capitalized.]

Italian-American, Indo-European [Capitalize both parts of a compound word made up of two proper nouns or adjectives.]

**REVIEW EXERCISE.** This exercise covers all capitalization rules presented in the chapter. Write lists of the words that should be capitalized in the following sentences. See Exercise 3 (page 414) for an example of the form in which these lists should be written.

1. The league of nations, an international association of countries created after world war I, has been compared with the united nations. The league was formed in january, 1920, in geneva, switzerland, under the leadership of the late president of the united states, woodrow wilson. The charter of the united nations was developed from proposals agreed upon at a conference held at dumbarton oaks, an estate in washington, d.c. In 1945 the dumbarton oaks proposals were put before the san francisco conference. The united nations charter was ratified on october 24, 1945.

2. The english writer oliver goldsmith was a "jack-of-all-literary-trades." He is remembered for a novel, *the vicar of wakefield,* and a well-loved poem, "the deserted village"; his play, *she stoops to conquer,* is still read and acted. He also wrote a *history of rome,* several biographies, a volume of essays, a series of letters, a history of england, and *the citizen of the world.* This versatile eighteenth-century writer, who

was a friend of dr. samuel johnson and of sir joshua reynolds, is buried in westminster abbey.

3. The science department of ellensville high school, through its director, dr. mcadoo, has said that juniors and seniors who wish to qualify for advanced-standing courses in chemistry or physics must maintain an average of eighty-five in earth science I or biology I.

4. Atlantic city, the nationally known seaside resort, is located on the southeastern coast of the state of new jersey about 140 miles south of the city of new york and 60 miles southeast of philadelphia. It is on an island called absecon beach. Famous for its boardwalk, shops, hotels, piers, and conventions, it is also the home of the miss america pageant.

5. All english-speaking students should know something about the history of their language. English and american english derive mainly from anglo-saxon, or old english, which was the language developed in britain by german tribes who invaded the island in the fifth century. English has been influenced and changed down through the years by many tongues such as danish, latin, norman or old french, greek, and even american indian. European and asian words have become a part of our vocabulary and science has brought new words into our always-changing language.

## SUMMARY STYLE SHEET

| | |
|---|---|
| Garden City | a city in Kansas |
| Yellowstone National Park | a national park |
| North Carolina | northern New Hampshire |
| the South | facing south |
| Pacific Ocean | an ocean voyage |
| Fifth Avenue | a broad avenue |
| Lions Club | a service club |
| Union Oil Company | an oil company |
| John Jay High School | a new high school |
| House of Commons | the lower house |
| Hotel Commodore | a hotel in New York |
| War Between the States | an internal war |
| Grand Central Station | a railroad station |

| | |
|---|---|
| Independence **D**ay | a **d**ay to celebrate freedom |
| the **J**unior **D**ance | a **d**ance given by **j**uniors |
| **S**panish, **G**erman, **E**nglish | **a**lgebra, **c**hemistry, **s**hop |
| United States **H**istory II | a course in **h**istory |
| Wrapped in fur, **W**inter comes. | **w**inter, **s**pring, **s**ummer, **f**all, **a**utumn |
| Ford **t**ruck | |
| a **C**atholic, a **S**wiss | |
| **D**ean Oakes | Dr. Oakes, the **d**ean |
| the **P**resident of the U.S. | our company **p**resident |
| the **S**enator | the oldest **s**enator |
| Ask **F**ather, **C**ousin Sue. | his **f**ather, Mary's **c**ousin |
| **A P**ortrait of the **A**rtist | |
| the **R**eader's **D**igest | |
| **G**od in **H**is goodness | the **g**ods of mythology |
| Representative-**e**lect Watt | |

# Punctuation

## End Marks and Commas

When we listen to ordinary speech, we do not hear sounds or words alone; we hear groups of words that we understand as phrases, clauses, or full sentences. We are able to hear these groups of words because the speaker stresses certain words, puts in pauses where they are needed, and changes pitch of voice according to the sentence sense.

When we write a sentence, we show these pauses by using marks of punctuation. Not all punctuation conforms to the pauses we use in speech; some, like the sen.icolon, are used in a traditional way to show grammatical relationships that cannot be expressed by the voice alone. Others, however, match the rise and fall of our voices, called inflection, and the stops, or pauses, we use to separate groups.

In speech, when we want to show that a thought is complete, our voice drops in pitch and we make a long pause. In writing, this full stop is indicated by a period. When we make a shorter pause, we show a break in thought, such as a nonessential clause or a word or a phrase in apposition. A comma — sometimes a dash or parentheses — indicates this half stop in writing. In asking a question, the tendency is to raise the voice before coming to a full stop; a question mark represents this in writing.

The way we use our voice is often a guide to proper punctuation, but if we depended only on marks that indicate speech pauses we would soon find them inadequate. Writing is more formal than speech and shows relationships that are not used in speaking. For example, a semicolon tells the reader that two clauses, which could be separate sentences, are closely related and should be understood as a unit. Other marks of punctuation, such as quotation marks, apostrophes, colons, are used to prevent misreading or to point out special ways of using words — as in showing dialogue, titles of poems, dates, and time.

For many years English writing was marked by extremely full and detailed punctuation that now seems excessive to us. Too much punctuation interferes with easy reading, just as a speaker who continually pauses or stops is hard to understand. Overpunctuation can be avoided by remembering to use a mark of punctuation for only two reasons: (1) because meaning demands it, or (2) because conventional usage requires it. If a sentence is unclear to begin with, punctuation will not clarify it. If you find yourself struggling with the punctuation of a particular sentence, ask yourself whether the trouble lies in your arrangement of phrases or choice of words. The problem can often be eliminated by recasting the sentence.

The following chapters provide rules for the use of all the marks of punctuation that you will normally need, and exercises to help you remember these rules.

## END MARKS

In written English, an end mark, or full stop, indicates the close of a sentence. The choice of the correct end mark is not a difficult one. However, if you find that you often omit end marks, you should review the rules, examples, and exercises on run-on sentences in Chapter 11.

**24a. A statement is followed by a period.**

EXAMPLE   As you leave, turn out the light.

**24b. An abbreviation or initial is followed by a period.**

EXAMPLES   U.A.R.          United Arab Republic
           Jan.            January

Mr.          Mister
A.D.        *anno Domini* (or "in the year of the Lord")
W. C. Handy    William Christopher Handy

## 24c. A question is followed by a question mark.

EXAMPLE    Who is going with you?

**(1) Use the question mark after a direct question only; do not use it after a declarative sentence containing an indirect question.**

CORRECT    She wants to know who is going with you. [a declarative sentence containing an indirect question]

**(2) Orders and requests are often put in question form out of courtesy, even when no real question is intended. Such a question may be followed by either a period or a question mark, though it is wise to use the question mark as a rule.**

CORRECT    Will you please call me at my home?
               Will you please call me at my home.

**(3) A question mark should be placed inside quotation marks when the quotation is a question. Otherwise, it should be placed outside quotation marks.**

EXAMPLES    My little sister is going through a stage in which it seems that the only thing she can say is, "Who cares?" [The quotation is a question.]

Did the witness use the words, "I saw Marie Ward enter the house"? [The quotation is not a question. The whole sentence, however, is a question.]

## 24d. An exclamation is followed by an exclamation mark.

EXAMPLES    Bravo! [emphatic interjection]
               What a terrific game! [emphatic phrase]
               I cannot believe it! [emphatic sentence]
               Shut that door! [emphatic command]

**(1) An interjection at the beginning of a sentence is almost always followed by a comma.**

CUSTOMARY   Oh, no, don't tell me!

RARE   Oh! No! Don't tell me!

**(2) An exclamation mark should be placed inside quotation marks when the quotation itself is an exclamation. Otherwise, it should be placed outside the quotation marks.**

EXAMPLES   "Block that kick!" the crowd shouted in unison.

Don't tell me, "Get ready"!

**(3) Do not use an exclamation mark unless a statement is obviously emphatic.**

INCORRECT   The party was a lot of fun!

CORRECT   The party was a lot of fun.

**EXERCISE 1.** All of the periods, exclamation marks, and question marks have been omitted from the following passage. When you find such an omission, write the number of the line in which it occurs. After each number, copy the word or words in that line which you think should be followed by end marks. After each word, write the end mark required. If quotation marks should precede or follow the end mark, write them in the proper place. If a new sentence should begin after the end mark, write the first word of that sentence, giving it a capital letter. Be very careful to write the words after the number of the line in which they appear. Not all lines require end marks; some need two.

EXAMPLE   1  "What did you think of the game" I asked Sally as
             2  we left the field
             3  "It was an exciting game," she replied "it would
             4  have been better though if we'd won"

             1. *game?"*
             2. *field.*
             3. *replied. "It*
             4. *won."*

1      One night last week the whole gang gathered at my house
2   to tell the truth, no one seemed to be having a very good
3   time — everyone was just sitting around "What shall I do
4   now." I asked myself
5      Just as this thought entered my head, Jack bounced out
6   of his chair
7      "This is a party" he exclaimed in a disgusted tone "Let's
8   dance"
9      Jack loves to dance, and I do, too
10     No one responded to him everyone just sat back and
11  said nothing Sue shrugged her shoulders
12    "You're the beat generation all right" Jack continued in
13  a sarcastic tone "How did you spend the afternoon — mowing
14  lawns"
15    "For your information," Sue replied, "my afternoon was
16  spent cleaning my room I'm pooped"
17    "I ran errands all day for my parents you know what
18  that's like," Harry added as he moved from the couch and
19  stretched out on the floor picking up a pillow, Nancy placed
20  it under his head as she did this, Harry turned on his side
21  and closed his eyes
22    "This party is dying a slow death, if it isn't already dead,"
23  Jack mumbled "can't someone think of something to do"
24    "Let's play Detective," Tom suggested dryly from his
25  comfortable chair, "and Jack can be the first victim"
26    "How about it, Jack" Sue added "that's the best idea
27  I've heard all evening"
28    "You kids make me sick" Jack exploded "All you want
29  to do is lie around let's *do* something"
30    To tell the truth, my sympathy was with Jack I wracked
31  my brain to try to think of what to say next
32    "How about charades" I asked hopefully, but I am sure
33  a tone of desperation showed through
34    Tom and Sue groaned
35    "Horrors, don't mention charades" Nancy cried "You
36  have to think to play that Look at Harry," she pointed
37  toward his recumbent body "is he in any condition to
38  think"
39    Harry rolled over without opening his eyes
40    "Well, then, how about a game of Monopoly" Jack asked
41    More groans from Tom and Sue this time Nancy added
42  one, too

43    Jack went over to the record player, picked out the loud-
44    est song he could find, and then set up the volume as high
45    as it would go
46        "Turn that thing off" Tom shouted above the blare
47        "A person can't sleep in peace around here," Harry
48    complained, rolling over again
49        "Please, Jack," Nancy begged, "be quiet you're waking
50    Harry"
51        As he turned off the record player, Jack gave me a
52    questioning look I am sure that I heard his unspoken
53    words correctly they were "let's get out of here" I nodded
54    "Yes"
55        I know that it is not polite to leave a party, especially
56    when you are the host, but what could I do For weeks I had
57    been hoping that Jack and I would go out, but we had never
58    gotten around to it
59        "In fact," I said to myself happily as Jack and I headed
60    toward town in his parents' car, "Nancy and the rest of the
61    gang were darn good friends to help me out like this"
62        They wouldn't mind being left alone

## THE COMMA

Next to end marks, the comma is the most frequently used
mark of punctuation. It groups words that belong together
and separates those that do not. It is also used in conventional ways that have little to do with meaning.

### Items in a Series

### 24e. Use commas to separate items in a series.

EXAMPLES    The guidance counselor recommended that I take
English, algebra, chemistry, and Latin. [words in
a series]

Will you spend your vacation in the mountains, on
the lake, or at the seashore? [phrases in a series]

On the day before our College Boards, our teacher
suggested that we go home, that we eat a good dinner, that we take a relaxing bath, and that we get to
bed early. [clauses in a series]

**(1) Do not place a comma before or after a series.**

INCORRECT   The coach expects, obedience, hard work, and
quick thinking, from every person on the team.

CORRECT   The coach expects obedience, hard work, and
quick thinking from every person on the team.

EXCEPTION   The abbreviation *etc.* is always followed by a comma
unless it occurs at the end of a sentence.

EXAMPLE   Bring food, comfortable shoes, a sleeping bag, etc.,
for the overnight hike.

**(2) When the words** *and, or,* **or** *nor* **join the last two items
in a series, the comma before the conjunction is sometimes
omitted. Follow the practice prescribed by your teacher.
Never omit the final comma, however, if such an omission
will make the sentence unclear.**

UNCLEAR   Zinnias come in many colors: yellow, orange, purple,
magenta, red and white.   [Do zinnias come in five or
six colors? If the answer is "six," then a comma should
be used after *red.*]

CLEAR   Zinnias come in many colors: yellow, orange, purple,
magenta, red, and white.

▶ **NOTE**   Words customarily used in pairs are set off as one
item in a series: *pancakes and syrup, bread and butter, profit
and loss, hat and coat, pork and beans,* etc.

EXAMPLE   The "great American breakfast" consists of orange
juice, ham and eggs, toast, and coffee.

**(3) Do not use commas when all the items of a series are
linked by** *and, or,* **or** *nor.*

EXAMPLES   Mother and Father and Jane and I all flew.

The forecasters could not make up their minds — they
predicted sunshine or clouds or showers.

## 24f. Use commas to separate two or more adjectives that modify the same noun.

EXAMPLE   She is a young, dynamic, creative woman.

▶ **NOTE**   A comma is unnecessary before a modifier so closely associated with the noun that the two words are thought of as one. (Two words this closely related are referred to as an open compound: *disc jockey, young man, movie actor.*)

EXAMPLE   She is a dynamic, creative young woman.

One device that is used to determine when two adjectives modify the noun equally is the substitution of *and* for the possible comma: *dynamic (and) creative young woman.* If this can be done, then a comma is called for. Another test is that a comma is needed if the order of the adjectives can be reversed: *She is a creative, dynamic young woman.*

**EXERCISE 2.**  Some of the following sentences contain series requiring commas. Number your paper 1–10. Copy after the proper number the words in each sentence that should be followed by a comma, placing the comma after the word. Watch for sentences in which the inclusion or omission of a comma affects the meaning. Be prepared to explain the punctuation that you use. If a sentence does not require any commas, write *C* after the number.

 1. The dull dreary morning sky looked ominous to the members of the mountain-climbing expedition.

 2. The article about Gertrude Stein considered her social background her style and her theories of poetry.

 3. He was formerly on the staff of the embassies in Moscow, Berlin, Vienna, and Madrid.

 4. We had a most delicious luncheon: cold consommé chicken à la king garden asparagus freshly baked biscuits French ice cream and black coffee.

 5. My birthday gifts included a new coat with a hat to match a dress of the same color a handbag and shoes of very soft leather and a gift certificate for fifty dollars.

 6. After its last meeting, the student council suggested that monitors be stationed in the halls that discipline problems be tried before a student court and that seniors be dismissed from class one minute before the last bell of the day.

 7. All water pistols firecrackers paper airplanes etc. are outlawed as of September.

8. This outdoor furniture comes in various color combinations:
   red and white green and black yellow and brown and blue
   and silver.

9. Have you ever experienced such a miserably cold wet summer?

10. Infinite patience an inquiring mind and a sense of humor
    are assets in any profession.

## Commas Between Independent Clauses

**24g. Use a comma before** *and, but, or, nor, for, yet*
**when they join independent clauses.**

EXAMPLES   We subscribe to seven magazines, and I find it impossible to read all of them every month.

Marisol was born in France, but she grew up in South America.

Mr. Ballin is a popular teacher, for he is known to be fair, and he has a sense of humor.

Rule 24g applies to compound *sentences*, not compound *verbs*, compound *subjects*, and the like. In the examples below, commas should not be used.

EXAMPLES   I ordered four pairs of mittens but received only three pairs.   [compound verb]

What we hope for and what we get are usually two quite different things.   [compound subject]

My sister did her undergraduate work at Cornell and her graduate work at Yale.   [compound object]

► **NOTE**   Rule 24g is always correct; however, writers are allowed freedom in its application. When two independent clauses joined by a conjunction are very short and closely connected in thought, the comma between them may be omitted.

EXAMPLES   The curtain rose and I was "on."

I'll meet you but I'll be late.

The comma should never be omitted if a sentence is unclear without it.

NOT CLEAR   I'll wait for Stephen and Ana can go with you.

[Most readers would have to go over this sentence twice before realizing that the writer is not saying *I'll wait for Stephen and Ana.*]

CLEAR   I'll wait for Stephen, and Ana can go with you.

*You are expected to follow Rule 24g in all instances in the exercises in this book.*

## Nonessential Elements

**24h. Use commas to set off nonessential clauses and nonessential participial phrases.**

A nonessential clause or phrase[1] is exactly what the adjective says it is—not essential. Such a clause may be used to describe something, to explain something, or to add extra information, but it can be omitted without changing the basic (essential) meaning of the sentence.

NONESSENTIAL   Margaret Mead, who is a disciple of Ruth Benedict, is a noted anthropologist.

The basic meaning of this sentence is *Margaret Mead is a noted anthropologist.* The subordinate clause *who is a disciple of Ruth Benedict* can be dropped without changing this basic meaning in any way because it simply adds a bit of information to the sentence. We call this latter clause *nonessential* because it does not restrict or limit the words that it modifies (*Margaret Mead*). Most clauses that modify proper nouns are nonessential.

Now consider the sentence that you have just read.

ESSENTIAL   Most clauses **that modify proper nouns** are nonessential.

Notice what happens to the meaning of the sentence if we omit the subordinate clause; we are left with *Most clauses are nonessential.* Obviously, this is not the meaning intended by the writer. In this sentence, omitting the subordinate clause *does* change the meaning since the clause

[1] Nonessential phrases and clauses are also called *unrestrictive* or *nonrestrictive*.

(*that modify proper nouns*) is essential to the meaning. We call this clause *essential* because it restricts or limits the word that it modifies (*clauses*); that is, it tells us that those *clauses that modify proper nouns* — and only those clauses — are almost always nonessential.

NONESSENTIAL The author of *Blackberry Winter*, **who is Margaret Mead,** is a noted anthropologist. [*The author of* Blackberry Winter *is a noted anthropologist* is the basic meaning of the sentence; therefore, *commas.*]

ESSENTIAL The early experiences **that Margaret Mead had as an anthropologist** are recorded in her book *Blackberry Winter.* [*The early experiences are recorded in her book* Blackberry Winter is *not* the basic meaning of the sentence; therefore, *no commas.*]

NONESSENTIAL American drama, **which began its development later than the American novel,** underwent a renaissance in the 1920's.

ESSENTIAL The one dramatist **who was most responsible for the renaissance** was Eugene O'Neill.

Understanding the difference between essential and nonessential clauses can be a valuable help in expressing the exact meaning that you have in mind. If commas were never used, some clauses could often be interpreted as either essential or nonessential.

EXAMPLE Mystery story readers (,) who appreciate suspense(,) will enjoy the works of Agatha Christie.

Notice the commas in parentheses. If these commas are included in the sentence, we have one meaning; if they are omitted, we have another, and very different, meaning. When commas are used, the writer is saying that *every* mystery story reader will enjoy Agatha Christie; the information in the subordinate clause merely explains *why* they will do so. Without the commas, however, the subordinate clause is essential and the meaning of the sentence is that only those who especially appreciate suspense will enjoy reading Christie; others may not.

## Participial Phrases

Participial phrases, like clauses, may be nonessential or essential. To differentiate nonessential from essential phrases, use the same tests that you have applied to clauses. When in doubt, read the sentence without the phrase; if the sentence still has the same basic meaning, the phrase is nonessential and should be set off by commas.

NONESSENTIAL   The President, knowing the need for drastic action, declared the entire state a disaster area. [If *knowing the need for drastic action* is omitted, the meaning of the sentence is not changed.]

ESSENTIAL   Anyone knowing the condition of the region will approve the President's action. [The phrase *knowing the condition of the region* is necessary to make the meaning clear.]

NONESSENTIAL   Rosemary Casals, known to many Americans, plays an excellent tennis game.

ESSENTIAL   A Casals match enjoyed by many took place in the 1973 Family Circle tournament.

**EXERCISE 3.**  Some of the sentences in this exercise contain nonessential phrases and clauses; others contain essential phrases and clauses. None of the sentences are ambiguous; that is, the italicized groups of words *must* be either nonessential or essential. Number your paper 1–20. If the italicized phrase or clause is essential, write *E* after the proper number; if it is nonessential, write *Commas* to indicate that you would use commas in this sentence.

1. Anyone *wishing to join the Biology Club on its field trip* should notify the secretary before ten o'clock tomorrow.
2. Alfalfa *which returns nitrogen to the soil* is used extensively in crop rotation.
3. The symphony *that Beethoven called the "Eroica"* was composed to celebrate the memory of a great man.
4. From the composer's letters, we know that the "great man" *whom he had in mind* was Napoleon Bonaparte.
5. Natalie Curtis *always interested in American Indian music* was an early recorder of American Indian songs.

6. That newborn snakes can live for months without food is a fact *known to few people.*

7. The musician *who founded the annual music festival in Puerto Rico* was Pablo Casals.

8. Semantics *which is concerned with the meanings of words and their effects on human behavior* is an interesting study for high school students.

9. Their house *which is perched on the bluff* is completely modern in design and materials.

10. All persons *applying for the position of camp counselor* must have had previous experience.

11. The new highway is the one *that skirts the city.*

12. Latin America covers an area *stretching from Mexico to Cape Horn.*

13. The Cabinet *which includes heads of executive departments* advises the President on national and international affairs.

14. Some of the hikers *unaccustomed to the fast pace* fell behind soon after we started the climb.

15. The new requirements apply to any student *who wishes to take an honors course.*

16. The new car *looking better than ever in the bright sunlight* raced down the empty highway.

17. The man *living next door* is a retired admiral.

18. Novels and short stories *that attempt to recreate life as it is* do not always end happily.

19. The comments *printed as footnotes in the second edition* make amusing reading.

20. Mrs. Peabody *who loved the movies* always brought her own popcorn.

## Introductory Elements

### 24i. Use a comma after certain introductory elements.

**(1) Use a comma after words such as *well, yes, no, why,* etc., when they begin a sentence.**

EXAMPLES  Why, I can't believe it!

No, it's impossible to leave now.

Well, I will think it over.

Yes, I can join you tomorrow.

## (2) Use a comma after an introductory participial phrase.

EXAMPLES    Rapping her gavel on the table, Shirley called the meeting to order.   [present participle]

Struck by lightning, the ancient oak tree crashed to the ground.   [past participle]

► **NOTE**   Remember that verb forms ending in *–ing* may also be verbal nouns, or gerunds (see page 48). When a gerund phrase is used as the subject of a sentence, do not mistake it for an introductory participial phrase.

EXAMPLES    **Reading late into the night** is a favorite pastime of mine.   [The gerund phrase, *Reading late into the night,* is the subject of the sentence.]

**Reading late into the night,** I enjoyed the peace and quiet absent during the daytime.   [The introductory participial phrase modifies *I.*]

## (3) Use a comma after a succession of introductory prepositional phrases.

EXAMPLE    During the first half of our trip down the Mississippi, all five of us were seasick.

► **NOTE**   A single introductory prepositional phrase need not be followed by a comma unless it is parenthetical (*on the other hand, in general*) or the comma helps to make the meaning clear.

EXAMPLES    In Paris, jaywalking is not a punishable offense. [Without the comma, a hasty reader might misunderstand this sentence.]

On the other hand, jaywalking in New York City is a misdemeanor.   [parenthetical expression]

## (4) Use a comma after an introductory adverb clause.

EXAMPLES    While the hardcover edition of the book was still on the best-seller list, a paperback edition was published.

Because that magazine often contains clever satires and parodies, we sometimes read it in English class.

A subordinate clause that follows an independent clause is not usually set off by a comma.

EXAMPLE   Some of the hot pools in Yellowstone National Park were destroyed when an earthquake shook the area in 1959.

**EXERCISE 4.**   This exercise covers all comma rules to this point in the chapter. Number your paper 1–10. Copy after the proper number the words in each sentence that should be followed by a comma, then place a comma after each of these words.

1. If I had known that it was going to be such hard work I might not have taken the junior course in creative writing.
2. Mrs. Gladstone who was teaching the course that year was the teacher I had had in sophomore English and I thought I could gain a lot from taking her course.
3. Well after a few weeks of assignments I realized that there was a lot more to writing a story than putting words down on paper.
4. Because the stories in our literature anthology seemed so short simple and easy to read I had thought it would be a breeze.
5. At first I decided to write a football story but then I realized that I really did not know enough about football never having played the game.
6. After discarding polo and ice hockey for the same reason I got an inspiration.
7. I would write a story about the War Between the States for we had been studying it in history.
8. When I tried to imagine how a young Confederate soldier would feel about having to fight in the Battle of Gettysburg I was at a loss again.
9. My difficulty was that I had never been in the South and had never been a soldier; I was a young peaceable high school girl living in a quiet country town in New England.
10. When I was ready to give up I remembered that the best way to write is to choose a subject that you know about have experienced or have discovered for yourself.

## Interrupters

**24j.** **Use commas to set off expressions that interrupt the sentence.**

To set off an expression takes two commas unless the expression comes first or last in the sentence.

**(1) Appositives and appositive phrases are usually set off by commas.**

An appositive is a word — with or without modifiers — that follows a noun or a pronoun and identifies or explains it. An appositive phrase consists of an appositive and its modifiers.

EXAMPLES     Claude McKay's *Banjo,* the book I have often told you about, was first published in 1929, the year the Great Depression began.
Have you met Mr. Luro, our new Spanish teacher?

When an appositive is so closely related to the word it modifies that it appears to be part of that word, no comma is necessary. An appositive of this kind is called a restrictive appositive. It is usually one word.

EXAMPLES     her cousin Arleen
the French writer Colette
my friend Boris
the word *dichotomy*

**(2) Words used in direct address are set off by commas.**

EXAMPLES     Helen, did you hear what I said?
I know, Ramón, that you will do well.
What is your chief complaint, children?

**(3) Parenthetical expressions are set off by commas.**

Many words and phrases are used parenthetically. Such expressions may serve as explanations or qualifications, but they do not affect the grammatical construction of the sentence in which they appear. The following list contains a few of the most commonly used parenthetical expressions.

after all                                incidentally
as a matter of fact                      in fact
by the way                               in the first place
consequently                             naturally
for example                              nevertheless
however                                  on the other hand
I believe (hope, think, etc.)            therefore

EXAMPLES   As a matter of fact, I was just going to call you.

That is, of course, only one opinion.

Why don't you come, too?

Of course, these expressions need not be used parenthetically. When they are not, do not set them off by commas.

EXAMPLES   It is, in my opinion, an excellent book. [parenthetical]

Are you interested in my opinion of the book? [not parenthetical]

► NOTE  A contrasting expression introduced by *not* is parenthetical and should be set off by commas.

EXAMPLE   It is the humidity, not the heat, that is so exhausting.

Subrule (3) is often deliberately not followed for several reasons. First, a writer may omit the commas setting off a parenthetical expression in order to avoid overpunctuating a sentence. Second, and of great importance, is the writer's intention. When you wish the reader to pause, to consider the expression as parenthetical, set it off; if not, leave it unpunctuated. You will always be safe, however, if you follow subrule (3).

**EXERCISE 5.** This exercise covers the four kinds of interrupters discussed in the preceding pages. Copy the following sentences, and insert commas wherever needed.

1. I think they would be surprised to learn that rules are not as a matter of fact made to be broken.

2. Ms. Grant's office the one at the end of the hall contains most if not all the books you will need.

3. Some of Eugene O'Neill's early plays moody one-act dramas of the sea established his reputation with at least one important group the critics.

4. Now ladies and gentlemen of the jury the time has come to consider the facts and to reach a just decision.

5. Some novels such as *Moby Dick* and *The Red Badge of Courage* are more than just the adventure stories they appear to be on the surface.

6. Martha my first cousin told Fred her brother that my sister Jane wanted to meet Fred's friend Larry.

7. Mark Twain was not merely a clown and entertainer but a great novelist perhaps the greatest of his time and place.

8. Mrs. Phillips the principal of our high school has one outstanding characteristic: she always tries I think to be fair to the students.

9. It is the pressure of getting work in on time not the work itself that gets on my nerves.

10. Why may I ask did you promise to keep the secret when as a matter of fact you knew you were not going to do so?

## Conventional Uses

### 24k. Use a comma in certain conventional situations.

**(1) Use a comma to separate items in dates and addresses.**

EXAMPLES   The reunion was held on Wednesday, June 16, 1965.

Helene's new address is 35 Rumsen Street, Hiram, Ohio 44234.   [Notice that the zip code number follows the name of the state without punctuation.]

► NOTE   When only the month and year are given, no punctuation is necessary.

EXAMPLE   In July 1976 we celebrated the two-hundredth anniversary of the United States.

When the items are joined by a preposition, commas are not used.

It is **on** Route 64 **near** Princeton, New Jersey.

**(2) Use a comma after the salutation of a friendly letter and after the closing of any letter.**

EXAMPLES   Dear Rosa,          Sincerely yours,

## Unnecessary Commas

**24l. Do not use unnecessary commas.**

One of the greatest comma faults is the overuse of the comma, and the commonest example of this is separation of the subject and the verb by a comma, particularly when the subject is followed by a series of phrases or clauses.

INCORRECT   The coach's sharp command to the players in the field, was drowned out by the cheering crowd. [*Command* is the subject; it must not be separated by a comma from the verb *was drowned*.]

CORRECT   The coach's sharp command to the players in the field was drowned out by the cheering crowd.

▶ **NOTE**   Although at first glance the comma following a non-essential clause or phrase may seem to separate the subject and verb, this is really not so, since nonessential elements in the middle of a sentence are set off, that is, preceded and followed by commas.

The pitcher, who was batting only .250, hit the second home run of the day.

If you remember that a nonessential element in the *middle* of a sentence must always have *two* commas, you will have little difficulty with this rule.

Although the comma can be used to advantage by a writer who is aware of the effect of making something par-enthetical, too often commas are put in where a young writer "feels" they should be. True, commas do reflect speech pauses, but not every pause in a spoken line is indicated by a comma. If you remember the rules you have learned in this chapter and apply them to your writing, there will be little chance of your overusing this very use-ful device.

**REVIEW EXERCISE.** This exercise covers end marks and all comma uses. Copy each sentence, inserting punctuation and capitalization where necessary.

1. When Dr Hayden the county medical officer arrived at the scene of the wreck she ordered the area cleared set up an emergency-aid station and at once began to treat the injured.
2. First performed on March 11 1959 on Broadway New York Lorraine Hansberry's play *A Raisin in the Sun* which was later made into a movie was awarded the New York Drama Critics Circle Award.
3. Although the tennis court looked ragged Maria's mother settling back observed that it wouldn't take us more than a few hours to have it looking clean smooth and brand-new.
4. Well driving on this road we cannot possibly get to Rutland Vermont for the map shows that we are following a route which will take us westward to Whitehall New York.
5. On her walk through the streets of her old neighborhood she was astonished to find apartment houses theaters and supermarkets in places where she remembered empty lots or woods or tiny one-family houses.
6. A house may be the perfect retreat from the struggles of daily living but why does it have to be above ground when an underground house has so many advantages?
7. Protected from wind rain and cold an underground house will have low fuel bills.
8. The owner will not have to pay for exterior painting which is necessary every few years on a surface house.
9. On a fine saturday morning in early spring you won't have to stay home mow the lawn wash the windows etc. for there'll be no windows or lawn.
10. If the Congress of this country ever decides that people have to move underground to save space I'll be the first to go.

## SUMMARY OF THE USES OF THE COMMA

24e. Use commas to separate items in a series.
24f. Use commas to separate two or more adjectives that modify the same noun.

24g. Use a comma before <u>and</u>, <u>but</u>, <u>or</u>, <u>nor</u>, <u>for</u>, <u>yet</u> when they join independent clauses.

24h. Use commas to set off nonessential clauses and nonessential participial phrases.

24i. Use a comma after certain introductory elements.

(1) After words such as <u>well</u>, <u>yes</u>, <u>no</u>, <u>why</u>, etc., when they begin a sentence

(2) After an introductory participial phrase

(3) After a succession of introductory prepositional phrases

(4) After an introductory adverb clause

24j. Use commas to set off expressions that interrupt the sentence.

(1) Appositives

(2) Words in direct address

(3) Parenthetical expressions

24k. Use a comma in certain conventional situations.

(1) To separate items in dates and addresses

(2) After the salutation of a friendly letter and the closing of any letter

24l. Do not use unnecessary commas.

**Chapter**  **25**

# Punctuation

## Other Marks of Punctuation

The basic punctuation tools have been given in the last chapter. With end marks and commas alone, you can probably punctuate most of the sentences you write, and your meaning will be clear. However, just as you have learned to express complex thoughts in complex sentences, so you can learn to use effectively the punctuation signals given in this chapter. Many of their uses will be conventional, but many will also help you to write more involved sentences clearly.

## THE SEMICOLON

The semicolon has often been described as either a weak period or a strong comma; in other words, it is part period and part comma. The most common use of the semicolon is to indicate a close relationship between two independent clauses.

**25a. Use a semicolon between independent clauses not joined by** *and, but, for, or, nor, yet.*

EXAMPLES   The last day of summer vacation finally arrived; reluctantly we prepared for the first day of a new school year.

She was willing to compromise; you were not.

Do not use a semicolon to join independent clauses unless

there is a close relationship in thought between the main ideas of the clauses.

NONSTANDARD   She enjoys ice skating; she learned how to roller skate when she was a mere child.

STANDARD   She enjoys ice skating. She learned how to roller skate when she was a mere child.

## 25b. Use a semicolon between independent clauses joined by the words *accordingly, also, besides, consequently, furthermore, hence, however, indeed, instead, moreover, nevertheless, otherwise, similarly, still, therefore, thus, for example, for instance, that is, in fact.*

EXAMPLES   Paula did well in two subjects; **consequently,** she will have a high average at the end of the year.

My mother is a basketball fan; **in fact,** she has not missed a single home game in the last three years.

Today we do not use such comparisons as "most unkindest cut of all"; Elizabethan plays, **however,** contain many double comparisons.

When the connectives mentioned in this rule are at the beginning of a clause, the use of a comma after them is optional except for *that is, for example,* and *for instance,* which are always followed by a comma. When they are clearly parenthetical (interrupters), they are followed by a comma. The word *however* is almost always followed by a comma.

## 25c. A semicolon (rather than a comma) may be needed to separate independent clauses if there are commas within the clauses.

EXAMPLE   In the seventeenth century, the era of such distinguished prose writers as Sir Thomas Browne, John Donne, and Jeremy Taylor, the balanced compound sentence using commas and semicolons reached a high degree of perfection and popularity; but the tendency of many writers today is to use a fast-moving style with shorter sentences and fewer commas and semicolons.   [commas within clauses]

**25d. Use a semicolon between items in a series if the items contain commas.**

EXAMPLE    The three top seniors in this year's class have the following four-year averages: Marvin Chan, 94.8; Ruth Ann Cummins, 93.6; and Joan Dorf, 92.8.

# THE COLON

**25e. Use a colon to mean "note what follows."**

**(1) Use a colon before a list of items, especially after expressions like *as follows* and *the following*.**

EXAMPLES    The application for membership in the Nine-Hole Club asked the following questions: How well do you play golf? Have you ever been in a championship game? What other sports do you play? [list introduced by "the following"]

Don't miss the following items that will be on sale during the first week in June: ice skates, skis, snow shoes, parkas, ski pants, mittens, etc.

▶ **NOTE**    When a list follows immediately after a verb or preposition, do not use the colon.

EXAMPLES    When she went to camp, she had to take blankets, sheets, toilet articles, a flashlight, and poison ivy lotion. [list follows the verb *take*]

Our school board provides the students with free books, book covers, a notebook cover, notebook paper, yellow pads, and one pencil every six weeks. [list follows the preposition *with*]

**(2) Use a colon before a long, formal statement or quotation.**

EXAMPLES    Patrick Henry concluded his revolutionary speech before the Virginia House of Burgesses with these ringing words: Is life so dear, or peace so sweet as to be purchased at the price of chains and slavery? Forbid it, Almighty God! I know not what course others may take; but, as for me, give me liberty or give me death! [Note that a formal statement like this need not be enclosed in quotation marks.]

Here are the four *main* uses of the comma: (1) to prevent misreading; (2) to separate items in a series; (3) to set off expressions which interrupt the sentence; and (4) to set off introductory phrases and clauses.

▶ **NOTE** The first word of a formal statement following a colon is generally capitalized; however, in the case of informal statements (see sentence above and (3) below), the first word often starts with a small letter.

**(3) Use a colon between independent clauses when the second clause explains or restates the idea of the first.**

EXAMPLES   The graduate was nervous about leaving for college: she felt safe, secure, and happy in her home town.

The reasons for the success of the play are obvious: it has fine actors, witty dialogue, and tuneful music.

## 25f. Use a colon in certain conventional situations.

**(1) Use a colon between the hour and the minute when you write the time.**

EXAMPLE   3:30 A.M.

**(2) Use a colon between chapter and verse in referring to passages from the Bible.**

EXAMPLE   Genesis 4:2

**(3) Use a colon between volume and number or between volume and page number of a periodical.**

EXAMPLES   *The American Scholar* 26:3   [volume and number]
*The American Scholar* 26: 289–302   [volume and page numbers]

**(4) Use a colon after the salutation of a business letter.**

EXAMPLES   Dear Mrs. Rodriguez:        Dear Madam:
Dear Sir:                  Gentlemen:

# THE DASH

**25g. Use the dash to indicate an abrupt break in thought.**

EXAMPLES    The way the argument started was stupid—but why bring it up again?—the problem has been settled.

A majority of the graduating class—fifty-five percent, in fact—is going on to higher education.

**25h. Use a dash to set off parenthetical material.**

EXAMPLE    According to the Constitution, only one person—and that is the President—can appoint justices to the Supreme Court.

**25i. Use a dash to mean *namely, in other words, that is,* and similar expressions that precede explanations.**

EXAMPLE    Her decision not to resign was based on one thought— she enjoys teaching science to teen-agers.

The dash and colon are often interchangeable in this use. A dash may be considered a little more emphatic than a colon. If the dash is overused, it loses its emphasis.

# PARENTHESES

**25j. Use parentheses to enclose informative or explanatory matter that is added to a sentence but is not considered of major importance.**

The material enclosed by parentheses may range from a single word or number to a short sentence.

EXAMPLES    Harriet Tubman (1820-1913) is remembered for her work on the Underground Railroad.

In the United States, the term *bank holiday* (in England the words mean *legal holiday*) refers to the closing of all banks by Franklin Delano Roosevelt on March 6, 1933.

▶ **NOTE** For setting off incidental matter, commas, dashes, and parentheses are frequently interchangeable. Commas and dashes are more common than parentheses.

**(1) Be sure that any material enclosed in parentheses can be omitted without changing the basic meaning and construction of the sentence.**

IMPROPER USE OF PARENTHESES   George Eliot (whose real name was Mary Ann Evans) wrote poems and several well-known novels. [The idea in parentheses would be better as a nonessential clause set off by commas.]

**(2) Punctuation marks are used within parentheses when they belong with the parenthetical matter. Punctuation marks that belong with the main part of the sentence are placed outside of the closing parenthesis.**

EXAMPLES   My mother's favorite quotation ("Life is real! Life is earnest!") is from "A Psalm of Life" by Henry Wadsworth Longfellow.

During the time when the Articles of Confederation were in effect (1781–1789), many states had tariff barriers against neighboring states.

# BRACKETS

In ordinary composition you will have practically no use for brackets. Commas, dashes, and parentheses are preferable as ways of setting off parenthetical matter.

**25k. Use brackets to enclose explanations within parentheses or in quoted material when the explanation is not part of the quotation.**

EXAMPLE   As the noted author explained to an overflow audience last night, "Much of the writing by the Irish in the twentieth century has been about the effects of the Seventeen [the Irish Revolution of 1917] on the young people of that time."

# UNDERLINING (ITALICS)

**25l. Use underlining (italics) for titles of books, periodicals, newspapers, works of art, ships, etc.**

EXAMPLES     Pride and Prejudice

Praying Hands, Bolero, the Sun

the Chicago Sun-Times or the Chicago Sun-Times,

Atlantic Monthly, Saturday Review/World

Nautilus (ship), Congressional Limited (train),

Freedom VII (spacecraft)

The use of quotation marks for titles is now generally limited to short compositions such as stories and short poems and parts of books such as chapters or articles.

EXAMPLE     Did you see that article "Immunology" in Time last
week?

It is sometimes necessary to call special attention to a particular word or expression. For this purpose printers use a slanting type called *italic*. In handwritten or typewritten manuscripts, underlining serves the same purpose. Thus, a title printed this way:

*Pride and Prejudice*

would look like this in a typewritten manuscript:

Pride and Prejudice

**25m. Use underlining (italics) for words and letters referred to as such and for foreign words.**

EXAMPLES     I sometimes have trouble deciding whether to use
imply or infer in a given situation.

Among the most common of spelling errors is the
confusion of ie and ei.

Our new gym has the Latin motto Mens sana in
corpore sano written above the entrance.

**EXERCISE 1.** This exercise covers semicolons, colons,

dashes, parentheses, brackets, and underlining. Copy the sentences, inserting the correct punctuation.

1. If you are planning to spend your vacation at home, let me know if your plans are not set, would you like to spend a month with us cruising Long Island Sound in my parents' boat, the Sea Bee?

2. Do you think you can punctuate the following "As Caesar loved me, I weep for him as he was fortunate, I rejoice at it as he was valiant, I honor him but as he was ambitious, I slew him"?

3. The substitution of a specific for a general expression the specific expression must, of course, be appropriate generally improves the style of a composition by increasing its vividness and immediacy.

4. In his address before the Chamber of Commerce, Mayor O'Malley warned "Unless our citizens learn to work together, this great project the proposed Wilson Memorial Dam will be placed farther up the river, where it will not benefit us."

5. I finally remembered where I had read that article comparing Romeo and Juliet and West Side Story it appeared in the New York Times last spring.

6. *The Little Foxes,* a play by Lillian Hellman its title by the way is taken from the Song of Solomon 2 15 had a remarkable effect upon Maxine last year it may have been the reading of this play that helped her decide to major in drama at Yale next year.

7. The position of underdeveloped countries underdeveloped in comparison with the industrialized nations of the West creates a special type of problem in the cold war for instance Soviet aggression in the Near East and Africa may best be countered by economic rather than military measures see Are We Winning the Cold War?

8. The playwright handles her material or should I say her lack of material quite well I must admit, however, that she does not adequately fill the time between 7 30 and 10 30.

9. After reading a few books of criticism, I thought I had better learn a few words of Latin and Greek in order to understand what the critics were saying when they mentioned the following in medias res, carpe diem, and hubris.

10. A hiker or camper setting out for the woods should remember these rules carry a compass, know how to use it, and don't panic.

## QUOTATION MARKS

### 25n. Use quotation marks to enclose a direct quotation—a person's exact words.

DIRECT QUOTATION    Mrs. Billings said, "The test was perfectly fair."

Do not use quotation marks to enclose an indirect quotation—one that does not give a speaker's exact words.

INDIRECT QUOTATION    Mrs. Billings said that the test was perfectly fair.

Remember that *enclose* means placing quotation marks at both the beginning and the end of a direct quotation. Omission of quotation marks at the end of a quotation is a common error.

**(1) A direct quotation begins with a capital letter.**

EXAMPLE    When the game was over, the coach said, "We'll have the victory celebration at my house."

EXCEPTION    If the quotation is only a fragment of a sentence, do not begin it with a capital letter.

What is your interpretation of Shakespeare's reference to "the marriage of true minds"?

**(2) When a quoted sentence is divided into two parts by an interrupting expression such as *she said* or *I asked,* the second part begins with a small letter.**

EXAMPLES    "In less than five minutes," Mary said, "the messenger will be here for the package."

"Will you," she asked, "go to the post office for me?"

If the second part of a broken quotation is a new sentence, it begins with a capital letter.

"Come home soon," Mother said. "Dinner will be ready in half an hour."

**(3) A direct quotation is set off from the rest of the sentence by commas or by a question mark or exclamation point.**

EXAMPLES   "Watch out!" he cried.

She asked, "Did you get the license plate number?"

► **NOTE**   If the quotation is only a phrase, do not set it off by commas.

He felt, as he looked through the windows of the deserted house, that he knew what "through a glass darkly" meant.

**(4) When used with quotation marks, the other marks of punctuation are placed according to the following rules:**

1. *Commas and periods are always placed inside the closing quotation marks.*

EXAMPLE   "As a matter of fact," she added, "it's warm enough to swim today."

2. *Semicolons and colons are always placed outside the closing quotation marks.*

EXAMPLES   Gloria promised, "I'll certainly go to the dance with you"; however, that was three weeks ago.

You must admit one thing about deliveries marked "rush order": they always do arrive, eventually.

3. *Question marks and exclamation points are placed inside the closing quotation marks if they belong with the quotation; otherwise they are placed outside.*

EXAMPLES   "Who was that on the phone?" my mother asked.

"Kill the umpire!" shouted the crowd.

Didn't you say yesterday, "I'll never be late again"?

Get out of here with your "I'm awfully sorry"!

To avoid overpunctuating, no more than one comma or end mark is used at the end of a quotation.

INCORRECT   The teacher asked, "In what Millay poem do you

find the quote, 'It gives a lovely light.' "?   [two end marks—a period and a question mark]

CORRECT   The teacher asked, "In what Millay poem do you find the quote, 'It gives a lovely light'"?

**(5) When a quoted passage consists of more than one paragraph, place quotation marks at the beginning of each paragraph and at the end of the entire passage. Do not place quotation marks at the end of any paragraph but the last.**

► NOTE   A long quotation is often set off from the rest of the text so as to be easily recognizable as quoted matter. Thus, the entire passage may be indented; in printed matter it may be set in small type; and in typewritten copy it may be single-spaced instead of double-spaced. *When a quotation has been identified as such by any of these devices, no quotation marks are necessary.*

**(6) Use single quotation marks to enclose a quotation within a quotation.**

EXAMPLE   "What do you suppose she meant when she said, 'You'll see tomorrow'?" Tom asked. [Notice the placement of the question mark. It belongs with the quotation as a whole, but not with the inner quotation; therefore, it falls inside the double quotation marks, but outside the single ones.]

**(7) When you write dialogue (two or more persons carrying on a conversation), begin a new paragraph every time the speaker changes.**

EXAMPLE   "Has anything happened, Carmen?" Mrs. Sanchez asked. "You look so happy."

"Oh yes, Mother," replied Carmen. "A very wonderful thing has happened. But I want to wait and tell the whole family together." She sat down on the sofa and began to leaf through a magazine.

"I can tell you what it is, Mother," said Carmen's little brother Ernesto. "Carmen won a scholarship to Columbia University. She just received the news today."

**25o. Use quotation marks to enclose titles of chapters, articles, other parts of books or magazines, short poems, short stories, and songs.**

EXAMPLES    For me, the highlights in this month's *Harper's* were the article "New Directions in Foreign Policy" and the poem "Wind from the Mountains."

Last night I read "The World Was New," which is the first chapter from the book *Fifth Chinese Daughter* by Jade Snow Wong.

**25p. Use quotation marks to enclose slang words, technical terms, and other expressions that are unusual in standard English.**

Use this device sparingly.

EXAMPLES    This year, for the first time, I have begun to enjoy "longhair" music.

Designers of modern books often "bleed" illustrations; that is, they allow pictures to run to the sides, tops, or bottoms of the pages.

**EXERCISE 2.**   Copy the following sentences, inserting quotation marks and other required punctuation.

1. Each month in the Farm Journal there is a feature called Ideas That Make Kitchens Convenient
2. Do you keep up with the news Mr. Green asked through the newspapers television radio or all of these mediums
3. Our teacher quotes Willa Cather's words there are only two or three human stories, and they go on repeating themselves as fiercely as if they had never happened before.
4. Can you tell me where I can find the poem Snow-Bound Jane asked the librarian.
5. On the stock exchange, the phrase cutting a melon has nothing to do with breakfast fruit it means simply that stockholders are receiving a large extra dividend.
6. You don't know the half of it the mechanic said gloomily your engine block is cracked too
7. The words every man for himself may describe the way most

of us actually behave but don't you think we'd be happier if we followed the words of Matthew 7 12 whatsoever ye would that men should do to you, do ye even so to them

8. Perhaps Lincoln's finest memorial is the poem When Lilacs Last in the Door Yard Bloom'd in Walt Whitman's book Sequel to Drum-Taps.

9. Did you say I'll be there at eight or I'll be there late?

10. Ms. Hammer warned us that the movie was in her own words a parody of the novel furthermore she advised us not to waste our money and time by seeing it.

## THE APOSTROPHE

### 25q. To form the possessive case of a singular noun, add an apostrophe and an *s*.

EXAMPLES    boy's hat        Helen's dress
            the boss's office   for heaven's sake

When a word of more than one syllable ends in an *s* sound, the singular possessive may be formed by adding the apostrophe alone. This omission avoids the awkward hiss of repeated *s* sounds.

EXAMPLES    the witness' testimony
           for conscience' sake

### (1) To form the possessive case of a plural noun ending in *s*, add only the apostrophe.

EXAMPLES    the girls' hats
           the marines' marching songs

► **NOTE**  The few plural nouns that do not end in *s* form the possessive by adding an apostrophe and an *s* just as singular nouns do.

EXAMPLES    men's clothing
           children's room

### (2) Personal pronouns in the possessive case (*his, hers, its, ours, yours, theirs, whose*) do not require an apostrophe.

INCORRECT   The victory was their's.
  CORRECT   The victory was **theirs.**

INCORRECT   The nation must protect it's people.
  CORRECT   The nation must protect **its** people.

INCORRECT   That's the boy who's bicycle I borrowed.
  CORRECT   That's the boy **whose** bicycle I borrowed.

**(3) Indefinite pronouns (one, everyone, everybody, etc.) in the possessive case require an apostrophe and an s.**

EXAMPLES   One's choice of a career is important.

This must be somebody's coat.

► **NOTE** In such forms as *anyone else, somebody else,* etc., the correct possessives are *anyone else's, somebody else's,* etc. The word *oneself* has no apostrophe.

**EXERCISE 3.** Copy the italicized words in the following list in two columns. Label the first column "Singular Possessive" and write the singular possessive form of each word in this column. Label the second column "Plural Possessive" and write the plural possessive form of each word.

EXAMPLE   1. *bird* song

| Singular Possessive | Plural Possessive |
|---|---|
| 1. *bird's* | *birds'* |

1. *student* opinion        6. *Burns* house
2. *horse* saddles          7. *woman* plan
3. *goose* feathers         8. *baby* wish
4. *sister* wardrobe        9. *reader* attention
5. *boss* letter           10. *state* rights

**EXERCISE 4.** Number your paper 1–20. If the possessive case in each item in the list has been correctly formed, write *C* after the proper number. If it has been incorrectly formed, write the correct form.

1. It is her's.              3. that boys' car
2. womens' coats            4. Who's is it?

5. fly's flight
6. scissors' blades
7. mice's tails
8. childrens' games
9. oxen's yokes
10. the Smith's invitation
11. companies plans
12. a man's hope
13. leaves' color
14. It is somebody's else.
15. soldiers' rations
16. it's shrill bark
17. That is their's.
18. churches' picnic
19. the Whites' plane
20. a horses' hooves

**(4) In hyphenated words, names of organizations and business firms, and words showing joint possession, only the last word is possessive in form.**

EXAMPLES    father-in-law's business
secretary-treasurer's report
Ralph Merrill and Company's products
Roz and Denise's boat

When the second word in a group of words showing joint possession is a possessive pronoun, the first word is also possessive.

INCORRECT   Jane and my car
CORRECT   Jane's and my car

**(5) When two or more persons possess something individually, each of their names takes the possessive form.**

EXAMPLES    Baldwin's and Ellison's writings
the buyer's and seller's signatures

**(6) The words *minute, hour, day, week, month, year,* etc., when used as possessive adjectives, require an apostrophe. Words indicating amount in cents or dollars, used as possessive adjectives, require apostrophes.**

EXAMPLES    a week's delay, four weeks' delay
this year's crop, those years' crops
one cent's worth, ten cents' worth
a dollar's worth, five dollars' worth

**EXERCISE 5.**  In the following list the possessive relationship is expressed by means of a phrase. Change each so that the possessive case of the noun or pronoun will be used to express the same relationship. Write the answers.

EXAMPLE 1. visit of mother-in-law
    1. *mother-in-law's visit*

1. boat of Juan and Geraldo
2. soft skin of babies
3. homes of my brothers-in-law
4. song of sailors
5. rest of two weeks
6. garage of Capra and Cooley
7. worth of ten million dollars
8. agreement of the gentlemen
9. singing of the birds
10. plans of the school board
11. locker room of the players
12. horses of Lynn and Bob
13. delay of six months
14. signatures of driver and witness
15. bookstore of New Hope
16. name of it
17. flooding of the river
18. hope of everyone else
19. wishes of the people
20. atmosphere of Michigan Boulevard

**25r. Use an apostrophe to show where letters have been omitted in a contraction.**

A contraction is a word made up of two words combined into one by omitting one or more letters.

EXAMPLES doesn't    *for*    does not
         we've      *for*    we have
         can't      *for*    cannot

Notice that the apostrophe always falls at the exact place at which a letter or letters have been omitted.

► **NOTE** The most common error in the use of the apostrophe in a contraction comes from the confusion of *it's,* which means *it is,* with the possessive form *its* (*its* atmosphere), which has no apostrophe. Another common error is the insertion of the apostrophe in the wrong place: *ca'nt* for *can't, does'nt* for *doesn't.*

**25s. Use the apostrophe and *s* to form the plural of letters, numbers, and signs, and of words referred to as words.**

EXAMPLES　There are two *s*'s and two *l*'s in *misspelled*.

I think the answer should have two *4*'s in it.

That happened back in the 1960's.

The last exercise had more +'s than 0's.

Can't you use fewer *so*'s and *and so*'s in your writing?

# THE HYPHEN

Hyphens function in two ways: (1) to form compounds; (2) to divide words at the end of a line. The hyphen is a flexible linking mark. By using the hyphen, the writer can take two words or parts of words, join them with a hyphen, and make a third word that has its own concept or meaning that is different from the meaning of the original words. As an example, let us consider the word *teen-age*. *Teen* is part of the words *thirteen, fourteen,* etc. *Age* is another word. When we join *teen* to *age,* we arrive at *teen-age,* a new word that means an age that is within or spans seven years: thirteen through nineteen. There are few invariable rules for the use of hyphens in compound words. The following somewhat oversimplified rules will, however, be useful in answering certain problems in the use of the hyphen.

## 25t. Use a hyphen to divide a word at the end of a line.

For rules on dividing words at the end of a line, see "Manuscript Form," pages 468–69.

## 25u. Use a hyphen with compound numbers from *twenty-one* to *ninety-nine* and with fractions used as adjectives.

EXAMPLES　five hundred and **forty-one**

**three-quarter**-length stockings

a **two-thirds** majority　[**two-thirds** is used as an adjective modifying *majority*] two thirds of the voters  [*thirds* is a noun modified by *two*]

## 25v. Use a hyphen with the prefixes *ex–*, *self–*, *all–*, with the suffix *–elect*, and with all prefixes before a proper noun or proper adjective.

EXAMPLES   ex-champion          mid-September
           self-confidence      trans-Canadian
           mayor-elect          pre-Renaissance

## 25w. Hyphenate a compound adjective when it precedes the word it modifies.

EXAMPLES   the well-known actor      The actor was well
                                     known.

           the soft-spoken woman     The woman was soft
                                     spoken.

► NOTE   Do not use a hyphen if one of the modifiers is an adverb ending in *–ly*.

EXAMPLE   a heavily loaded truck

## 25x. Use a hyphen to prevent confusion or awkwardness.

EXAMPLES   semi-invalid   [prevents awkwardness of *semiinvalid*]
           re-cover a floor   [prevents confusion with *recover*]
           re-form a line   [prevents confusion with *reform*]
           re-mark the term papers   [prevents confusion with *remark*]

**EXERCISE 6.** Number your paper 1–33. Change the following, inserting apostrophes where they are needed, changing the phrasal possessives to the possessive case, and adding the necessary hyphens. Some of the items are correct.

1. cars of Allan and Joe
2. the sons of my sisters-in-law
3. preRenaissance literature
4. editorial page of the *Times*
5. Its a lie, isnt it?

6. two thirds of the vote
7. Does'nt its tail wag?
8. Use fewer *and*s and *but*s.
9. well liked personality
10. Shes had straight *A*s this year.
11. They're our's.
12. recover the floor with tile
13. The Jazz Age was the 1920's and 30's.
14. a solidly-built bookcase
15. Its you'r turn.
16. ex champion's valor
17. party of Ann and Peggy
18. It's eight oclock.
19. ballet length dress
20. Whose that with you?
21. catalogue of Denver Dry-goods
22. the seven hundred pages of the book
23. widely known school
24. Its true that Marys leaving.
25. Whats' happening?
26. the squeak of the mouse
27. record of the all star team
28. Isn't you're name Sue?
29. Well call it sixty five cents worth.
30. two hundred and sixty four pounds
31. Her 9s look like 7s.
32. three-fourths of a cup
33. the poetry of Gwendolyn Brooks

**REVIEW EXERCISE.** Most of the needed punctuation and capitalization has been omitted from the following passages. Copy the passage assigned to you, making every required change that you can find. (In paragraphing, the only changes you need to make are those required by dialogue.) When you are in doubt about a particular punctuation or capitalization problem, don't guess. Look up the rule.

1

The origins of most sports are unknown try as we may we cannot say exactly when or where or how such games as baseball football and golf were first played. There is however one exception to this rule the game of basketball. Historians of sport know precisely where basketball began they know precisely when it began and perhaps the most interesting fact of all they know the name of the man who invented it Dr James Naismith in the winter of 1891–92 Dr. Naismith who was then an instructor at the y m c a training college now called springfield college in springfield massachusetts had a problem on his hands. The football season was over the baseball season had not yet begun his students needed indoor exercise at a competitive sport but apparently no such sport existed working with the materials at hand naismith set himself the task of creating a new indoor sport he fastened two peach baskets to the walls at opposite ends of his gymnasium and using a soccer ball he devised the game that we call basketball today Like his equipment his rules were based upon his material for example he started with eighteen available players and the first rule he wrote read as follows there shall be nine players on each side imagine eighteen players set loose on a modern basketball court.

2

Where's Ann my father asked dropping his paper to his lap I looked up from my homework this was going to be good. Oh shes out I heard my mother say did you want her for anything No nothing special just wondered where she was

Silence returned to the room and I returned sadly to my work was that going to be all oh by the way Marge said my father casually where did you say shed gone its after 10 00 you know. As a matter of fact I didn't say my mother returned to working on her manuscript then she added Anns over at Sallys house theyre having some kind of committee meeting about the charity benefit. Did you say sallys house isnt that out on twenty-first street My father was beginning to speak with a little more interest why its an hours trip from here whens the girl going to get home Dont worry Frank my mother spoke more softly than ever Ann wont be long she asked if she could borrow my car what my father asked Your car again Marge do you realize whats going on Ann had the car on Saturday on one evening last week I forget whether it was Tuesday or Wednesday and now tonight thats three times in let me see a little over a week When I was a senior in high school I couldn't carry on like that now it was my mothers turn oh yes you could and you did she added Freeport high school hasnt changed that much since you and I went there how do you suppose we used to go to each other's house and what about the dates you took me out on in your fathers car this was better than I had expected it was far better certainly than my history II textbook which was lying open on my desk. Then somewhat subdued my father said well you shouldnt bring up prehistoric memories hc smiled at her and I thought I heard a chuckle then he picked up his paper rustled it fiercely for a moment and concentrated once again on the freeport chronicle.

Chapter **26**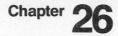

# Manuscript Form

## Rules for Preparing a Final Draft

As most students well know, the appearance and correctness of a manuscript—regardless of content—are important. Very often they make the difference between an *A* and a *B,* between a *B* and a *C,* or between a passing grade and a failure. A sloppily written manuscript with misspelled words and other careless errors says two things to the reader: (1) this student was not interested enough to proofread, to check, to revise; (2) this student has no pride in quality work. The correct preparation of a manuscript is every writer's responsibility. You should follow standard practice in writing or typing your manuscript, just as you follow standard practice in spelling and usage. In this chapter you will find the basic rules of standard manuscript form, from the first draft to the final paper submitted for the teacher's corrections and evaluation.

## THE MANUSCRIPT

*Paper and ink.* Write on standard size ($8 \times 10\frac{1}{2}''$) lined paper. Use black, blue, or blue-black ink. Follow the school policy on the use of both sides of the paper and skipping of lines.

If you typewrite, use standard size ($8\frac{1}{2} \times 11''$) white typewriting paper. Type double space, using a black ribbon. Do *not* type on both sides of the paper. Consider

**463**

using paper with special erasing qualities, especially if you are not an accomplished typist.

*The title.* Place the title in the center of the first line of a ruled page and skip a line between the title and the beginning of the composition. In a typewritten composition the title should be placed about two inches below the top of the page. Do not underline the title; do not enclose the title in quotation marks unless it is a quotation.

*Margins.* Leave a margin of at least one-and-a-quarter inches at the left and one inch at the right side of the paper. The left-hand margin must be even; the right-hand margin should be as even as possible. Leave a margin of at least one inch at the top and the bottom of all pages after the first.

*Indention.* Indent the first line of every paragraph about one inch from the left-hand margin; in typing, indent these lines five spaces.

Indent long quotations one inch or five spaces from both the left- and right-hand margins; in typewritten work, a quotation treated in this way should be single-spaced. The first line of each paragraph in an indented quotation should be further indented from the quotation's left-hand margin. If a long quotation is indented and clearly identified, quotation marks may be omitted.

*Labeling and numbering pages.* Follow the school policy on the labeling and numbering of pages. One common practice is to label the first page by writing your name, the name or number of the course, and the date in the upper right-hand corner. This information should be given on three separate lines, one below the other. Number all pages, except the first, with Arabic numerals in the upper right-hand corners (remembering to allow for the first page in your numbering). It is a good practice to write your name beneath the page number on each sheet.

EXAMPLE          Aline Brown

                 English III

                 September 16, 1977

                                        4

                               Aline Brown

*General Appearance.* Do not spoil the appearance of your composition with cross-outs and insertions between lines; do not use margins for changes or additions. If corrections are long or if they cannot be made neatly, rewrite the entire page. In typewritten work, do not sacrifice neatness for speed; retype any page containing excessive strike-overs or messy erasures.

## REVISING THE FIRST DRAFT

Every composition should be written at least twice: as a first draft and as a final manuscript. The first draft is your copy, meant for your eyes alone. The process of revision is an extremely important stage in the writing of a composition. It should never be done casually or hastily. Plan the revision of your first draft in three distinct steps: (1) Evaluate the content and the general organization of the entire composition; (2) Eliminate badly constructed sentences and poorly chosen words; (3) Check the mechanics. Use the checklist on pages 465–66 as a guide in revising the first draft. With repeated use, the checklist will become so clearly fixed in your mind that you will follow it automatically. *After the final draft has been written, proofread your manuscript carefully for careless copying errors.*

When the revision is completed, write the composition in its final form. Be sure to proofread the final draft. On the following pages, you will find rules for the treatment of abbreviations, numbers, and word division. Other aspects of manuscript form are treated elsewhere in this book; for example, footnotes and bibliographical references are discussed in Chapter 21. Whenever you are uncertain about a specific feature of manuscript form, consult the index.

## CHECKLIST FOR REVISION

### Evaluate:

Quality of material (effectiveness, relevance, etc.)
General organization (sequence of ideas)

Division into paragraphs (Check your topic sentences.)
Transitions (within and between paragraphs)
Variety of sentence structure

**Eliminate:**

Errors in grammatical usage (agreement, pronouns,
verbs, adjectives, and adverbs)
Sentence fragments and run-on sentences
Awkward sentences
Confusing sentences
Wordiness
Clichés (trite expressions)

**Check:**

Spelling
Punctuation (Watch the placement of the apostrophe.
Don't omit final quotation marks.)
Capital letters
Hyphenation (especially the division of words at the
ends of lines)

## 26a. In compositions, do not use abbreviations except in certain special instances in which abbreviations are customary.

INCORRECT    During Sheila's 1st yr. at the Univ. of Ala., she
devoted most of her spare time to tennis & track;
then, one Fri. aft. in Apr., she announced to a friend
at the Chem. Bldg., "I've decided to become a
premed major!"

CORRECT    During Sheila's first year at the University of Alabama, she devoted most of her spare time to tennis
and track; then, one Friday afternoon in April,
she announced to a friend at the Chemistry Building, "I've decided to become a premed major!"

**(1) The following abbreviations are customary before a name: *Mr., Messrs., Mrs., Ms., Dr., Rev., St. (Saint).* The following abbreviations are customary after a name: *Jr., Sr.* The college degrees *B.S., Ph.D.,* etc., may be abbreviated whether they are used with a name or not.**

NONSTANDARD  Mother asked me to tell the dr. that jr. feels much better today.

STANDARD  Mother asked me to tell the doctor that Junior feels much better today.

STANDARD  Dr. Herbert Simms, Jr., has a sister, Alice Simms, Ph.D.

STANDARD  Holders of the Ph.D. degree are properly addressed as "Doctor."

**(2) The following abbreviations are acceptable in all writing:**
*A.D.* **(***A.D.* **1066);** *B.C.* **(44** *B.C.***);** *A.M.* **or** *P.M.* **(2:30** *P.M.***);** *etc.* **(and so forth);** *i.e.* **(that is);** *e.g.* **(for example).**[1] **Generally understood abbreviations for government agencies are acceptable:** *AEC, HEW, FBI* **(notice that periods are not used with these abbreviations).**

EXAMPLES  Cleopatra died in 30 B.C.

The AEC made a momentous decision last month.

## Numbers

### 26b. Do not begin a sentence with a numeral.

NONSTANDARD  342 students must commute to our high school every day.

STANDARD  Three hundred and forty-two students must commute to our high school every day.

### 26c. Spell out numbers of one or two words. Write numbers of more than two words as numerals.

EXAMPLES  2,031,427; 1867; $100.26

two million; ten cents; ninety dollars; seventy-nine

EXCEPTIONS  In statistical and technical writing, *all* numbers are generally written as numerals. All page numbers are written as numerals (*page 10*). Numbers representing dates do not follow this rule. See Rule 26e.

[1] For other common abbreviations, see pages 372–74.

**26d. Hyphenate all compound (two-word) numbers from** *twenty-one* **to** *ninety-nine.* **Do not hyphenate a fraction unless it is used as an adjective.**

EXAMPLES  We counted **twenty-two** guests at Juanita's party.

He won by a **two-thirds** majority.

**Two thirds** of the girls in this class are brunettes.

**26e. Write out numbers like** *third, forty-first,* **etc., rather than writing them as numerals with letter endings (3rd, 41st, etc.).**

EXAMPLE  My mom and dad celebrated their **twenty-fourth** wedding anniversary last week.

EXCEPTION  Street numbers may be either written out or written as numerals with letter endings.

Jane lives at 363 West **37th** Street (or **Thirty-seventh** Street).

In dates, numerals *only* are used when the name of a month precedes the date. When the date precedes the name of the month or stands alone, either write out the number or use a numeral with a letter ending.

EXAMPLES  My birthday is December **21.**

We shall see you on the **12th** (or **twelfth**) of July.

## Dividing a Word at the End of a Line

If it is necessary to divide a word, it should be divided between *syllables.* (A syllable is a letter or group of letters pronounced as a single sound.) Your dictionary gives the correct syllable division of every word it contains. Whenever you are in doubt on a syllabication problem, consult the dictionary. A great many of these problems can be solved by the application of the following simple rules.

**26f. Divide a word at the end of a line between pronounceable parts only. One-syllable words should never be divided.**

INCORRECT     play–ed [one-syllable word]
  CORRECT     **played**

INCORRECT     stat-ionary [parts not pronounceable]
  CORRECT     **sta-tionary**

### 26g. A word having double consonants should be divided between the consonants.

EXAMPLES     control-ling
                       bil-lion

Words like *sell–ing* and *less–er* are exceptions. See Rule 26i regarding prefixes and suffixes.

### 26h. Do not divide a word so that a single letter stands alone. If possible, do not divide a word so that only two letters are carried over to the next line.

AWKWARD     i-solate
  BETTER     **iso-late**

AWKWARD     democra-cy
  BETTER     **democ-racy**

### 26i. Words having prefixes and suffixes should be divided between the prefix and the root of the word or between the root of the word and the suffix.

EXAMPLES     inter-jection; dis-mantle; over-joyed
                       sing-ing; good-ness; cheer-ful; tell-ing

## CORRECTION SYMBOLS

We learn how to write by recognizing and correcting our own errors, but often we do not recognize our errors until they are pointed out by a teacher. More often than not, your compositions will be returned to you with marginal notations by your teacher indicating errors and corrections. Learn the meanings of these notations; make the corrections they call for. This kind of practice—and lots of it—

is an indispensable part of learning to write English effectively.

## Correction Symbols Used by Teachers

| | |
|---|---|
| **ms** | error in manuscript form or neatness |
| **cap** | error in use of capital letter(s) |
| **p** | error in punctuation |
| **sp** | error in spelling |
| **frag** | sentence fragment |
| **ss** | error in sentence structure |
| **k** | awkward sentence |
| **rs** | run-on sentence |
| **nc** | not clear |
| **ref** | unclear reference of pronoun |
| **gr** | error in grammar |
| **w** | error in word choice |
| **¶** | Begin a new paragraph here. |
| **t** | error in tense |
| **∧** | You have omitted something. |

### Example of Marginal Notations by a Teacher

Growing up in a big city is not entirely

 different from a small town. Because people
live in small communities within the city.

 Each of these communities compose only two
or three city blocks. Children living there
soon learn where everything is. They know
the schools and the churches, the supermarket, delicatessen, drugstore, bakery,
clothing store, stationery store, and of
coarse the ice cream and candy store.
Proprietors know there regular customers by

*ref*

*p, gr*
name, and the customers know all about
them. Children make friends among the
neighbors children who they play with in
the street or at local playgrounds. Adults

*sp*
on a summer evening sit outside there brown-
stones discussing problems and politics,

*frag*
watching the traffic and children. Just as
neighbors do anywhere. Until they are teen-
agers, young people rarely explore the huge

*rs, sp*
city around them, they remain in there own
"village."

### Passage Corrected by the Student

Growing up in a big city is not entirely

*s,s, frag*
different from a small town, Because people
*growing up in*    *b*
live in small communities within the city.

*gr, w*
Each of these communities compose only two
*comprises*
or three city blocks. Children living there
soon learn where everything is. They know
the schools and the churches, the supermarket, delicatessen, drugstore, bakery,
clothing store, stationery store, and of

*sp*
coarse the ice cream and candy store.
*course*

*sp*
Proprietors know there regular customers by
*their*
name, and the customers know all about

*ref*
them. Children make friends among the
*the proprietors*

*p, gr*
neighbors' children who they play with in
*whom*
the street or at local playgrounds. Adults

*sp*      on a summer evening sit outside ~~there~~ *their* brown-

stones discussing problems and politics,

*frag*    watching the traffic and children, just as

neighbors do anywhere. Until they are teen-

agers, young people rarely explore the huge

*rs, sp*   city around them. They remain in ~~there~~ *their* own

"village."

# Aids to Good English

# PART SIX

# Chapter 27

# The Library

### Arrangement and Resources of the Library

Today, every well-equipped high school (and many elementary schools) has an extensive library with books, pamphlets, magazines, reference books, and other valuable sources of information. Libraries are, moreover, sufficiently alike so that when you become familiar with one, you can easily find your way in others.

In this chapter you will learn the following important facts about library organization:

1. The arrangement of books in the library.
2. The arrangement and uses of the card catalogue.
3. The names and functions of the parts of a book.
4. The use of the *Readers' Guide to Periodical Literature.*
5. The use of the vertical file.
6. The location of items in your library.

## ARRANGEMENT OF BOOKS IN THE LIBRARY

### 27a. Learn the arrangement of books.

### Fiction

By this time you have already learned that books of fiction (novels and short stories) are arranged on the fiction shelves alphabetically by the author. When there are two or more books by the same author, they are arranged alphabetically by title. *Day and Night,* by Virginia Woolf, would come before her *Mrs. Dalloway,* and both of these would precede her *To the Lighthouse.*

When you want to find out whether or not your library has a copy of a particular book, look for it, by author or title, in the card catalogue. If the book you want is listed in the catalogue but is not on the shelves, ask the librarian about it. Another student may have borrowed it; it may be in the library being repaired; it may be on "reserve" for special class use. If possible, ask the librarian to put your name on the waiting list. When the book comes in, or is available for circulation again, the librarian will notify you.

## Nonfiction: The Dewey Decimal System

In 1876 Melvil Dewey, an American librarian, devised the system we now use for classifying nonfiction books.[1] In this system every book is placed in a certain class and is identified by a number placed on the back of the book, near the bottom. There are ten large subject classifications, and any book can be fitted into one of them. Within each large class there can be an unlimited number of subdivisions. Since a decimal point plays an important part in the numbering of the books, the plan is given the name Dewey decimal system.

A valuable feature of this system is that all books on the same subject may be found together on the library shelves. Once you have learned the class number of the subject you are interested in, you can go to that section of shelves in the library and find all the books in the library on this subject grouped in one place.

The ten major subject classifications and their numbers are listed on the following page.

[1] The Library of Congress system of cataloguing is not described here because it is not common in high school libraries.

| 000–099 | General Works (encyclopedias, periodicals, handbooks, bibliographies, etc.) |
| 100–199 | Philosophy (includes psychology, conduct, etc.) |
| 200–299 | Religion (includes mythology) |
| 300–399 | Social Sciences (education, economics, government, law, occupations, communications) |
| 400–499 | Language (dictionaries, grammars, the study of language and languages) |
| 500–599 | Science (mathematics, chemistry, physics, astronomy, geology, biology, zoology, etc.) |
| 600–699 | Applied Science, or Technology (agriculture, engineering, aviation, inventions, manufacturing, and commercial operations) |
| 700–799 | The Arts and Recreation (sculpture, painting, music, architecture, photography, sports) |
| 800–899 | Literature (poetry, plays, orations, essays in English and foreign languages. Does not include novels or short stories, which are on the *fiction* shelves.) |
| 900–909 930–999 | History |
| 910–919 | Travel |
| 920–929 | Biography (arranged alphabetically by name of subject of biography) |

Each class is subdivided as the need arises. For example, the large 500–599 class is devoted to Science. Each science is further classified as follows: ·

| 500–509 | General Science |
| 510–519 | Mathematics |
| 520–529 | Astronomy |
| 530–539 | Physics |
| 540–549 | Chemistry |
| 550–559 | Geology |
| 560–569 | Paleontology |
| 570–579 | Anthropology and Biology |
| 580–589 | Botany |
| 590–599 | Zoology |

This subdivision can be broken down even further. For example, Mathematics has the following categories:

510–519    Mathematics
511    Arithmetic
512    Algebra
513    Geometry
514    Trigonometry

When books have the same class number, they are distinguished from one another by the first letter of the author's name. Thus, a book on plane geometry by Limond C. Stone would have the number 513.1 and the capital letter S under the number stamped on the back of the book: $\frac{513.1}{S}$. This number, including the first letter of the author's last name, is known as the book's *call number*. To find the call number of a book, look up the book in the card catalogue.

## LOCATING INFORMATION IN THE LIBRARY

### The Card Catalogue

The card catalogue is a cabinet containing drawers filled with alphabetically arranged cards. In most libraries the catalogue holds at least three cards for each book in the library: one or more *author cards,* the *title card,* and one or more *subject cards. Guide cards* help you locate your books more easily.

### 27b. Learn the uses of the card catalogue.

### The Author Card

The *author card* has the name of the author in bold-faced type on the top line. If you know an author's name and wish to find a book by that author in the library, you may look for the last name in the card catalogue. There you will find all the books by that author which your library owns. Cards for books *about* an author follow cards for books *by* an author. Thus, all the books by Sinclair Lewis, the novelist, will be arranged alphabetically. Following these might come the biography of Lewis by Mark Schorer.

## Catalogue Cards

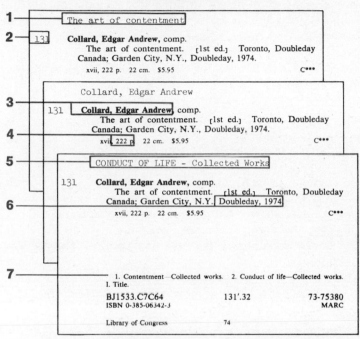

**1** — The art of contentment

**2** — 131   **Collard, Edgar Andrew,** comp.
    The art of contentment.   [1st ed.]   Toronto, Doubleday
Canada; Garden City, N.Y., Doubleday, 1974.
    xvii, 222 p.   22 cm.   $5.95        C•••

**3** — Collard, Edgar Andrew

131   **Collard, Edgar Andrew,** comp.
    The art of contentment.   [1st ed.]   Toronto, Doubleday
Canada; Garden City, N.Y., Doubleday, 1974.

**4** — xvii, 222 p.   22 cm.   $5.95        C•••

**5** — CONDUCT OF LIFE - Collected Works

131   **Collard, Edgar Andrew,** comp.
    The art of contentment.   [1st ed.]   Toronto, Doubleday
Canada; Garden City, N.Y., Doubleday, 1974.

**6** — xvii, 222 p.   22 cm.   $5.95        C•••

**7** — 1. Contentment—Collected works.   2. Conduct of life—Collected works.
I. Title.
BJ1533.C7C64          131'.32          73-75380
ISBN 0-385-06342-3                               MARC
Library of Congress         74

## Top to bottom: title, author, and subject cards

*From top to bottom: title card, author card, and subject card*

1. Title
2. Call number
3. Author
4. Number of pages
5. Subject
6. Publisher and date of publication
7. Other headings under which the book is listed (In some libraries this book might be shelved with books on other related subjects.)

## The Title Card

The *title card* has the book's title at the top. The quickest way to find a book in the catalogue is to look it up under its title. There may be many books by the same author and hence many cards to go through if you look among the author cards. If you know the exact title, however, you have only one card to hunt for. Titles beginning with *a, an, the* are listed by the word following these articles. For example, the title card for *The Invisible Man* would be found under **I**.

## The Subject Card

The *subject card* has at the top, usually in capital letters, the subject with which the book deals. Such subjects may be anything from Archaeology to Zymurgy. Subject cards are very helpful when you wish to read a number of books on the same subject but do not know any specific authors or titles. As a coin collector, you may wish to know all the books your library has on numismatics. The subject cards under that heading will tell you how richly stocked your library is in this field. As the illustrations show, some books may be included in more than one subject area.

## Information Given on a Catalogue Card

By studying the sample cards, you will learn a great deal about a book even before you see it. In addition to the title, author, and call number of the book, the card may also supply the following information:

1. *Facts about authorship:* full name of the author; names of joint authors and illustrators, if any. (When a book has several authors, there is a separate author card for each one.)

2. *Facts about publication:* the name of the publisher; the date of publication.

3. *Facts about the book:* number of pages; whether the book contains illustrations, diagrams, etc.

In addition to title, author, and subject cards, there are also specialized cards for certain uses.

## "See" and "See Also" Cards

Cards in the catalogue which refer you to other cards are called "see" cards and "see also" cards. They often help you find exactly what you are seeking. For instance, suppose you have chosen to look up books on penicillin. Looking under "Penicillin" in the card catalogue, you find "see Antibiotics." This means that the card catalogue of your library does not list any books under "Penicillin" but does list them under the heading "Antibiotics." A "see" card tells you that any books on the subject are under another heading.

```
Penicillin, see Antibiotics
```

```
Voyages and Travels, see also
    Adventures and Adventurers
    Discoveries (in geography)
    Explorers
```

For another example, imagine you are looking for books about voyages and travels and you have found some listed under the subject heading "Voyages and Travels." Under that heading you may also find a "see also" card advising you to look under the subject headings "Adventures and Adventurers," "Discoveries (in geography)," and "Explorers." Here you will find additional titles on your subject. A "see also" card tells you that there is additional material in other places.

## Analytic Cards

In addition to the three types of cards already described (author, title, subject) some libraries have *analytic* cards which are helpful for finding the location of short stories, plays, or articles in books. These analytic cards are of three types — *author, title,* and *subject.* They tell you in which collection of plays a particular play is found. An analytic card may also tell you where a chapter on a certain subject may be found in a book.

## SUMMARY

The card catalogue is a valuable library tool which may be used for the following purposes:

1. To find out whether a certain book is owned by your library
2. To find the call number of a book
3. To find out what books by a certain author are in the library
4. To find out what books on a certain subject are in the library
5. To find out which book or books contain a certain play, short story, or essay
6. To find out certain facts about a book's authorship, publication, illustrations, size, etc.

**EXERCISE 1.** Using the card catalogue in your library, find the title, author, and call number of the following. Write them on your paper.

1. A book about automation
2. A book about Maria Mitchell
3. A book about African nationalism
4. A biography of Queen Victoria
5. A book containing a one-act play by J. M. Synge, *Riders to*

*the Sea,* or a one-act play by John Galsworthy, *The Little Man,* or another one-act play by either of these authors

6. A book about the first trip to the moon
7. A book about basketball
8. A book about acting or one about directing or writing a play
9. A book about gardening
10. A book about getting into the college of your choice
11. A one-volume history of England
12. A book about the Presidency

**EXERCISE 2.** Using the card catalogue, find answers to the following questions. Write the answers.

1. Does your library have any books by the poet Edna St. Vincent Millay? If so, give the titles and call numbers.
2. Give the title, author, publisher, and publication date of a book about either Langston Hughes or John F. Kennedy.
3. Does the library own the complete plays of George Bernard Shaw or Lillian Hellman? Give the exact title and publisher of the books.
4. Give the title, author, and date of publication of a book of recent (within the past five years) one-act plays.
5. How many books by Iris Murdoch does your library own? List titles and dates of publication.

## The Parts of a Book

For some readers the only important part of a book is the text itself. Discriminating readers, however, know that the author and the publisher have given them more than the text. They use the information supplied in the table of contents, the index, and the bibliography to help them get the most out of their reading. In this section you will learn the parts of a book and what information each supplies. Not all the parts described below are in all books, but you should learn the use of each.

**27c. Learn the names and the functions of the parts of a book.**

## The Frontispiece

The frontispiece is a full-page illustration. It usually faces the title page.

## The Title Page

The title page gives the complete title, the subtitle, if there is one, the complete name of the author or editor (and sometimes a position or title if it is a textbook or work of nonfiction), the name of the publisher, and the place of publication.

## The Copyright Page

On the reverse side of the title page is the copyright page. Information on this page includes the year the book was copyrighted and the name of the copyright holder. To obtain a copyright, the author or publisher must send two copies of the book, a certain fee, and information about the book to the Register of Copyrights in Washington, D.C. That office then issues a copyright, which grants the owner exclusive right to print the book or any part of it for a period of twenty-eight years. At the end of that period, the copyright may be renewed for another twenty-eight years. Sometimes publishers secure a copyright in their own name, sometimes in the name of the author. Anyone reproducing substantial portions of the book without the permission of the copyright owner is committing a criminal offense and is liable to a suit in court.

A series of dates printed on the copyright page, such as "Copyright 1958, 1960, 1962," means that the original copyright was obtained in 1958. In 1960 and 1962 new material was added and a new copyright secured to cover the material. The date of the last copyright is important when you are buying such books as an encyclopedia, a dictionary, or a book on science.

Sometimes a book has a large sale and is reprinted frequently. Publishers sometimes indicate on this page which printing of the book this volume represents. Do not confuse a new copyright date with a new printing date. The former tells when the book was revised; the latter, when it was merely reprinted.

## The Preface, Foreword, Introduction

These terms refer to matter at the beginning of a book in which the author or someone else (a general editor of a series) speaks directly to the reader. Generally these terms are used interchangeably. Some books may have both a preface and an introduction. In that case, the preface is usually about the particular book; the introduction is more general and may deal with the subject as a whole or the purpose of the series. In the preface, as in this book, the author may indicate the purpose or the scope of the book, or the author may give information that will help the reader. When others have helped the author, acknowledgment is usually made here.

## The Table of Contents

The list of chapters, their subdivisions, and the corresponding pages make up the table of contents. Wise readers examine the table of contents before reading the book to gain an overall view of the content and organization of the entire work. Instead of reading the whole book, they may turn to the portion in which they are interested.

## Lists of Illustrations (maps, diagrams, charts, etc.)

If you read a modern biography, you will probably find a list of photographs with page numbers after the table of contents. Other books, such as atlases, history texts, and art books, may use diagrams, charts, maps, as well as drawings and photographs. When a book has almost as much illustrative material as text, you will often find separate lists of maps, pictures, and charts at the back of the book, preceding the index.

## The Appendix

The appendix contains additional material which the author did not wish to include in the body of the book. A book on American history might contain in the appendix the Declaration of Independence, the Constitution, and the Atlantic Charter. A book on science might have the periodic table of elements and other scientific data.

## The Glossary

A glossary, usually at the end of the book, is a list of definitions of difficult or technical words used in the book. Foreign language texts almost always contain a glossary.

## The Bibliography

Sometimes the author prepares a list of books which were consulted or which are recommended for further reading. Such lists may appear at the end of each chapter or at the end of the book.

## The Index

The index is an alphabetical list, with page numbers, of topics treated in the book. It is much more detailed than the table of contents and is useful for finding quickly the page on which certain topics are discussed. Since an index lists every reference to a topic and tells how many pages are devoted to it, many readers who want information on a particular topic will turn first to the index to see how well the subject is covered in that particular book.

## The End Papers

The pages pasted inside the front and back covers of the book are the end papers. Occasionally maps, other illustrations, or pertinent materials are found there. The end papers of a book on Shakespeare, for example, might have a map of Elizabethan London; the end papers of a book on Joan of Arc might have a map of medieval France.

**EXERCISE 3.** Write answers to the following questions.

1. Why would a book on television copyrighted in 1949 not be very helpful today?
2. Why do modern plays not contain glossaries while an annotated edition of an Elizabethan play almost always does?
3. If you wanted to read about the Battle of Okinawa in a one-volume history of World War II, would you use the table of contents or the index to determine how thoroughly the topic was covered?
4. What parts of a nonfiction book are absent in a work of fiction?
5. Where might you expect a dedication to come – at the beginning or end of the book?

Using *this textbook* as your source of information, answer the following:

6. On what page do the names of the authors appear?
7. When was the second edition copyrighted? The first edition?
8. By what firm was this book published? Where is the firm located?
9. After reading the Preface, write in a sentence or two the primary purpose of the book.
10. What material is contained on the end papers?

## The *Readers' Guide*

Since most of the reference work you will do in high school deals with current rather than historical subjects, you will probably use more magazines than books in preparing a research paper. If you had to look through every issue of every magazine published in order to find an article on your topic, you would probably spend more hours in the library than in the classroom. A guide is needed. That book is the *Readers' Guide to Periodical Literature*.

HOOPER, L. O. — author entry
Market comment. See issues of Forbes
HOPE, Bob — article by author
Jokes that made presidents laugh. il por Sat
Eve Post 246:40-1 Ja '74

*about* — article about author
Bob Hope's scrapbook: Thanks for the
memories; with captions by B. Hope. J. N.
Bell. il pors Good H. 178:58-63+ Ja '74 *

HOPE, Norman V.
Origins of church-state separation in America. Educ Digest 39:54-6 Ja '74

HOPKINS, John — title of article
Find your way home. Criticism
America 130:33 Ja 19 '74 * — title and issue
Nation 218:187-8 F 9 '74 * of magazine
New Repub 170:22 Ja 26 '74 *

HORITA, A. See Quock, R. M. jt auth

HORMAY, August L.
How to have more game. T. Trueblood. il
Field & S 78:24+ Ja '74 *

HORMONES — subject entry
Thymus hormone is isolated. il Sci N 105:52
Ja 26 '74

*See also* — "see also"
Parathyroid hormone cross reference

HORMONES, Sex
Female steroid hormones and target cell
nuclei. B. W. O'Malley and A. R. Means. — volume number
bibl il Science 183:610-20 F 15 '74 — page references

HORN ISLAND
Message from a desert island. J. Madson.
il Audubon 76:56-69 Ja '74 — date of issue

HORN players — descriptions of article
View from the second horn; the new Ameri-
can-born musicians: tired of playing second
fiddle. H. Epstein. pors N Y Times Mag
p 10-11+ Ja 20 '74; Discussion. p7+ F 17
'74

HORNE, Alexander J. and Goldman, C. R.
Suppression of nitrogen fixation by blue-green
algae in a eutrophic lake with trace additions of copper. bibl il Science 183:409-11
F 1 '74

HORNS (animals)
Stories sheep horns tell. J. O'Connor. il Outdoor Life 153:76-9+ F '74

HOROWITZ, Irving Louis
Capitalism, communism and multinational-
ism. il Society 11:32-6+ bibl(p 104) Ja '74

HORSE breeding
And they used to call him sexy; doubtful fer-
tility of Riva Ridge and Secretariat. W.
Tower and W. F. Reed. il Sports Illus 40:
26-8+ F 18 '74

HORSEBACK trips
Don't spare the horses; T. Roosevelt's phys-
ical fitness test ride. C. T. Grayson, Jr. il
Am Heritage 25:78-80 F '74 — "see" cross reference

HORSEMEAT. See Meat

HORSES, Miniature. See Ponies

HORSES, Race — secondary subject heading
Breeding
*See* Horse breeding

HORTON, Luci
Slice of life drawn from the ghetto. il pors
Ebony 29:80-2+ F '74

HORWITZ, Carey A.
(ed) Books to come (cont) Lib J 99:395-421
F 1 '74

HOSE
*See also*
Garden hose

From *Readers' Guide to Periodical Literature,* March 10, 1974, Vol. 74. Reprinted by permission of the H. W. Wilson Company.

**27d.** **Learn to use the** *Readers' Guide to Periodical Literature.*

In the *Readers' Guide,* articles from more than 175 magazines are indexed alphabetically by subjects and authors. You may look up the subject in which you are interested and find articles that have been written on it and the magazines in which they appeared.

Magazine stories (from such magazines as *Atlantic, Harper's, McCall's,* etc.) are listed by title and by author; the complete entry is given with the author listing only. Poems and plays are listed by author. Articles *about* moving pictures and plays are listed under the subject headings MOVING PICTURE PLAYS AND DRAMAS, beneath the subheading **Criticisms, plots, etc.**

The *Readers' Guide* is published in paper-covered pamphlets twice a month from September to June and monthly in July and August. Occasionally during the year a cumulative issue is published that includes the articles listed in preceding months as well as those for the current month. At the end of the year, a large volume is published containing all entries for the year. Every two years a volume covering a two-year period is published.

You must remember, however, that the usefulness of the *Readers' Guide* is limited by the availability to you of the magazines to which it refers you. When you are taking down references from the *Readers' Guide,* you should know what magazines your library has. You should know, too, whether the library has kept back issues of all these magazines or only of certain ones, and for how many years back it has the magazines.

A sample excerpt from the *Readers' Guide* is reproduced on page 488. You can probably understand most of the abbreviations used, but if you cannot, you will find a complete list with explanations in the front of the *Readers' Guide* itself.

**EXERCISE 4.** Write answers to the following questions.

1. Does your library have a list of the magazines to which it

subscribes? Does the list give the dates of back numbers on file? If so, for what years does the library have back numbers of either *Time* or *Atlantic?*

2. Where are the back numbers of magazines kept in your library? How do you get the particular issue you want?

3. Where are the volumes of the *Readers' Guide* kept in your library? What is the latest monthly issue?

4. You are interested in a special career and wish to read some recent articles about opportunities in this field. Consult the *Readers' Guide* and copy the information for at least five articles that you could get in your own library on this subject.

5. The *Readers' Guide* gives you considerable information about each article listed. Copy the data given about a review of a television play or motion picture. Show that you understand the abbreviations by spelling out all of them.

## The Vertical File

### 27e. Learn the nature and proper use of the vertical file.

Many times a subject you would like to read more about is too current to be found in a book. You may have read magazine articles on the subject, but often these articles are too brief to be anything more than an introduction to a topic. Another source of information is the pamphlet, a paper-covered booklet on contemporary subjects that discusses a topic in more detail than a magazine article. It may sometimes be the size of a small book and often contains charts, diagrams, and other illustrative material. Pamphlets are published by government agencies, welfare organizations, political groups, industrial concerns, educational institutions, historical societies, etc.

Your librarian files such pamphlets, as well as interesting clippings and pictures from magazines and newspapers, in a special cabinet usually referred to as the vertical file. Each of these pamphlets is placed in a special folder which is given a topic label. For up-to-the-minute material, both printed and pictorial, you will find the vertical file very useful. Consult your librarian to see whether a file folder is available on the topic you are studying.

### 27f. Learn the location of items in your library.

To make full use of your school or public library, you should know the exact location of the principal items you wish to use. If you know exactly where to go for the information you want, you can save both the librarian and yourself a lot of time.

**EXERCISE 5.** Be prepared to state the location in your school or public library of each of the following:

1. The desk where books are charged out and returned
2. The card catalogue
3. The fiction shelves
4. The biography shelves
5. The science section
6. The reserved-book shelf and the new-book shelf
7. The encyclopedias
8. The vertical file
9. The back numbers of magazines
10. The *Readers' Guide*

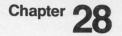

# Reference Books

## The Principal Reference Books and Their Uses

A distinguished professor of chemistry astonished her class one day when she was unable to answer a rather simple question. "I don't know the answer," she admitted, "but I know exactly where I can look it up. That, to me, is more important than having all the answers in my head."

Through its many reference books a modern, well-equipped library can give you answers to almost any question you can think of.

Become familiar with the location in the library and the contents of all the reference books discussed in this chapter. Do not be satisfied with knowing only that you can get some information from an encyclopedia. You will be a more successful student if you know which reference book is the best source for the kind of information you want.

## ENCYCLOPEDIAS

Most students know the encyclopedia as a set of many volumes, located in a special section of the library, and frequently in use. These books contain information on almost any branch of knowledge. Dozens of scholars, working for years, contribute to the making of an encyclopedia. These experts are identified and their qualifications are described in the front of the encyclopedia; their standing in their fields is one indication of the caliber of the encyclopedia.

Since most encyclopedias give an overall view of a subject in general articles, reading one article is usually not enough for accurate research. In order to find all the information that your encyclopedia has on a subject, consult the index, which is usually in the last volume. For example, if you were looking up the Declaration of Independence in the *Encyclopedia Americana* you would find an article several pages long in the D volume which would give a history of the writing and the complete text of the document. After you had read this, you could turn to the index and find references to many other articles that discuss some aspect of the Declaration. You would also find a list of the signers and the volumes where their biographies could be found.

When the *Encyclopaedia Britannica* expanded to thirty volumes in 1974, it introduced a new method of arrangement. The first volume became an introduction to the rest of the encyclopedia. The *Micropaedia* (shorter articles) occupies the next ten volumes; the *Macropaedia* (longer articles) occupies the final nineteen volumes. Many of the *Macropaedia* articles are longer than full-length books. This offers three solutions to different levels of curiosity. The introductory volume is a fine channel for general curiosity; it discusses the most general areas of knowledge and explains the various ways in which they have been subdivided into more and more specialized areas, suggesting ways of pursuing various questions throughout the rest of the encyclopedia. The *Micropaedia* articles explain more particular questions in detail, with generous cross-referencing to the *Macropaedia,* where exhaustive answers can be found.

Most encyclopedias are kept up-to-date in two ways. First, each printing usually represents some minor revisions —political changes, deaths, etc.—and every few years a major revision is produced. Second, most encyclopedias publish an annual volume, or yearbook, which includes major events of the year and important changes or additions to the general body of knowledge. A new discovery in biology or physics, for example, would probably appear first in a yearbook and later in a major revision.

Investigate the encyclopedias in your school and public library. Among them you may find:

## Encyclopedias in Many Volumes

*Collier's Encyclopedia*
>24 volumes
>Bibliography and index in Volume 24
>Publishes *Collier's Yearbook*

*Encyclopaedia Britannica*
>30 volumes
>Cross-referencing throughout *Micropaedia*
>Publishes the *Britannica Book of the Year*

*Encyclopedia Americana*
>30 volumes
>Index in Volume 30
>Publishes the *Americana Annual*

*Encyclopedia International*
>20 volumes
>Index in Volume 20
>Publishes the *Encyclopedia International Yearbook*

*World Book Encyclopedia*
>22 volumes
>Research Guide and Index in Volume 22
>Publishes an annual supplement

## One- and Two-Volume Encyclopedias

For brief, handy accounts of a subject, a "desk" encyclopedia in one or two volumes is adequate. Three of the better-known works of this kind are the *Columbia Encyclopedia,* the *Columbia-Viking Concise Encyclopedia,* and the *Lincoln Library of Essential Information.* The *Lincoln*

*Library* has two volumes arranged in broad areas of knowledge explained in its opening pages, as well as a thorough index. The *Columbia* and *Columbia-Viking* are arranged with their articles in alphabetical order, like a dictionary.

# GENERAL REFERENCE BOOKS

## Yearbooks and Almanacs

*World Almanac and Book of Facts*
*Information Please Almanac*
*The Official Associated Press Almanac*
*Statesman's Yearbook*

Although almanacs are published yearly, remember that they tell about the year preceding their date: a 1978 almanac contains information about 1977.

All four of these books are fully indexed. They contain statistical and factual information subject to constant change, like census tables, economic statistics, the results of elections and athletic and artistic competitions, the winners of all sorts of awards, and summaries of important current events. The *Statesman's Yearbook* is particularly concerned with governments and information of particular value to governments; it begins with information about international affairs and moves on to information about individual nations. *The Official Associated Press Almanac* includes encyclopedic articles on various important aspects of the current year. The *World Almanac* is the most popular and is especially valuable for its brevity; the *Information Please Almanac* is a bit less abbreviated and sometimes easier to read.

## Atlases

Although an atlas is primarily a book of maps showing political and geological divisions of the world, there is much more to be found in any atlas than the current boundaries of nations and states. Climate, food production, ethnic distribution, languages, health, kinds of industry for every continent and country are only part of the information given in a good atlas.

Before you consult any modern atlas, check the copyright date. Since World War II the political divisions of the world have changed so rapidly that only a recent atlas will be of any help to the student who is looking for information about troubled areas of the globe.

### General Atlases

    *The Encyclopædia Britannica Atlas*
    *Hammond Contemporary World Atlas*
    *National Geographic World Atlas*
    *New York Times Atlas of the World*
    *Rand McNally New Cosmopolitan World Atlas*

Some atlases show the world of the past. These are historical atlases and are valuable for students of history.

### Historical Atlases

    Lord's *Historical Atlas of the United States*
    Shepherd's *Historical Atlas*

## BIOGRAPHICAL REFERENCE BOOKS

Many reference books in your library are devoted to the lives of people of the past and present. Like the general encyclopedias, reference books about people are sometimes available in sets or as individual volumes.

### General Biography

#### Current Biography

This is issued monthly and is concerned with outstanding personalities of our own time. Their activities are usually in the current headlines. Thus, if England gets a new queen or Iran a new shah, you may expect a biographical sketch and frequently a photograph of the new dignitary.

Published monthly in paper covers, the year's issues are cumulated in one bound volume. By using the cumulative index in each issue, you can find biographies that have appeared in other issues and in other years. A separate index includes biographies from 1940 to 1970. Biographies are also indexed by professions.

### The Dictionary of American Biography (20 volumes)

Great Americans who are no longer living are included from all areas of arts, sciences, politics, industry. The articles are somewhat longer than their equivalents in ordinary encyclopedias. Naturally, many more distinguished Americans are to be found here than in a general reference encyclopedia, which has to include information concerning the great people of all countries. Supplementary volumes, of which three have been published, keep the dictionary relatively up-to-date.

### The Dictionary of National Biography

This many-volume reference work presents information about the lives of distinguished English people who are no longer living.

### The New Century Cyclopedia of Names (3 volumes)

This comprehensive reference work lists 100,000 proper names of every description, including persons, places, events, literary works and characters, works of art, and mythological and legendary persons and places. Consulting this book first will often save you a lot of time in looking up a proper name.

### Webster's Biographical Dictionary

In one volume this book lists more than 40,000 biographies of famous men and women through the ages. Each alphabetical entry gives more information than you would find in a general dictionary, but the articles are obviously shorter than those in an encyclopedia. For quick reference, and for a guide to pronunciation of proper names, this is a helpful work.

### Who's Who

This has long been the most frequently consulted book of facts about distinguished living British and Commonwealth persons. The kinds of facts you may expect to find are: date of birth, parentage, schooling, publications (if an author), public offices (if an official), accomplishments in the professional field, name of spouse, and children. Occasionally non-British people are included if they are very prominent. This one-volume work comes out annually. For distinguished persons no longer living, consult *Who Was Who.*

### Who's Who in America

This volume, published every two years, lists distinguished living Americans. The latest edition has over 50,000 entries.

## Books About Authors

Although authors' lives are included in all biographical reference books and encyclopedias, the following books treat authors only.

*The Writers Directory*
Magill's *Cyclopedia of World Authors*
*Twentieth Century Authors,* with supplements, by Kunitz and Haycraft
*American Authors 1600–1900,* by Kunitz and Haycraft
*British Authors Before 1800,* by Kunitz and Haycraft
*British Authors of the Nineteenth Century,* by Kunitz and Haycraft

*The Writers Directory* lists briefly about 18,000 of today's writers, and is published every two years. Its articles are more concise and a little more formal than those in the other books listed above. Magill's *Cyclopedia* is a popular worldwide reference book, and includes pictures of the authors, as the Kunitz and Haycraft books do.

# LITERARY REFERENCE BOOKS

You have already learned something about the available biographical reference books on authors. For information about literary works, including material on plots, characters, sources, and quotations, you can consult one of the following:

## Books of Quotations

### Bartlett's *Familiar Quotations*

Bartlett's has been in use for over a century, with many revisions, and is the most familiar reference book of quotations. The quotations and the index occupy almost equal parts of the book. Quotations are given under the authors' names in chronological order, according to when the quotation was written. You might look up an author and read all the quotations under the author's name, or look up a key word in the quotation to discover who the author was and what the quotation was from, or what its exact wording should be. Wondering who wrote "Absence makes the heart grow fonder," for example, you might look up *absence* (or *heart,* or *fonder*) in the index. You would find "makes the heart grow fonder" in a list of cross-references giving the page number to check, and on that page of the edition you are using you would find that Thomas Haynes Bayly wrote it, as a line of his *Isle of Beauty.*

### Stevenson's *Home Book of Quotations* and *Home Book of Proverbs, Maxims, and Familiar Phrases*

These books are arranged on an entirely different principle. Instead of being grouped by author, the quotations are grouped by subject matter so that all quotes about love or courage or learning are together. This arrangement makes the books particularly useful when you are writing a speech or an essay and want to find appropriate quotations on a particular subject.

## Indexes and Collections of Poetry

### *Granger's Index to Poetry* (sixth edition)

Occasionally you want to locate not a quotation but an entire short work. If the selection is a poem, *Granger's Index* will help you to locate it. Suppose you would like to find a book containing the poems "The Wreck of the Hesperus" and "The Chambered Nautilus." Looking for these titles in *Granger's,* you find listed in code (which is explained in the front of the book) the titles of a number of books containing the poems. You can then use the card catalogue in the library to find one of the books containing these two poems.

An index of authors and an index of first lines help you find the poem if you do not know the title. Two supplements cover newer collections of poetry.

Stevenson's *Home Book of Verse* and *Home Book of Modern Verse*
Van Doren's *An Anthology of World Poetry*
Untermeyer's *Modern American Poetry* and *Modern British Poetry*

The books listed above are only a few of the collections of poems that are found in many libraries. The Stevenson volumes are arranged by subjects; the Van Doren book by countries. Untermeyer arranges the authors in chronological order. All have indexes of authors, titles, and first lines.

## OTHER REFERENCE BOOKS

There are many other reference books that you may find in your library on literature and other subjects. If your teacher asks you to report on any of the following books, be sure to include the title of the book, number of volumes, publication date, a brief description of contents and arrangement of material, and the principal use of the book in reference work.

## Literature

*American Authors and Books*
*Book Review Digest*
*Bulfinch's Mythology*
*Cambridge History of American Literature*
*Cambridge History of English Literature*
*Guide to Great Plays* by J. T. Shipley
*Index to One-Act Plays*
*Index to Plays*
*Index to Short Stories*
*The New Century Classical Handbook*
*Oxford Companion to American Literature*
*Oxford Companion to Classical Literature*
*Oxford Companion to English Literature*

## Grammar and Usage

*A Dictionary of Contemporary American Usage* by Bergen
   and Cornelia Evans
*American Usage: The Consensus* by Roy H. Copperud

## History and Social Studies

*Dictionary of American History* by J. T. Adams
*The Dictionary of Dates* by Helen R. Keller
*Encyclopedia of American History* by R. B. Morris
*Encyclopedia of the Social Sciences*
*Encyclopedia of World History* by W. L. Langer
*Historical Statistics of the United States*
*Statistical Abstract of the United States*
*Webster's Geographical Dictionary*

## Science and Mathematics

*Mathematics Dictionary*, edited by Glenn and R. C. James
*McGraw-Hill Encyclopedia of Science*
Van Nostrand's *Scientific Encyclopedia*

## Music and Art

*Grove's Dictionary of Music and Musicians*
*Harvard Dictionary of Music*
*The McGraw-Hill Encyclopedia of World Art*
*The New College Encyclopedia of Music*, edited by Westrup
   and Harrison
*Oxford Companion to Music*

*Vasari's Lives of the Painters, Sculptors, and Architects* (four paperback volumes)

### Colleges and Universities

*American Universities and Colleges*
*College Blue Book*
*Comparative Guide to American Colleges*
*Lovejoy's College Guide*
*New American Guide to Colleges* by G. R. Hawes

**EXERCISE.** Indicate the reference book or books you would use to find the information requested below.

1. A list of last year's winners of the Nobel Prizes.
2. The prime ministers of Ghana, Nigeria, and Tanzania.
3. The countries that border on Albania.
4. The name of the poem which begins "The world is too much with us."
5. The contemporary reviews of Willa Cather's *Death Comes for the Archbishop*.
6. The important rivers and mountains in Nepal.
7. A brief list of facts about Eleanor Roosevelt.
8. A map of the Roman Empire under Augustus.
9. The current presidents of M.I.T., N.Y.U., and Princeton.
10. A book containing Susan Glaspell's one-act play *Trifles*.
11. An informative article on Greek civilization by an acknowledged authority.
12. A brief sketch of a person who was elected to high office in any foreign land a few months ago.
13. The definition of an unusual musical term.
14. Current linguistic opinion about the propriety of using *it's me* in formal English.
15. The name of a poem of which you know a familiar line.

# Chapter 29

# The Dictionary

## Content and Uses of Dictionaries

Norman Douglas, the author of *South Wind,* once wrote to his friend Muriel Draper, "Do you learn a column of the dictionary every day by heart? Well, you should." Several years later she wrote Douglas the following invitation, which wittily suggests that she had followed his advice:

Dearest Doug:

I have married, marrow, Mars, Marsala, Marseillaise, marsh, marshal, Marshalsea, marsupial, mart, martello, martial, Martin Paul Draper and live at 19 Edith Grove, grovel, grow, growl, growth, groyne, grub, grudge, gruel, gruesome, gruff, grumble, grume, grummet, grumpy, Grundyism, grunt, Gruyère, grysbok. Will you come to tea, teach, league, teak, teal, teamster, teapot, tear, tearing, tease, teasel, technic at once (I have got some excellent wine), and stay to dine, dingdong, ding-hey, dingo, dinosaur, dinothere, dint, diocese, dioptric, dioxide, dip—

Yours—

Muriel Draper[1]

No one expects you to follow Douglas' advice literally, although you could learn a great deal by doing so. You do not have to memorize all the information in a dictionary, but you should know what kind of information is there and

---

[1] From *Music at Midnight* by Muriel Draper. Copyright 1929 by Muriel Draper; renewed 1957 by Paul Draper. Reprinted by permission of Harper & Row, Publishers, Inc.

how to find it. You should also know something about the way in which dictionaries are made and their purpose.

The first great dictionary of the English language was compiled by Samuel Johnson in 1755. The first American dictionary, published in 1806, was also the work of one man—Noah Webster. Modern dictionaries, like *Webster's Third New International Dictionary, Webster's New World Dictionary of the American Language, The Random House Dictionary of the English Language: The Unabridged Edition,* and *The Oxford English Dictionary,* represent the cooperative efforts of hundreds of scholars and take many years to prepare. The essential method is the same, however, whether carried out by one person or many. Dictionary makers collect all of the information they can about the way English speakers use their language and record it in a form convenient for reference. Although Johnson and Webster were able to bring together an astonishing amount of evidence on which to base their initial definitions, modern dictionaries with large staffs and modern methods are naturally able to collect much more. In general, the more separate uses of words examined in the preparation of a dictionary, the better the dictionary is likely to be.

A dictionary is a record of the usage of words—their meanings, spellings, pronunciations, histories, and forms. Its purpose is to show you how a large number of users of English have pronounced or spelled a word, what they have meant by it, and under what circumstances they have used it. This is not the same thing as telling you how to use a word—a dictionary is a record of usage, not a body of laws. Since you use words to communicate with others, it is essential that you know what words mean to other people, and what associations they may have with them. A dictionary cannot tell you what word to use—only you know what it is you want to say. What a good dictionary can do, however, is provide you with the information you need to make up your own mind.

To get a clearer idea of the way in which dictionary makers go about their work, try your hand at writing a definition of your own for the blank word in the following exercise.

**EXERCISE 1.** The following sentences illustrate the use of a single common word. The word itself has been omitted from the sentence and in its place the word BLANK has been substituted. Like many common words, the one that BLANK stands for has a number of different meanings. You will need, therefore, to sort out these separate meanings. Begin by copying each sentence on a separate slip of paper, and then group the ones with similar meanings together. When you are satisfied with your grouping of the slips, write a brief definition for each different meaning of BLANK or BLANKS. Before you are finished, you should be able to guess the word.

1. Deciphering the ancient document was a difficult task because so many of the BLANKS had been obliterated.
2. You can see from her portrait that she was a person with a great deal of BLANK.
3. The Masquers are looking for a play that has an equal number of male and female BLANKS.
4. A headline writer has to bear in mind the number of BLANKS that will fit in a single line.
5. Mrs. Dillon, who drives an ancient electric car and keeps a seal in her swimming pool, is one of our town's better-known BLANKS.
6. Persons of bad BLANK need not apply for jobs in banks.
7. It is difficult to play the part of a BLANK that you cannot understand or sympathize with.
8. Scholars cannot decide whether the BLANK means "seven" or "last winter."
9. Team sports are supposed to be better at developing BLANK than such games as checkers, billiards, and Scrabble.
10. The BLANK I found most amusing was the spy who wanted everyone to like him.
11. In some languages, many BLANKS are really pictures.
12. What a BLANK that Joy Adams is!

# KINDS OF DICTIONARIES

## 29a. Know the kinds of dictionaries.

Excluding the many special dictionaries—dictionaries of scientific terms, foreign language dictionaries, etc.—there are two main kinds of dictionaries with which you should be familiar: the large, *unabridged* dictionary, which you will probably use mainly in libraries; and the "college-size" dictionary, which you should have at hand whenever you study.

You should know that the small, pocket-sized dictionaries sold in stationery and drugstores may help you with common word meanings and spellings, but are not as dependable as scholarly, complete, up-to-date works.

## Unabridged Dictionaries

The largest dictionaries—those containing over 300,000 words—are called *unabridged* dictionaries. *Unabridged* means that a dictionary is not a cut-down version of some larger dictionary. The best known and most available of these are:

> *The Oxford English Dictionary,* Oxford University Press, New York
>
> *The Random House Dictionary of the English Language: The Unabridged Edition,* Random House, New York
>
> *Webster's Third New International Dictionary,* G. & C. Merriam Company, Springfield, Massachusetts

An unabridged dictionary has entries for about two to three times as many words as a college dictionary, and the entries are likely to be longer and more detailed, and to distinguish finer shades of meaning. It simply contains more information than a college dictionary. For example, you will stand a better chance of finding in it a word that is unfamiliar to you but familiar to people in some other part of the world, a word that has a particular meaning in a certain part of the country, or an old or obsolete meaning of a word. *Webster's Third* and the *"O.E.D."* (the *Oxford*) also provide actual quotations showing the use of a word.

## College Dictionaries

The most practical dictionary for everyday use is the college dictionary. Dictionaries of this kind usually contain entries for between 100,000 and 160,000 words. Because it is easier to revise a college dictionary than an unabridged dictionary, the former is more likely to be up-to-date. Dictionary makers, who have students in mind when they prepare college dictionaries, are careful to include useful guides to spelling, capitalization, punctuation, research paper techniques, etc. The college dictionaries listed below are reputable and well known.

> *American Heritage Dictionary of the English Language,* American Heritage Publishing Company, Inc., New York, and Houghton Mifflin Co., Boston
>
> *The Random House College Dictionary,* Random House, New York
>
> *Webster's New Collegiate Dictionary,* G. & C. Merriam Company, Springfield, Massachusetts
>
> *Webster's New World Dictionary of the American Language, Second College Edition, Complete Reference Edition,* World Publishing Company, Cleveland

# CONTENT AND ARRANGEMENT OF DICTIONARIES

## 29b. Become familiar with the content and arrangement of dictionaries.

Most people consult the dictionary only when they want the meaning, the spelling, or the pronunciation of an unfamiliar word. To confine your use of the dictionary thus is to shortchange yourself. Dictionaries can provide you with many other kinds of information. This section will point out some of these additional resources. The more often you turn to the dictionary, the richer will become your knowledge, not only of words, but of all branches of human knowledge — from numismatics to ichthyology.

Although all good dictionaries contain essentially the same kinds of information, they sometimes vary in arrangement and in their manner of presenting the information. There are differences also in the position of abbreviations and foreign words and phrases. Familiarizing yourself with the arrangement of your dictionary will save you a great deal of time and enable you to appreciate your dictionary more fully.

The following exercises apply to almost all standard dictionaries for senior high schools.

**EXERCISE 2.** Using the dictionary with which you have been provided, write the answers to the following questions. This exercise is designed to familiarize you with the contents and arrangement of your dictionary. The table of contents of that book will help you find some of the answers.

1. What is the full title of the dictionary?
2. Who is the publisher?
3. What is the latest copyright date?
4. Is there a section on pronunciation? What is it called? On what pages does it appear?
5. If there is a section explaining the *purpose* of the dictionary, for what group of readers is it intended? What are some of its special features? On what pages does this section appear?
6. Where can you find abbreviations — in the body of the text or in the back of the book? If they are in a separate section, give the name of that section and its page numbers.
7. Where do you find signs and symbols? If they are in a separate section, give the name and pages.
8. Where are spelling rules indicated, if such a section exists?
9. Where can you find the rules for punctuation and capitalization?
10. What kind of illustrations are there? Are there any in color?
11. Where do you look for Jane Addams, Galileo, and Jung — in the main body of the text or in a special biographical section?

12. How do you find the location and length of the Kabul—in the main body of the text or in a special section? Give the pages of that section.

13. Can you locate characters in fiction or in mythology? Give the pages of any special section that contains such information.

14. How do you find the meaning of *pro bono publico, tout de suite,* and similar foreign expressions?

15. What other features does your dictionary have?

**EXERCISE 3.** Look up in your dictionary the answers to the following questions and write them in a column on your paper. After each answer write the page number on which you found it.

1. What does the abbreviation *R.S.V.P.* mean? (Give the English meaning.)

2. What is the population of Bombay (at the time your dictionary was published)?

3. What was the occupation of Sarah Siddons?

4. Who was Minerva?

5. What is the meaning of the French expression *pièce de résistance?*

6. What are the plurals of the following words: *addendum, adieu, axis, crisis, datum, dilettante?*

7. How did the word *Tory* come to have its present meaning?

8. Where is Nepal?

9. Where would such spellings as *armour, clamour, labour, odour* be preferred today?

10. How does your dictionary indicate the sound of the first vowel in the word *tale?*

## DICTIONARY INFORMATION ABOUT A WORD

**29c. Learn to use the vocabulary entries.**

The words listed in alphabetical order in the main part of the dictionary are referred to as "vocabulary entries." There is, as you would expect, more information about each word in a large, unabridged dictionary than in a college dictionary, and still more than in one of the small paperbound dictionaries. Remember that the unabridged is the richest in information.

## Spelling

When you are in doubt about a spelling, you should turn to the dictionary almost automatically. When there are two acceptable spellings, the more common spelling is generally given first. If the forms are of equal or nearly equal standing, they are separated by a comma or by the word *or:* **labor, labour.** If the spellings are not at all equal in frequency of occurrence, the word *also* will precede the less common spelling: **envelope** *also* **envelop.** British preferences are often given following the American spellings, set off by a comma: **analyze, analyse; peddler, pedlar; armor, armour.**

Occasionally the spelling of the various forms of a word presents a problem to you. The dictionary helps to solve it. You may learn, for example, that the plural of *erratum* is *errata.* Are you unsure about the past tense of *prefer, ricochet, benefit?* The dictionary conveniently answers your questions with *preferred, ricocheted,* and *benefited.*

## Capitalization

Proper nouns and adjectives are given with capital letters in the dictionary. If such words are sometimes used with a lower-case initial, that usage is noted.

## Syllabication

When you divide a word at the end of a line, you must divide it according to its syllables. A dictionary indicates the syllables in a word by placing a centered dot (·) or a space between them.

## Pronunciation

Dictionaries indicate the pronunciation of words by means of accent marks and respellings which show clearly how the words should sound. The respellings are necessary because our alphabet uses more than two hundred combinations of letters to represent the forty-two or forty-three sounds of English. Each letter or special symbol used in the respellings always stands for the same sound. The sounds represented by the various letters and other symbols in the respelling are shown on a key that usually appears at the front of the dictionary and at the bottom of every pair of facing pages. Since different dictionaries use different systems of indicating pronunciation, it is essential that you familiarize yourself with the key and notes on pronunciation in your own dictionary. The examples on the following pages show different systems for representing pronunciation.

> **stu·dent** (stōōd/ʰnt, styōōd/-), *n.* **1.** a person formally engaged in learning, esp. one enrolled in an institution of secondary or higher education. **2.** any person who studies, investigates, or carefully examines a subject. —*adj.* **3.** of, by, or pertaining to students, esp. of colleges or universities: *a student song; a student demonstration.* [late ME < L *studēnt-* (s. of *studēns,* prp.) = *stud-* (s. of *studēre* to take pains) + *-ēnt-* -ENT; r. *studiant* < MF] —**Syn. 1, 2.** See **pupil¹.**

From the *Random House College Dictionary,* Revised Edition. Copyright © 1968, 1975 by Random House, Inc. Used by permission.

When a word may be pronounced in more than one way, dictionaries give other correct pronunciations. The first syllable of *student,* above, may be given either the flat *oo* sound or the pointed *you* sound. There are several different methods of showing accentuation, too.

## Part of Speech

The dictionary indicates the part of speech of each word by means of common abbreviations:

> **school¹** (skōōl) *n. Abbr.* **s., S., sch. 1.** An institution for the instruction of children. **2.** An institution for instruction in a skill or business. **3.** A college or university. **4.** An institution within a college or university for instruction in a specialized

field. **5.** The student body of an educational institution. **6.** A place of instruction; the building or group of buildings in which instruction is given or in which students work and live. **7.** The process of being educated; especially, formal education comprising a planned series of courses over a number of years. **8.** A session of instruction. **9.** A group of persons, especially intellectuals or artists, whose thought, work, or style demonstrates some common influence or unifying belief. **10.** A class of people distinguished by a convention of manner, custom, or opinion. **11.** The education provided by a set of circumstances or experiences. **12.** A division comprising several grades or classes in a private school. **13.** The prescribed regulations and drill instructions applying to individuals or to a unit of an army or navy. —*tr.v.* **schooled, schooling, schools. 1.** To instruct; educate. **2.** To train; discipline. —See Synonyms at **teach.** [Middle English *scole,* Old English *scōl,* from Medieval Latin *scōla,* from Latin *schola,* leisure, school, from Greek *skholē,* leisure (devoted to learning), lecture, school. See **segh-** in Appendix.*]

From *The American Heritage Dictionary of the English Language,* © 1969, 1970, 1973, 1975, American Heritage Publishing Company, Inc. Used by permission.

Here *n.* (noun) precedes definitions of the noun *school,* and *tr. v.* (transitive verb) precedes the definitions of the transitive verb *school.* (Some dictionaries have different, full entries for these different parts of speech, even under the same word.)

## Inflected Forms

The dictionary gives other forms of a word whenever there is an important reason for this information. These forms are called *inflected* or *inflectional* forms. They may be of several kinds:

The plural of a word when formed irregularly: **crisis;** *pl.* **crises**

The feminine form of a foreign word: **alumnus;** *fem.* **alumna**

The principal parts of an irregular verb: **bring; brought; brought**

Comparative and superlative forms of an adjective or adverb if formed irregularly: **bad; worse; worst**

Case forms of pronouns: **who;** *possessive* **whose;** *objective* **whom**

## Derivation, or Etymology

One of the most fascinating studies in connection with words is their derivation, or etymology. Most dictionaries indicate the history of a word. By means of abbreviations, they show the language from which it came and what its original meaning was. With its half million words, English has drawn upon almost all modern and ancient languages. Consider the following:

| | |
|---|---|
| *ginger* (Sanskrit) | *fjord* (Norwegian) |
| *alibi* (Latin) | *tycoon* (Chinese) |
| *bizarre* (French) | *ukulele* (Polynesian) |
| *paradise* (Persian) | *skunk* (American Indian) |
| *obbligato* (Italian) | *kimono* (Japanese) |
| *zwieback* (German) | *cravat* (Croatian) |
| *algebra* (Arabic) | *czardas* (Hungarian) |

In addition to the derivation of words from other languages, the dictionary gives you the origin of recently coined words, hundreds of which come into the language yearly. If you know the source and the original meaning of a word, you may have a better idea of its present meaning and especially of its subtle connotations.

**free·dom** \\'frēdəm\\ *n* -s [ME *fredom*, fr. OE *frēodōm*, fr. *frēo* free + *-dōm* -dom] **1 :** the quality or state of being free: as **a :** the quality or state of not being coerced or constrained by fate, necessity, or circumstances in one's choices or actions ⟨the philosophical implications of the play theory are found in its opposition of ~ and necessity, of spontancity and order —John Dewey⟩ **b** (1) **:** the status of the will as an uncaused cause of human actions **:** the absence of antecedent causal determination of human decisions (2) **:** self-realization or spiritual self-fulfillment that is not incompatible with the existence of natural causes of the will-act **:** SELF-DETERMINATION

From *Webster's Third New International Dictionary,* © 1971 by G. & C. Merriam Co., Publishers of the Merriam-Webster Dictionaries. Used by permission.

The common English word *freedom* comes, the entry above shows, from Middle English (ME), and it got into Middle English through Old English (OE). It is one of our oldest root words. The abbreviations in your dictionary will tell you how the many other languages are identified in etymology entries. Some dictionaries list the etymology at the beginning of the entry; some list it at the end. All the information abbreviated in the etymological entry can be learned easily once you are familiar with the dictionary's system of abbreviation.

## Meanings

Most English words have more than one meaning. A good dictionary will provide all of the important definitions, numbering each one separately.

> **growth** (grōth) *n.* **1.** the process of growing or developing; specif., *a*) gradual development toward maturity *b*) formation and development **2.** *a*) degree of increase in size, weight, power, etc. *b*) the full extent of such increase **3.** something that grows or has grown [a thick *growth* of grass] **4.** an outgrowth or offshoot **5.** a tumor or other abnormal mass of tissue developed in or on the body

From *Webster's New World Dictionary*, Second College Edition. Copyright © 1974 by William Collins & World Publishing Co., Inc. Used by permission.

Here the meanings are listed in more or less chronological order—the order of the word's etymology, from what it meant when it was first used to what it means today. Some dictionaries list meanings in the order of frequency of use —they move from the most common meaning to the least common meaning. Most dictionaries list extremely technical meanings of words last, where they often fall no matter which order is used.

When you are looking up a word in your dictionary, read through the entire list until you find the meaning that exactly fits the context in which the word appears in your book. Many students have misused words all their lives because they settled for the first entry in their dictionaries, without realizing that there were several other meanings. The richer your understanding of all the meanings of words, the greater will be your power to understand and use language.

## Restrictive Labels

Most of the words defined in a dictionary belong to the general vocabulary of standard English. Some words, as well as some special meanings of otherwise standard words, require special treatment, and these usually appear with a label. There are three main kinds of labels: *subject* labels, which specify that a word has a particular meaning in a certain field: *Law, Med., Aeron.* (Aeronautics), etc.; *geographical* labels, which indicate the area in which a particular word, meaning, or pronunciation is principally used: Brit., SW U.S. (Southwest U.S.); and *usage* labels, which characterize a word as to its level of usage: *informal, slang, nonstandard,* etc.

Usage labels provide a good general guide to usage, but every writer must learn to make judgments about these matters on the basis of careful observation. Assigning a label such as *slang* or *informal* is necessarily a subjective judgment on the part of the definer, and not all dictionaries agree about labeling the same word.

Often a vocabulary entry in a dictionary will include synonyms for the word, and sometimes it will include antonyms. Synonyms are words which are more or less closely related in meaning to the word being defined. Antonyms are words which are opposite in meaning to the word being defined.

> **hin·der**[1] (hin′dər) *vt.* [ME. *hindren* < OE. *hindrian,* lit., to keep or hold back (akin to G. *hindern*) < base of ff.]
> **1.** to keep back; restrain; get in the way of; prevent; stop **2.** to make difficult for; thwart; impede; frustrate —*vi.* to delay action; be a hindrance
> *SYN.*—**hinder** implies a holding back of something about to begin and connotes a thwarting of progress *[hindered* by a lack of education*]*; **obstruct** implies a retarding of passage or progress by placing obstacles in the way *[*to *obstruct* the passage of a bill by a filibuster*]*; **block** implies the complete, but not necessarily permanent, obstruction of a passage or progress *[*the road was *blocked* by a landslide*]*; **impede** suggests a slowing up of movement or progress by interfering with the normal action *[*tight garters *impede* the circulation of the blood*]*; **bar** implies an obstructing as if by means of a barrier *[*he was *barred* from the club*]* See also DELAY —*ANT.* **advance, further**

From *Webster's New World Dictionary,* Second College Edition. Copyright © 1974 by William Collins & World Publishing Co., Inc. Used by permission.

Here, following the abbreviation SYN., the distinctions between synonyms are explained. The synonyms are *hinder, obstruct, block, impede,* and *bar.* Following the abbreviation ANT., two antonyms are given: *advance* and *further.*

Besides the dictionary, there are several books of synonyms, of which the best known is *Roget's Thesaurus.* This book and other synonym dictionaries are discussed on pages 518–19.

## Illustrations

Dictionaries illustrate many words that cannot be easily

visualized. To most of us, a helmet may suggest a covering for the head in playing football, but *Webster's Third New International Dictionary* pictures those used for lacrosse and polo as well as several others used in wars throughout history. Many scientific illustrations are particularly helpful to students beginning their study of the sciences.

**EXERCISE 4.** This exercise is designed to test your knowledge of the information given about a word in the dictionary. With your dictionary before you, begin work at the teacher's signal. Find the answers to the following questions and write them on your paper. While your speed indicates to some degree your efficiency in using the dictionary, accuracy is more important.

1. Which is the preferred spelling in the United States: *defence* or *defense?*
2. Copy the correct pronunciation of *phlegmatic,* including diacritical marks. Be able to pronounce it correctly.
3. What are the comparative and superlative degrees of *little?* of *many?*
4. Copy the word *dexterity,* dividing it correctly into syllables.
5. How many different meanings are given in your dictionary for the word *horse?*
6. What restrictive label, if any, does your dictionary give for the word *guy,* meaning "fellow"?
7. Which meanings, if any, of the verb *bounce* have been labeled as slang?
8. What is the difference in meaning between *prophecy* and *prophesy?*
9. How did *gerrymander* get its meaning?
10. Who was the legendary character Guinevere?
11. From what language is the word *echo* derived?
12. What restrictive label is given the word *eftsoons?*
13. What restrictive label, if any, is given the word *bamboozle?*
14. In your own words, give the information about Pandora as a character in Greek mythology.
15. From what language did the word *dog* come into English?

## Other Information in Dictionaries

### 29d. Learn to use the information entries.

In addition to information about words, most dictionaries give a great many facts about people and places. Such information may appear in the body of the dictionary or it may be collected in a special section.

## Important Persons

The dictionary usually gives the following biographical data about important persons:

1. *Name:* correct spelling, pronunciation, and the first name
2. *Dates of birth and death*
3. *Nationality*
4. *Why famous*

> **Wil·son** (wil′sən), *n.* **1. Edmund,** 1895–1972, U.S. literary and social critic. **2. Henry** (*Jeremiah Jones Colbath*), 1812–1875, U.S. politician: vice president of the U.S. 1873–75. **3. (James) Harold,** born 1916, British statesman: prime minister 1964–70 and since 1974. **4. John** ("*Christopher North*"), 1785–1854, Scottish poet, journalist, and critic. **5. (Thomas) Wood·row** (wŏŏd′rō), 1856–1924, 28th president of the U.S. 1913–21: Nobel peace prize 1919. **6. Mount,** a mountain in SW California. 5710 ft. **7.** a city in E North Carolina. 29,347 (1970).

From the *Random House College Dictionary*, Revised Edition. Copyright © 1968, 1975 by Random House, Inc. Used by permission.

The biographical information in a dictionary cannot always be up-to-date for contemporary figures. A more promising source of information about contemporaries is *Who's Who* or *Who's Who in America* (see page 498).

## Important Places

In listing geographical place-names (like Mount Wilson or Wilson, North Carolina, above) the dictionary usually gives the following information:

1. *Name:* spelling, pronunciation
2. *Identification:* whether a city, country, lake, mountain, river, etc.
3. *Location*

4. *Size:* population, if a city or country; area in square miles, if a country or territory or body of water; length, if a river; height, if a mountain, etc.

5. *Importance:* If a city is a capital of a state or country, this fact will be indicated, sometimes by a star or an asterisk. The capital of a country or state will also be given under the name of the country or state.

6. *Historical or other interesting information of importance:* Thus, for Gettysburg, Pennsylvania, almost all dictionaries mention the Union victory in the War Between the States just before the Fourth of July, 1863.

7. *Governing or controlling country:* Thus, for the British Virgin Islands, a dictionary entry will say "a British colony."

# DICTIONARIES OF SYNONYMS

## 29e. Learn to use the special dictionaries.

In addition to the general dictionaries of the English language, there are many special books that are useful to anyone who does much writing. Among these are books of synonyms. They help you to find just the right word when you are in doubt as to which word to use, and they help you to vary your choice of words so that you do not have to keep using the same words over and over. Three of the best known of these books of synonyms are listed below.

Fernald, James C., *Funk and Wagnalls Standard Handbook of Synonyms, Antonyms, and Prepositions*

This standard book lists in alphabetical order most of the words you would wish to use and gives synonyms and antonyms for them.

*Roget's Thesaurus of the English Language in Dictionary Form*

*Roget's Thesaurus* has been the best known of the synonym books. Now published in an inexpensive paperback edition, it stands beside the dictionary on many student desks.

*Webster's Dictionary of Synonyms*

This book of synonyms and antonyms is especially valuable for its detailed explanations of the distinctions between words of similar meaning. Like the Fernald and Roget books, it is also a handy reference volume for authors in search of a word.

**EXERCISE 5.** Like Exercise 4, this will test your knowledge of the information given in the dictionary. At the teacher's signal, look up the answers to the following questions and write them on your paper. Although speed is desirable, accuracy is more important.

1. Find two synonyms for the word *mercy.*
2. Write the plural of *consensus.*
3. Write the comparative and superlative of *well.*
4. What is the capital of Iceland?
5. What is the population of Cádiz?
6. When did Queen Elizabeth I reign?
7. What was Galileo's full name?
8. What was the real name of George Sand?
9. What is the meaning of the abbreviation *TKO?*
10. Copy the pronunciation of *predilection* which is listed first in your dictionary. Use diacritical marks.
11. What symbol is used in medicine for beginning a prescription?
12. Write the plural of *basis.*
13. What is the meaning of the Latin phrase *carpe diem?*
14. What is the rule for forming the plural of letters, figures, and signs?
15. Why is Trafalgar famous?

**EXERCISE 6.** Look up the origins of the following words and be prepared to write or tell about them in class.

1. assassin
2. sick
3. bedlam
4. pedestal
5. boycott
6. curfew
7. infant
8. juggernaut
9. maudlin
10. sabotage

# Chapter 30

# Vocabulary

## Meaning Through Context
## and Word Analysis

An effective and large vocabulary can be one of your most valuable assets in high school, in college, and in your future vocation or profession. Studies have shown that a large vocabulary goes hand in hand with responsibility and success in the business world. Scholarship and college entrance examinations place great emphasis on vocabulary. Tests for men and women entering the armed forces also have large sections devoted to word knowledge. It is obvious, therefore, that for your immediate and future success you owe it to yourself to build as large a vocabulary as possible.

The main things you should know about words—how to find clues to meaning in context and in the formation of words—are reviewed in this chapter. But before you begin the chapter itself, take the following diagnostic test.

### Diagnostic Test

Number your paper 1–25. After the proper number, write the letter of the word or expression that comes closest to the meaning of the italicized word.

1. to *abrogate* a law: a. violate; b. enact; c. ignore; d. record; e. annul

2. an *altruistic* action: a. unusual; b. spontaneous; c. unselfish; d. brave; e. blameworthy

3. an *astute* lawyer: a. shrewd; b. unethical; c. criminal; d. experienced; e. amateur

4. a *bellicose* measure: a. warlike; b. cowardly; c. infamous; d. sudden; e. alarming

5. the *calumnies* of the political campaign: a. speeches; b. promises; c. candidates; d. agitations; e. false charges

6. the two substances will *coalesce:* a. fuse together; b. neutralize each other; c. stay inert; d. disappear; e. sink

7. reacting with *consternation:* a. extreme pride; b. amazed alarm; c. inactive sluggishness; d. slow hesitation; e. calm decision

8. feeling genuine *contrition:* a. lasting comfort; b. intense anger; c. sudden shock; d. repentance; e. wild humor

9. to *corroborate* the answer: a. question; b. deny; c. confirm; d. repeat; e. broadcast

10. a *didactic* passage: a. sarcastic; b. instructional; c. unclear; d. unnecessary; e. learned

11. living a *dissolute* life: a. exciting; b. very short; c. virtuous; d. religious; e. immoral

12. to *enervate* the patient: a. strengthen; b. cure; c. occupy; d. examine; e. weaken

13. marked by *ennui:* a. enthusiasm; b. strength; c. boredom; d. sickness; e. excitement

14. to *excise* the tissue: a. cut out; b. examine; c. cure; d. label; e. discolor

15. to *expunge* an answer: a. amplify; b. delete; c. accept; d. copy; e. request

16. a *heinous* offense: a. minor; b. infrequent; c. outrageous; d. penal; e. pardonable

17. these plants were *indigenous:* a. harmful; b. native; c. rare; d. colorful; e. hard to classify

18. these *insidious* reports: a. alarming; b. subtly harmful; c. laudatory; d. substantiated; e. subversive

19. to *jeopardize* our forces: a. immobilize; b. endanger; c. increase; d. surrender; e. notify

20. the *onerous* duties: a. neglected; b. daily; c. specialized; d. important; e. burdensome

21. to *plagiarize* the theme: a. copy dishonestly; b. forget; c. record; d. misunderstand; e. begin

22. a *recondite* fact: a. ancient; b. unimportant; c. little known; d. literary; e. magical

23. concerned with *secular* matters: a. nonreligious; b. regional; c. marital; d. trivial; e. financial

24. the *surveillance* of the police: a. watchful observation; b. needless cruelty; c. careless negligence; d. baffled uncertainty; e. thorough investigation

25. this disease is *ubiquitous:* a. very serious; b. almost unknown; c. bacterial; d. easily cured; e. found everywhere

# THE KINDS OF VOCABULARY

Before you study the ways to increase your vocabulary, you should understand what words your vocabulary includes. There are four kinds of vocabulary with which you deal. Two of them—your reading vocabulary and your listening vocabulary—are those which you use for understanding other people. They are called the *comprehension vocabulary.* You may know that such a sentence as "She was a voracious eater" means that she had a huge appetite or that such a sentence as "His ill-prepared and feeble effort was not a speech but rather a travesty of a speech" means that his attempt was an inferior imitation of a speech. Although these words are part of your comprehension vocabulary, they may not be part of your *use vocabulary,* which consists of the other kinds of vocabulary, the words you use in speaking and those you use in writing. One authority has estimated that the high school graduate has a use vocabulary of 15,000 words. You understand many more words than you use in your speaking and writing.

# HOW OUR VOCABULARIES ARE FORMED

No child is born with a vocabulary; children learn words by listening—to parents, older brothers and sisters, friends, teachers. Today television introduces children to the special words of science, politics, music, and art long before they see any of them in print.

Whether or not you are aware of it, all your life you

will be acquiring words through the ear. Hence, one of the best ways to increase your comprehension vocabulary is to be an alert, attentive listener. Frequently the sense of the conversation, if you pay careful attention, will give you some idea of the meaning of words you hear for the first time. Learning new words in this way is called "getting the meaning from the *context*."

In addition to listening, reading is a rich source of new words. Every issue of a daily newspaper, every magazine, and every book you read will have words that are new to you. Sometimes the written context — like the heard context — will help you get some idea of the meaning of a word, but for the exact meaning there is no substitute for the dictionary. (In Chapter 29 you can quickly review the many ways in which a good dictionary can help you enlarge your vocabulary.)

## 30a. Look for context clues to meaning.

You have learned many thousands of words by understanding their meaning from their *context*. The *context* is the words and sentences that surround the unfamiliar word. For example, suppose you read, "The astronomer focused the telescope on the planet Mars," and you do not know the word *focused*. Your understanding of the words *astronomer, telescope,* and *planet* gives you a strong clue to the meaning of *focused:* "brought together rays of light for a clear image." The astronomer adjusted the telescope so that Mars could be seen clearly.

**EXERCISE 1.** Number your paper 1–10. After each number, copy the italicized words from the sentences which follow, and write a short definition of each based on the clues you find in the context. You may check your definitions with the dictionary later, if you wish.

1. Instead of *ameliorating* it, this treatment seemed to make the disease worse.
2. To everybody's surprise, Rosa did not object to the plan; instead, she *acquiesced* at once.

3. There is little good, *arable* land in these hilly areas, and very few colonists try to plow or cultivate much of it.

4. Mr. Anderson was unpopular because he always tried to embarrass students with his sarcastic, *caustic* comments.

5. A feeling of tiredness and a series of aches in the joints and muscles are likely to be *concomitants* of a severe head cold.

6. Obviously the child is trying hard; we should encourage her to continue instead of *disparaging* her unsuccessful efforts.

7. Her mother was very ill, her husband had just lost his position, the children were having their troubles at school, and Mrs. Roberts was naturally nervous and *distraught*.

8. Human beings are essentially *gregarious;* they always like to band together and are usually afraid of solitude.

9. Several state departments of agriculture have cooperated with the federal government in drives to *extirpate* poison ivy and other harmful plants.

10. But even the ridiculously low price of one hundred dollars for the car *elicited* no offers to buy from the crowd.

**EXERCISE 2.** Number your paper 1–10 and copy the corresponding italicized word after each number. After each word, write a short definition based on your understanding of the context.

As for the Japanese, they sought for Chinese civilization at various times, and absorbed and (1) *assimilated* it with skill, yet always managed to give the borrowed product a (2) *distinctive* national individuality, until now and then it would have been difficult to assert that the teacher still remained more advanced than the pupil. Nevertheless, the flow of (3) *diffusion* continued one-way. Whether it was coining money or drinking tea or printing books or a different Buddhist (4) *sect* or a new style of painting landscapes, it was always China that (5) *originated,* Japan that followed. The lag might be one century or two centuries or six, but it was always Japan that was behind. The Japanese did exercise (6) *option* about their acceptance, and simply rejected a good-sized series of Chinese traits. Where they had something of their own, however, as in the native Shinto cult, or where they gave something of Chinese origin a new twist or value, as in fine swordmaking, these originalities of theirs never passed out of Japan back into China. This does not mean that Japanese products and (7) *devisings* were invariably inferior. They could hardly all have been so, and assuredly were not. Essentially it was Chinese (8) *self-sufficience,* quiet (9) *arrogance* about the superiority of their own culture, that prevented important return diffusion. Here, then, it was an attitude which was effective as a block; whereas the long (10) *retardation* of Japan, like that of Britain at the opposite end of the great Eurasiatic land mass, was due primarily to its extreme marginal position.[1]

## Common Clues to Meaning

Although a particular sentence may provide a clue to the meaning of a word in any number of ways, there are three types of clues to meaning that are extremely helpful.

### Supplied Definitions

Often authors will use wording that is familiar and natural to them but that may not be clear to all of their readers. Anticipating this lack of familiarity, they will often add a definition for the sake of clarity. These definitions may be preceded by such expressions as *in other words* or *that is* or simply by a comma which introduces a synonym in apposition.

For example, you may read that on a particular point the foreign policy of another nation is "an enigma, a puzzle." From this you understand that the writer has first used the word *enigma,* then clarified the meaning by adding the more easily understood synonym *puzzle.* Sometimes full definitions are given in complete sentences. A science writer may mention *symbiosis* and then follow with a sentence like "Symbiosis is the more-or-less close and intimate association or union of dissimilar life forms." In the following examples, the definitions or explanations are italicized and the words defined are in bold-faced type.

[1] From *Anthropology* by A. L. Kroeber. Reprinted by permission of Harcourt Brace Jovanovich, Inc. and George G. Harrap & Company Ltd.

He was told to avoid strong **condiments,** or *seasonings,* for his food.

Lorraine studied **ethnology,** that is, *the science dealing with the cultures of various peoples.*

But James's **forte,** or *strong point,* was not playing the piano.

The young divinity student usually takes a course in how to compose a **homily,** or *sermon.*

The candidate delivered a *long, bitter speech* — a regular **tirade** — against her opponent.   [Here the explanation precedes the unfamiliar word.]

## Words Used in Contrast

Often a writer wishes to show the extent of a subject and does so by mentioning the extremes: "This action was praised from Maine to Hawaii, from Florida to Alaska." Sometimes the writer will seek emphasis by using both positive and negative statements: "The room was not warm at all; rather, it was bitter cold." Such balances of extremes and contrasts are clues to meaning. If we read that "From the smallest hamlet to the largest metropolis people came flocking to volunteer," we have a good idea about the meanings of *hamlet* and *metropolis.*

EXAMPLES  There was nothing at all praiseworthy about her action; it was entirely **despicable** from start to finish. [*Despicable* is contrasted with *praiseworthy.* Since it is preceded by the word *entirely,* it probably means something completely the opposite of praiseworthy.]

She did not treat the proposal with her usual delay or hesitation; she accepted it with uncharacteristic **celerity.**  [In this instance the modifiers *usual* and *uncharacteristic* help us to determine the meaning of the contrasted word *celerity* — *swiftness* or *speed* are possibilities.]

Contrasting words are often introduced by *but, not, rather than,* and *however.* Sometimes *or* is used, but this can be confusing, since *or* may introduce a synonym as well as an antonym.

EXAMPLES   We were asked to precede the band, or lead the way.
[*or* introducing a synonym]

Will the students progress or retrogress under the
new program of studies?   [*or* introducing an antonym]

Contrasts often offer a clue to meaning, but, as in the
examples above, they can sometimes be misleading. Always
look for other clues before making your final choice of
meanings.

## Words Similar in Meaning

Very frequently a word is used in a context that shows
quite clearly what that word means. In the sentence "Her
aunt's *benevolence* was well known because of the generosity with which she contributed to charities," it is easy
to decide that *benevolence* means something like "kindly,
generous actions." Again, in the sentence, "They were
naturally *solicitous* about the child's health and were taking every precaution against a return of the disease,"
*solicitous* must mean "showing care and concern." You
will find many sentences like these that will help you add
to your vocabulary if you read them carefully and thoughtfully.

**EXERCISE 3.** Number your paper 1–10, and after each
number, copy the italicized word. Give a brief definition
in your own words, based on the context.

1. She was extremely *ingenuous,* not at all sophisticated.
2. Instead of being an expert, Sharon turned out to be a mere
   *dilettante,* a person who dabbled at music and art in a superficial way.
3. It is sometimes hard for us to imagine how life has changed
   in the past four hundred years; it would be a great *anachronism* to picture Columbus reading a daily paper.
4. In this lawsuit the parties had been acting entirely independently of each other and without knowledge of each
   other's plans; they had not been acting in *collusion.*

5. The long vacation did not strengthen or invigorate her; instead it left her thoroughly *enervated*.

6. The *tortuous* passage through the cave was filled with all kinds of twists and turns.

7. Naturally, Ella, who was an attractive and pleasant girl to begin with, was viewed as a heroine after her exploit, and she received a good deal of *adulation* from her friends.

8. You must play down his weak points instead of *accentuating* them.

9. A law should not be *immutable;* rather, it should be changed when the times and the people demand it.

10. Fifty years ago, the first-year high school student learned elementary Latin, world history, and the *rudiments* of geometry and trigonometry.

**EXERCISE 4.**   The following passage, written by a naturalist, contains a variety of context clues. Study the whole passage and then write your own definitions for the italicized words. Consult your dictionary only after you have written your own definitions.

The cliché often used for the forest is "cathedral-like." The comparison is (1) *inevitable:* the cool, dim light, the utter stillness, the massive grandeur of the trunks of forest giants, often supported by great buttresses and (2) *interspersed* with the straight, clean columns of palms and smaller trees; the Gothic detail of the thick, richly carved, woody (3) *lianas* plastered against trunks or looping down from the canopy above. Awe and wonder come easily in the forest, sometimes (4) *exultation*—sometimes, for a man alone there, fear. Man is out of scale: the forest is too vast, too impersonal, too variegated, too deeply shadowed. Here man needs his fellow man for (5) *reassurance*. Alone, he has lost all significance.

The rain forest is perhaps more truly a silent world than the sea. The wind scarcely (6) *penetrates;* it is not only silent, it is still. All sound then gains a curiously (7) *enhanced* mystery. A sudden crack—what could have made it? An (8) *inexplicable* gurgle. A single, clear peal—that was a bird, probably a trogon. A whistle, impossible to identify. But mostly silence. The silence becomes (9) *infectious;* I remember sometimes trying to blend into this world by moving along a trail without rustling a leaf

with my foot or popping a twig. But more often I purposely
(10) *scuffled,* broke noisily through this forest where I didn't
belong, tried to advertise my presence both to reassure myself
and to warn the creatures of the forest that a stranger was there—
I had no desire to surprise a fer-de-lance.[1]

### 30b. Look up unfamiliar words in the dictionary.

How often should you turn to the dictionary when you
are not sure about a word? Certainly it is not necessary
every time you encounter a strange word; many of them
you will understand from context. If the book you are
reading is your own, you may underline the unfamiliar
words and look them up later. *Do not underline a school
textbook or library book.* Of course, if you have no idea of
the meaning of a word, you should certainly look it up in
the dictionary. Once you have found the meaning you
want, read the whole definition, since most words have a
range of different meanings.

Suppose you read about "a *dilapidated* mansion," but
you don't know what *dilapidated* means. You may have
studied Latin and remember that *lapis, lapidis* means *stone.*
That gives you a small clue, but not a very helpful one. If
there is nothing in the context to explain the word, you
need to turn to the dictionary.

In your dictionary you would discover something like
the following:

di·lap′i·dat′ed (dĭ·lăp′ĭ·dāt′ĕd), *adj.* Reduced to or fallen into
ruin or decay.

A "dilapidated mansion," then, is one that has fallen
into ruin or decay, as if stone after stone had gradually
fallen away.

### 30c. Keep a vocabulary notebook.

Having learned a new word, you should not stop there.
To insure that the word will become a permanent part of

[1] From *The Forest and the Sea* by Marston Bates. Copyright 1960 by
Marston Bates. Reprinted by permission of Random House, Inc.

your vocabulary, write it in your notebook. Follow it with its pronunciation, the sentence in which you first found it, and its definition. You will find that keeping a list of new words will result in noticeable vocabulary growth.

# WORD ANALYSIS

### 30d. Use your knowledge of prefixes, suffixes, and roots.

In general, English words are of two kinds: those that can be analyzed into smaller parts (*untimely, suburban*) and those that cannot (*time, face, feel*). The words of the first kind, which can be divided, are made up of parts called prefixes, roots, and suffixes. Because these parts with broad general meanings remain essentially the same in many different words, knowing something about word analysis can help you to figure out the meaning of an unfamiliar word. However, there are some difficulties that make it unwise to depend entirely on word analysis for clues to meaning. It is not always easy to tell whether a particular group of letters is really the prefix or suffix it appears to be. The *-er* in *painter* is a suffix, but the *-er* in *summer* is not. To be certain, you have to know something about the origin of the word. Moreover, the original force of a combination of word parts may no longer have much to do with the modern meaning of a word. For these and other reasons, absolute dependence on word analysis would lead you to make as many bad guesses as good ones.

There are, however, some good reasons for having a general knowledge of the way English words are formed. Word analysis helps you to understand the peculiarities of English spelling and the connection between the related forms of a particular word. (Knowing about related forms often enables you to learn four or five new words as easily as one.) Also, word analysis gives you useful practice in taking a close look at words. In reading, we pass very quickly over words, hardly noticing more than their general shape. This is all very well for words you know well, but close examination is called for with unfamiliar ones. Most important of all, word analysis offers the key to the origin of English words. Since so many cultures have contributed to the vocabulary of English the study of word origins is a fascinating one. Further, people should know something about the history as well as the use of their words. After all, building a vocabulary is a kind of collecting, differing from the collection of stamps or coins in being less expensive and more useful. No collector worth the name is content to possess a specimen and know nothing about it. Word analysis will tell you a great deal about the words you add to your collection.

## How Words Are Divided

Many words that can be divided have two or more parts: a core called a *root* and one or more parts added to it. The parts that are added are called *affixes*—literally, "something fixed or attached to something else." An affix added before the root is called a *prefix;* one added after the root is called a *suffix.* A word may have one or more affixes of either kind, or several of both kinds. Only compound words like *baseball* and *post office* have more than one root. A root with no affixes at all is incapable of being divided. A word consisting of a root only is one like *stone* or *true,* to which word analysis does not apply.

The following table shows some typical combinations of affixes (prefixes and suffixes) and roots.

| PREFIX[ES] | ROOT | SUFFIX[ES] | EXAMPLE |
|---|---|---|---|
| dis– | put– | –able | disputable |
| post– | war | | postwar |
| | sole | –ly | solely |
| | soft | –en, –ing | softening |
| il– | leg– | –ible | illegible |
| un– | self | –ish, –ly | unselfishly |
| under– | hand | –ed | underhanded |
| | bliss | –ful | blissful |

Roots are often independent words, as in the case of *war, self,* and *hand* in the table above. They are then called *free forms*. But some roots, like *–clude* in *conclude,* are not words by themselves. Such roots are called *bound forms*. Most affixes are bound forms.

## Prefixes

Prefixes have broad general meanings like *not, under,* and *against,* and a particular one of them may appear in hundreds of different words. Often their meanings are hard to interpret, since many prefixes have more than one meaning. In general, a knowledge of prefixes will help you to know when to double consonants in such words as *misspell, overrun,* and *interrupt.* Many of the prefixes in the following list have several different spellings in order to fit with various roots.

| PREFIX | MEANING | EXAMPLES |
|---|---|---|
| *Old English* | | |
| a– | in, on, of, up, to | abed, afoot |
| for– | away, off, from | forget, forswear |
| fore– | before, previous | foretell, forefathers |
| mis– | bad, poorly, not | misspell, misfire |
| un– | not, opposing | unfold, untrue |
| *Latin* | | |
| ab– | from, away, off | abdicate, abjure |
| ante– | before, previous | antecedent, antedate |
| bi– | two, twice | bisect, biennial |
| circum– | around | circumspect, circumference |
| com– | with, together, very | commotion, complicate |
| contra– | against, opposing | contradict, contravene |
| dis– | away, off, down, not | dissent, disappear |
| ex– | out | extract |
| in– | not, opposing | incapable, ineligible |
| inter– | among, between | intercede, interrupt |
| post– | after, following | postpone, postscript |
| pre– | before | prevent, preclude |
| re– | back, backward, again | revoke, recur |
| retro– | back, backward | retrospect, retrograde |
| sub– | under, beneath | subjugate, substitute |
| trans– | across, beyond, over | transact, transport |

*Greek*

| | | |
|---|---|---|
| a– | without, lacking | atheist, agnostic |
| anti– | against, opposing | antipathy, antitoxin |
| apo– | from, away | apology, apostate |
| cata– | down, away, thoroughly | catastrophe, cataclysm |
| dia– | through, across, apart | diameter, diagnose |
| hyper– | excessive, over | hypercritical, hypertension |
| hypo– | under, beneath | hypodermic, hypothesis |
| pro– | before | prognosis, program |
| sym– | with, together | sympathy, symphony |

**EXERCISE 5.**  Copy the following words, using a slant line (/) to separate the prefix from the rest of the word. Then give the meaning of the English word. Be ready to explain the connection between the meaning of the prefix and the present meaning of the word.

EXAMPLE   1. antithesis
          1. *anti / thesis (direct contrast of ideas)*

1. abnegation
2. circumvent
3. hyperactive
4. intermittent
5. sublimate
6. submit
7. translation
8. unnatural
9. misfortune
10. external

**EXERCISE 6.**  Find and write on your paper two words that contain each of the following prefixes: *ab–, com–, dis–, ex–, in–, inter–, pre–, re–.* Use words other than those given as examples in the preceding lists.

## Suffixes

Suffixes, you will recall, are affixes added after the root, or at the end of a word. There are two main kinds of suffixes: those that provide a grammatical signal of some kind but do not greatly alter the basic meaning of the word and those that, by being added, create new words. The endings *–s, –ed,* and *–ing* are suffixes of the first kind; by adding them to *work* (*works, worked, working*) we indicate something about number and tense, but we do not change the essential meaning of the word. This kind of suffix is a *grammatical* suffix.

Grammatical suffixes are important in grammar, but in vocabulary we are more concerned with the second kind of suffixes—those that make new words. By adding *–ful* to *thank,* we get a different word: *thankful.* Adding *–hood* to *girl* gives us *girlhood,* again a different word. Suffixes that change meaning in this way are called *derivational* suffixes. Notice in the following examples that the addition of a derivational suffix often gives a new part of speech as well as a new meaning.

| ROOT | SUFFIX | RESULT |
|------|--------|--------|
| friend (n.) | –ly | friendly (adj.) |
| critic (n.) | –ize | criticize (v.) |
| prefer (v.) | –ence | preference (n.) |
| child (n.) | –hood | childhood (n.) |

Since derivational suffixes so often determine the part of speech of English words, we can classify them according to the parts of speech.

| NOUN SUFFIXES | MEANING | EXAMPLES |
|---------------|---------|----------|
| *Old English* | | |
| –dom | state, rank, condition | serfdom, wisdom |
| –er | doer, maker | hunter, dancer |
| –hood | state, condition | manhood, statehood |
| –ness | quality, state | greatness, tallness |
| –th | act, state, quality | warmth, width |
| *Foreign (Latin, French, Greek)* | | |
| –age | process, state, rank | passage, bondage |
| –ance | act, condition, fact | acceptance, vigilance |
| –ard | one that does (esp. excessively) | drunkard, wizard |
| –ate | rank, office | delegate, primate |
| –ation | action, state, result | occupation, starvation |
| –cy | state, condition | accuracy, captaincy |
| –er | doer, dealer in, result | baker, diner, rejoinder |
| –ess | feminine | waitress, lioness |
| –ion | action, result, state | union, fusion |

| -ism | act, manner, doctrine | barbarism, socialism |
| -ist | doer, believer | monopolist, socialist |
| -ition | action, state, result | sedition, expedition |
| -ity | state, quality, condition | acidity, civility |
| -ment | means, result, action | refreshment, disappointment |
| -or | doer, office, action | juror, elevator, honor |
| -tude | quality, state, result | magnitude, fortitude |
| -ty | quality, state | enmity, activity |

| ADJECTIVE SUFFIXES | MEANING | EXAMPLES |
| --- | --- | --- |

*Old English*

| -en | made of, like | wooden, ashen |
| -ful | full of, marked by | thankful, zestful |
| -ish | suggesting, like | churlish, childish |
| -less | lacking, without | hopeless, countless |
| -like | like, similar | childlike, dreamlike |
| -ly | like, of the nature of | friendly, queenly |
| -some | apt to, showing | tiresome, lonesome |
| -ward | in the direction of | backward, homeward |

*Foreign*

| -able | able, likely | capable, tolerable |
| -ate | having, showing | separate, desolate |
| -esque | in the style of, like | picturesque, grotesque |
| -fic | making, causing | terrific, beatific |
| -ible | able, likely, fit | edible, possible, divisible |
| -ous | marked by, given to | religious, riotous |

| VERB SUFFIXES | MEANING | EXAMPLES |
| --- | --- | --- |

*Old English*

| -en | cause to be, become | deepen, strengthen |

*Foreign*

| -ate | become, form, treat | animate, sublimate |
| -esce | become, grow, continue | convalesce, acquiesce |
| -fy | make, cause, cause to have | glorify, fortify |
| -ish | do, make, perform | punish, finish |
| -ize | make, cause to be, treat with | sterilize, motorize, criticize |

**EXERCISE 7.** Using slant lines (/), separate the suffix from the rest of the words below. Then write a brief definition of the word.

EXAMPLE  1. beastly
1. *beast/ly* (*like a beast*)

1. identify
2. certitude
3. modernize
4. apelike
5. jealously

6. eulogize
7. eatable
8. capricious
9. peerage
10. festivity

## Roots

A root is the core of a word—the part to which prefixes and suffixes are added. To find the root, you usually have only to remove any affix there may be. For example, removal of the affixes *a–* and *–ous* from *amorphous* leaves us with *–morph–,* a root meaning "form or shape." The root *–clysm–,* meaning "falling," remains after we remove the prefix *cata–,* meaning "down," from *cataclysm.*

Roots have more specific and definite meanings than either prefixes or suffixes, and a particular root appears in fewer different words. The following list contains some of the common roots in English.

| ROOT | MEANING | EXAMPLES |
|---|---|---|
| *Latin* | | |
| –ag–, –act– | do, drive, impel | agent, reaction |
| –am–, –amic– | friend, love | amatory, amicable |
| –aqu– | water | aquatic, aqueduct, aquarium |
| –aud–, –audit– | hear | audible, auditorium |
| –ben–, –bene– | well, good | benefit, benediction |
| –capit– | head | capital, decapitate |
| –carn– | flesh | carnal, carnivorous |
| –cent– | hundred | century, percent |
| –clud–, –clus– | close, shut | conclude, seclusion |
| –cogn– | know, be acquainted | recognize, cognizant |
| –cred– | belief, trust | incredible, credulity |
| –crypt– | hidden, secret | crypt, cryptic |

| –duc–, –duct– | lead | educate, conductor |
| –fer– | bear, yield | transfer, fertile |
| –fid– | belief, faith | fidelity, perfidious |
| –fin– | end, limit | final, indefinite |
| –frag–, –fract– | break | fragment, fraction, fragile |
| –gen– | birth, kind, origin | generate, congenital |
| –junct– | join | junction, disjunctive |
| –jud– | judge | prejudice, adjudicate |
| –jug– | join, yoke | conjugal, conjugate |
| –loc– | place | locus, locale |
| –magn– | large | magnitude, magnify |
| –man–, –manu– | hand | manicure, manual |
| –mor–, –mort– | die, death | mortuary, immortal |
| –omni– | all | omnipotent, omnivorous |
| –pater–, –patr– | father | paternal, patrimony, patriarchy |
| –port– | carry, bear | transport, importation |
| –prim– | first, early | primitive, primordial |
| –punct– | point | punctuation, punctilious |
| –sci– | know, knowledge | omniscient, prescience |
| –scrib–, –script– | write | inscribe, proscribe, manuscript |
| –spec–, –spic–, –spect– | look, see | suspicious, circumspect |
| –spir– | breath, breathe | expire, inspiration, respiration |
| –tract– | draw, pull | traction, extractor, tractable |
| –uni– | one | unity, uniform |
| –vid–, –vis– | see | evident, vision |
| –vit– | life | vitality, vitamin |

*Greek*

| –anthrop– | man | anthropology, misanthropic |
| –arch– | ancient, chief | archaeology, monarch |
| –astr–, –aster– | star | astronomy, asterisk |
| –auto– | self | autonomy, automobile, autocracy |
| –biblio– | book | bibliography, bibliophile |
| –bio– | life | biology, autobiography |

| ROOT | MEANING | EXAMPLES |
|------|---------|----------|
| –chrom– | color | chromatic, chromosome |
| –chron– | time | synchronize, anachronism, chronometer |
| –dem–, –demo– | people | democracy, epidemic |
| –gen– | kind, race | eugenics, genesis |
| –geo– | earth | geography, geology |
| –gram– | write, writing | grammar, telegram |
| –graph– | write, writing | orthography, geography |
| –hydr– | water | hydrogen, dehydrate |
| –log– | word, study | epilogue, theology, logic |
| –micr– | small | microbe, microscope |
| –mon– | one, single | monogamy, monologue |
| –neo– | new | neologism, neolithic |
| –pan– | all, entire | panorama, pandemonium |
| –phil– | like, love | philanthropic, philosophy |
| –poly– | many | polygon, polygamy |
| –soph– | wise, wisdom | philosophy, sophomore |
| –zo– | animal | zoology, protozoa |

**EXERCISE 8.** With the help of your dictionary, find two English words—other than those given above—containing each of the following roots.

1. –am–
2. –aud–
3. –bene–
4. –cent–
5. –cred–
6. –fin–
7. –port–
8. –sci–
9. –spect–
10. –vid–

**EXERCISE 9.** Follow the instructions for Exercise 8.

1. –arch–
2. –auto–
3. –bio–
4. –chron–
5. –demo–
6. –geo–
7. –gram–
8. –mon–
9. –phil–
10. –poly–

## Word List

The words in the list below may be the basis of your vo-

cabulary study this year. In many of them you will recognize the Old English, Latin, and Greek word parts you
have just studied. Make it a habit to learn unfamiliar words
from this list regularly; ten each week is a practical number.

abeyance
abnegation
abrogate
accentuate
acquiesce
acquisitive
adulation
affinity
aggrandize
allegory

allusion
altercation
altruistic
ameliorate
anachronism
anathema
animosity
anomaly
antithesis
aphorism

approbation
aquiline
arable
archipelago
arduous
argosy
ascetic
atrophy
auspicious
automation

avow
banal
bane

beleaguer
bellicose
blazon
bode
bravado
broach
bullion

bumptious
bureaucracy
cadaverous
calumny
castigate
caustic
celerity
chauvinistic
choleric
circumscribe

circumvent
clandestine
climactic
coalesce
coalition
cogitation
collateral
colloquy
collusion
commensurate

commiseration
complement
comprehensive
conclave
concomitant
condiment

confederation
configuration
congenital
congruent

connotation
consensus
consonant
consternation
constituent
consummate
contemptuous
contrition
convivial
convoke

corollary
correlate
corroborate
credence
credulous
crystallize
culpable
cumbersome
debacle
debility

defray
degenerate
delineate
demeanor
denote
deprecate
depreciate
dereliction
desecrate

desist

despicable
deterrent
detrimental
devastation
dictum
didactic
diffident
digress
dilettante
disconsolate

discrepancy
disparage
disparate
dissemble
dissimulation
dissolute
distend
distraught
duplicity
duress

efficacious
effusion
egregious
elation
elicit
emanate
emendation
emissary
enervate
enigma

ennui
enthrall
entity
epicurean
epilogue
epithet
equivocal

erroneous
erudite
esoteric

espionage
ethnology
evangelist
evasive
evoke
evolve
excerpt
excise
excoriate
exhaustive

exodus
exonerate
expatriate
expletive
expound
expunge
extant
extenuate
extirpate
extraneous

exude
faction
factious
fallible
fatuous
felicitous
festoon
fetid
filch
finesse

fiord
flay
foible
foment
foreshadow

forte
fortuitous
fresco
fulminate
fulsome

gainsay
gambol
germane
gibe
goad
gratuitous
haphazard
hardihood
herculean
hiatus

homily
hyperbole
hypochondriac
iconoclast
idiosyncrasy
ignominy
immemorial
immutable
imperious
implacable

impregnable
impotent
impromptu
impunity
incalculable
incendiary
inception
inchoate
incipient
incredulous

indigenous
inexorable
inexplicable

inflexible
influx
ingratiate
inhibition
innocuous
inordinate
insatiable

insidious
insoluble
intangible
interminable
interpose
intermittent
intimidate
inundate
inure
invariably

inveigle
irascible
iridescent
irreducible
irrevocable
jeopardize
laconic
legerdemain
litigation
longevity

lucrative
lugubrious

machination
malevolent
mellifluous
mercurial
mesmerism
missal
moot
munificent

nadir
nebulous
neolithic
nostalgic
nostrum
obnoxious
obsequious
obtrude
omnivorous
onerous

oracular
oscillate
ostensible
palliate
panacea
patrimony
penury
perfunctory
pernicious
philistine

precipitate

predecessor
prerogative
profligate
progeny
propagate
propensity
protagonist
purport
rapacity

rationalize
recondite
rectitude
relegate
reprisal
reticent
rudiment
sanctimonious
sartorial
satyr

scrutinize
secular
sequester
shibboleth
sluice
solicitous
specious
spurious
stigmatize
stoic

# Chapter 31

# Spelling

## Improving Your Spelling

Spelling correctly is a bugaboo to many students; it is so difficult for them that they have adopted the defeatist's attitude of "Good spellers are born, not made." Some good spellers may be born that way, but it is a fact that poor spellers, even very poor spellers, can improve their skill through understanding the nature of words, through study, and through developing their memory. Of greater importance than this, however, a student must want to learn to spell correctly. The will to improve is absolutely necessary.

Learning to spell with accuracy is no easy task. English spelling is neither logical nor consistent. Almost every spelling rule seems to have its exceptions.

You should work on the improvement of your spelling habits through using a combination of rules and good practices. In time your stock of memorized spellings will grow large enough to meet all the ordinary needs of everyday writing, and you will be able to handle the spelling of new or unfamiliar words with confidence.

One of the most important spelling rules is *Care enough to be careful.* Care in writing and in proofreading what you have written will eliminate errors in the spelling of simple words like *too, their, its,* which account for so many of every teacher's corrections on compositions.

The discussions, rules, and exercises in this chapter suggest a number of things you can do to improve your spelling.

# GOOD SPELLING HABITS

If the following good spelling habits are developed, improvement is bound to result.

(1) Keep a list of your spelling errors.
(2) Use the dictionary as a spelling aid.
(3) Learn to spell by syllables.
(4) Learn a few helpful spelling rules.
(5) Learn to distinguish between words that are often confused.
(6) Learn lists of commonly misspelled words.

1. *Keep a list of your spelling errors.* Each of us has special spelling problems. Set aside a part of your notebook for lists of words that you repeatedly misspell and of new words that seem difficult to you. If possible, keep these lists in either one of the following two orders: (1) a rough alphabetical order, using a separate loose-leaf page for each letter so that you can easily find specific words; or (2) according to general types of spelling errors: for instance, a page each for the *ie* and *ei* rule, adding prefixes and suffixes, plurals, hyphens, troublesome silent letters, homonyms, your own special spelling demons, etc. Method two is particularly helpful because it constantly reinforces spelling rules and practices. Whenever you have time, restudy your lists as part of a campaign to overcome your personal spelling problems.

2. *Use the dictionary as a spelling aid.* The only sure way to find out how to spell a word is to look it up.

Whenever you have any doubt whatever about the spelling of a word, consult the dictionary for the spelling that seems most likely to you. If you do not find the word at once, try other spellings. Check the definition to be certain that you have located the right word rather than a homonym or a similar-sounding word. When more than one spelling is given, find and use the preferred form. To determine the preferred spelling of a word, see page 510.

3. *Learn to spell by syllables.* Short words, with the exception of a comparatively brief list of so-called spelling demons, are easier to spell correctly than long ones. Some

long words, such as *notwithstanding,* break down into short, easily spelled words; others, like *satisfactorily,* break down into combinations of short syllables. In both cases, the job of spelling the entire word is much simplified.

Pronouncing words correctly will also help with spelling. If you say *liberry* and *athalete* and *artic* instead of lǐ'brěr'ǐ and ăth'lēt and ärk'tǐk, the chances are that you will also misspell these words. Look up pronunciations in the dictionary. Learn pronunciation symbols.

**EXERCISE 1.** Write the syllables of each of the following words, using hyphens to separate the syllables from one another. Do this exercise without looking up the words in the dictionary. Your divisions of these words may or may not correspond exactly with the dictionary syllabication; what is important is that (1) each syllable is a single sound; (2) separately, each has the same pronunciation that it has in the entire word; and (3) all letters are included and no letters are added.

1. adversary
2. alias
3. barbarous
4. chimney
5. costume
6. deficit
7. genuine
8. gondola
9. incidentally
10. inventory

**EXERCISE 2.** Follow the directions for Exercise 1.

1. integral
2. lamentable
3. maintenance
4. plebiscite
5. probably
6. temperature
7. chandelier
8. vehemently
9. preferable
10. incongruous

# SPELLING RULES

**4. *Learn a few helpful spelling rules.*** The first few rules given below are simple, useful, and important. Like most spelling rules, they have their exceptions; but the exceptions are not difficult and are easily mastered. Once you have learned these rules, they should keep you from making certain common spelling errors; in addition, the rules will assist you in determining the spelling of unfamiliar words. By spending some time and effort now, you will save time and gain accuracy later on.

## *ie* and *ei*

### 31a. Write *ie* when the sound is long *e*, except after *c*.

EXAMPLES   believe, field, niece     ceiling, receive, conceit
EXCEPTIONS   seize, either, neither, weird

### Write *ei* when the sound is not long *e*, especially when the sound is long *a*.

EXAMPLES   freight, weight, reign     forfeit, height
EXCEPTIONS   friend, mischief, conscience

**EXERCISE 3.** The blanks in the following words stand for the letters *ei* or *ie*. Write out the words, filling in the blanks with the correct letters. Be prepared to explain how Rule 31a applies to each word.

| | | |
|---|---|---|
| 1. dec . . . ve | 9. gr . . . vous | 17. perc . . . ve |
| 2. ch . . . ftain | 10. r . . . gn | 18. sl . . . gh |
| 3. v . . . l | 11. pr . . . st | 19. bes . . . ge |
| 4. h . . . r | 12. bel . . . f | 20. shr . . . k |
| 5. rec . . . pt | 13. p . . . rce | 21. var . . . d |
| 6. counterf . . . t | 14. w . . . ght | 22. . . . ght |
| 7. gr . . . f | 15. l . . . sure | 23. cash . . . r |
| 8. th . . . r | 16. bel . . . ve | 24. y . . . ld |

## *–cede, –ceed,* and *–sede*

### 31b. Only one English word ends in *–sede—supersede;* only three words end in *–ceed—exceed, proceed, succeed;* all other words of similar sound end in *–cede.*

EXAMPLES   precede, recede, secede, accede, concede

## Adding Prefixes

A *prefix* is one or more letters or syllables added to the beginning of a word to change its meaning.

**31c. When a prefix is added to a word, the spelling of the word itself remains the same.**

EXAMPLES   dis + satisfy = dissatisfy
mis + spell = misspell
in + numerable = innumerable
il + legible = illegible
im + mature = immature
re + commend = recommend

## Adding Suffixes

A *suffix* is one or more letters or syllables added to the end of a word to change its meaning.

**31d. When the suffixes *–ness* and *–ly* are added to a word, the spelling of the word itself is not changed.**

EXAMPLES   plain + ness = plainness
casual + ly = casually

EXCEPTIONS   Words ending in *y* usually change the *y* to *i* before *–ness* and *–ly:* empty — emptiness; heavy — heaviness; busy — busily; ordinary — ordinarily. One-syllable adjectives ending in *y*, however, generally follow Rule 31d: dry — dryness; shy — shyly.

**EXERCISE 4.** Spell out each of the words described below.

1. mis + inform
2. in + numerable
3. un + open
4. habitual + ly
5. dis + agree
6. il + legal
7. final + ly
8. happy + ness
9. stubborn + ness
10. crafty + ly
11. re + commend
12. real + ly
13. in + animate
14. merry + ly
15. dis + appoint
16. im + movable
17. dis + appear
18. hearty + ly
19. over + anxious
20. dis + similar

## 31e. Drop the final *e* before a suffix beginning with a vowel.

EXAMPLES    care + ing = caring          dose + age = dosage
love + able = lovable       bride + al = bridal

EXCEPTIONS    (1) To prevent a change in pronunciation, words ending in a soft *c* or *g* preceding a final *e* generally retain the *e* before a suffix beginning with *a* or *o* in order to retain the soft sound: noticeable, peaceable, courageous. (2) Words ending in *ie* change this combination to *y* before –*ing:* lie—lying.

## 31f. Keep the final *e* before a suffix beginning with a consonant.

EXAMPLES    love + ly = lovely               hope + ful = hopeful
place + ment = placement      care + less = careless

EXCEPTIONS    truly, argument, acknowledgment, judgment

## 31g. With words ending in *y* preceded by a consonant, change the *y* to *i* before any suffix not beginning with *i*.

EXAMPLES    accompany + ment = accompaniment

plenty + ful = plentiful

satisfy + es = satisfies

BUT    intensify + ing = intensifying

modify + ing = modifying

**EXERCISE 5.**    Spell out each of the words indicated below. Be ready to state the rule for each word.

1. merry + ment
2. dilatory + ness
3. beauty + fy
4. modify + cation
5. sure + ly

6. study + ing
7. hurry + ing
8. occupy + ed
9. ally + es
10. pity + ful

## 31h. Double the final consonant before a suffix that begins with a vowel If both of the following conditions exist: (1) the word has only one syllable or is accented on the last syllable; (2) the word ends in a single consonant preceded by a single vowel.

EXAMPLES    swim + ing = swimming   [one-syllable word]

confer + ed = conferred   [accent on last syllable; single consonant and single vowel]

benefit + ed = benefited   [accent not on last syllable]

confer + ence = con'ference   [accent shifted; consonant not doubled]

**EXERCISE 6.**   Spell out each of the words indicated below. Be ready to state the rule for each word.

1. plan + ed
2. defer + ence
3. die + ing
4. achieve + ment
5. trod + en
6. shape + less
7. propel + er
8. seize + ure
9. definite + ly
10. due + ly
11. desire + able
12. rob + ery
13. sense + ible
14. write + ing
15. plane + ing
16. nine + ty
17. profit + able
18. shape + ing
19. lose + ing
20. argue + ment
21. control + ing
22. prepare + ing
23. fame + ous
24. create + or

# THE PLURAL OF NOUNS

**31i. Observe the rules for the spelling of nouns.**

**(1) The regular way to form the plural of a noun is to add an *s*.**

EXAMPLES   dog, dogs      book, books      horse, horses

**(2) The plural of some nouns is formed by adding *es*.**

Add *es* to form the plural of nouns ending in *s, sh, ch, z,* and *x*. The *e* is necessary to make the plural forms pronounceable.

EXAMPLES    dress, dresses                dish, dishes
            sandwich, sandwiches         fox, foxes
            bus, buses                   waltz, waltzes

**(3) The plural of nouns ending in *y preceded by a consonant* is formed by changing the *y* to *i* and adding *es*.**

EXAMPLES    country, countries     fly, flies
                forgery, forgeries     theory, theories
                comedy, comedies     salary, salaries

**(4) The plural of nouns ending in *y preceded by a vowel* is formed by adding an *s*.**

EXAMPLES    boy, boys          journey, journeys
                monkey, monkeys    toy, toys
                tray, trays         buoy, buoys

**(5) The plural of most nouns ending in *f* or *fe* is formed by adding *s*. The plural of some nouns ending in *f* or *fe* is formed by changing the *f* to *v* and adding *s* or *es*.**

EXAMPLES    Add *s:*   gulf, gulfs     safe, safes
                         roof, roofs    kerchief, kerchiefs

                Change *f* to *v* and add *s* or *es:*
                         leaf, leaves    wife, wives
                         shelf, shelves   knife, knives

**(6) The plural of some nouns ending in *o preceded by a vowel* is formed by adding *s;* the plural of most nouns ending in *o preceded by a consonant* is formed by adding *es*.**

EXAMPLES    *o* following a vowel:
                studio, studios    radio, radios

                *o* following a consonant:
                potato, potatoes   hero, heroes

EXCEPTIONS    Some nouns ending in *o* preceded by a consonant form the plural in the regular way, by adding *s*. Most nouns ending in *o* and referring to music belong in this class.

EXAMPLES    soprano, sopranos    solo, solos
                piano, pianos       concerto, concertos
                dynamo, dynamos   silo, silos

**(7) The plural of a few nouns is formed in irregular ways.**

EXAMPLES    child, child**ren**    tooth, teeth    goose, geese
                woman, women    mouse, mice    ox, oxen

**(8) The plural of compound nouns written as one word is formed by adding *s* or *es*.**

EXAMPLES    spoonful, spoonfuls      cupful, cupfuls
                leftover, leftovers      strongbox, strongboxes

**(9) The plural of compound nouns consisting of a noun plus a modifier is formed by making the modified word plural.**

To determine the word that is modified in a compound word, make each of the parts plural. The modified word is the one that tells what the entire compound is or does. Thus the plural of *notary public* is *notaries public* (they are *notaries,* not *publics*); the plural of *mother-in-law* is *mothers-in-law* (they are *mothers,* not *laws*); etc.

EXAMPLES    runner-up, runners-up
                editor in chief, editors in chief
                lieutenant governor, lieutenant governors
                poet laureate, poets laureate

**(10) The plural of a few compound nouns is formed in irregular ways.**

EXAMPLES    drive-in, drive-ins      six-year-old, six-year-olds
                stand-by, stand-bys      tie-up, tie-ups

**(11) Some nouns are the same in the singular and the plural.**

EXAMPLES    sheep, deer, trout, salmon, Japanese, fowl

**(12) The plural of some foreign words is formed as in the original language.**

EXAMPLES    alumnus, alumni [masculine]
                alumna, alumnae [feminine]
                analysis, analyses
                phenomenon, phenomena

**(13) The plural of other foreign words may be formed either as in the foreign language or by adding *s* or *es*.**

EXAMPLES    index, indices *or* indexes

appendix, appendices *or* appendixes

► **NOTE** In certain words the English plural is the preferred one, for example, *formulas,* not *formulae.* **Whenever** you are in doubt about which plural to use, turn to your dictionary.

**(14) The plural of numbers, letters, signs, and words considered as words is formed by adding an apostrophe and an** *s.*

EXAMPLES    two *s*'s        two *4*'s
              *and*'s       *that*'s
              +'s          0's
              *so*'s       1960's

**EXERCISE 7.** Write the plural form of each of the following words. Be prepared to explain your spelling on the basis of Rule 31i (1–14).

| | |
|---|---|
| 1. gulf | 13. taboo |
| 2. penny | 14. right of way |
| 3. father-in-law | 15. try |
| 4. valley | 16. corps |
| 5. county | 17. shelf |
| 6. who | 18. echo |
| 7. solo | 19. elk |
| 8. life | 20. ox |
| 9. scissors | 21. politics |
| 10. larva | 22. niece |
| 11. perch | 23. push-up |
| 12. 1900 | 24. turkey |

**EXERCISE 8.** This exercise reviews all the spelling rules covered up to this point. By referring to the rules on the preceding pages, explain the spelling of each of the following:

| | |
|---|---|
| 1. proceed | 5. rodeos |
| 2. perseverance (final *e* dropped) | 6. senators-elect |
| 3. lovely | 7. trading (final *e* dropped) |
| 4. fierce | 8. parentheses |
| | 9. teaspoonfuls |

| | |
|---|---|
| 10. biggest | 18. package |
| 11. two *c*'s | 19. iciness |
| 12. wheels | 20. obligation (final *e* dropped) |
| 13. illegible | 21. conceive |
| 14. happiness | 22. immature |
| 15. liberally | 23. changeable |
| 16. handkerchief | 24. secede |
| 17. wharves | 25. freight |

## WORDS OFTEN CONFUSED

**5. *Learn to distinguish between words that are often confused.*** Some present spelling problems because they sound alike but have different meanings and, usually, different spellings. Like other students, you have probably run into difficulty with such pairs of words as *capital-capitol* and *stationary-stationery.* Most of the paired words in the following lists are frequently confused even though they are not pronounced exactly alike, for example, *desert-dessert.*

In the following lists, each word is defined and used in a sentence; for some words special problems of usage or pronunciation are indicated. Study these definitions and examples carefully; do the exercises to test your understanding of the words and to fix their meanings and spellings in your mind.

Some word pairs present problems that are primarily those of usage rather than meaning; these words are discussed in the "Glossary of Usage" (pages 174–91).

| | |
|---|---|
| **already** | *previously*<br>We have *already* studied that chapter. |
| **all ready** | *all prepared* or *in readiness*<br>Are you *all ready* for the exam? |
| | |
| **altar** | *a table or stand at which religious rites are performed*<br>This is the *altar* used in the Communion service. |
| **alter** | *to change*<br>Do not *alter* your plans on my account. |

**altogether**   *entirely*
The President is *altogether* opposed to the bill.

**all together**   *everyone in one group or place*
My family will be *all together* at Thanksgiving.

---

**ascent**   *a rise; a climb*
The *ascent* of the balloon was followed by radar.

**assent**   *consent*
Will they *assent* to our proposal?
Our last proposal won their *assent*.

---

**born**   *given life*
Ynes Mexia was *born* in Washington, D. C.

**borne**   *carried; endured*
She has *borne* her troubles better than we thought
    she would.

---

**brake**   *a device for stopping or slowing down*
An automobile *brake* will overheat if used too
    often.

**break**   *to shatter or come apart*
Borrow my mirror, but don't *break* it.

---

**capital**   *a city which is the seat of government of a
    country or state; also, money used to carry
    on a business*
Washington is the *capital* of the United States.
The company has a *capital* of $100,000.

**capitol**   *building in which a legislature meets* (often
    cap.)
Our Senate and House of Representatives meet in
    the *Capitol* in Washington.

---

**clothes**   *garments; wearing apparel*
I'd like to buy some summer *clothes*.

**cloths**   *pieces of cloth; fabrics*
Use these *cloths* to clean the car.

---

**EXERCISE 9.** Number your paper 1–20. After each number, write the correct one of the two words in parentheses in the corresponding sentence.

1. Mary has joined the (Altar, Alter) Society of her church.
2. The baby was (born, borne) on her mother's back.
3. The course was (all together, altogether) changed.
4. The state plans to (altar, alter) the route of the new highway.
5. Are you (all ready, already) for the big game?
6. Their (ascent, assent) was given on the first vote.
7. The largest city in the state is often its (capital, capitol).
8. After graduation, we will probably never be (all together, altogether) again as a class.
9. They had (all ready, already) left when we arrived.
10. Do you know the amount of their (capital, capitol) investment?
11. Did you, too, (ascent, assent) to that miserable practical joke?
12. The automatic (brake, break) failed.
13. The anxieties (born, borne) by the flood victims were unbelievable.
14. My mother keeps all of her torn sheets for cleaning (clothes, cloths).
15. The trees are (all ready, already) bare.
16. Did you buy all of those new (clothes, cloths) for your trousseau?
17. We watched the (ascent, assent) of the mountain climbers through a small telescope.
18. After it burned to the ground, the (capital, capitol) was rebuilt as a modern skyscraper.
19. My leaving at this time is (all together, altogether) out of the question.
20. Do you think that it is possible for someone's heart to (brake, break)?

---

**coarse**     *rough; crude; not fine*
His *coarse* language and manners kept him from getting the job.
The driveway was covered with *coarse* sand.

**course**        *path of action; passage* or *way; study* or *group of studies; part of a meal*
We approve of the *course* you have taken.
Jerry's parents go to the golf *course* every Saturday.
The *course* in American history lasts a full year.
My favorite main *course* is roast chicken.

**complement**   *something that completes or makes whole*
A good shortstop is needed to *complement* the team. [to make the team complete]
The *complement* of 30° is 60°. [the angle needed to make a complete 90° right angle]

**compliment**   *praise*
Nancy's performance deserved the *compliments* that it received.
I want to *compliment* you on your costume.

**council,**     *a group assembled for conferences or legislation; each member is a* council
**councilor**
The Student *Council* meets this afternoon.
The queen's *councilors* could not agree.

**counsel,**     *advice* or *to advise; a giver of advice is a* coun-
**counselor**    *selor*
Only a wise *counselor* can give good *counsel*.

**des'ert**      *a dry or barren land*
Irrigation has brought new life to the *desert*.

**desert'**      *to leave or abandon*
A good soldier never *deserts* his post.

**dessert'**     *the last course of a meal*
My favorite *dessert* is pie à la mode.

**formally**     *in a strict or dignified manner; according to strict rules*
The mayor will *formally* open the new recreation center on Wednesday.

**formerly**     *previously; in the past*
Mrs. Dong was *formerly* head of the history department at Lakeville High School.

**ingenious**  *clever; resourceful; skillful*
      Carla has an *ingenious* plan to earn some money
       this summer.

**ingenuous**  *innocent; trusting; frank*
      Ian is as *ingenuous* as a ten-year-old child.

---

**its**  [possessive form of *it*]
      Our city must increase *its* water supply.

**it's**  [contraction of *it is*]
      *It's* almost time for the bell.

---

**later**  *more late; at a subsequent time*
      It's true that I wasn't on time, but you were *later*.
      I'll see you *later*.

**latter**  *the second of two*
      Dr. Edwards can see you in the morning or the
       afternoon, but the *latter* is more convenient for
       her.

---

**lead**  [present tense] *to go first; guide*
      We want you to *lead* us.

**led**  [past tense of *lead*]
      Elaine *led* the way and we followed.

**lead**  [lĕd] *a heavy metal;* also, *graphite in a pencil.*
      Nuclear reactors are often shielded with *lead*.

---

**EXERCISE 10.** Number your paper 1–20. After each number, write the correct one of the two words in each of the parentheses in the corresponding sentence.

1. Court is (formally, formerly) opened with the bailiff's cry of "Oyez, Oyez!"

2. When her painting was purchased by the museum, the artist received many (complements, compliments).

3. One of my father's favorite sayings is "What's next — (desert, dessert) or (desert, dessert) the table?"

4. The discovery and development of rayon required an (ingenious, ingenuous) mind.

5. Leslie C. Freeman, (formally, formerly) mayor of Lakeville, is running for state senator.

6. Members of Student (Council, Counsel) should exemplify the highest type of school spirit, but do they?

7. King Henry (lead, led) his troops into battle.

8. I enjoy both chicken and steak but prefer the (later, latter).

9. One of the guidance (councilor's, counselor's) jobs is to (lead, led) students into the proper (coarse, course) of study.

10. José has spent three summers as a camp (councilor, counselor).

11. (Its, It's) about time for the mare to have her foal.

12. Have you tried out the new municipal golf (coarse, course)?

13. The treasurer (counciled, counseled) the club not to waste (its, it's) limited funds.

14. Many engineering schools are beginning to introduce (coarses, courses) in the humanities.

15. The master of ceremonies referred to Mrs. Hawke's (ingenious, ingenuous) manner that concealed an iron will.

16. My little sister acts as if (desert, dessert) were the main (coarse, course).

17. Do you like the song "(Its, It's) Later Than You Think"?

18. The (complement, compliment) of the division was brought up from the rear to the front lines.

19. Great areas of ocean floor which were (formally, formerly) unexplored are now known to be like a vast underwater (desert, dessert).

20. The expression "a diamond in the rough" means that a (coarse, course) exterior masks an interior quality.

---

**loose**     *free; unfastened; not tight or firm*
That *loose* wheel on your bike will give you trouble someday.
Clothes with a *loose* fit are stylish now.

**lose**     [pronounced lōōz] *to suffer the loss of*
You seem to *lose* everything you borrow from me.

---

**miner**     *a worker in a mine*
American *miners* lead the world in the production of coal.

**minor**   *under legal age; also, smaller or less important (as opposed to major)*
Normally, a *minor* is not permitted to sign a legal paper.
Let's not list the *minor* objections to the plan.

**moral**   *good or virtuous; also, a lesson taught by a story or event*
Good conduct is based upon *moral* principles.
The *moral* of the story is plain.

**morale**   *spirit; mental condition*
Teamwork is impossible without good *morale*.

**peace**   *calmness (as opposed to strife or war)*
Disarmament is an important step toward *peace*.

**piece**   *a part or portion of something*
You've had four *pieces* of cake already!

**personal**   *individual; private*
My *personal* opinion has nothing to do with the case.

**personnel**   *a group of people employed in the same work or service; a staff*
Most large companies prefer to find their executive *personnel* among college graduates.

**plain**   *not fancy; undecorated; also, a large area of flat land; also, clear*
*Plain* dresses are sometimes the most expensive.
Many Western movies are set in the Great *Plains*.
Does my explanation make things *plain* to you?

**plane**   *a flat surface; also, a woodworking tool; also, an airplane*
Some problems in physics deal with bodies on an inclined *plane*.
Use this *plane* to make the wood smooth.
We watched the *plane* circle for its landing.

**principal**   *head of a school [noun]; also, chief or most important among several things*

The *principal* will address the entire student body tomorrow.

Florida and California are our *principal* orange-growing states.

**principle** *a rule of conduct; also, a basic or general truth*

The *principle* of the Golden Rule is found in many religions.

This machine operates on a new *principle*.

---

**quiet** *still; silent*

The library is not as *quiet* as it should be.

**quite** *completely or entirely; also, considerably or very*

Are you *quite* finished?

Anne is *quite* a courageous girl.

---

**route** *a road; a way to go*

This highway is the shortest *route* to the mountains.

**rout** *a disorderly flight; to put to flight*

What began as an orderly retreat ended as a *rout*.

---

**EXERCISE 11.** Number your paper 1–20. After each number, write the correct one of the two words in parentheses in the corresponding sentence.

1. The salary schedule is posted on the bulletin board next to the office of the (personal, personnel) director.
2. Literature and composition are the (principal, principle) parts of the course.
3. Automation in the coal fields has put thousands of (miners, minors) out of work.
4. Coral has a sign that she puts on her desk in the library; it reads: "(Quiet, Quite) please. Genius at work."
5. The (principals, principles) of mathematics are basic to those of the other sciences.
6. Each of Aesop's *Fables* ends with a pat (moral, morale).
7. The treasure hunt led us on a circuitous (rout, route) from one end of the park to the other.

8. After it was worked out in class, the solution of the trig problem seemed (quiet, quite) (plain, plane) to all of us.
9. When Kurt's (plain, plane) failed to return, the (moral, morale) of his outfit sank to zero.
10. As long as you are a (miner, minor), you are not responsible for debts.
11. The diver found an old chest filled with jewels and (peaces, pieces) of eight.
12. Follow the marked (rout, route) or you will surely (loose, lose) your way.
13. Some of the new regulations, though good in (principal, principle), are difficult to enforce.
14. The treeless (plain, plane) stretched as far as the eye could see.
15. The (principal, principle) that underlies the company's choice of (personal, personnel) is "An educated person is usually willing to learn more."
16. The sports columnist described last Saturday's game as a (rout, route) for our team.
17. To forestall infection, always take care of (miner, minor) cuts and burns.
18. The foremost aim of the United Nations is the establishment of international (peace, piece).
19. The accident that completely demolished the car was caused by a (loose, lose) cotter pin worth ten cents.
20. With the adoption of the Eighteenth Amendment, the (principal, principle) that it is possible and desirable to legislate (morals, morales) was about to be severely tested.

| | |
|---|---|
| **stationary** | *in a fixed position*<br>The new state power plant contains large *stationary* engines. |
| **stationery** | *writing materials, especially paper*<br>Save your best *stationery* for important letters. |
| **straight** | *not crooked or curved; direct*<br>If you can't draw a *straight* line, use a ruler. |
| **strait** | *channel between two large bodies of water;* also (plural), *difficulty; distress* |

The *Strait* of Gibraltar links the Mediterranean Sea and the Atlantic Ocean.

My parents have always helped me when I was in bad *straits*.

---

**than**  [conjunction; used mainly in comparisons]
Loretta is taller *than* I.

**then**  adverb meaning *at that time; soon afterward*
We lived on Garden Street until last year, and *then* we moved to our new house.

---

**there**  *at that place*
I will be *there* when you arrive.

**their**  [possessive form of *they*]
Did your friends bring *their* bathing suits?

**they're**  [contraction of *they are*]
*They're* the ones to watch.

---

**to**  [a preposition that indicates direction, degree, connection, etc.; also, part of the infinitive form of a verb]
Let's go *to* the movies.
Suddenly, a bird began *to* sing.

**too**  adverb meaning *more than enough; also*
Is it *too* far to walk?
You, *too*, are invited to the party.

**two**  *one + one*
There are *two* flavors: vanilla and chocolate.

---

**waist**  *middle part of the body*
These trousers are too tight at the *waist*.

**waste**  *useless spending; unused or useless material; also, to spend idly or uselessly*
The movie was simply a *waste* of time.
Don't *waste* your money on books like that.

---

**weather**  *atmospheric conditions*
We had good *weather* for the picnic.

**whether**  [a conjunction that expresses an alternative]
I don't know *whether* he's been delayed or *whether* he isn't coming at all.

---

**who's**  [contraction of *who is; who has*]
*Who's* going to play the lead in the show?
*Who's* been using my typewriter?

**whose**  [possessive form of *who*]
*Whose* sweater is this?

---

**your**  [possessive form of *you*]
Is this *your* book?

**you're**  [contraction of *you are*]
I hope *you're* able to go with us.

---

**EXERCISE 12.** Number your paper 1–20. After each number write the correct one of the two words in each of the parentheses in the corresponding sentence.

1. Watching and listening (to, too) television indiscriminately can be a (waist, waste) of precious time.
2. (Their, There) Great Dane is taller and heavier (than, then) (your, you're) Sicilian donkey.
3. The roof of the stadium is not (stationary, stationery) but can be put up or taken down as needed.
4. (Weather, Whether) or not I will be able (to, too) go (to, too) college depends on (to, too, two) things: money, and money.
5. (Your, You're) right (to, too) act is determined by (weather, whether) or not (your, you're) actions are damaging to the general welfare.
6. (Who's, Whose) planning on writing a paper on Ida Tarbell?
7. If that is not (your, you're) car, (who's, whose) is it— (there's, theirs)?
8. The Bering (Straight, Strait) is a mere fifty-four miles wide.
9. Remind Carol and Tom (to, too) bring (their, there) own frankfurters for the picnic.
10. What did (your, you're) family say when you told them about the scholarship (your, you're) going to get?
11. (Your, You're) mistaken; I have never been (their, there, they're).

12. What styles of (stationary, stationery) did you order for the class project?

13. "What a (waist, waste)!" Joan exclaimed as she looked at all the spoiled food in the broken refrigerator.

14. Never had we seen such (straight, strait) and towering trees as those in the experimental forest.

15. I'd rather be shot (than, then) do it, but after taking that last test, I'm afraid I'll have (to, too, two) take a course this summer, (to, too).

16. Is that (peace, piece) of garden statuary (stationary, stationery)?

17. Of the (too, two) horses, I'd select the chestnut rather (than, then) the bay.

18. (Who's, Whose) the new teacher I just saw in the corridor?

19. "(Your, You're) just the person I'm looking for," said Ms. Shaw. "(Your, You're) assignment for yesterday is missing."

20. Half of India could be fed on the food that is (waisted, wasted) every year in the United States.

**REVIEW EXERCISE.**   Write a sentence using correctly each of the words in the preceding list, beginning on page 552. You will have seventy-four sentences in all. Follow the order of the list. For related forms of words, such as *council, councilor,* you need use only one word.

## COMMONLY MISSPELLED WORDS

**6. *Learn lists of commonly misspelled words*.** Frequent short spelling tests are an effective means of fixing correct spellings in your mind. On the following pages you will find a list of 300 commonly misspelled words. Taking no more than twenty at a time, have these words dictated to you. Study the ones you miss and record them in your list of spelling errors. When you have studied them (divided them into syllables and practiced writing each word several times), write them again from dictation. Spelling tests should be written, not oral.

## *Three Hundred Spelling Words*[1]

accidentally
accommodate
accurate
acknowledgment
acquaintance
across

aerial
aisle
all right
always

amateur
analyze
annihilate
anonymous
apologize
appearance
appreciate
approaching
appropriate
approval

arctic
argument
arrangement
assassinate
association
athletics
atomic
attach
attack
attention

auxiliary
awful
awkward
bachelor
banana

bargain
basketball
battalion
beggar
beginning

believe
benefited
bicycle
biscuit
bookkeeper
breathe
bruise
bulletin
bureau
business

calendar
campaign
candidate
caricature
catastrophe
cellophane
cemetery
ceremony
chaperon
classroom

college
colonel
colossal
column
commission
committee
comparatively
compel
competitive
completely

complexion
conscience
conscientious
consensus
contemptible
convenience
copies
cordially
corps
correspondence

corroborate
courageous
courteous
criticism
criticize
cylinder
decide
decision
defense
definitely

dependent
descendant
descent
description
desirable
develop
dictionary
different
dining
diphtheria

disappear
disappoint
discipline
discuss
disease

[1] The list does not include the words listed on pages 552–62.

dissatisfied
divided
doesn't
economical
ecstasy

efficient
eighth
eligible
embarrass
emphasize
endeavor
environment
equipped
especially
etiquette

exaggerate
excellent
exercise
exhausted
exhilaration
existence
expense
extraordinary
familiar
fascinating

fatigue
February
feminine
fiery
financial
foreign
forfeit
fourth
fragile
generally

genius
government
governor

grammar
grateful
grievance
guarantee
guard
gymnasium
handkerchief

happened
harass
haven't
height
heroes
hindrance
hoping
horizon
hospital
humorous

imitation
immediately
inconvenience
indispensable
inevitable
influence
initial
inoculate
insofar (as)
interpreted

irrelevant
irresistible
kerosene
laboratory
leisure
license
lightning
likelihood
literacy
loneliness

losing

luxurious
maintenance
maneuver
marriage
matinee
medicine
medieval
mentioned
microphone

minimum
mischievous
missile
misspelled
mortgage
movable
municipal
murmuring
necessary
negotiations

nickel
ninety
ninth
noticeable
nuclear
nuisance
occasionally
occur
occurred
omitted

opinion
opportunity
optimistic
pamphlet
parallel
paralysis
parliament
particularly
pastime
perhaps

permanent
permissible
perseverance
personally
perspiration
persuade
playwright
pleasant
pneumonia
possess

possibility
practice
preference
prejudice
privilege
probably
procedure
professor
pronunciation
propaganda

propeller
prophecy
psychology
pursue
questionnaire
realize
receive

recognize
recommend
referred

rehearse
reign
relief
repetition
representative
restaurant
rhythm
satisfactorily
schedule
scissors

seize
semester
separate
sergeant
shining
siege
similar
sincerely
souvenir
specimen

strategy
subtle
success

sufficient
suppress
surprised
syllable
sympathy
symphony
synonym

tariff
television
temperament
temperature
thoroughly
tomorrow
tournament
traffic
tragedy
transferred

twelfth
tyranny
undoubtedly
unforgettable
unnecessary
vacuum
vengeance
vicinity
villain
weird

# American
# English

**PART SEVEN**

# Chapter 32

# American English

One of the first things anyone notices about language is that different groups of people speak the same language differently. English people speak differently from Americans, and New Yorkers speak differently from Texans. You may even have noticed that special groups such as fishers, miners, or railroad workers have a special vocabulary that they use among themselves. If you are very observant, you might have noticed that different social classes often use different varieties of language.

This situation, like most things in our world, is the result of a historical process. Whenever groups of people are separated by distance, by different occupations, or by class in such a way that communication between groups is infrequent, each group develops a form of the common language that is peculiar to itself. Because languages are constantly changing, speakers separated from one another by time or class or job are likely to change their way of speaking in different ways, and in time the changes produce varieties, or *dialects,* of the native language.

In this chapter, you will study the history and movement of the various groups who make up the speakers of American English, for it is this movement that results in the differences between American and other varieties of English and between the dialects of American English itself.

# AMERICAN ENGLISH DIALECTS

The history of American English begins with the physical separation of two groups of speakers: those who remained in England and those who came to America. In tracing the history of the colonists' language, we must realize that the colonists came from many different parts of Britain and, accordingly, spoke as many dialects of British English. In addition, they settled in separate communities which had very little contact with each other. Thus, because most of these communities were composed of speakers of various British dialects, no one of them was quite like any other language group anywhere. Ultimately, it was from these differing communities that most of the rest of the United States was settled, and it was from their dialects that modern American English dialects developed.

## Eastern New England and Southern

The five most clearly definable regions of the United States can be traced to four early centers of population. The first two of these — eastern New England and the coastal, or tidewater, region of the Southeast — share certain similarities in their linguistic development. In the first place both have contributed relatively little to the major streams of migration by which the rest of the country was settled. The early growth of important industries in New England, the development of the great commercial center of Boston, and the establishment of fishing, whaling, and sealing ports all tended to keep New England's energies turned toward the sea and toward its own growth. Charleston and Richmond and the plantation economy of the Southeast had much the same effect on that area. Because few settlers left these parts to go further inland, the dialects have remained relatively confined to the coastal areas of the East and South.

Secondly, the economic and cultural importance of these two regions gave their dialects a social importance not shared by other areas. Until recent times at least, the tidewater dialect in the South and the eastern New England

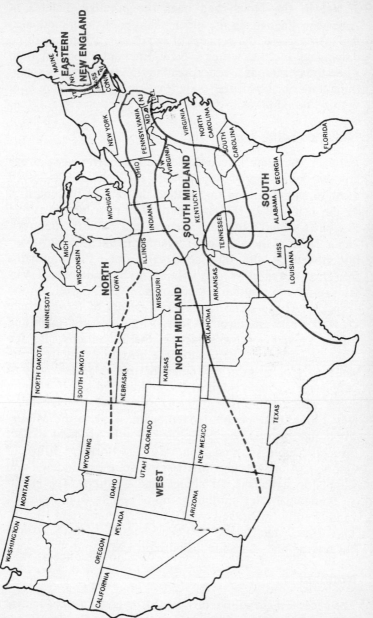

**American English Dialect Regions**

dialect in the North had been the prestige dialects of American English. In the older schoolbooks and dictionaries, for example, the concept of standard English was often influenced by the writer's New England pronunciation. Even today there is a widespread notion that there is something superior about the New England way of saying *aunt* with a "broad *a*" as in *father*.

## Midland: South and North

Between the New England and the southern coastal areas lay two other population centers through which flowed most of the migration that settled the rest of the country. In the first half of the eighteenth century a large wave of Scotch-Irish left Northern Ireland and came to Pennsylvania. Most of them did not stay long in that area, however, but moved on, this time southward along the mountains into the valleys of West Virginia, the Shenandoah of Virginia, and the southern piedmonts of the Carolinas and Georgia. At the same time, some groups of these people crossed westward through West Virginia to the Ohio and others moved southwest across the mountains into the Tennessee Valley. Because these people came from the same part of Britain, the result of this migration was to people the upland region of the middle and south Atlantic states with a group that spoke approximately the same dialect. Later these people moved again, west to the Mississippi and beyond, carrying their South Midland dialect through Tennessee and Kentucky, the northern fringe of Georgia, Alabama, and Mississippi, southern Indiana and Illinois, to Arkansas, Oklahoma, and southern Missouri.

Somewhat later another group of people from Pennsylvania went westward to central Ohio, Indiana, and Illinois. This area, which starts in Pennsylvania, forms a distinct but related dialect region called North Midland.

## Northern

The second main source of westward migration was central and northern New York and western New England. This group went by way of the Erie Canal, the Great Lakes, and overland through northern Pennsylvania, Ohio, Indiana, and Illinois to Michigan, Wisconsin, and beyond. This area makes up the modern American dialect region called Northern.

## The Mississippi and Beyond

Although we have described the source and to some extent the area of the five major dialect regions — New England, Northern, North Midland, South Midland, and Southern — we have said very little about the dialects of the regions west of the Mississippi. In general, the Southern dialect has extended along the Gulf of Mexico as far west as Texas, and Northern and Midland — with much mixing and crossing — have reached in parallel bands west to the Pacific. However, as a result of northward movements of South Midland settlers and southwestward movements of Northern settlers, the areas have become so mixed that any definite statement about them is open to question and is probably of no great value. As is so often the case in questions of dialect distribution, the dialect areas of the United States are very much more distinct in those parts of the country that have been settled longest.

**EXERCISE 1.** To test your knowledge of what you have just read, write short answers to the following questions.

1. List at least two things that lead to the growth of differences between dialects.
2. Why is it difficult to relate a particular American English dialect to a particular British English dialect?
3. List the five main dialect regions of American English and write one or two short sentences about the source and extent of each.

# CHARACTERISTICS OF AMERICAN ENGLISH

Even in the East, where they are most distinct, the dialects of American English do not show such great differences from one another as do those of many older language areas. Also, in many places throughout the country, the distinguishing features of the local dialects are disappearing as a result of education, television, radio, and movies, all of which present speakers with a relatively uniform model. Because of this pattern, language researchers often choose to investigate the speech of older persons in a dialect area to determine the differences in vocabulary, sounds, and grammar that distinguish the dialects. Much of this language research can be found in the *Linguistic Atlas of the United States and Canada.*

## Vocabulary

Dialect differences in vocabulary are most often found among words that are handed down orally. For example,

| ENE[1] | N | NM | SM | S |
|---|---|---|---|---|
| brook | creek | creek, run | branch, run | branch |
| nightcrawler | angleworm | fishworm | redworm, fishworm | fishing worm |
| darning needle (i.e., the dragonfly) | darning needle | snake feeder | snake doctor, snake feeder | snake doctor |
| bonny clabber | lobbered milk | clabber (milk) | clabber (milk) | clabber |
| spider (i.e., frying pan) | spider | skillet | skillet | spider |
| carry | carry | pack | pack | tote |
| white bread | white bread | white bread | lightbread | lightbread |
| (corn) husks | husks | husks | shucks | shucks |

Most of these words are household terms, farmyard terms, names of foods, common animals, children's games, and so forth. Occasionally, however, terms for new things are developed independently in different regions, and these

[1] The abbreviations used here and throughout this chapter are ENE (Eastern New England), N (North), NM (North Midland), SM (South Midland), S (South).

differences are preserved for a considerable time. Examples are the terms *movie show* and *central,* now generally being replaced by *movie* and (*telephone*) *operator,* and words associated with the modern superhighway. The highway itself is, in different areas, *thruway, parkway,* and *turnpike;* the area at the edge of the paved strip may be the *verge* or *shoulder;* and an intersection with another road may be an *exit* or *interchange.*

## Pronunciation

Probably the first time you noticed another way of speaking, or dialect, it was brought to your attention by a different pronunciation. This is the most obvious area of dialect difference and one that persists when vocabulary and grammar have become uniform. The following list of characteristic sound features of our five dialects can be used as a test for yourself and your class to see how closely you conform to the dialect in your area. If there are differences, they can probably be traced to your parents' dialect or to the influence of education and mass media.

1. The absence of noticeable *r* sounds at the end of a word like *far* or *father* and before consonants in such words as *card, heard, fort,* etc. [S and ENE]

2. An $\overline{oo}$ sound, like the vowel of *food,* in words like *Tuesday, duty, new.* [ENE, NM, and N]

3. The vowels of *horse* and *hoarse, morning* and *mourning* are, respectively, "aw" and "oh," as "hawrse — hohrse." [N, S, and SM]

4. The vowel of *path, half, dance* is similar to the vowel of *father.* The same vowel is regularly heard also (long and without the *r*) in words like *barn* and *yard.* [ENE]

5. The vowel of *on, off, fog, frog,* and *wash* is "aw." [M and S. A shorter, but similar, sound is found in ENE.]

The vowel of *on, off,* etc., is like the vowel of *father.* [N]

6. The sound represented by the *s* in *greasy* and in the verb *grease* is the "ss" sound in *hiss.* [ENE, N, and NM]

The *s* in *greasy* and *grease* has a "z" sound. [SM and S]

7. The *ou* of *house* is made up of an "ah" plus an "oo." [ENE, N, NM]

The *ou* of *house* is made up of the short *a* in *cat* plus an "oo." [SM, S]

8. The title *Mrs.* is pronounced as one syllable with a "z"—"Mizz." [This is a notable characteristic of the S and parts of SM. Other areas pronounce this as "mississ" or "mizziz."]

## Grammar

Grammar in American dialects is much less varied than pronunciation and vocabulary; furthermore, many of the differences are limited to nonstandard speech idioms. The following phrases and expressions are characteristic of the five dialect regions.

1. The past tense form *waked up* and the phrase *all to once* are features especially characteristic of ENE. Elsewhere *woke up* and *all at once* are more common.

2. Common to ENE and the whole of the Northern region are *sick to* (one's) *stomach*, (he's not) *to home*, (you) *hadn't ought* (to do it), *begin* and *see* as past tense forms.

3. The past tense form *seen* is found most often in the Midland area, but is spreading into the North. Also typical of Midland speech are the second person plural pronoun *you-uns*, (this is) *all the further* (I go), *wait on you* (i.e., "wait for you"), *want off* (i.e., "want to get off"), *a quarter till* (twelve).

4. Forms typical of SM are the *sun raised*, the past tense form *shrinkt*, the pronouns *ourn, yourn, hisn*, etc. (for *ours, yours, his*, etc.).

5. Common to S and SM are the second person plural pronoun *you-all*, *might could* (i.e., "might be able to"), the use of *done* in (she) *done* (told you), (he) *used to didn't* (like tomatoes), the ending *–es*, pronounced *–iz*, after *–st*, *–sp*, *–sk* in *postes, fistes, waspes, taskes*.

6. Typical of S are *belongs to be* (i.e., "ought to be"), *fell out the bed*, (I won't go) *on account of* (I wasn't asked).

## "Standard" American

For American English some such description of the dialects as we have given is an essential part of any description of the language. This is probably more true of American English than of the great majority of the widely known languages of the world. In British English, French, Italian, or Spanish, to name a few, one particular dialect has, as a result of political, social, and economic forces, become a standard form of the language which is taught in the schools and used more or less uniformly throughout the country. In the United States, however, no single dialect has yet achieved this status. It seems probable that, under the influence of radio, television, and motion pictures, a kind of "standard" is beginning to emerge. This somewhat vaguely defined dialect avoids the more regionally limited vocabulary items and grammatical forms and favors a pronunciation that is Northern with some mixture of North Midland. However, it is still true that speakers in the various dialect regions of the United States continue to use the pronunciations of their region no matter how well educated they may be. Certainly, few public speakers in Boston, Charleston, or New Orleans, for example, feel any necessity to make their speech conform to that of a network TV announcer.

**EXERCISE 2.** Make a brief dialect survey of your classmates or of members of your community. If you find differences between their speech and the speech of your area, try to explain why. These items will help you.

1. How are the following groups of words pronounced? (See the text, pages 575–76, for the pronunciation of some of these.)
   a. dew, new, Tuesday
   b. loud, mountain, house (noun), house (verb)
   c. horse, hoarse; forty, fourteen
   d. poor, your [an "oh" vowel is common in S and SM]
   e. on, hog, fog
   f. Mary, merry, marry [This is said with the vowels of *late, wet,* and *hat* in some areas, like the S; in other

areas, for example, Midland, these are all said with the same vowel sound, that of *wet*.]

2. What is the usual term for the following? Are other terms known? (The terms supplied as answers suggest how varied the responses can be; they are not the only terms known.) In asking questions of this kind, try to avoid suggesting the possible answer.

    a. a container for liquid having a bail or movable handle: *pail, bucket.*

    b. the area of the house between the front steps and the front door: *porch, stoop, piazza.*

    c. the fresh cheese made from strained milk curd: *cottage cheese, Dutch cheese, smearcase.*

    d. a sweet cake made by frying in deep fat: *doughnut, fried cake, raised doughnut, cake doughnut.*

    e. the window curtain that rolls down from the top: *roller shades, blinds, shades.*

    f. a bed covering made of two layers of cloth filled with cotton: *comfort(er), quilt.*

    g. a top covering for the bed: *counterpane, coverlid, bed spread.*

    h. the "collar bone" of a chicken: *wishbone, pull bone, pulley bone.*

# LOAN WORDS

Insofar as there is a "standard" American English, it is a standard that includes a variety of possible forms, especially in the area of pronunciation. This, however, is only one of the things that distinguishes American English from other varieties of the language. In vocabulary especially, there are features that are peculiar to the language of the whole country and not just one region. One of these features is the variety of loan words brought into American English as a result of the numerous contacts throughout our history with speakers of other languages.

## American Indian Loan Words

The first group of these loan words is borrowed from the

American Indian languages of North America. Like all word borrowings, these loan words reflect the nature of the contacts between two peoples. On the simplest level they consist almost entirely of names of places, animals and plants, foods, and things from Indian culture. The largest group is the place-names that occur in every conceivable form as the names of rivers, lakes, creeks, mountains and hills, streets, parks, towns, counties, and states. Some idea of their frequency may be seen from the fact that the names of at least twenty-six of the fifty states are Indian in origin.

The treatment of the Indian words shows considerable variety. Shortening and adaptation to English sound patterns is usual in direct borrowings, such as *Mackinaw* from *michilimackinac* and *Cheyenne* from *shahiyena.* Probably the majority of Indian place-names are tribal or personal or descriptive names given to places by whites with some knowledge of Indian names or languages. Personal names of well-known Indians are preserved in the names of cities such as *Pontiac* and *Osceola,* tribal names in *Miami, Huron,* or *Mandan.* Descriptive names were either left in an approximation of their original form, as *Chicago,* "place of wild onions," or translated into an English equivalent, as the *Big Horn* or the *Yellowstone* rivers. The latter is in fact a double translation, deriving from the French *roche jaune,* which is in turn a rendering of an Indian name *mitsiadazi.*

Apart from place-names, the list of Indian loan words in current American English is relatively short, especially in comparison with the total number of borrowings that have at some time been in use. Following the complete settlement of the country, the great decline in significant contacts between Indian and settler resulted in equally great loss of Indian terms from the vocabulary. Surviving common words still reflect the nature of the settlers' relations with the Indians. They learned and borrowed the names of new plants and animals (*hickory, squash, chipmunk, skunk*) and the names of new foods (*hominy, pone, succotash*). Usually, they kept some form of an Indian word for things associated with the Indian culture (*papoose, moccasin, tomahawk*).

Many of these terms have undergone interesting changes since their adoption into English. One such change is the alteration of the form of the original in order to bring it closer to a form familiar to a speaker of English. Two examples are the Algonquin words *wuchak* and *muskwessu,* which, after their adoption into English, were changed to *woodchuck* and *muskrat.* Since the woodchuck lives in or near woods, and since the muskrat is, in fact, a rodent that gives off a musky odor, users of English found it plausible to alter the Indian forms to suit their own concepts of what they thought the names ought to be.

Another type of change is semantic, that is, it affects the meaning of a word. Interesting examples of this are *powwow* and *mugwump. Powwow* was originally a term for "medicine man." Soon, however, it came to be applied to ceremonies at which magic or "medicine" was practiced. Later it was generalized to refer to any council of Indians or conference with them, and finally it was extended to its present sense of any conference or gathering for discussions of almost any kind. The second term, *mugwump,* originally meant "great chief," but, perhaps as a result of its sound, soon came to have comic or playful overtones. In 1884 it was applied to the "rump" Republicans who left the party to support the Democratic candidate, Cleveland. Following this, it acquired the generally favorable sense of an independent in politics. Recently, however, it has again become a somewhat unflattering term for a political opportunist who hopes to benefit by giving support to both sides. This sense has been imaginatively rationalized by deriving the term from the name of a supposed bird who "sits on the fence with its mug on one side and its 'wump' on the other."

## Loan Words from Other Languages

In addition to the Indian loan words in American English there are, of course, large numbers from a variety of other languages. These are the result of contacts between the English-speaking community and communities of speakers of other languages established either by immigration or by original settlement in areas later taken over by the United States—for example, the Spanish settlements in the Southwest and California and French communities in Louisiana and Maine. Successive waves of immigration in the nineteenth century, first from Germany, later from Scandinavia, and in the 1890's and after from South European and Slavic countries, brought millions of immigrants and hundreds of new words to American English.

## French

The earliest of these contacts were with the French, though French borrowings, of course, went on over a long period of time. A number of the loans from French (*bayou, toboggan, caribou*) were originally Indian words adopted first by the French before passing into English. The greater part of the remaining words are, like these, terms for things either newly found or newly developed in the new world— things that were peculiar enough to America so that new names were needed for them. They include names for plants and animals (*gopher, pumpkin*), foods (*chowder, jambalaya*), features of the land (*butte, coulee, levee, prairie*). Others include *bureau* (furniture), *depot* (railway station), *portage, charivari, lacrosse, parlay, picayune*.

## Spanish

The majority of loan words from Spanish are of later date, many deriving from relatively late nineteenth-century contacts with the ranching culture of the Southwest and Mexico but some traceable to South American or Central American Spanish. Borrowings include words for peculiar types of clothing (*chaps, poncho, sombrero*), architectural features (*adobe, patio, plaza, pueblo*), ranching terms (*cinch, corral, lariat, lasso, ranch, rodeo, stampede*), plants and animals (*alfalfa, mesquite, bronco, burro, coyote, mustang*), foods (*chile con carne, tamale, tortilla*), and a variety of other terms (*canyon, filibuster, savvy, stevedore, tornado*).

Like Indian words, Spanish loan words were often changed to make them sound more like familiar English syllables or words. In the Mexican Spanish word *juzgado* ("minor court"), the *j* would have sounded to English ears rather like an *h,* and the *d* in some Mexican dialects would have been entirely lost. Thus, with the stress shifted in English fashion to the first syllable, it became in American English, quite reasonably, *hoosegow.* Similarly, Spanish *vamos* ("let's go") was altered at two separate times into different Anglicized forms and acquired in the process two different senses in English: *vamoose* ("leave hurriedly") and *mosey* ("move along or stroll"). The first syllable of *vaquero,* "cowboy," pronounced with initial *b* in Spanish, was changed to the familiar English *buck* by the natural association of cowboys with *buck*ing horses, resulting in the American English word *buckaroo.* The Spanish word *galon,* meaning "braid," originally applied to sombreros decorated with numerous braids at the base of the crown, was mistakenly associated with the English word *gallon,* producing in English *ten* (or *five*) *gallon hat.* As a result the word is often mistakenly thought to derive from the capacity of the hat for holding water.

## German

In the seventeenth and eighteenth centuries there were extensive migrations from Germany into areas of Pennsylvania. The communities established there remained almost completely separated in language and culture from their neighbors. In the course of time, the language of these communities, now known as Pennsylvania Dutch (derived from the German word *Deutsch* meaning "German"), has been greatly affected by linguistic change, especially by the introduction of English vocabulary. But in spite of this, these people have been so close-knit that even now, after nearly 200 years, it is estimated that at least one fourth of the population of this section of the state still speak this variety of German.

In the second quarter of the nineteenth century and again in the 1880's, additional very large waves of German immigrants settled principally in the cities of the Northeast and Midwest. Here, until quite recent times, large communities of German-speaking Americans maintained their own schools, churches, and even newspapers. The influence of both of these settlements on the English language appears to have been primarily in the areas of food, drink, and social activities. Some of the loan words in this area are *delicatessen, frankfurter, hamburger, noodle, pretzel,* and *sauerkraut.* In addition to these, a number of other borrowings testify to the English-speaking American's ability to recognize and adopt a useful and picturesque term upon hearing one: *bum, fresh* ("impudent"), *loafer, nix, ouch, phooey, spiel.*

## Other Languages

The variety of borrowings from other languages is nearly as great as the variety of national origins. Italian, for example, contributes the names of many foods—*spaghetti, ravioli, pizza.* From Scandinavian we have *smorgasbord,* and from Dutch, *cookie, waffle, boss, dumb* ("stupid"), *spook.* Finally, from the several African languages we have a variety of words, several of which are fairly well known outside local areas of the South—*gumbo, goober, voodoo, juke* (box).

## Americanisms

Another distinctive feature of American English is the presence of considerable numbers of expressions not found in other varieties of English—or at least not until introduced by American movies and television programs. The very large number of these Americanisms, or new coinages from native English materials, can be seen by looking at the *Dictionary of Americanisms,* published by the University of Chicago Press. This dictionary consists of 1,911 pages of definitions and includes many tens of thousands of items, each of which is a word, a compound, or a special sense or meaning that appeared for the first time in American English.

This peculiarly American vocabulary is a subject that has aroused a remarkable amount of comment, much of it prejudiced, ill-informed, and even foolish. Comparative judgments are always dangerous, but it would appear that American, as contrasted with British English, has been much more active in the creation of new words and senses. Many of these creations are perfectly sober terms that excite little attention and pass pretty much unnoticed. Examples of these are *caption* (words beneath a picture or cartoon), *schedule* (a plan of working or action, a timetable), *pocketbook* (a purse), *excelsior* (fine wood shavings used as packing material), *headlight* (light on the front of a vehicle), *chicken wire* (wire mesh used to form an enclosure for chickens), *belittle* (to disparage). But many, too, are picturesque coinages of slang or the uninhibited creations of the street and the world of commerce, all of which, in our society, move quickly into the pages of the popular newspapers and magazines and from there into general usage. It is this kind of Americanism that is noticed by the casual critic, who at once concludes that the American vocabulary is composed chiefly of words like *louse up, go-getter, groceteria* and *cheeseburger heaven*. True, this is an interesting, vigorous, and distinctive element in American English; we should not conclude, however, that it is the only one.

## Generalization and Specialization

Very many Americanisms are special developments of words that already existed in British English. In some of these, American English broadened, or *generalized,* the earlier sense. In British English, for example, *laundry* referred only to the place where the washing is done; in American English the term has been generalized to include also the articles to be washed, that is, "take the laundry to the laundry." In British English *pie* originally referred only to a type of pastry filled with meat, but in American English it may also—and usually does—refer to one filled with fruit or some flavored sweet.

On the other hand, the opposite process may have taken place, and the usual meaning of a word may be more restricted, or *specialized,* in American English. Thus *corn* in Britain refers to grain in general, whereas in the United States is applied specifically to maize. A somewhat different kind of restriction is seen in *mean,* which in British English ranges in meaning from "low in social rank" through "petty or ignoble" to "stingy." In American English, however, it almost always means "ill natured" or "vicious." This is, of course, not merely a reduction in the breadth of meaning, but a loss (or near loss) of some senses and the addition of a new one. Similarly, in England *lumber* referred to a collection of more or less useless articles, as in the term *lumber room* for what Americans would call a *storeroom.* In America *lumber* came to be applied also to cut timber, a sense which soon entirely replaced the earlier one. In British English *homely* is a word with good connotation, meaning "simple, plain, or unpretentious; suited to the home"; in American English, however, the word has taken quite another direction and is generally an unfavorable term with meanings ranging from "plain in appearance" almost to "ugly."

## Technical Words

Another rich source of Americanisms is in the more or less technical areas where new terms have developed independently for things invented since the separation of America from Britain. In railroading we have in the United States *railroad* (British English *railway*), *conductor* (*guard*), *engineer* (*engine driver*), *freight train* (*goods train*), *cow catcher* (*plough*), *switch* (*points*). In automobile terms we have *windshield* (*windscreen*), *fender* (*wing*), *hood* (*bonnet*), *house trailer* (*caravan*). In other areas we have *streetcar* (*tram*), *flashlight* (*torch*), *long distance call* (*trunk call*), *wrench* (*spanner*), *thumbtack* (*drawing pin*), *installment plan* (*hire-purchase*), *hardware store* (*ironmongers*), and *five- and ten-cent store* (*bazaar*).

## Compound Words

Many of these American creations are compound words, which is the largest category of new formations. Some of these were created to name things met for the first time by Americans in their new country; others derive from special developments of a new civilization; and many are metaphorical expressions of attitudes taken by Americans toward features of their environment. All these types are found in the following: *catbird, cottonwood, log cabin, hired hand, lame duck, doubleheader, rain check, stopover, soap opera, ghost town, rat race, sweatshop, double-talk.*

## Other Ways of Adding Words

In addition to the development of new senses for old words and to the creation of new terms by compounding, American English very freely forms new words by adding suffixes, by shortening, and by combining elements in different ways. The old verb-forming suffix *–ize* and the suffixes *–ist* and *–ician,* indicating one who performs or specializes, are three of the numerous active word-forming suffixes in American English. Examples are *itemize, slenderize, hospitalize, receptionist, cornetist, beautician, mortician.* Shortening, or *clipping,* of long words is an old practice in English that continues to be active in America: *coed* (from *coeducational*), *prefab* (from *prefabricated*), *gym* (from *gymnasium*), *gas* (from *gasoline*), *pop* (from *soda pop*), *phone* (from *telephone*). *Blending,* or the combining of elements of two words into one, is especially popular in recent American English. Examples are *motel* (from *motor hotel*), *paratrooper* (from *parachute trooper*), *travelogue* (from *travel monologue*), *newscast* (from *news broadcast*), *telecast* (from *television broadcast*). A type of blending involving punning or other word play is popular in journalistic writing, though the resulting words usually have only a brief vogue. One example is the corner grocery store that changed its name to a *superette* (*super* from *supermarket* combined with *ette* meaning "little").

## THE RICHNESS OF OUR LANGUAGE

In these few pages we have given only a tiny sample of the enormous number of American English vocabulary creations. Many of these words are used for a short time and then disappear and are forgotten. Very many, however, survive, filling an important place in the vocabulary. So useful, indeed, are some of them that they are borrowed into British or other varieties of English, and may even be found as loan words in other languages. Signs reading *parking gratuit* may be seen in Paris, the *nightclub,* so spelled, is a European institution, the small lunch counter on a Greek boat in the Mediterranean is the *snackbar,* and a French-speaking Lebanese in Beirut has been heard to praise a pair of blue jeans as follows: "Ce sont des jolis cowboys."[1]

"Des jolis cowboys" — here is linguistic change in essence. The word itself, *cowboy,* is older than American English. But a wondrous change has been worked upon the original boy who herded his cows, doubtless on some peaceful upland English pasture. The word comes, in the American West, to refer to a hard-bitten ranch hand on a tough little horse, dressed in Levis, leather chaps, and ten-gallon hat, spending unpeaceful days and nights herding cattle, riding fence, and breaking horses. Locally, in the folklore of Tombstone, Arizona, the *cowboys* were the marauding outlaws famed as the rivals and enemies of Marshal Wyatt Earp. With the invention of Western fiction, the *cowboy* became a romantic figure, the last natural man — adventurous, brave, a dead shot, and a knight errant sworn to save the ranch and win the hand of the rancher's

[1] "What good-looking blue jeans."

daughter, the schoolteacher. With his translation to the movies, this figure achieves world renown as a type both in dress and behavior. His name, cowboy, is so well known that not only is it borrowed into other languages, but it is there extended to cover his most characteristic article of dress, his Levis. And hence "des jolis cowboys."

The growth of new languages or new dialects results from linguistic change accompanied by the separation of peoples and the passage of time and conditioned by the impact of new environments and social forces. The many senses of *cowboy* in American English illustrate this change in one of its aspects. Within the framework of American English, separation leads also to the development of varieties of language: varieties of pronunciation, of grammar, and of vocabulary. This is perhaps the most significant feature of American English: that there is no single variety that we may identify as a standard. Southern, Northern, Midland varieties, each has its standard, or socially acceptable, forms; each one is standard American English. And yet, together with their differences, they all have in common additional features that set American English as a whole apart from the other English dialects. These are, most notably, the vocabulary elements (the loan words, the new formations, the adaptations of old words) that have developed since the moment when these speakers were physically isolated into a single, separate group.

**EXERCISE 3.** It would be helpful for you, and interesting for the class, to make a notebook to record the material you gather for these questions.

1. Make a list of twenty words or terms that you think might be Americanisms. The best places to look for such terms will be in areas, occupations, or activities that have developed in the last few centuries. If you have Matthews' *Dictionary of Americanisms* in your library, check your list to see if your terms were, in fact, coined in America.

2. The following terms are all current in some part of the English-speaking world. Some are peculiar to a particular dialect of American English, some are Americanisms borrowed in Amer-

ica from one of the non-English languages spoken there, some have been created there out of English or foreign elements, some are not American English at all. Look up each one in a good dictionary and determine which of these categories it belongs to. *Webster's Third New International Dictionary* will have the necessary information on all of them.

chesterfield
hoarding
  (billboard)
kibitzer
groundnuts
banjo
cafeteria
tonic (soda pop)
cheeseburger

cruller (doughnut)
prairie
ringer (cowboy)
yam
snoop
spicket
county town
courthouse
  (county seat)

smearcase
croker sack
litterbug
spa (soda fountain)
mustang
groceteria
dog irons (andirons)
hamburger

# College Entrance
# and
# Other Examinations

Chapter **33**

# College Entrance and Other Examinations

## Tests of Vocabulary, Reading, and English Composition

No matter what your plans for the years following high school, it is more than likely that you will be asked to "take some tests." Many of the most commonly administered tests include measures of verbal fluency, reading comprehension, and/or grammar and composition.

Among the tests of this type used for college entrance, the best known are probably the *Scholastic Aptitude Test — Verbal,* or SAT-V, and the *English Composition Test,* or "English Achievement" test. Both of these tests are administered by the College Entrance Examination Board, or CEEB. Another well-known test is *The English Test* of the American College Testing Program (ACT).

Many schools and colleges do *not* require tests for admission, but do administer tests for placement in courses and for guidance purposes after you have registered. The military and other employers may also, on occasion, administer tests of English vocabulary, reading, or grammar when such skills can be shown to be important to success in the job.

Tests with the word *aptitude* in their titles are used mainly to predict future success, whether in school or on the job. They do not, on the whole, measure what you have learned in particular courses. They measure the

English language skills which you have been developing all your life through your habitual listening, reading, and speaking.

*Achievement* tests, on the other hand, concentrate on specific skills and understandings which you have learned in the courses taken to complete your academic program.

Cramming is *not* an appropriate or helpful way to prepare for tests of this nature. There are, however, a number of good test-taking practices which will help you to do your best on any test. These may be summarized as follows:

## SUMMARY OF TEST-TAKING PRACTICES

### 1. Take a positive approach to the test.

   a. Try to do your best even though you may be nervous. Don't panic.

   b. Regard lapses of memory as normal. If you "block" on a certain question, go on and come back to it later if you can.

   c. Don't expect to answer every question. Unlike teacher-made tests, some of the tests we are discussing are built so that the average student will answer only about half the questions correctly.

### 2. Use your time wisely.

   a. Look over the test before you start to work. Get a feel for its length and difficulty.

   b. Plan your time. If you have a time limit of 20 minutes for a 40-question test, check that you are on or beyond question 21 after 10 minutes. But don't be an excessive clock-watcher. Clock-watching uses up your time and heightens anxiety.

   c. Work rapidly but carefully. Answer the easy questions first. If you don't know an answer right away, leave it and go on. Easy questions "count" just as much as hard ones.

   d. If you have time after finishing the test, try some of the questions you left out the first time. Then go back and check all your answers.

**SUMMARY OF TEST-TAKING PRACTICES** (*continued*)

3. *Avoid careless errors.*

   a. Pay close attention to directions. Do the sample questions even though you're sure you understand the task.

   b. Read each question carefully. Be sure you know exactly what it is asking you to do.

   c. Look at all the choices before you answer. In many cases the correct answer is not *absolutely* correct; it is the *best* among the choices you have been given. Be sure to compare all the choices before picking the one you believe to be the best answer.

   d. Avoid careless mistakes in marking the answer sheet. Keep it lined up with the booklet if possible. Be sure you make your mark in the correct manner in the correct row for the question. The scoring machine can't tell when you were "off" by one question or one row.

   e. If you change an answer, be sure you erase the first answer thoroughly. If the machine "reads" both marks, it will count the question as unanswered.

One of the best ways to prepare for any test is to become familiar with the types of tasks you will be asked to perform. Many test questions will be similar to those on tests you have taken before. Others may be new to you. The purpose of this chapter is to show you some of these question types. When any test you take makes use of them you will, in a sense, be on familiar ground.

# TESTS OF WORD KNOWLEDGE OR VOCABULARY

Vocabulary tests measure your understanding of the meanings of words, either in isolation or in context. Often, the relationships among words—the way they are related in meaning—will be tested. Examples of three types of vocabulary questions follow.

## Word Meanings

The simplest type of vocabulary question simply asks you the meaning of a word. Usually, the format is an incomplete statement to which you add one of several choices to complete the meaning. The following is a sample question of this type.

EXAMPLE    **A** To whet one's appetite is to ——

     a wean it
     b salve it
     c sharpen it
     d appease it      Answer:[1]
     e dampen it     

Some questions ask for a choice between *phrases* explaining the word's meaning or use; others offer *single words* and ask you to choose a synonym of the key word.

**EXERCISE 1.**   Read the beginning of each sentence below and the choices that follow it. Choose the answer which best completes the sentence.[2]

**1** To secede is to ——

     a attain
     b follow
     c establish
     d withdraw

**2** An ingenious person is one who is ——

     a impudent
     b inventive
     c decisive
     d frank

---

[1] Answer: © *sharpen it.* When you have marked your answer sheet for ©, this is the way it will look. You will black in the circle containing the letter of the correct answer. Answers are shown this way for all sample test items throughout this chapter.

[2] Answers for this and all the following exercises will be found on pages 618–19.

**3** If something is superfluous, it is ——

  a necessary
  b shallow
  c excellent
  d excessive

**4** Your agreement with a decision is your ——

  a ascent
  b asset
  c assent
  d assist

**5** Something that is done inadvertently is probably done ——

  a accidentally
  b imaginatively
  c intentionally
  d maliciously

## Synonyms and Antonyms

In a test on synonyms or antonyms you are asked to select, from four or five choices, the word *most similar* in meaning (synonym) to the word given *or* the word *most nearly opposite* in meaning (antonym). *Pay attention!* These are sometimes mixed together. Careful reading will help you here. There are very few true synonyms or antonyms in English; the "correct" answer, therefore, is the one most nearly the same or most nearly the opposite in meaning — it need only be better than the other choices.

Following are three sample questions in which you are to find the word *most similar* in meaning (synonym) to the underlined word.

EXAMPLE    **A** <u>disclose</u>    a react
                                  b darken
                                  c resound
                                  d visualize
                                  e reveal

**B** <u>impediment</u>    a agreement
                          b obstacle
                          c idiot
                          d outline
                          e utterance

**C** <u>enervate</u>    a encourage
                        b enlarge
                        c bemoan
                        d weaken
                        e cut

Answers:

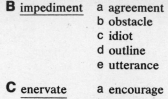

You will note that in the last question, a common misconception of the word's meaning is included among the choices. Many people are confused as to whether *enervate* means to take "nerve" away or to give it; hence *encourage* is given as an incorrect choice.

**EXERCISE 2.** For each of the following questions, choose the word *most nearly opposite* in meaning (antonym) to the underlined word.

**1** <u>chaotic</u>

   a confused
   b active
   c orderly
   d silent
   e cowardly

**2** <u>obstinate</u>

   a flexible
   b persistent
   c vague
   d obedient
   e extinct

**3** eradicate

   a refine
   b ratify
   c endorse
   d annihilate
   e establish

**4** pensive

   a careless
   b melancholy
   c sympathetic
   d exuberant
   e pleasant

**5** disperse

   a release
   b collect
   c destroy
   d produce
   e reinforce

## Verbal Analogies

Analogies are designed to measure your understanding of the relationships existing among words. Here is a sample set of directions and one question.

EXAMPLE   In the items below, the first and second words are related in a certain way. The third word is related in the same way to one of the four words which follow it. You are to choose the word related to the third word in the same way that the second word is related to the first.

   **A** *Inch* is to *foot* as *ounce* is to ——

      a weight
      b meter
      c yard
      d pound

Answer:

**A** ⓐ ⓑ ⓒ ●

In this sample question, the relationship tested is that of a unit of measurement to a larger unit in the same scale. An inch is a division of a foot. Hence, the correct answer is *pound* since an ounce is a division of a pound. *Weight* is an attractive wrong choice, since an ounce is a unit of weight, but the relationship is not parallel to that between *inch* and *foot.* If the first part of the analogy had been *inch* and *length,* then *weight* would have been the best answer.

Analogies may also be presented as shown in the following example.

EXAMPLE   Below is a list of five pairs of related words. Choose the pair of words whose relationship is most like that of the first pair.

**A** a  INCH: FOOT
　 b  weight: peck
　 c  ounce: pound
　 d  mile: length       Answer:
　 e  meter: yard        **A** ⓐ ⓑ ● ⓓ ⓔ

The same relationship is being measured here as was measured in the first example. *Ounce* is related to *pound* as *inch* is related to *foot.* But here you are to find the whole pair. In the first example, the first part of the second pair was given to you. If you are not familiar with analogies, it may help to turn them into sentences such as the one in the first example.

Suppose the first pair of words were *glance* and *gaze.* They are both "ways of looking at something." But a *glance* is a quick look, usually superficial or casual, while *gaze* has the idea of a long, careful, or thoughtful look. Which of these combinations, then, has the same relationship between the words?

EXAMPLE   **A** GLANCE: GAZE
　　　　　 a  blink: scowl
　　　　　 b  glimpse: stare

c skim: peek
d peruse: study

Answer:

**A** ⓐ ● ⓒ ⓓ

Option ⓑ would be the most similar pair to complete the analogy, since *glimpse* also implies a quick once-over, and *stare* gives the notion of a long and concentrated look. Another way to check your understanding of the analogy is to compare the first and third parts, and then check to see if the second and fourth parts have the same relationship. In the original example, this check would take the form: "*Inch* is to *ounce* as *foot* is to ——?"

**EXERCISE 3.** In the items below, the first and second words are related in a certain way. The third word is related in the same way to one of the five words which follow. Choose the word related to the third word in the same way as the second word is related to the first.

**1** *Head* is to *foot* as *cap* is to ——

  a toe
  b shoe
  c wig
  d ankle
  e bottle

**2** *Sphere* is to *axis* as *circle* is to ——

  a hypotenuse
  b square
  c radius
  d circumference
  e diameter

**3** *Canvas* is to *suede* as *cloth* is to ——

  a leather
  b cotton
  c fur
  d boot
  e tent

In the following items, choose the pair of words whose

relationship is most similar to that of the first pair given.

**4** speak : sing : :

   **a** paint : draw
   **b** run : walk
   **c** prose : poetry
   **d** move : dance
   **e** swim : sink

**5** nose : odor : :

   **a** mouth : speech
   **b** ear : sound
   **c** color : eye
   **d** hand : hold
   **e** foot : walk

# READING ACHIEVEMENT

Your grasp of the meaning of what you read, and your understanding of concepts presented in written form, are abilities that are often measured in tests for school or vocational guidance. Reading abilities are usually measured in one of the two ways described below.

## Sentence Completion

This question format could be called "fill in the blanks." Sentences are presented with one or two blanks, each indicating that a word has been left out. You are to choose, from the possible answers given, the one which fits best in the sentence.

EXAMPLE   **A** We laughed at the clown —— he performed funny tricks.

   **a** but
   **b** until
   **c** because
   **d** unless
   **e** although

Answer:
**A** ⓐ ⓑ ● ⓓ ⓔ

The sentence clearly calls for a conjunction, but the only one that makes any sense is *because*. Questions like this do not ask for the recall of information. Rather, they look for your ability to recognize the logic and coherence of the sentence — one aspect of comprehension.

## Reading Comprehension

The reading tests you are likely to be taking are not concerned with testing whether you understand, word by word, what you have read, but rather how well you can draw conclusions about what you read, and how well you can make judgments about it. The questions you will be asked about the passage you read should not require outside information, but should be based upon the information found within the paragraph itself. Here is a sample passage followed by three questions.

EXAMPLE   Two days after his sudden death on June 9, 1870, Charles Dickens was honored in a *New York Times* obituary covering more than five of the seven long columns on the front page. The length of this article accurately reflected Dickens' position among the American reading public of a century ago, when entire households waited anxiously from month to month to discover the fate of Little Nell, or Oliver Twist, or whichever Dickensian hero figured in the novel currently being serialized for United States audiences. In later years, the novelist's reputation diminished; critics dismissed him as a "popular" writer rather than a true craftsman. His remarkably vivid characterizations were considered caricatures, even though numerous outstanding writers such as Feodor Dostoevski, Joseph Conrad, and Henry James expressed their indebtedness to "the master." But during the 1940's, writers like Franz Kafka and Edmund Wilson brought readers to a fresh awareness of Dickens' unforgettable delineations of personalities whose very names — Scrooge, for instance — have assumed an independent meaning for people around the world. Readers today are also impressed by Dickens' vision, more than 100 years ago, of what the modern city was to become. For Dickens' London was a place of smoke and filth and a decaying social fabric, rather than the rich, bustling, upper-class London of virtually all his contemporaries.

**A** The main thrust of this article has to do with ——

  a  modern attitudes towards Dickens
  b  Dickens' descriptions of London
  c  changes in Dickens' literary reputation
  d  Dickens' treatment of fictional characters

**B** Dostoevski, Conrad, and James indicated that ——

  a  their writing was influenced by Dickens
  b  Dickens wrote for a lower-class public
  c  they had learned about London from Dickens
  d  Scrooge was a caricature

**C** Apparently other British authors of Dickens' day ——

  a  were upper-class Londoners
  b  ridiculed Dickens' London
  c  believed Dickens an expert on city life
  d  pictured London as an attractive place to live

Answers:

A  ⓐ ⓑ ● ⓓ
B  ● ⓑ ⓒ ⓓ
C  ⓐ ⓑ ⓒ ●

These sample questions are fairly typical of the kinds of questions that may be asked in reading comprehension tests. Question 1, for example, asks for the main idea of the passage. Question 2 asks for a restatement of an idea clearly stated in the passage. And question 3 asks for an inference which the reader must draw from the passage. Other types of questions often used in this type of test may ask the meaning of a term or phrase as used in the paragraph, a recognition of the author's intent, or the identification of bias, exaggeration, value judgments, or the like.

**EXERCISE 4.** After reading the following passage, answer the questions given at its conclusion.

1      Catbirds are good neighbors; they eat small fruit,
2   wild as well as cultivated, but they also eat insects, lots of
3   them. Thus they earn their keep in the garden. Catbirds
4   may be as tame as chickadees, and may sometimes even come
5   to your hand to beg for raisins. Spring is the best time of
6   year to listen for catbirds. However, only the male catbird
7   sings. While his mate is brooding the eggs, the male
8   has ample time to sing—and play the clown. A friendly
9   bird, the male catbird has a sense of humor, or something
10   like it. He is a mimic; he borrows music from other birds.
11   Sometimes he merely sits in a bush, well concealed, and
12   sings to himself, as though practicing. Other times he
13   seeks a human companion with whom he can have a con-
14   versation. He likes company, and he seems to need an audi-
15   ence. He is essentially a showoff. Try to imitate his own imi-
16   tations and he will come close, and then laugh at you.
17   The male catbird can be as musical as his cousins, the
18   brown thrasher and the mockingbird. But he doesn't stammer,
19   as the thrasher sometimes does. And he can break into the
20   middle of a song to jeer at his own performance, as the
21   mockingbird never does. He will sing part way through a
22   robin's choicest song, then break into squawking like a
23   barnyard hen or mewing like a cat. And after a pause he
24   will start another song, this time perhaps that of a
25   tanager. The catbird's songs are nearly always fragmented.
26   Perhaps you could say he sings for his supper. You can
27   never be sure whose song he is going to sing, but he will sing.[1]

**1** According to the article, the male catbird is different from the mockingbird because he ——

a interrupts his own singing
b stammers during his song
c imitates the songs of other birds
d likes human companionship

**2** A factual statement about catbirds, as opposed to an opinion or value judgment, appears on line ——

[1] Adapted from *The New York Times,* editorial of June 15, 1975, © 1975 by The New York Times Company. Reprinted by permission.

a 14
b 3
c 9
d 2

**3** As used in this paragraph, the word *brooding* (line 7) means ——

a sitting quietly and thoughtfully
b hovering or looming over
c sitting on or incubating
d being depressed and moody

**4** Apparently the catbird is most closely related to the ——

a chickadee
b brown thrasher
c tanager
d robin

**5** The phrase that best sums up the author's opinion of the male catbird appears in line ——

a 1
b 15
c 17
d 4

## ENGLISH COMPOSITION

Tests of composition are designed to measure, at least indirectly, your skills in the writing of English — skills that have been developed in your language arts program in school. Ideally, of course, the best way to "test" your writing skill is to have you write. For many reasons, however, this is not always practical, so multiple choice tests have been developed to measure your knowledge of correct spelling and usage, your skill in organizing material into a cohesive whole, and your sensitivity to nuances of tone, style, and choice of words. The paragraphs which follow give examples of some of the more commonly used methods of testing composition skills.

### Spelling

Spelling may be tested in any number of ways. One of the

most common formats consists of five words, one of which may be misspelled. You are to indicate the word spelled incorrectly or mark a choice indicating no errors. The questions usually test basic rules of spelling and misspellings of frequently used words; they are not generally "spelling bee" words. Another type of common spelling error derives from the misuse of homophones — words which sound alike but differ in spelling, such as *to, too,* and *two.* In this sort of test question, four phrases with different homophones will usually be given, and you will be asked to choose the phrase in which a homophone is used correctly or incorrectly. In the following sample, choose the phrase in which a homophone is incorrectly used:

EXAMPLE **A** a *too* hot
b grizzly *bear*
c *peace* of pie
d rough *seas*

Answer:
**A** ⓐ ⓑ ● ⓓ

**EXERCISE 5.** For each of the following questions, choose the one word which is misspelled. If no word is misspelled, mark the answer N for no error.

**1** a practice
b calender
c tomato
d already
N

**2** a freight
b anchor
c pursuade
d magazine
N

**3** a efficient
b personal
c implement
d hindrence
N

**4** a  irregular
b  separate
c  recommend
d  appearance
N

**5** a  abreviate
b  perturb
c  calorie
d  technique
N

**6** a  *mail* a letter
b  *site* a reference
c  *raze* a building
d  *reign* as king
N

**7** a  *pare* an apple
b  *tale* of woe
c  *hew* wood
d  *peel* of laughter
N

## Error Recognition

Another way of testing writing skills indirectly is to ask you to detect or correct errors in written passages. Some type of error recognition questions ask you only to indicate that an error has been made; others ask you to specify the type of error it is. Here are samples of three types of questions.

EXAMPLES  TYPE 1.

Mark the letter of the line containing an error in spelling, punctuation, capitalization, grammar, or usage. If there is no error, mark N for no error.

**A** a  Actually, bats are fascinating
b  animals. They are the only Mammals
c  living today that are able to fly.
N

Answer:

**A** ⓐ ● ⓒ Ⓝ

## TYPE 2.

Mark the letter of the underlined part that must be changed in order to make the sentence correct. (Be sure to note whether underlining includes the punctuation.) If there is no error, mark answer space e.

**B** During <u>the colonel period</u>, many colonies had
$\qquad$ a
<u>their own flags</u>, the <u>earliest of which</u> was
$\qquad$ b $\qquad$ c
based on <u>the British flag.</u> $\qquad$ <u>No error.</u>
$\qquad$ d $\qquad$ e

Answer:

**B** ● ⓑ ⓒ ⓓ ⓔ

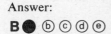

## TYPE 3.

Some of the sentences below contain errors; others are correct as they stand. For each sentence, mark your answer sheet:

a — if the sentence contains an incorrect choice of words (error in diction)

b — if the sentence is wordy (verbose or redundant)

c — if the sentence contains an overworked expression (cliché) or a mixed metaphor

d — if the sentence contains an error in grammar or structure

e — if the sentence is correct as it stands

**1** Each day it was a daily occurrence to see the mail truck arrive.

**2** The mass of detail is not penitent to the question at hand.

**3** The young woman was fit as a fiddle as she started work.

Answers:

**EXERCISE 6.** Following the appropriate set of directions, record your answers to each of the following questions.[1]

**TYPE I.** Mark the letter of the line containing an error in spelling, punctuation, capitalization, grammar, or usage. If there is no error, mark N for no error.

**1** a Ben Franklin was an excellent student,
  b but his father could not afford to send him
  c to Harvard college. He dropped out of school.
  N

**2** a For a short time he helped his father
  b make candels and cakes of soap from animal fat,
  c but Ben really wanted to go to sea.
  N

**3** a Finally, at 12 years of age, Ben Franklin
  b pledged himself to an apprenticeship the
  c most common type of schooling in the colonies.
  N

**4** a Ben learned all there was to know about
  b the printing trade from his brother, James.
  c He also wrote for the paper his brother published.
  N

**5** a Although the paper was very succesful, Ben
  b was unhappy. So, at 17 years of age,
  c he ran away to begin a new life for himself.
  N

**TYPE II.** Mark the letter of the underlined part that must be changed in order to make the sentence correct. (Be

[1] The factual ideas for all these sentences came from the July 1975 National Geographic article on Franklin.

sure to note whether the underlining includes the punctuation.) If there is no error, mark answer space e.

**6** Broke jobless and dirty, Ben landed in
             a
Philadelphia, in 1793. He started a business by
     b                 c
printing everything from business forms to

hymnals, and he became prosperous.        **No error.**
       d                               e

**7** Soon after he arrived in the City of Brotherly love,
                                 a
Franklin founded a four-page newspaper, which
                   b
was published weekly, as well as an almanac
            c
called "Poor Richard's."            **No error.**
       d                            e

**8** The young printer also founded a political
               a
club called the Junto. The members met discussing
     b                  c
the needs of the growing community.    **No error.**
          d                        e

**9** Once a project was chosen, Franklin published
                  a
articles in his paper. And signatures collected.
                         b
Then the Junto would petition the assembly
            c          d
for action.                    **No error.**
                                       e

**10** By such methods, Franklin and his friends
            a
attacked serious social problems. Many of the
        b
institutions they established were so useful
                         c
that they still thrive today.         **No error.**
       d                            e

**TYPE III.** Some of the sentences below contain errors; others are correct as they stand. For each sentence, mark your paper with one of the following letters as appropriate:

> a — if the sentence contains an incorrect choice of words (error in diction)
>
> b — if the sentence is wordy (verbose or redundant)
>
> c — if the sentence contains an overworked expression (cliché) or a mixed metaphor
>
> d — if the sentence contains an error in grammar or structure
>
> e — if the sentence is correct as it stands

**11** Franklin and his friends began a public academy which later became the University of Pennsylvania.

**12** They also founded a lending library where people which had paid a small membership fee could borrow books.

**13** Before any other fire insurance company had been founded, Franklin promoted the establishment of the insurance company which survives today as the oldest fire insurance company in existence at the present time.

**14** To reduce counterfeiting, Franklin devised paper money with the imprint of a leaf, since he had observed that no two leaves were identifiable.

**15** Last but not least among Franklin's contributions should be mentioned the Union Fire Company, Philadelphia's first volunteer fire department.

## Error Correction

Error correction questions indicate the inappropriate part of the sentence and ask you to choose a suitable correction from among the choices given you. Here are some samples.

EXAMPLES **A** Eating, drinking, and *to stay up* late at night were among her pleasures.

> a correct as it stands
> b she liked staying up
> c staying up
> d to remain up

**B** *On the snow-covered branch, two sparrows, they huddled close together.*

  **a** correct as it stands
  **b** On the snow-covered branch, two sparrows huddled close together.
  **c** On the snow-covered branch, two sparrows, huddled close together.
  **d** Closely, on the snow-covered branch, huddled the two sparrows together.

Answers:
**A** ⓐ ⓑ ● ⓓ
**B** ⓐ ● ⓒ ⓓ

## Sentence Revision

This type of question requires you to mentally restate a *correct* sentence, using a phrase that is given to you. Using the phrase will require change in other parts of the sentence as well. Then you must choose, from among the choices given you, a word or phrase that will appear somewhere in the restated sentence. (They may not necessarily follow directly after the given revision.) Study the sample given below.

EXAMPLE  **A** Sentence: When night came and the temperature fell, my parents lit the fire in the bedroom.

    Revision: Begin with *"Each night . . ."*

      **a** that the temperature
      **b** upon the temperature's
      **c** because the temperature
      **d** when the temperature

Answer:

**A** ⓐ ⓑ ⓒ ●

There will often be several ways the new sentence could be completed. If none of the choices given is in your revised sentence, think of another way to rephrase the sentence, and check the choices again. But be sure you do not change the meaning of the original sentence when you revise it.

**EXERCISE 7.** Following the appropriate directions, answer each of the following questions.

**Error Correction.** Choose the letter which indicates the best correction for the underlined part of each sentence. If the sentence is correct as it stands, mark d.

**1** The hour was indeed late in the evening when we started back homeward toward our own house.

    a We started back homeward when the hour was late.
    b It was very late evening when we started home.
    c We began when it was late in the evening to go home.
    d Correct as it stands

**2** Rain had been falling for several hours, this having caused the streams to rise.

    a which resulted in
    b which was responsible for
    c causing
    d Correct as it stands

**3** Our road home crossed an old covered bridge over a narrow stream.

    a homeward was by way of an old
    b necessitated our crossing over a
    c led us via a bridge which was an old
    d Correct as it stands

**4** We couldn't but hope that the bridge was still open.

    a couldn't hardly
    b could scarcely
    c could only
    d Correct as it stands

**5** When we arrived at the river's edge, the angry waters were to be seen swirling and were carrying branches along with them as they rushed past.

   a Swirling and carrying branches along with them, the angry waters were seen as they rushed past when we arrived at the river's edge.

   b When we arrived at the river's edge, we could see the angry waters swirling and carrying branches along with them as they rushed past.

   c Having arrived at the river's edge, the angry waters were swirling and carrying branches along with them as they rushed past.

   d Correct as it stands

**Sentence Revision.** Mentally revise each of the following sentences according to the instruction given for each. Then choose the letter of the phrase most likely to occur in the sentence as revised.

**6** Sentence: My friend said that she hoped the bridge would hold until we got across.

  Revision: Change the indirect quote to a direct quote.

    a "I hoped the bridge would hold until we got across."

    b "She hopes the bridge will hold until we get across."

    c "I hope the bridge will hold until we get across."

    d "She hopes the bridge would hold until we got across."

**7** Sentence: There was also a thick swirling fog. We finally arrived home safely.

  Revision: Rewrite these two sentences as a single sentence.

    a even though
    b so that
    c due to the
    d whereas

## Organizing Paragraphs

Another area of composition in which a student is generally tested is organization. The most frequent exercise designed to measure organizational ability is the scrambled paragraph. This exercise takes a paragraph from any type of subject matter and presents the sentences to you in random order. Your job is to figure out the correct order, the order which will rearrange them so as to make a well-knit paragraph. This you do to some extent by studying the sequence of ideas presented; but primarily you have to concern yourself with the transitional words and phrases.

Here is the way the directions are likely to go:

DIRECTIONS  Each group of sentences in this section is actually a paragraph presented in scrambled order. Each sentence in the group has a place in the paragraph; no sentence is to be left out. You are to read each group of sentences and decide the best order in which to put the sentences so as to form a well-organized paragraph.

Before trying to answer the questions which follow each group of sentences, jot down the correct order of the sentences in the margin of the test book. Then answer each of the questions by blackening the appropriate space on the answer sheet. Remember that you will receive credit only for answers marked on the answer sheet.

A sample paragraph follows:

EXAMPLE  **P** As you read, however, concentrate only on main ideas; don't try to remember everything.

**Q** If you develop an interest in what you read, you are more likely to remember the factual information in a passage.

**R** Finally, when you have completed the passage, pause to summarize the main ideas in your mind.

**S** You will have an even stronger motive for remembering those facts if you understand their importance to you.

**1** Which sentence did you put first?
a  sentence **P**
b  sentence **Q**

c   sentence **R**
d   sentence **S**

**2**  Which sentence did you put after sentence **S** ?

a   sentence **P**
b   sentence **Q**
c   sentence **R**
d   None of the above. Sentence **S** is last.

**3**  Which sentence did you put after sentence **Q** ?

a   sentence **P**
b   sentence **R**
c   sentence **S**
d   None of the above. Sentence **Q** is last.

Answers:

**1** ⓐ ● ⓒ ⓓ
**2** ● ⓑ ⓒ ⓓ
**3** ⓐ ⓑ ● ⓓ

Note the use of words such as *finally, however, even
stronger*. These words refer to previous statements. You
may also find clues in sentences using pronouns or adjectives clearly referring to some noun in a previous sentence
(*those* facts). Before you answer any of the questions, you
should determine the correct order for all the sentences
and write it down for your own reference. Most tests, however, will not ask you to give that order all at once. They
will be set up so as to give you credit for each correct
relationship you detect between the individual sentences.
If you were merely asked for the order itself, you would
lose all credit for a single mistake.

**EXERCISE 8.**   Read the following sentences carefully and
write down their correct order before answering the questions related to them. Then choose your answer for each
question that follows.

**P**  They should also use transitional words and phrases.
**Q**  Writers should indicate the logical relationships among ideas
in their essays.

**R** The first-rate writer, on the other hand, usually uses precise transitions to indicate relationships.

**S** Some writers have only two transitional words in their vocabulary: *and* and *but*.

**1** Which sentence did you put first?

  a **P**

  b **Q**

  c **R**

  d **S**

**2** Which sentence did you put after sentence **P**?

  a **Q**

  b **R**

  c **S**

  d Sentence **P** is last.

**3** Which sentence did you put after sentence **Q**?

  a **P**

  b **R**

  c **S**

  d Sentence **Q** is last.

**4** Which sentence did you put after sentence **R**?

  a **P**

  b **Q**

  c **S**

  d Sentence **R** is last.

**5** Which sentence did you put after sentence **S**?

  a **P**

  b **Q**

  c **R**

  d Sentence **S** is last.

## *Answers to Exercises*

| Ex. 1, p. 596 | Ex. 2, p. 598 | Ex. 3, p. 601 |
|---|---|---|
| 1 d | 1 c | 1 b |
| 2 b | 2 a | 2 e |
| 3 d | 3 e | 3 a |
| 4 c | 4 d | 4 d |
| 5 a | 5 b | 5 b |

Ex. 4, p. 605

1 a
2 d
3 c
4 b
5 b

Ex. 5, p. 607

1 b
2 c
3 d
4 N
5 a
6 b
7 d

Ex. 6, p. 610

1 c
2 b
3 b
4 N
5 a
6 a
7 a
8 c
9 b
10 e
11 e
12 d
13 b
14 a
15 c

Ex. 7, p. 614

1 b
2 c
3 d
4 c
5 b
6 c
7 a

Ex. 8, p. 617

1 b
2 c
3 a
4 d
5 c

Abbreviations
  acceptable in writing, 467
  of government agencies, 467
  of titles with names, 467
  punctuation of, 423–24
  used in source materials, 373–74
Abstract noun, defined, 5
Accent marks, 511
*Accept, except,* 175
Achievement tests, 593–94
Action verbs, 11–12
Active voice, 155–56
Addresses, commas with, 439
Adjective clauses, 59–60, 220
  defined, 59
  diagramed, 59–60
  relative pronoun in, 59–60
Adjective phrases, 42
Adjectives
  after linking verbs, 164
  comparison of, 168–72
  defined, 9
  distinguished from adverbs in usage, 163–65
  ending in *-ly,* 163–64
  nouns used as, 10
  predicate, 9, 35
  proper, 409
Adverb clauses, 63–64, 204–05
  defined, 63
  diagramed, 64
  introductory, commas with, 435–36
  subordinating conjunctions in, 65, 215–16
Adverb phrases, 43–44
Adverbs
  comparison of, 168–72
  defined, 15
  distinguished from adjectives in usage, 163–65
  not ending in *-ly,* 163–64
  nouns used as, 16
*Affect, effect,* 175

Affixes, 531
Agreement of pronoun and antecedent, 98–100
  antecedents joined by *and,* 98
  antecedents joined by *or, nor,* 100
  *each, either, everyone,* etc., 99
  in gender, 98
Agreement of subject and verb, 81–96
  after *here, there,* 91
  collective nouns, 92
  *doesn't, don't,* 96
  *each, either, everyone,* etc., 86
  *every, many a,* 96
  *measles, mathematics,* etc., 95
  predicate nominative, mistaken agreement with, 96
  *several, few, both, many,* 86
  *some, any, all, none, most,* 86–87
  subjects joined by *and,* 89
  subjects joined by *or, nor,* 89
  subjects of different number, 89–90
  titles of books, etc., 94
  *together with, as well as,* etc., 84
  words stating amount, 92–93
*All,* number of, 86–87
*All ready, already,* 552
*All the farther, all the faster,* 175–76
*Allusion, illusion,* 176
Almanacs, 495
*Altar, alter,* 552–53
*Altogether, all together,* 553
*Alumni, alumnae,* 176
Ambiguous reference, of pronouns, 227
*American Authors 1600–1900,* 498
American English, 569–88
  Americanisms, 583–87
    blending, 586
    clipping, 586
    generalization, 584–85

American English,
  Americanisms, *continued*
    specialization, 584–85
  characteristics of, 573–77
    grammar, 576
    pronunciation, 575–76
    vocabulary, 574–75
  dialects of, 569–73
  loan words in, 578–83
*American Heritage Dictionary of
  the English Language,* 80
*Among, between,* 179–80
*Amount, number,* 176–77
Analytic cards, in card catalogue,
  482
*And etc.,* 177
Antecedent
  agreement of pronoun with, 98
  defined, 6
Antonyms, in dictionaries, 515
*Any,* number of, 86–87
*Anybody, anyone,* number of, 86
*Anywheres, everywheres, nowheres,*
  177
Apostrophes, 455–59
  in compound words, 457
  in contractions, 458
  in names of business firms, 457
  in words showing joint posses-
    sion, 457
  plural of letters, numbers, etc.,
    458–59
  to form possessive case, 455–58
    of a plural noun, 455
    of a singular noun, 455
    of an indefinite pronoun, 456
    with personal pronouns, 455–
      56
  words indicating number or
    amount, 457
Appendix of a book, 486
Appositives
  as sentence fragments, 203–04
  case of, 117–18
  defined, 54
  diagramed, 55
  punctuation of, 437

Appropriateness, in usage, 75–76
Aptitude tests, 593–94
Articles, 9
*As,* case of pronoun after, 116
*As, like,* 186
*As if, like,* 186
*Ascent, assent,* 553
*At* (after *where*), 177
Atlases, 495–96
Author card, 478–79
Auxiliary verb = helping verb

*Bad, badly,* 166–67, 178–79
Bartlett's *Familiar Quotations,* 499
*Be*
  as linking verb, 12
  conjugation of, 146–47
  special nature of, 12
Because (after *reason is*), 179
*Being as, being that,* 179
*Beside, besides,* 179
*Between, among,* 179–80
Bibliography
  correct form of, 369–71
  function of, in a book, 486
  reference, in note-taking, 362
  sample of, 381
  working, 352–56
Biographical dictionaries, 497–98
Biographical reference books, 496–
  98
Blending, in formation of Ameri-
  canisms, 586
Body, of a business letter, 391
Book, parts of a, 483–87
Book review, 336–40
  characters, 337
  plot, 336
  setting, 337
  style, 337
  theme, 337–38
*Born, borne,* 553
*Both,* number of, 86
Brackets, use of, 448
*Brake, break,* 553
*Bring, take,* 180

*British Authors Before 1800,* 498
*British Authors of the Nineteenth Century,* 498
Business letter, 382–403
  body, 391
  closing, 392
  correct form, 383–84
  envelope, 392–93
  folding, 393–94
  heading, 386
  indention in, 383–85
    block, 384–85
    full block, 384, 385
    semiblock, 384, 385
  inside address, 386
  model of, 387
  of adjustment, 397–98
  of application, 399–401
  of inquiry, 395–96
  salutation, 386–91
  second page, 385–86
  signature, 392
  stationery and appearance, 382–83
  trite phrases in, 391
*Bust, busted,* 180

C or ©, meaning of, 373
*c.,* or *ca.,* meaning of, 373
Call number, 353–54
*Can't hardly, can't scarcely,* 180, 191–92
*Can't help but,* 192
*Capital, capitol,* 553
Capitalization, rules for standard usage, 407–21
  dictionary as guide to, 510
  of abbreviations, 409
  of business firms, 412–13
  of calendar items, 412–13
  of directions, 410–11
  of first word in a line of poetry, 408
  of first word in a quotation, 451
  of first word in a sentence, 408
  of geographical names, 410
  of government bodies and political parties, 412–13
  of historical events, periods, 412–13
  of *I* and *O,* 408
  of names of persons, 409–10
  of nouns derived from proper names, 411
  of organizations and institutions, 412–13
  of parts of compound word, 419
  of proper nouns and adjectives, 409–14
  of races, religions, 412–13
  of school subjects, 414
  of sections of the country, 410–11
  of *senior, sophomore,* etc., 414
  of ships, trains, etc., 412–13
  of special events, 412–13
  of titles of books, art works, 417–18
  of titles of persons, 416–17
  of words of family relationships, 417
  of words referring to Deity, 418
  summary style sheet for, 420–21
Card catalogue, 353, 478–82
  analytic cards, 482
  author card, 478–79
  information given on cards, 480–81
  "see" and "see also" cards, 481–82
  subject card, 480
  summary of uses, 482
  title card, 480
Case, 103–19
  defined, 103
  nominative, uses, of, 105–07
  objective, uses of, 108–10
  of appositives, 117–18
  of pronouns, 103–19
  of relative pronouns, 113
  possessive before gerund, 118–19

Case forms of personal pronouns, 104–05
-cede, -ceed, and -sede, 545
cf., meaning of, 373
ch., meaning of, 373
Chronological order, in a paragraph, 276–77
Civics, number of, 95
Clauses, 56–69
    adjective, 59–60, 220
    adverb, 63–64
    defined, 57
    elliptical, 65
    essential, 531–32
    independent, 57, 67–69
    infinitive, 53–54
    intervening, 83–84
    nonessential, 431–32
    noun, 61–63
    subordinate, 58–65, 220
Clincher sentence, 262
Clipping, in word formation, 586
Closing, of a business letter, 392
Clothes, cloths, 553
Coarse, course, 554–55
Coherence in the paragraph, 276–82
    arrangement of ideas, 276-82
        in chronological order, 276–77
        in order of importance, 278
        in spatial order, 277–78
    use of linking expressions and connectives, 279–82
Collective nouns
    defined, 5
    number of, 91
College entrance examinations, 593–619
Collier's Encyclopedia, 494
Colon, 445–46
    after salutation of business letter, 446
    before a formal statement, 445–46
    before a list, 445
    between independent clauses, 446

in numbers, 446
Columbia Encyclopedia, 494
Columbia-Viking Concise Encyclopedia, 494
Comma, 427–42
    after closing in letters, 440
    after introductory elements, 434–36
    after salutation in letters, 440
    between independent clauses, 430–31
    in a series, 427–28
    in dates and addresses, 439
    in direct address, 437
    summary of usage, 441–42
    unnecessary use of, 440
    with adjectives before noun, 428–29
    with appositives, 437
    with direct quotation, 452
    with interrupters, 437–38
    with nonessential clauses, phrases, 431–33
    with parenthetical expressions, 437–38
Comma splice = run-on sentence
Common noun, defined, 5
Comparative degree
    formation of, 169–70
    use of, 170–72
Compared and contrasted ideas, parallelism in, 243
Comparison of adjectives and adverbs, 168–72
    double, 171–72
    irregular, 170
Comparison or contrast, paragraphs developed by, 265–66
Complements, 30–36
    defined, 31
    direct object, 31–32
    indirect object, 32–33
    objective, 33–34
    predicate adjective, 35–36
    predicate nominative, 35--36
    subject, 34–36
Complement, compliment, 555

Complex sentence, 68–69
Complimentary close (closing), of a business letter, 392
Composition, 284–312
  assembling materials, 287, 352–58
  body, 297–98
  conclusion, 298–300
  formal, 348–49
  introduction, 296–97
  organizing materials (outlining), 287–94
  paragraphing, 301
  purpose, 287
  revising, 300–06
  selecting and limiting the subject, 285–86
  suggested topics for, 307–12
  summary of steps in, 307
  transitions, 301–02
  writing the first draft, 295–300
Composition tests, 606–18
Compound-complex sentence, 69
Compound noun, 5
Compound numbers, hyphenation of, 459–60
Compound object, 32–33
Compound sentence, 67
Compound subject, 27–28, 88–90
  defined, 27
  number of, 88–90
Compound verb, 28
Conclusion, of a composition, 298–300
Concluding sentence, 262
Concrete noun, defined, 5
Conditional clauses, conjunctions introducing, 215
Conjugation of verbs, 144–47
Conjunctions, 19–20
  between independent clauses, 68, 213
  coordinating, 19, 68, 242
  correlative, 19, 243
  defined, 19
  introducing adverb clause, 65
  kinds of, 19–20

  subordinating, 20, 65, 215–16
Conjunctive adverbs, 68
Connectives between coordinate ideas, 213–14
Connectives in the paragraph, 279–82
Context, getting meaning from, 523–27
Contractions, use of apostrophe in, 458
Contrasts in words, 526
Coordinate ideas
  clear relationship between, 213–14, 242–43
  parallelism in, 242–43
Coordinating conjunctions, 19, 213
Coordination, faulty, 222–23
Copyright date, 484–85
Copyright page, function of, 484–85
Correction symbols, 470
Correlative conjunctions
  in parallel constructions, 243
  list of, 19–20
Correlative constructions, parallelism in, 243
*Council, councilor,* 555
*Counsel, counselor,* 555
*Course, coarse,* 554–55
*Current Biography,* 496–97
*Cyclopedia of World Authors,* 498

Dangling modifiers, 237–38
Dash, uses of, 447
Dates
  commas with, 439
  writing numbers in, 467–68
Declarative sentence, 37
Degree, in comparison, 168–72
Demonstrative pronouns, 7
Dependent clause = subordinate clause
Derivation of a word, 512–13
*Des'ert, desert', dessert',* 555
Dewey decimal system, 476–78
Diagraming
  adjective clauses, 59–60

Diagraming, *continued*
adjective phrases, 42
adverb clauses, 64
adverb phrases, 43–44
appositives, 55
complex sentences, 68–69
compound sentences, 67
compound-complex sentences, 69
direct and indirect objects, 31–33
elliptical clauses, 65
gerund phrases, 49–50
gerunds, 49–50
infinitives, 53
noun clauses, 62
objective complements, 33
participial phrases, 46
participles, 46
predicate adjectives, 35
predicate nominatives, 35
prepositional phrases, 42–44
simple sentences, 67
subordinate clauses, 59–60, 62, 64, 65, 69
Dialects, of American English, 569–73
Dictionaries, 503–19
accent marks in, 511
arrangement and content of, 507–08
as guide to capitalization, 510
as guide to pronunciation, 511
as guide to spelling, 510
as guide to usage, 514–15
biographical, 496–98
college, 507
derivation of word, 512–13
illustrations, 515–16
in vocabulary study, 529
inflected forms in, 512
kinds of, 506–07
kinds of information in, 509–16, 517–18
of synonyms, 518–19
order of meanings in, 514
part of speech in, 511–12
restrictive labels in, 514–15
syllable division in, 510
synonyms in, 515
unabridged, 506–07
*Dictionary of American Biography,* 497
*Dictionary of National Biography,* 497
Direct address, punctuation of, 437
Direct object, 31–32
compound, 32
defined, 31
diagramed, 31–32
Direct quotation
capital letter with, 451
commas with, 452
from reference books, in note-taking, 462–63
quotation marks with, 451
Division of words into syllables, 468–69
*Doesn't,* agreement with subject, 96
*Done,* 180
*Don't*
agreement with subject, 96
for *doesn't,* 181
Double comparison, 171–72
Double negative, 181, 191–92
Double subject, 184

*Each,* number of, 86
*Economics,* number of, 95
*ed.,* meaning of, 373
*Effect, affect,* 175
*e.g.,* meaning of, 373
*ei, ie* (spelling), 545
*Either,* number of, 86
Ellipsis, 363
Elliptical clauses
case of pronoun in, 116
defined, 65
*Emigrate, immigrate,* 181
Emphasis in sentence, through subordination, 220
*Encyclopaedia Britannica,* 493–94
*Encyclopaedia Britannica Atlas,* 496

*Encyclopedia Americana,* 493–94
*Encyclopedia International,* 494
End marks, 423–24
End papers, function of, 486–87
Envelope, for business letter, 392–93
Essay, 327–35
  book review, 336–40
  informal personal, 328–29
  of opinion, 330
    choice of subject, 330
    factual evidence in, 331
    organizing, 331–32
    style and tone in, 332–35
      clarity, 332–33
      honesty, 333
      persuasiveness, 333
    testimony of authorities, 331
  précis, 341–44
Essential clause, phrase, 431–32
*et al.,* meaning of, 373
*etc.,* 177
*Every,* number of subject preceded by, 96
*Everybody,* number of, 86
*Everyone,* number of, 86
*Everywheres, anywheres,* 177
Examinations, 593–619
  achievement, 593–94
  aptitude, 593–94
  composition, 606–18
  reading, 602–06
  vocabulary, 595–602
*Except, accept,* 175
Exclamation mark, 424–25
  in relation to quotation marks, 425
Exclamatory sentence, 37
Expletive, 29

*f., ff.,* meaning of, 373
Fact and opinion, 331
Fallacies, 313–25
  attacking the man instead of the issues (*ad hominem*), 322–23

circular thinking—begging the question, 325
  "either-or," 324–25
  false analogy, 318–19
  in cause-and-effect reasoning, 317–18
  overgeneralizing, 313–16
    and prejudice, 316
  rationalizing, 323–24
Faulty coordination, 222–23
*Few,* number of, 86
*Fewer, less,* 181
Footnotes, 367–69
  abbreviations for, 373–74
  bibliographical data in, 367
  form of, 367–68
  *ibid.,* 368–69
  numbering, 367
Foreword, function of, 485
Formal standard English, 77–78
*Formally, formerly,* 555
Fractions
  hyphenation of, 467–68
  number of, 92–93
Fragments = sentence fragments
Frontispiece of a book, 484
Future perfect tense, 150
Future tense, use of, 149

Gender, agreement in, 98–99
General reference, 228–29
Generalization, and the scientific hypothesis, 315–16
Geographical names, capitalization of, 410
Gerund
  as object of preposition, 48
  as object of verb, 48
  as predicate nominative, 48
  as subject, 48
  defined, 48
  diagramed, 49–50
  modifiers and complements of, 49–50
  possessive case with, 118–19

Gerund phrase
  defined, 49–50
  makeup of, 49–50
Glossary, function of, 486
Glossary of Usage, 174–92
*Good, well,* 167, 181–82
Grammar
  distinguished from usage, 75
  of American English dialects, 576
*Granger's Index to Poetry,* 500

*Had of,* 184
*Had ought, hadn't ought,* 184
*Hammond Contemporary World
  Atlas,* 496
*Hardly,* 184, 192
*Haven't but, haven't only,* 192
*He, she, they,* as double subject,
  184
Heading, business letter, 386
Helping verbs, 13–14
*Here,* not subject of sentence, 29
Historical present, 148
Hyphen, 459–60
  in compound adjectives, 460
  in compound numbers and frac-
    tions, 459–60
  in dividing words at the end of a
    line, 459
  with prefixes and suffixes, 460

*ibid.,* meaning of, 368, 373
*i.e.,* meaning of, 373
*ie, ei* (spelling), 545
*Illusion, allusion,* 176
*Immigrate, emigrate,* 181
Imperative mood, 159
*Imply, infer,* 184–85
*In, into,* 185
Indefinite pronouns
  list of, 8
  misuse of *it, they, you,* 232
  number of, 85–87
Independent clause, 57, 67–69
Index of a book, 486

Indicative mood, 159–60
Indirect object, 31–33
  compound, 33
  defined, 32
  diagrammed, 33
  not part of prepositional phrase,
    32
Indirect quotation, 451
*Infer, imply,* 184–85
Infinitive
  as principal part of verbs, 123
  as verbal, 51–54
  clause, 53–54
  defined, 51
  distinguished from prepositional
    phrases, 51
  modifiers and complements of,
    51, 53
  perfect, 154
  present, 154
  subject of, 54
Infinitive phrase
  as sentence fragment, 204
  defined, 53
  diagrammed, 53
  makeup of, 53–54
Inflected forms of a work, in dic-
  tionaries, 512
Informal standard English, 78–79
*Information Please Almanac,* 495
*Ingenious, ingenuous,* 556
Inside address of business letter,
  386, 387–89
Intensive pronouns, 6
Interjections, 20–21
Interrogative pronouns, 7
Interrogative sentence, 37
Interrupters, commas with, 437–38
*Into, in,* 185
Intransitive verbs, 12
Introduction of a book, 485
Introduction of a composition,
  296–97
Introductory clauses and phrases,
  punctuation of, 434–36
Irregular comparison, 170
Irregular verbs, 124–31

Irregular verbs, *continued*
  defined, 124
  list of, 125–26
  principal parts of, 124–31
*It*
  as an expletive, 29
  indefinite use of, 232
It is *me . . . him, them,* etc., 107
Italics (underlining), 449
  for foreign words, words re-
    ferred to as words, etc., 449
  for titles, 449
*Its, it's,* 556

Joint possession, use of apostrophe
  in, 457
*Jr.,* capitalization of, 409

*Kind, sort, type,* 185
*Kind of a, sort of a,* 185

*l., ll.,* meaning of, 373
*Later, latter,* 556
*Lay, lie,* 136–38
*Lead, led,* 556
*Leave, let,* 185–86
*Less, fewer,* 181
Letter of adjustment or complaint,
  397–98
Letter of application, 399–401
Letter of inquiry, request, 395–96
Letter writing, 382–403
  (*See also* Business letter.)
Levels of usage, 75–80
  (*See also* Standard English, Non-
    standard English.)
Library, 475–91
  arrangement of, 475–76
  call number, 479
  card catalogue, 478–82
  Dewey decimal system, 476–78
  fiction, 475–76
  locating information, 478–91
  nonfiction, 476–78

parts of a book, 483–87
*Readers' Guide,* 487–89
vertical file, 490–91
(*See also* Reference books.)
*Lie, lay,* 136–38
*Like, as,* 186
*Like, as if,* 186
Limiting the subject
  of a composition, 285–86
  of a research paper, 349–52
*Lincoln Library,* 494–95
Linking expressions, 279–82
Linking verbs, 12–13, 122–23
List of illustrations, in a book, 485
Loan words, in American English,
  578–83
*loc. cit.,* meaning of, 373
*Loose, lose,* 557
*Lord's Historical Atlas of the
  United States,* 496

*Macropaedia,* 493
Magazine articles, listed in *Readers'
  Guide,* 487–89
Main clause = independent clause
Manuscript form, 463–72
  abbreviations, 466–67
  correction symbols, 469–72
  division of words, 468–69
  indention, 464
  margins, 464
  neatness, 463, 465
  numbering pages, 464
  paper and ink, 463–64
  placement of title, 464
  revision checklist, 465–66
  syllabication, 468–69
  writing numbers, 467–68
*Many,* number of, 86
*Many a,* number of subject preceded by, 96
*Mathematics,* number of, 95
Meaning of a word in dictionaries,
  514
*Measles,* number of, 95
*Micropaedia,* 493

*Miner, minor,* 557–58

Misplaced modifiers, 235–36

Modifiers
dangling, 237–38
defined, 9
misplaced, 235–36
squinting, 239
two-way, 239

Mood, of verbs, 159

*Moral, morale,* 558

*Most,* number of, 86–87

*ms., mss.,* meaning of, 374

*Much,* 86

*Mumps,* number of, 95

*Myself, ourselves,* 117


*National Geographic World Atlas,* 496

*N.B.,* meaning of, 374

*n.d.,* meaning of, 374

*Neither,* number of, 86

*New Century Cyclopedia of Names,* 497

*New York Times Atlas of the World,* 496

*No, nothing, none,* 192

*No one,* number of, 86

*Nobody,* number of, 86

Nominative case, uses of, 105–07

*None*
in double negative, 191
number of, 86–87

Nonessential clauses, phrases, 431–32

Nonrestrictive = nonessential

Nonstandard English, 79–80

*Nor,* case of subjects joined by, 89–90

Note-taking, for research papers, 360–64

Noun clause, 61–63
defined, 61
diagramed, 62

Nouns, 5, 10, 548–51
abstract, 5
collective, 5
common, 5
compound, 5
concrete, 5
defined, 5
number of, 81
plural of, 548–51
possessive case of, 455–58
proper, 5, 409
used as adjectives, 10
used as adverbs, 16

*Nowheres, anywheres, everywheres,* 177

Number, agreement in, 81–90, 98–100

*Number, amount,* 176–77

Numbers
at beginning of sentence, 467
compound, hyphen with, 468
in dates and addresses, 468
in fractions used as adjectives, 468
of more than two words, 467


Object
direct, 31–32
indirect, 31–33
of gerund, 48–49
of infinitive, 51–53
of participle, 46
of preposition, 18, 41, 110
of verb, 11, 31–32, 108
retained, 156

Object complement = direct, indirect object

Object of preposition
case of, 110
defined, 18

Object of verb
case of, 108–09
defined, 11
diagramed, 31–33

Objective case, uses of, 108–10

Objective complement, 33–34

*Of (could of, had of),* 180, 187–88

*Off of,* 188

*Official Associated Press Almanac,* 495

*One,* number of, 86

*op. cit.,* meaning of, 374

*Or, nor*
number of subjects joined by, 89–90
with *either, neither,* 188

*Others,* 86

*Ought (had ought),* 184

*Ourselves, myself,* 117

Outlining, 291–94, 359–60, 364–65
for research paper, 359–60, 364–65
parallelism of topics, 293
rules for form, 291–94
sentence outline, 292
topic outline, 292–94

Overgeneralizing, fallacy of, 313–16

*Oxford English Dictionary,* 506


*p., pp.,* meaning of, 374

Paragraph, 259–83
arrangement of details in, 276–78
coherence in, 276–82
concluding sentence, 262
connectives in, 281–82
defined, 259
developed by comparison and contrast, 265–66
developed by combination of methods, 268
developed by definition, 267–68
developed by examples, 264–65
developed by facts, 263
developed by incident, 265
developed by reasons, 266–67
length of, 260
linking expressions in, 279–80
methods of development of, 263–68
topic sentence, 260–62
transitions between, 301–02
transitions within, 281–82
unity in, 273–74

Parallelism, in outlines, 293

Parallelism, in sentences, 242–46
compared and contrasted ideas, 243
coordinate ideas, 242–43
correlative constructions, 243–44
repetition of article, preposition, pronoun, 245–46

Parentheses, uses of, 447–48

Parenthetical expressions, commas with, 437–38

Participial phrase
defined, 46
diagramed, 46
essential, 531–32
introductory, 434
makeup of, 46
nonessential, 431
punctuation of, 431, 433

Participle
defined, 45
distinguished from verb, 45
in verb phrase, 45
modified by adverb, 45
modifiers, complements of, 46
present and past, 45

Parts of speech, 3–22
adjective, 9–10
adverb, 15–16
conjunction, 19–20
interjection, 20–21
labeled in dictionaries, 511–12
noun, 5
preposition, 18
pronoun, 5–8
same word as different parts of speech, 21
summary of, 22
verb, 11–14

Passive voice, 157–58

Past participle, 123–31

Past perfect tense, 150

Past tense, 149

*Peace, piece,* 558

Perfect infinitive, 154

Period, 423–24
after abbreviations, 423–24

Period, *continued*
  as end mark, 423
Person, agreement in, 90
*Personal, personnel,* 558
Personal pronouns
  case forms of, 103–10
  correct use of, 105–110
  defined, 6
  list of, 104–05
  possessive case of, 104
Phrase, 40–55
  adjective, 42
  adverb, 43–44
  appositive, 54–55
  dangling, 237–38
  defined, 41
  fragment, 202–03
  gerund, 49–50
  infinitive, 53
  intervening, 83–84
  modifying two words, 240
  participial, 46
  prepositional, 41–44
  verb, 13–14
  verbal, 44–54
*Physics,* number of, 95
*Piece, peace,* 558
*Plain, plane,* 558
Pluperfect = past perfect tense
Plural
  defined, 81
  of letters, numbers, words as
    words, etc., 458–59
  of nouns, 548–51
*Politics, mathematics,* number of,
    95
Positive degree, 169
Possessive case
  before a gerund, 118–19
  formation of, 455–58
*Post hoc* reasoning, 317–18
Précis writing, 341–44
Predicate
  compound, 28
  defined, 26
  simple, defined, 27
  (*See also* Verb.)

Predicate adjective
  compound, 35
  defined, 35
  diagramed, 35
  position of in normal word order,
    36
Predicate nominative
  case of, 106–07
  compound, 35
  defined, 35
  diagramed, 35
Preface, function of, 485
Prefixes, in word analysis, 530–33
Preliminary outline, of a research
    paper, 359–60
Prepositional phrase, 41–44
  defined, 41
  diagramed, 42, 43–44
  introductory, comma with, 435
  used as adjective, 42
  used as adverb, 43–44
Prepositions
  defined, 18
  list of, 18
  object of, 18, 41, 110
  of more than one word, 18
Present infinitive, 154
Present participle, 123
Present perfect tense, 149
Present subjunctive, 160
Present tense, 148
*Principal, principle,* 558–59
Principal parts of verbs, 123–26
Pronouns
  antecedent of, 7, 98
  as transitional devices, 280
  case forms of, 103–16, 117–19
  case of in an incomplete con-
    struction, 116
  correct use of, 103–19
  defined, 5
  demonstrative, 7
  distinguished from adjectives, 9–
    10
  ending in *-self, -selves,* 6, 117
  indefinite, 8
  indefinite use of *it,.they, you,* 232

Pronouns, *continued*
  intensive, 6, 7
  interrogative, 7
  personal, 6
  possessive, 6
  reflexive, 6, 7
  relative, 7, 59–60
Pronoun reference, 226–32
  ambiguous, 227
  general, 228–29
  indefinite use of *it, they, you,* 232
  weak, 230–31
Pronunciation
  accent in, 511
  dictionary as guide to, 511
  in American English dialects,
    575–76
Proper adjectives, capitalization of,
  409–14
Punctuation
  after an abbreviation, 423–24
  apostrophe, 455–59
  brackets, 448
  colon, 445–46
  comma, 427–42
  dash, 447
  end marks, 423–25
  exclamation mark, 424–25
  hyphen, 459–60
  italics (underlining), 449
  parentheses, 447–48
  period, 523–24
  question mark, 524
  quotation marks, 451–54
  semicolon, 443–45
  underlining (italics), 449
  (*See also* individual marks.)

Question mark
  as end mark, 524
  in relation to quotation marks,
    424, 452
*Quiet, quite,* 559
Quotation marks, 451–54
  for a quotation within a quota-
    tion, 453
  for direct quotations, 451–53
  in a quotation of more than one
    paragraph, 453
  in dialogue, 453
  in note-taking, 363
  other marks of punctuation with,
    452–53
  to enclose slang words, etc., 454
  to enclose titles, 454
Quotations
  books of, 499
  in note-taking, 362–63
  punctuation with, 451–54
*q.v.,* meaning of, 374

*Raise, rise,* 142
*Rand McNally New Cosmopolitan
  World Atlas,* 496
*Random House Dictionary of the
  English Language,* 506
*Readers' Guide to Periodical Liter-
  ature,* 354, 487–89
Reading tests, 602–06
*Reason is because,* 179
Reference books, 492–502
  almanacs, 495
  atlases, 495–96
  authors, 498
  biographical, 496–98
  dictionaries, 503–19
  dictionaries of synonyms, 518–
    19
  encyclopedias, 492–95
  indexes, 500
  literary, 499
  miscellaneous, 500–02
  yearbooks, 495
Reference of pronouns, 226–32
  ambiguous, 227
  general, 228–29
  indefinite use of *it, they, you,* 232
  weak, 230–31
Reflexive pronouns, 6, 7
Regular verbs, 124
Relative pronouns, 7, 59–60

Relative pronouns, *continued*
case of, 113–15
defined, 7
function in clause, 59–60, 114–15
list of, 7
Repetition of key word, as transitional device, 280–81
Research paper, 348–81
abbreviations used in source materials, 373–74
areas for research, 349
availability of source material, 350–51
bibliography, final form of, 369–71
cover, 372
final draft, 366
final outline, 364–65, 372
first draft, 365–66
footnotes, 367–69
note-taking, 360–64
preliminary outline, 359–60
sample pages from, 375–81
selecting and limiting the subject, 349–52
selecting suitable reference books, 354–55
seven steps in writing, 349
statement of purpose, 359
title page, 372
working bibliography, 352–58
cards in, 355–56
*Respectfully, respectively,* 189
Restrictive clause= essential clause
Restrictive labels in dictionaries, 514–15
Résumé, 201, 402–03
Retained object, 156
Revising a composition, 300–06
Revision checklist, 465–66
*Rise, raise,* 142
*Roget's Thesaurus,* 518
Roots, in word analysis, 536–38
*Route, rout,* 559
Run-on sentence, 207–08

Salutation
for dignitaries, high officials, *et al.,* 389–91
in business letters, 386–91
*Scarcely,* 189, 191
*Scissors,* number of, 95
*-sede, -cede,* and *-ceed,* 545
"See" and "see also" cards, 481–82
*-self, -selves,* pronouns ending in, 117
Semicolon, 443–45
between independent clauses containing commas, 444
between independent clauses joined by *for example, nevertheless, therefore,* etc., 444
between independent clauses not joined by *and, but,* etc., 443–44
in series, 445
Sentence
beginning with *there, here,* 29
classification
by purpose, 36–37
by structure, 66–69
completeness, 198–200
complex, 68–69
compound, 67
compound-complex, 69
concluding, of a paragraph, 262
declarative, 37
defined, 25, 199
diagraming, 31–33, 35
exclamatory, 37
fragments, 200–05
imperative, 37
interrogative, 37
parts of, 24–36
patterns, summary of, 38–39
predicate of, 26–27
run-on, 207–08
simple, 67
stringy, 254–56
subject of, 26–27
topic, 260–68
variety, 248–56

Sentence fragments, 200–05
Sentence outline, 292
Sentence patterns, summary of, 38–39
Series
  commas in, 427–28
  semicolons in, 445
*Set, sit,* 140–41
*Several,* number of, 86
*Shall, will,* 189
*She, they, he,* as double subject, 184
Shepherd's *Historical Atlas,* 496
*sic,* meaning of, 374
Signature, in a business letter, 392
Simple predicate, defined, 27
Simple sentence, defined, 67
Simple subject, defined, 27
Single quotation marks, uses of, 453
*Sit, set,* 140–41
Slang, labeled in dictionaries, 514–15
*Slow, slowly,* 167, 189
Slug, 361–62
*So,* overuse of, 189
*Some,* number of, 86–87
*Some, somewhat,* 190
*Somebody, someone,* number of, 86
*Sort, type, kind,* 185
*Sort of a, kind of a,* 185
Source material, for research
  abbreviations in, 373–74
  acknowledgment of, 367–69
  availability of, 350–51
Spatial order, in paragraph, 277–78
Specialization, in word formation, 584–85
Spelling, 542–66
  dictionary as guide to, 510, 543
  distinguishing words that sound alike, 552–62
  formation of plurals, 548–51
  how to improve, 542–44
  list of spelling words, 564–66
  rules
    doubling final consonant, 547–58

final *e,* 547
*ie, ei,* 545
words with prefixes and suffixes, 546–48
Squinting modifiers, 239
*Sr.,* capitalization of, 409
"Standard" American English, 577
Standard English, 76–79
  formal, 77–78
  informal, 78–79
State-of-being verb = linking verb
*Statesman's Yearbook,* 495
*Stationary, stationery,* 560
Stationery, for business letters, 382
Stevenson's *Home Book of Quotations,* and *Familiar Phrases,* 499
*Straight, strait,* 560
Stringy style, ways of correcting, 254–56
Subject card, 480
Subject complements, 12, 34–36
  (*See also* Predicate adjective, Predicate nominative.)
Subject of infinitive, 53
Subject of a sentence
  agreement of verb with, 81–90
  complete, 27
  compound, 27
  defined, 26
  how to find, 28–29
    in a question, 29
    in commands or requests, 28
    in sentences beginning with *there, here,* 29
  never in a phrase, 29
  simple, 27
  understood, 28
Subjunctive mood, 159–60
Subordinate clause, 58–65
  adjective, 59–60, 220
  adverb, 63–64
  as sentence fragment, 204–05
  clear relationship to main clause, 215–16
  defined, 57, 58

Subordinate clause, *continued*
  noun, 61–63
  relative pronouns in, 59–60, 114–15
  without introductory word, 62
Subordinate ideas, 214–15
Subordinating conjunctions
  defined, 20
  expressing time, cause or reason, purpose or result, condition, 215–16
  list of, 20, 65
Suffixes, in word analysis, 533–35
Superlative degree
  formation of, 169–70
  use of, 170–72
Supplied definitions, 525–26
Syllabication
  dictionary as authority on, 510
  rules for, 468–69
Symbols used in correcting compositions, 470
Synonyms
  dictionaries of, 518–19
  dictionary as authority on, 515

Table of contents, function of, 485
*Tactics*, number of, 95
*Take, bring*, 180
Tense, of verbs, 144–54
  sequence of, 151–53
  special problems with, 151–54
  uses of each, 147–50
Test-taking practices, summary of, 594–95
*Than*, case of pronoun after, 116
*Than, then*, 561
*That, who, which*, 191
*Their, there, they're*, 561
*Them*, 190
*There*
  as an expletive, 29
  never the subject of a sentence, 29, 91
*There, their, they're*, 561
*These kind, those kind*, 190
*They*, indefinite use of, 232

*They, she, he*, as double subject, 184
*This here, that there*, 190
Title card, 480
Title page, function of, 484
Titles
  italicized, 449
  number of, 94
  personal, capitalization of, 416–17
  quotation marks with, 454
*To, too, two*, 561
Topic outline, 292–94
Topic sentence, of a paragraph, 260–68
  defined, 260
  development of, 263
    by combination of methods, 268
    by comparison and contrast, 265–66
    by definition, 267
    by examples, 264–65
    by facts, 263–64
    by incident, 265
    by reasons, 266–67
  position of, 260–62
Transitions between paragraphs, 301–02
Transitions within paragraphs, 280–81
Transitive verbs, 11
*Trousers*, number of, 95
*Twentieth Century Authors*, 498
Two-way (Squinting) modifiers, 239
*Type, kind, sort*, 185
*Type, type of*, 190

Underlining (italics), 449
  for foreign words, words as words, etc., 449
  for titles, 449
Understood subject, 28
Unity in the paragraph, 273–74
Usage
  distinguished from grammar, 75

Usage, *continued*
   glossary of, 174–92
   labels in dictionaries, 514–15
   levels of, 75–80
   sources of information on, 80
   standard, 76–79
     formal, 77–78
     informal, 78–79
     nonstandard, 79–80

Variety in sentences
   length and structure, 252–53
   sentence openings, 249–50
   using subordination, 254–56
Verbs, 11–14, 122–60
   action, 11–12
   agreement with subject, 81–90
   as simple predicates, 27
   auxiliary = helping verbs
   *be*
     conjunction of, 146–47
     special nature of, 12
   compound, 28
   defined, 11
   emphatic form, 148, 149
   helping, 13–14
   intransitive, 12
   irregular, 124–31
   *lie, lay,* 136–38
   linking, 12–13, 122–23
     defined, 12–13
     function of, 12–13, 122–23
     list of, 13
   mood, defined, 159
   phrase, defined, 13
   principal parts of, 123–31
   progressive form, 147
   regular, 124
   *rise, raise,* 142
   *see,* conjunction of, 144–46
   *sit, set,* 140–41
   state of being = linking verb
   subjunctive mood, 159–60
   tense, 144–54
   transitive, 11

   unnecessary shifts in tense, 151–53
   voice, 155–58
Verbal phrases
   gerund, 49–50
   infinitive, 53
   participle, 46
Vertical file, 490–91
*Vide,* meaning of, 374
Vocabulary, 520–41
   context clues, 523–27
   dictionary study, 529
   kinds of, 522
   notebook, 529
   of American English dialects, 574–75
   prefixes, list of, 532–33
   roots, list of, 536–38
   suffixes, list of, 534–35
   word analysis, 530–38
   word list, 538–41
Vocabulary tests, 595–602
Voice, active and passive, 155–58

*Waist, waste,* 561
*Ways* (for *way*), 190
Weak reference, 230–31
*Weather, whether,* 561
*Webster's Biographical Dictionary,* 497–98
*Webster's New Collegiate Dictionary,* 507
*Webster's New World Dictionary,* 507
*Webster's Third New International Dictionary,* 506
*Well, good,* 167, 181–82
*Were,* as subjunctive, 159–60
*When, where,* in definitions, 190–91
*Where* (for *that*), 191
*Which, that, who,* 191
*Who, which, that,* 191
*Who, whom,* 113–15
*Who's Who,* 498
*Who's Who in America,* 498
*Who's, whose,* 562

*Whose,* as relative, 59
*Will, shall,* 189
Word analysis, 530–38
Working bibliography for a research paper, 352–56
*World Almanac and Book of Facts,* 495
*World Book Encyclopedia,* 494

*Would have,* avoid use of, 153
*Writers Directory,* 498

Yearbooks, 495
*You,* indefinite use of, 232
*Your, you're,* 562

# TAB KEY INDEX

▶ **GRAMMAR**

## The Parts of Speech

| | |
|---|---|
| 1a | the noun, 5 |
| 1b | the pronoun, 5 |
| 1c | the adjective, 9 |
| 1d | the verb, 11 |
| 1e | the adverb, 15 |
| 1f | the preposition, 18 |
| 1g | the conjunction, 19 |
| 1h | the interjection, 20 |

## The Parts of a Sentence

| | |
|---|---|
| 2a | sentence defined, 25 |
| 2b-f | subjects & predicates, 26–28 |
| 2g | direct object, 31 |
| 2h | indirect object, 32 |
| 2i | predicate nominative, 35 |
| 2j | predicate adjective, 35 |
| 2k | sentences classified by purpose, 36 |

## The Phrase

| | |
|---|---|
| 3a | phrase defined, 41 |
| 3b-d | prepositional phrase, 41–43 |
| 3e | participle defined, 45 |
| 3f | participial phrase, 46 |
| 3g | gerund defined, 48 |
| 3h | gerund phrase, 49 |
| 3i | infinitive defined, 51 |
| 3j | infinitive phrase, 53 |
| 3k | appositives, 54–55 |

## The Clause

| | |
|---|---|
| 4a | clause defined, 57 |
| 4b | adjective clause, 59 |
| 4c | relative pronoun, 59 |
| 4d | noun clause, 61 |
| 4e | adverb clause, 63 |
| 4f | subordinating conjunction, 65 |
| 4g | sentences classified by structure, 66–69 |

▶ **USAGE**

## The Varieties of English

## Correct Agreement

| | |
|---|---|
| 6a | singular & plural number, 81 |
| 6b | verb agrees with subject, 82 |
| 6c | intervening expression between subject & verb, 84 |
| 6d-f | indefinite pronouns, 86 |
| 6g-i | compound subjects, 89 |
| 6j | verb before subject, 91 |
| 6k | collective nouns, 92 |
| 6l | expressions stating amount, 92 |
| 6m | titles, 94 |
| 6n | singular nouns plural in form, 94 |
| 6o | predicate nominative & agreement, 96 |
| 6p | *every* & *many a*, 96 |
| 6q | *doesn't* & *don't*, 96 |
| 6r | agreement of pronoun & antecedent, 98–100 |

## Correct Pronoun Usage

| | |
|---|---|
| 7a | case forms, 103 |
| 7b-c | nominative case, 105, 106 |
| 7d-e | objective case, 108, 110 |
| 7f | *who* & *whom*, 114 |
| 7g | case after *than* & *as*, 116 |
| 7h | pronouns in *-self, -selves*, 117 |
| 7i | case of appositives, 117 |

7j possessives before gerunds, 118

## Correct Verb Usage

8a irregular verbs, 126
8b tense, 144
8c-f tense usage, 147–50, 153, 154
8g passive voice, 157
8h subjunctive, 160

## Correct Use of Modifiers

9a-b modifiers following verbs, 164, 165
9c comparison defined, 168–70
9d comparing two things, 170
9e *other* & *else*, 171
9f double comparisons, 171

## Glossary of Usage

## COMPOSITION: SENTENCE STRUCTURE

## Complete Sentences

11a sentence fragment, 201
11b attaching fragments, 204
11c run-on sentences, 208

## Coordination and Subordination

12a clear relationships, 216
12b subordinating ideas, 220
12c correcting relationships, 222

## Clear Reference

13a avoiding unclear references, 226–31
13b avoiding indefinite references, 232

## Placement of Modifiers

14a misplaced modifier, 235
14b dangling modifier, 237

## Parallel Structure

15a parallel ideas, 242
15b placement of conjunctions, 243
15c repetition when necessary, 245

## Sentence Variety

16a varied beginnings, 249
16b varied structure & length, 252
16c avoiding "stringy" style, 254–55

## COMPOSITION: PARAGRAPHS AND LONGER PAPERS

## The Paragraph

17a paragraph defined, 259
17b topic sentence defined, 260
17c paragraph development, 263–68
17d unified paragraph, 273
17e coherent paragraph, 276
17f linking expressions, 279

## The Whole Composition

18a selecting a subject, 285–87
18b-c organizing material, 288, 290
18d outlining, 291–93
18e writing the first draft, 295
18f revising the first draft, 300–03
18g completing the revision, 303

**19** Clear Thinking

**20** Exercises in Writing Prose

**21** The Research Paper

21a selecting a subject, 349
21b limiting the subject, 350
21c working bibliography, 352
21d stating the purpose, 358
21e preliminary outline, 359
21f taking notes, 360
21g final outline, 364
21h first draft, 365
21i final draft, 366

**22** The Business Letter

22a standard practice, 382–86
22b types of business letters, 395

▶ **MECHANICS**

**23** Capitalization

23a first word in sentence, 408
23b O & I, 408
23c proper nouns & adjectives, 409–14
23d titles, 416–17
23e words referring to Deity, 418
23f compound words, 419

**24** Punctuation

24a-b periods, 423
24c question marks, 424
24d exclamation marks, 424–25
24e commas in series, 427–28
24f commas between adjectives, 428
24g commas between clauses, 430
24h commas with nonessential elements, 431

24i commas with introductory elements, 434–35
24j commas with interrupters, 437
24k conventional uses of commas, 439–40
24l unnecessary commas, 440

**25** Punctuation

25a-d semicolons, 443–45
25e-f colons, 445–46
25g-i dashes, 447
25j parentheses, 447–48
25k brackets, 448
25l underlining titles, 449
25m underlining words as words, 449
25n direct quotations, 451–53
25o quotation marks with titles, 454
25p quotation marks with unusual terms, 454
25q apostrophe for possessives, 455–57
25r apostrophe for omissions, 458
25s apostrophe for plurals, 458
25t-x hyphens, 459–60

**26** Manuscript Form

26a abbreviations, 466–67
26b numerals, 467
26c-e numbers, 467–68
26f-i dividing words, 468–69

▶ **AIDS TO GOOD ENGLISH**

**27** The Library

27a arrangement, 475
27b uses of card catalogue, 478
27c parts of a book, 483
27d Readers' Guide, 489

27e  vertical file, 490
27f  learn location of items, 491

## 28 Reference Books

## 29 The Dictionary

29a  kinds of dictionaries, 506
29b  content & arrangement, 507
29c  vocabulary entries, 509
29d  information entries, 517
29e  special dictionaries, 518

## 30 Vocabulary

30a  context clues, 523
30b  using the dictionary, 529
30c  vocabulary notebook, 529
30d  prefixes, suffixes, & roots, 530

## 31 Spelling

31a  *ie & ei,* 545
31b  *-cede, -ceed,* & *-sede,* 545
31c  adding prefixes, 546
31d-h  adding suffixes, 546–47
31i  forming plurals, 548–51

## AMERICAN ENGLISH

## 32 American English

## COLLEGE ENTRANCE AND OTHER EXAMINATIONS

## 33 College Entrance and Other Examinations

## CORRECTION SYMBOLS

| | |
|---|---|
| ms | error in manuscript form or neatness |
| cap | error in use of capital letters |
| p | error in punctuation |
| sp | error in spelling |
| frag | sentence fragment |
| ss | error in sentence structure |
| k | awkward sentence |
| nc | not clear |
| ref | unclear reference of pronoun |
| rs | run-on sentence |
| gr | error in grammar |
| w | error in word choice |
| ¶ | You should have begun a new paragraph here. |
| t | error in tense |
| ʌ | You have omitted something. |

G
H
I
J